2021

杭州统计年鉴

HANGZHOU STATISTICAL YEARBOOK

杭州

2021 统计年鉴

HANGZHOU STATISTICAL YEARBOOK

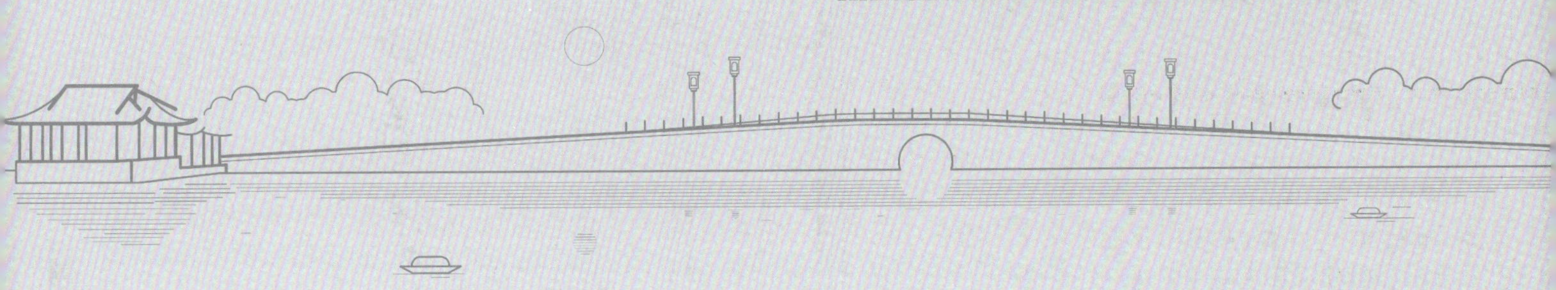

杭 州 市 统 计 局
国家统计局杭州调查队
杭州市社会经济调查队

中国统计出版社
China Statistics Press

图书在版编目（CIP）数据

杭州统计年鉴. 2021 = Hangzhou Statistical Yearbook 2021 : 汉英对照 / 杭州市统计局, 国家统计局杭州调查队, 杭州市社会经济调查队编. -- 北京 : 中国统计出版社, 2021.10
ISBN 978-7-5037-9618-0

Ⅰ. ①杭… Ⅱ. ①杭… ②国… ③杭… Ⅲ. ①统计资料－杭州－2021－年鉴－汉、英 Ⅳ. ①C832.551-54

中国版本图书馆CIP数据核字(2021)第164276号

杭州统计年鉴—2021

作　　者/ 杭州市统计局
　　　　　国家统计局杭州调查队
　　　　　杭州市社会经济调查队
责任编辑/ 钟钰
装帧设计/ 张子杰
出版发行/ 中国统计出版社有限公司
地　　址/ 北京市丰台区西三环南路甲6号
邮政编码/ 100073
电　　话/ 邮购（010）63376909　书店（010）68783171
网　　址/ http://www.zgtjcbs.com
印　　刷/ 浙江新中商务印刷有限公司
经　　销/ 新华书店
开　　本/ 890mm×1240mm　1/16
字　　数/ 1017千字
印　　张/ 28　彩页0.75
版　　别/ 2021年11月第1版
版　　次/ 2021年11月第1次印刷
定　　价/ 300.00元　Price: 300.00yuan(RMB)

统计年鉴

HANGZHOU STATISTICAL YEARBOOK

2021 编委会和编辑人员

统计年鉴

HANGZHOU STATISTICAL YEARBOOK

2021 Editorial Board and Staff

编者说明

一、《杭州统计年鉴—2021》是一部信息密集的资料性年刊。本年鉴系统收集了全市和各区、县（市）2020年经济和社会各方面的统计数据，以及多个重要历史年份和近年全市主要统计数据。

二、本年鉴分为13个篇章：综合；人口和就业人员；农业；工业、能源；建筑业；交通运输、邮电；固定资产投资；批发、零售贸易和住宿餐饮业；对外经济、旅游；财政、金融、保险；城市建设、环境保护；科技、教育、文化、卫生、体育；人民生活、物价、民政。为便于读者使用，各篇章附有简要说明和主要统计指标解释。

三、本年鉴中涉及历史数据，均以最新版本为准；本年鉴中部分数据合计数或相对数由于单位取舍不同而产生的计算误差，均未做机械调整。

四、2001年起，萧山、余杭撤市建区，市区数据含萧山、余杭区；2014年起富阳撤市建区，市区数据包括富阳区；2017年起临安撤市建区，市区数据包括临安区。2019年起区县分组新增钱塘新区，萧山区数据未做特殊说明的均含托管在钱塘新区的街道数据。

五、本年鉴表中符号使用说明：“－”表示这一栏没有数字；“…”表示该数字不足本表最小计量单位；“#”表示其中的主要项；“空格”表示该项统计数据不详或无该项数据；“＊”表示表下有注解。

六、本年鉴所使用的度量衡单位均采用国际统一标准计量单位，金额除特别标明外，均以人民币计量。

七、《杭州统计年鉴》公开出版以来，受到了社会各界的关心和支持，对此我们深表谢意。限于我们的水平，欢迎各界人士继续对年鉴的不足之处给予批评指正，帮助我们进一步提高统计年鉴的编辑工作，更好地为社会各界服务（网址：http：//tjj. hangzhou. gov. cn）。

Editorial Note

Ⅰ. *Hangzhou Statistical Yearbook 2021* is an informative annual which contains very comprehensive statistics of Hangzhou's social and economic development in 2020, and selected data of recent years and some historically important years.

Ⅱ. This yearbook is composed of 13 chapters: 1. General Survey; 2. Population and Employment; 3. Agriculture; 4. Industry and Energy; 5. Construction; 6. Transportation, Post and Telecommunications; 7. Investment in Fixed Assets; 8. Wholesale and Retail Trade and Hotel and Catering Trade; 9. Foreign Economic Cooperation and Tourism; 10. Finance, Banking and Insurance; 11. Urban Construction and Environmental Protection; 12. Science and Technology, Education, Culture, Public Health and Sports; 13. People's Livelihood, Price Indices and Civil Administration. To facilitate readers, each chaper provides brief introduction and explanatory notes on main statistical indicators.

Ⅲ. Please refer to the newly published version of the yearbook for updated historical data. Statistical discrepancies on totals and relative figures due to rounding are not adjusted in the yearbook.

Ⅳ. Because of the change of urban administrative division, the data of Xiaoshan District and Yuhang District have been included into the urban districts since 2001, and it is the same for Fuyang District since 2014, Lin'an District since 2017. Qiantang New Area has been added into classification of districts and counties since 2019. Figures of Xiaoshan District without special explanation all include districts under administered by Qiantang New Area.

Ⅴ. Notations used in this yearbook: "—" indicates that the column has no figure; "…" indicates that the figure is not large enough to be measured with the smallest unit in the table; "#" indicates that the date are unknown, or are not available; "blank" indicates the major items of the total; " * " indicates "see footnotes below".

Ⅵ. International standard units of measurement are applied in this yearbook, all amounts are denominated in RMB, unless otherwise indicated.

Ⅶ. Since published openly, previous editions of *Hangzhou Statistical Yearbook* have been widely concerned and supported, for which we are very grateful. In order to get further improvement in the yearbook editing, we welcome all candid comments and criticism from our readers (website: http://tjj.hangzhou.gov.cn).

目　　录
Contents

一、综合
Ⅰ. General Survey

二、人口和就业人员
Ⅱ. Population and Employment

三、农业

Ⅲ. Agriculture

四、工业、能源
Ⅳ. Industry and Energy

五、建筑业
Ⅴ. Construction

六、交通运输、邮电
Ⅵ. Transportation, Post and Telecommunications

七、固定资产投资
Ⅶ. Investment in Fixed Assets

八、批发、零售贸易和住宿餐饮业

Ⅷ. Wholesale and Retail Trade and Hotel and Catering Trade

九、对外经济、旅游

Ⅸ. Foreign Economic Cooperation and Tourism

十、财政、金融、保险
X. Finance, Banking and Insurance

十一、城市建设、环境保护

Ⅺ. Urban Construction and Environmental Protection

十二、科技、教育、文化、卫生、体育

Ⅻ. Science and Technology, Education, Culture, Public Health and Sports

十三、人民生活、物价、民政

XIII. People's Livelihood, Price Indices and Civil Administration

2020 年杭州市国民经济和社会发展统计公报

杭 州 市 统 计 局
国家统计局杭州调查队
（2021 年 3 月 18 日）

2020 年，面对严峻复杂的国内外形势，特别是新冠肺炎疫情的严重冲击，杭州坚持以习近平新时代中国特色社会主义思想为指导，坚定不移实施新发展理念，以强有力举措抓"六稳"、促"六保"、拓"六新"，以自身发展的确定性全力对冲外部环境的不确定性，决胜高水平全面建成小康社会取得历史性成就，高质量发展走出坚实步伐，为开启全面建设社会主义现代化新征程奠定坚实基础。

一、综合

（一）经济增长。

初步核算，2020 年杭州实现地区生产总值 16106 亿元，比上年增长 3.9%。分产业看，第一产业增加值 326 亿元，下降 1.1%；第二产业增加值 4821 亿元，增长 2.3%；第三产业增加值 10959 亿元，增长 5.0%。三次产业结构为 2.0∶29.9∶68.0（经最终核实，2019 年杭州 GDP 修订为 15419 亿元，比上年增长 6.8%，三次产业增加值结构为 2.1∶31.4∶66.5）。

数字经济赋能发展。全年以新产业、新业态、新模式为主要特征的"三新"经济增加值占 GDP 的 35.5%。数字经济核心产业增加值 4290 亿元，增长 13.3%，高于 GDP 增速 9.4 个百分点，占 GDP 的 26.6%。电子信息产品制造、软件与信息服务、数字内容和机器人产业分别增长 14.7%、12.9%、12.7% 和 12.3%。规模以上工业中，高新技术产业、战略性新兴产业、装备制造业增加值分别增长 8.6%、8.1% 和 11.8%。

民营经济活力持续增强。全年民营经济增加值 9855 亿元，占 GDP 的 61.2%，比上年提高 0.2 个百分点。民营企业货物出口 2589 亿元，增长 5.8%，占出口总额的 70.1%。年末，全市私营企业 67.8 万户，比上年末增长 8.4%；个体工商户 65.9 万户，增长 9.5%。

（二）发展质效。

全年全员劳动生产率为 21.9 万元/人；规模以上工业全员劳动生产率 34.0 万元/人。

全年财政总收入 3854.2 亿元，增长 5.6%；一般公共预算收入 2093.4 亿元，增长 6.5%，其中税收收入 1978.6 亿元，增长 10.5%，占一般公共预算收入的 94.5%。一般公共预算支出 2069.7 亿元，增长 6.0%，其中民生支出 1583.6 亿元，占一般公共预算支出的 76.5%。

规模以上工业企业利润总额 1302 亿元，规模以上服务业企业利润总额 2451 亿元。

（三）市场价格。

全年市区居民消费价格比上年上涨 2.1%，其中食品烟酒类价格上涨 6.9%。商品零售价格上涨 0.9%。工业生产者出厂价格下降 2.5%，工业生产者购进价格下降 3.9%。

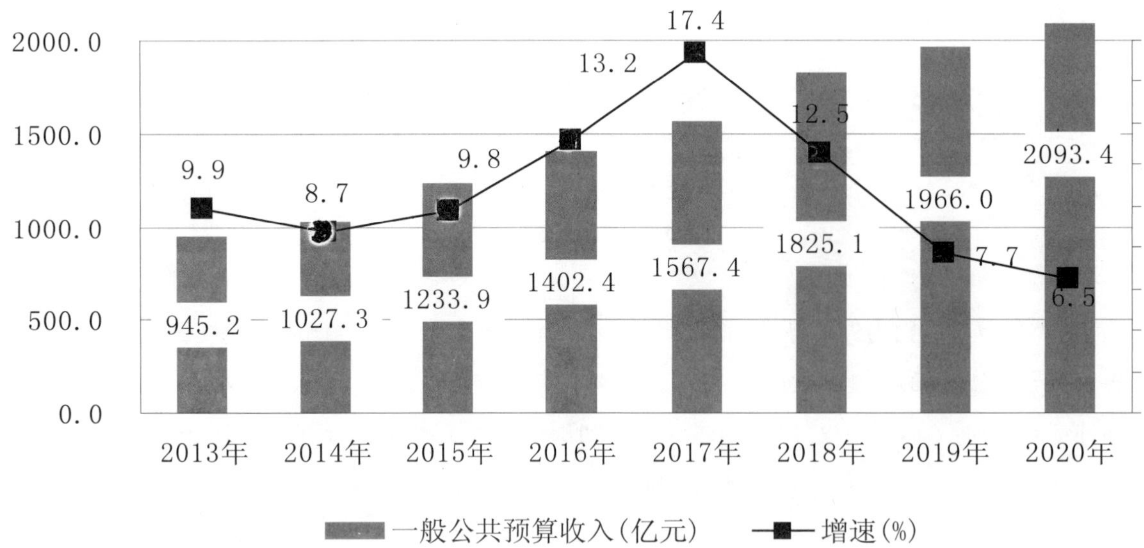

2013 －2020 年一般公共预算收入及增速

市区居民消费价格涨跌幅度(%)

项　　目	2019 年	2020 年
市区居民消费价格	3.1	2.1
其中:食品烟酒	6.3	6.9
其中:食品	7.9	8.9
其中:粮食	1.1	1.7
鲜菜	3.4	2.0
畜肉类	23.1	36.7
衣着	1.3	0.1
居住	0.9	-0.3
生活用品及服务	3.0	3.1
交通和通信	-1.0	-3.4
教育文化和娱乐	4.3	1.7
医疗保健	7.0	3.1
其他用品和服务	2.8	3.8

(四)人口就业。

全年人口出生率为 9.92‰,自然增长率为 4.63‰。全市新增城镇就业人员 69.05 万人,安置失业人员再就业 3.44 万人。年末城镇登记失业率 2.4%。

二、农业和农村

全年农林牧渔业增加值 334 亿元,下降 0.9%。

全年粮食总产量 50.9 万吨,增长 2.4%;蔬菜产量 347.7 万吨,增长 1.8%;水果产量 83.1 万吨,增长 0.6%;水产品产量 19.3 万吨,下降 4.8%;肉类产量 11.0 万吨,下降 44.0%。市级“菜篮子”基地 563 个,其中新建 21

个。新启动4个省级重点历史文化村、70个美丽乡村精品村、9个风情小镇。“大下姜乡村振兴联合体”入选全国12个乡村典型案例。农家乐(民宿)接待游客7153万人次,实现经营收入65亿元。农村电商销售额165亿元,增长15.7%。

全年1922个行政村集体经济总收入超过30万元、经营性收入超过20万元,占比达100%。市县两级美丽乡村行政村覆盖率达54.5%。

三、工业和建筑业

全年工业增加值4221亿元,增长2.6%,其中规模以上工业增加值3467亿元,增长3.8%。八大高耗能行业增加值占比20.4%,占比下降3.2个百分点。17个传统制造业增加值下降3.1%。规模以上工业总产值14712亿元,出口交货值1874亿元。新产品产值率40.0%,工业产品产销率为98.6%。集成电路、工业机器人、光缆等列入国家“三新”统计的产品产量分别增长62.7%、45.4%和32.1%。

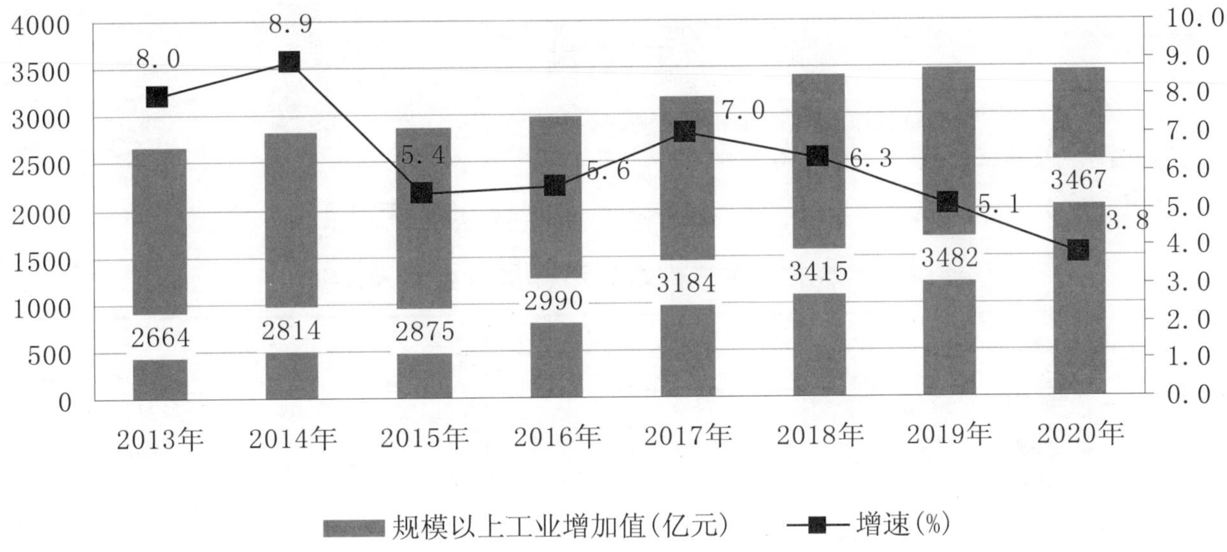

2013-2020年规模以上工业增加值及增速

全年建筑业增加值601亿元,增长0.2%。

四、交通运输和邮电

全年交通运输、仓储和邮政业增加值392亿元,下降1.8%。

全年货运量4.2亿吨,增长9.1%。客运量1.2亿人次,下降41.7%。至年末萧山国际机场开通航线336条,其中国际航线69条,港澳台航线6条。航空客运吞吐量达2822万人次,下降29.6%;货物吞吐量80.2万吨,增长16.2%。地铁客运量5.8亿人次,下降8.1%。

年末社会机动车保有量311.9万辆,增长4.8%。非营运汽车保有量258.4万辆,增长4.9%,其中私人汽车227.5万辆,增长5.2%。

全年邮政企业和规模以上快递服务企业实现业务收入450.0亿元,增长11.9%,其中快递业务收入367.0亿元,增长12.3%。年末固定电话用户204.55万户,移动电话用户1868.9万户,固定互联网宽带接入用户547.58万户。

2020 年各种运输方式完成货运量和客运量

指　　标	绝对数	比上年增长(%)
全社会货运量(万吨)	41944	9.1
铁路(万吨)	578	7.6
公路(万吨)	34837	3.1
水路(万吨)	6483	59.2
航空(万吨)	46	11.9
全社会客运量(万人次)	12183	-41.7
铁路(万人次)	5895	-33.6
公路(万人次)	4535	-51.6
水路(万人次)	339	-44.4
航空(万人次)	1414	-30.8

五、金融

全年金融业增加值 2038 亿元,增长 10.6%。

年末金融机构本外币存款余额 54246.5 亿元,增长 19.8%;贷款余额 49799.3 亿元,增长 17.9%。

2020 年末金融机构本外币存贷款余额及增速

指　　标	年末数(亿元)	比上年末增长(%)
各项存款余额	54246.5	19.8
其中:住户存款	14398.1	21.0
非金融企业存款	24934.8	23.0
各项贷款余额	49799.3	17.9
其中:住户贷款	20428.8	23.7
企(事)业单位贷款	29021.3	14.4
其中:短期贷款	9012.7	11.1
中长期贷款	17194.5	17.1
票据融资	1849.9	13.7

年末上市公司 218 家,其中境内上市 161 家;全年新增上市公司 28 家,IPO 融资 509.1 亿元,增长 213.6%。年末中小板上市公司 34 家,创业板上市公司 46 家。

全年保费收入 964.4 亿元,增长 14.0%,其中财产险保费收入 260.8 亿元,人身险保费收入 703.6 亿元,支付各类保险赔款 264.6 亿元,增长 8.9%,其中财产险 155.2 亿元,人身险 109.5 亿元。

六、固定资产投资和房地产业

(一)固定资产投资。

全年固定资产投资增长 6.8%,其中民间投资增长 3.4%,基础设施投资增长 7.7%,交通投资增长 6.6%。从产业投向看,第二产业投资增长 6.2%,其中工业投资增长 6.9%;第三产业投资增长 6.8%。高新技术产业投资增长 10.0%。

(二)房地产业。

全年房地产业增加值1226亿元,增长3.9%。

全年房地产开发投资增长5.3%,其中住宅投资增长0.8%,办公楼投资增长11.5%,商业营业用房投资增长3.5%。年末房屋施工面积13310万平方米,增长11.0%;新开工面积3543万平方米,增长45.5%;竣工面积1799万平方米,增长4.1%。商品房销售面积1699万平方米,增长12.3%;商品房销售额4595亿元,增长17.1%。

2020年房地产开发和销售主要指标

指　　标	实绩数	比上年末增长(%)
房地产开发施工面积(万平方米)	13310	11.0
其中:住宅(万平方米)	6959	11.1
房地产开发竣工面积(万平方米)	1799	4.1
其中:住宅(万平方米)	934	-3.1
商品房销售面积(万平方米)	1699	12.3
其中:住宅(万平方米)	1472	14.6

七、国内贸易

全年批发和零售业增加值1272亿元,增长2.3%;住宿和餐饮业增加值213亿元,下降10.6%。

全年社会消费品零售总额6055亿元,下降3.5%,按消费类型统计,商品零售5060亿元,下降2.4%,餐饮收入995亿元,下降8.5%。在限额以上批零企业商品零售额中,化妆品、文化办公用品和日用品零售额分别增长10.4%、10.3%和10.3%;新能源汽车、智能家用电器和音像器材等升级类商品消费分别增长24.2%和12.8%。限额以上批零单位通过公共网络实现的商品零售增长15.4%。

全年各类商品市场617个,全年交易额3431亿元。

八、对外经济

(一)对外贸易。

全年货物进出口总额5934亿元,增长5.9%。其中出口3693亿元,增长2.1%;进口2241亿元,增长12.9%。高新技术产品出口649亿元,增长14.1%;机电产品出口1659亿元,增长4.1%。对"一带一路"沿线国家出口1170亿元,占出口总额31.7%。对美国、欧盟28国出口分别增长5.7%和8.5%;对日本、韩国出口分别下降4.9%和1.8%。服务贸易出口138.4亿美元,增长10.8%。

全年跨境电商进出口总额1084.2亿元,增长13.9%。其中出口756.8亿元、进口327.4亿元,分别增长14.9%和11.6%。

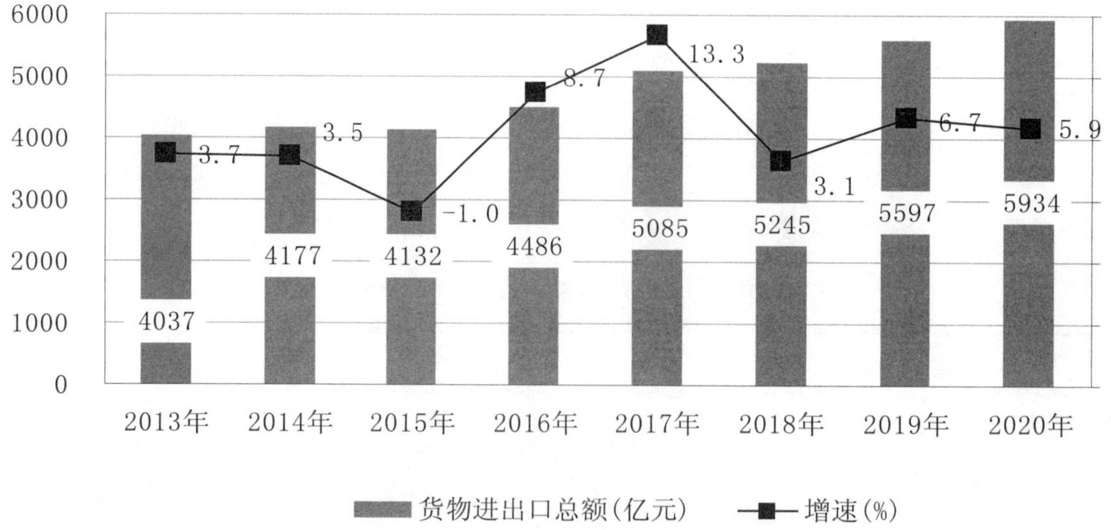

2013－2020 年货物进出口总额及增速

(二)利用外资。

全年新引进外商投资项目 804 个,其中总投资 3000 万美元以上项目 98 个。实际利用外资 72.0 亿美元,增长 17.5%,其中第二产业实际利用外资 23.3 亿美元,增长 218.8%,第三产业实际利用外资 48.7 亿美元,下降 9.7%。至年末,126 家世界 500 强企业来杭投资 222 个项目。

(三)对外合作。

年末全市设立各类境外投资企业(机构)2445 个,增长 9.3%。对外承包工程和劳务合作营业额 18.6 亿美元,下降 31.9%。离岸服务外包合同执行额 77.7 亿美元,增长 8.1%。

九、人民生活和社会保障

(一)人民生活。

全年全市居民人均可支配收入 61879 元,增长 4.4%,扣除价格因素实际增长 2.3%。按常住地分,城镇、农村居民人均可支配收入分别为 68666 元和 38700 元,增长 3.9% 和 6.7%,扣除价格因素增长 1.8% 和 4.5%。低收入农户人均可支配收入增长 13.7%。

全年全市居民人均消费支出 38235 元,下降 4.5%。按常住地分,城镇、农村居民人均消费支出分别为 41916 元和 25664 元,下降 4.9% 和 2.4 %。

2020 年全市城乡居民人均收支主要指标

指标名称	全体居民		城镇居民		农村居民	
	绝对数(元)	比上年增长(%)	绝对数(元)	比上年增长(%)	绝对数(元)	比上年增长(%)
人均可支配收入	61879	4.4	68666	3.9	38700	6.7
(一)工资性收入	36014	5.5	39720	5.0	23359	8.1
(二)经营净收入	6446	－2.1	5640	－3.6	9196	1.4
(三)财产净收入	8235	1.5	10182	1.4	1586	0.8
(四)转移净收入	11184	7.2	13124	6.4	4559	13.6
人均消费支出	38235	－4.5	41916	－4.9	25664	－2.4

年末城镇居民人均住房建筑面积39.3平方米,每百户居民家庭拥有家用汽车65.3辆、空调252.2台、家用电脑90.6台,分别增长4.3%、0.8%和0.9%。农村居民人均住房建筑面积75.5平方米,每百户居民家庭拥有家用汽车54.9辆、空调211.6台、家用电脑61.3台,分别增长4.2%、0.1%和1.8%。

(二)社会保障。

年末职工基本养老保险参保人数、城镇职工基本医疗保险参保人数分别为751.5万人和713.5万人,增长6.7%和6.3%;年末失业保险、职工工伤保险参保人数分别为523.5万人和633.4万人,增长7.6%和13.8%。主城区居民最低生活保障标准调整至每人每月1102元,增长5.9%。年末全市最低生活保障对象9.88万人,全年发放困难家庭救助金10.81亿元,增长21.8%。

社会保障相关待遇标准

	2019年	2020年
失业保险金最低标准(市区城镇居民)	1608元/月	1608元/月
城乡最低生活保障标准(市区,不含临安)	1041元/月	1102元/月
城乡最低生活保障标准(桐庐、建德)	833元/月	882元/月
城乡最低生活保障标准(淳安)	833元/月	955元/月
城乡最低生活保障标准(临安)	989元/月	1102元/月
职工最低工资标准(市区)	2010元/月	2010元/月

(三)社会福利。

年末全市拥有城乡社区居家养老服务照料中心2910个。拥有各类福利院、敬老院330所,床位7.58万张,收养人员3.55万人。儿童福利机构8个,床位1040张。全年发行各类福利彩票24.7亿元,下降18.4%。

十、科学技术和教育

(一)科学技术。

全年研究与试验发展(R&D)经费支出与生产总值之比为3.59%。财政一般公共预算支出中科技支出144.3亿元,占一般公共预算支出的7.0%。

全年发明专利申请量和发明专利授权量分别为55297件和17327件,增长27.7%和47.5%。累计拥有市级以上企业技术中心817家,其中国家级45家;国家技术创新示范企业11家,省级技术创新示范企业11家。科技企业孵化器209家,其中国家级41家,省级107家。众创空间181家,其中国家级68家,省级144家。全年签订技术合同总量16307项520.3亿元。

(二)教育。

年末全市拥有普通高等学校40所,在校学生55.1万人,增加3.2万人,其中研究生8.5万人,高等教育毛入学率70.04%;普通高中91所,在校学生12.5万人,增加0.7万人;职高和中等专业学校37所,在校学生6.4万人,增加0.2万人;初中280所,在校学生24.9万人,增加0.5万人,初中毕业生升入各类高中比例为99.76%;小学496所,在校学生64.5万人,增加2.8万人;幼儿园1049所,在园幼儿37.5万人,增加2.5万人,学前三年幼儿入园率为99.15%。流动人口随迁子女在本市义务教育学校就读28.5万人。各级各类中外合作办学项目74个,其中市属高校项目8个,高中段学校项目7个。

十一、文化旅游、卫生健康和体育

（一）文化旅游。

全年文化产业增加值2285亿元，增长8.2%。年末全市文化馆（含省）15个，公共图书馆（含省）15个，剧场（含省）11个，音乐厅（含省）12个，博物馆、纪念馆78个，全国重点文物保护单位48处。全年制作电视剧5部199集，原创动画片26733分钟。放映电影116万场次，电影票款收入4.8亿元。年末有线电视注册用户310.7万户。

全年旅游休闲产业增加值999亿元，下降16.3%。旅游总收入3335.4亿元，下降16.7%；旅游总人数17573.1万人次，下降15.6%，其中接待入境过夜游客14.3万人次，下降87.4%。年末各类旅行社926家，增长3.5%。星级宾馆119家，其中五星级23家。A级景区111个，其中5A级3个。

（二）卫生健康。

全年健康产业增加值1156亿元，增长8.3%。年末拥有各类医疗卫生机构5675个，其中医院353个。各类专业卫生技术人员13.4万人，其中执业（助理）医师5.1万人，注册护士5.9万人，分别增长7.5%、8.6%和9.1%。拥有床位9.0万张，其中医院床位8.4万张，分别增长5.3%和5.9%。全市医疗机构完成诊疗人数15404万人次，增长5.2%。全市基层就诊率67%，县域就诊率90.1%。全市婴儿死亡率和5岁以下儿童死亡率分别为1.87‰和2.88‰。孕产妇死亡率为1.68人/10万。

（三）体育。

全年运动员获得全国性奖牌204枚，其中金牌56枚，银牌75枚。成功举办杭州马拉松、横渡钱塘江、全国全民体能大赛总决赛等10余项大型品牌体育赛事活动。完成6个游泳池、8个足球场、23个省级社区多功能运动场升级工程。

全年销售体育彩票29.5亿元，下降13.25%。

十二、城市建设

全年境内公路总里程达到16919公里，其中高速公路801公里。年末主城区公共交通运营线路367条，其中新辟线路24条，优化线路29条。地铁运营里程306.3公里，在建里程210公里。

全市用电量808亿千瓦时，下降1.1%，其中三次产业用电664亿千瓦时，下降2.2%；城乡居民生活用电144亿千瓦时，增长4.7%。

全市新建成停车泊位10.2万个，其中公共泊位1.3万个。

十三、环境保护和安全生产

全年市区年平均气温18.3℃，比上年高0.3℃；总降水量1664毫米，比上年增加14毫米。

全年市区空气优良天数334天，优良率91.3%。市区细颗粒物（$PM_{2.5}$）平均浓度29.8微克/立方米。二氧化氮年均浓度值38微克/立方米，下降7.3%；二氧化硫年均浓度值6微克/立方米，下降14.3%。地表水国考断面达到或优于Ⅲ类比例100%，省考断面达到或优于Ⅲ类比例100%，同比提高3.1个百分点。

全年共发生各类生产安全事故171起、死亡136人，分别下降25.3%和28.4%。

公报注释：

1. 本公报所列各项数据为年度初步数据。部分数据因四舍五入原因，存在分项与合计不等的情况。

2. 全市地区生产总值和各产业增加值绝对数按现行价格计算，增长速度按不变价格计算；三次产业划分执行国家统计局2018年修订的《三次产业划分规定(2012)》。

3. 规模以上服务业企业：辖区内年营业收入2000万元及以上服务业法人单位。包括：交通运输、仓储和邮政业，信息传输、软件和信息技术服务业，水利、环境和公共设施管理业三个门类和卫生行业大类。辖区内年营业收入1000万元及以上服务业法人单位。包括：租赁和商务服务业，科学研究和技术服务业，教育三个门类，以及物业管理、房地产中介服务、房地产租赁经营和其他房地产业四个行业小类。辖区内年营业收入500万元及以上服务业法人单位。包括：居民服务、修理和其他服务业，文化、体育和娱乐业两个门类，以及社会工作行业大类。

资料来源：

本公报中城镇新增就业、登记失业率、社会保障数据来自市人力社保局；私营企业、个体工商户、专利数据来自市市场监管局；财政数据来自市财政局；农业园区、美丽乡村、农家乐(民宿)数据来自市农业农村局；教育数据来自市教育局；货物进出口数据来自钱江海关；低保、社会服务和救助、福利彩票数据来自市民政局；公路里程、公交运营线路数据来自市交通局；航空客运吞吐量、货邮吞吐量、通航线路数据来自萧山机场；地铁运营数据来自市地铁集团；停车泊位数据来自市建委；生态建设、环境监测数据来自市生态环境局；各类事故发生起数、死亡人数来自市应急管理局；实际利用外资数据来自市投资促进局；对外承包工程、服务贸易数据来自市商务局；用电量数据来自国网杭州供电公司；户籍人口、机动车拥有数据来自市公安局；邮政业务数据来自市邮政管理局；货币金融数据来自人民银行杭州中心支行；保险业数据来自中国保监会浙江监管局；博物馆、纪念馆数据来自市园林文物局；科技创新、高新技术企业、研发中心、众创空间数据来自市科技局；旅游、艺术表演团体、公共图书馆、文化馆数据来自市文化广电旅游局；电影、动画片数据来自市委宣传部；上市公司数据来自市金融办；卫生数据来自市卫生健康委员会；医疗保险数据来自市医疗保障局；体育数据来自市体育局；建设用地数据来自市规划和自然资源局；森林覆盖率数据来自市林业水利局；企业技术中心、技术创新示范数据来自市经济和信息化局；固定电话用户、移动电话用户和(固定)互联网宽带接入用户数据来自市信息基础设施建设(5G试点城市建设)工作领导小组办公室；价格、城乡居民收支、人均住房面积、百户居民耐用品数据来自国家统计局杭州调查队；其他数据均来自市统计局。

Statistical Communiqué of Hangzhou on the 2020 National Economic and Social Development

Hangzhou Municipal Bureau of Statistics
Hangzhou Survey Office of National Bureau of Statistics
March,2021

In 2020, faced with the severe and complicated domestic and international situation, especially the severe impact of the novel coronavirus pneumonia epidemic, Hangzhou persisted in the guidance of Xi Jinping's Thought on Socialism with Chinese Characteristics in the New Era, unswervingly implemented the new development concept; took strong measures to stabilize employment, finance, foreign trade, foreign investment, investment and expectations; promoted the protection of residents' employment, basic people's livelihood, market players, food and energy security, industrial chain and supply chain stability and grassroots operation; exploited new infrastructure, new technology, new materials, new equipment, new products and new business formats; fully hedged against the uncertainty of the external environment with the certainty of its own development, secured a decisive victory in building a moderately prosperous society in an all – round way at a high level and achieved historic achievements, high – quality development took a solid step, and laid a solid foundation for starting a new journey of building socialist modernization in an all – round way.

I. General Outlook

Economic Aggregate

The gross domestic product (GDP) of the year was 1610. 6 billion yuan, up by 3. 9% over the previous year. Of this total, the added value of the primary industry was 32. 6 billion yuan with an annual decrease of 1. 1%, that of the secondary industry was 482. 1 billion yuan with an annual increase of 2. 3%, and the tertiary industry was 1095. 9 billion yuan with an annual increase of 5. 0%. The proportions of the three industries was adjusted to 2. 0 : 229. 9 : 268. 0 (According to the final verification, the gross domestic product (GDP) of Hangzhou in 2019 was adjusted to 1541. 9 billion yuan, up by 6. 8% over the previous year, the proportions of the three industries was 2. 1:231. 4:266. 5).

Digital economy empowered development. The added value of "three new" economic, which characterized by new industries, new business formats and new models, accounted for 35. 5% of GDP throughout the year.

The added value of digital economy core industry was 429. 0 billion yuan, up by 13. 3%, which was 9. 4 percentage points higher than the GDP growth rate and accounted for 26. 6% of GDP. Electronic information product manufacturing industry, software and information service industry, digital content industry and robot Industry increased by 14. 7%、12. 9%、12. 7% and 12. 3% respectively. Among the industrial enterprises above designated size, the added value of high – tech industry, strategic emerging industry and equipment manufacturing industry increased by 8. 6%, 8. 1% and 11. 8%, respectively.

The vitality of the private economy continued to increase. The added value of the private economy was 985. 5 billion yuan, accounting for 61. 2% of GDP which is 0. 2 percentage points higher than the previous year. The export of goods by private enterprises was 258. 9 billion yuan, up by 5. 8%, accounting for 70. 1% of the total exports. At the year end, there were 678 thousand private enterprises and 659 thousand individual businesses, up by 8. 4% and 9. 5% respectively.

Development quality and efficiency

The annual labor productivity of all employees was expected to be 21. 9 thousand yuan/person; the labor productivity of all employees in industrial enterprises above designated size was 34 thousand yuan/person.

The general fiscal revenue of the city reached 385. 42 billion yuan, up by 5. 6%. The general budgetary revenue of the local government was 209. 34 billion yuan, up by 6. 5%; of which, the tax revenue was 197. 86 billion yuan, up by 10. 5%, accounting for 94. 5% of the general public budget revenue. The fiscal expenditure of the local government was 206. 97 billion yuan, up by 6. 0%; of which, the fiscal expenditure for promoting people's livelihood reached 158. 36 billion yuan, accounting for 76. 5% of the fiscal expenditure of the local government.

The total profit of industrial enterprises above designated size was 130. 2 billion yuan, and the total profit of service enterprises above designated size was 245. 1 billion yuan.

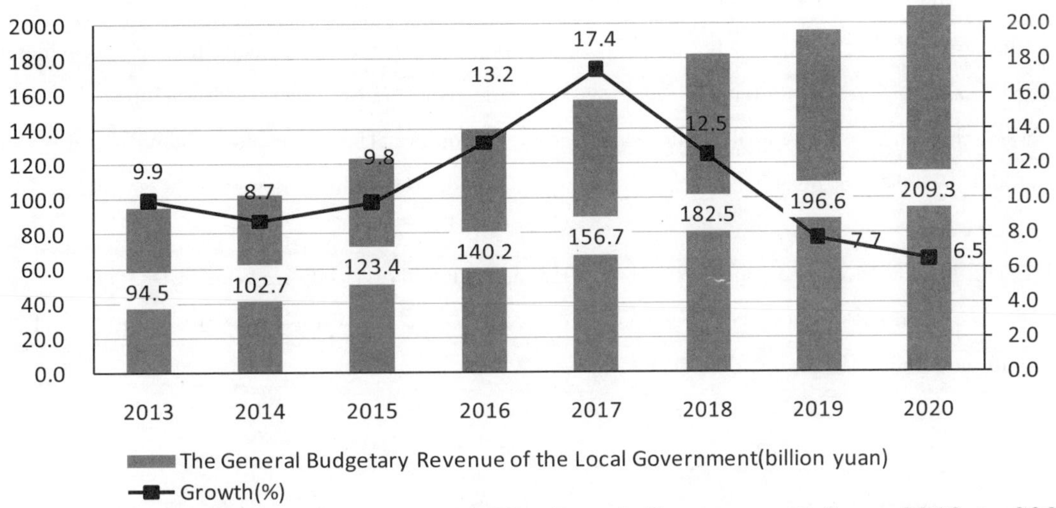

The General Budgetary Revenue of The Local Government from 2013 to 2020

Commodity Price

The consumer price in urban area went up by 2. 1% over the previous year; of which, the price of food and tobacco went up by 6. 9%. The commodity retail price went up by 0. 9%. The producer price for industrial products went down by 2. 5%, the purchasing price for industrial producers went down by 3. 9%.

The Changes of Consumer Price in Urban District (%)

Item	2019	2020
General level of consumer price in urban district	3.1	2.1
1. Food and Tobacco	6.3	6.9
Of which: Food	7.9	8.9
Of which: Grain	1.1	1.7
Fresh Vegetables	3.4	2.0
Meat	23.1	36.7
2. Clothing	1.3	0.1
3. Residence	0.9	-0.3
4. Daily necessities and Services	3.0	3.1
5. Transportation and Communication	-1.0	-3.4
6. Education, Culture and Entertainment	4.3	1.7
7. Health Care	7.0	3.1
8. Other supplies and Services	2.8	3.8

Population and Employment

The annual birth rate was 9. 92‰, and the natural growth rate of population was 4. 63‰. The newly employed people in urban area increased 690. 5 thousand, and 34. 4 thousand unemployed people were re – employed. The registered urban unemployment rate was 2. 4% at the year end.

II. Agriculture and Rural Area

The added value of agriculture, forestry, animal husbandry and fishery achieved 33. 4 billion yuan, down by 0. 9%.
The total output of grain was 0. 509 million tons, up by 2. 4% ; the output of vegetable was 3. 463 million tons, up by 1. 8% ; the output of fruit was 0. 831 million tons, up by 0. 6% ; the output of aquatic products was 0. 193 million tons, down by 4. 8% ;and the output of meat was 0. 110 million tons, down by 44. 0%. There were 563 municipal vegetable bases in Hangzhou, of which 21 were newly built. Hangzhou newly launched the construction of 4 provincial – level key historical and cultural villages, 70 municipal – level boutique villages and 9 folk towns. "Big Xiajiang Rural Revitalization Consortium" was selected into 12 typical rural cases across the country. The farmhouse (home hostel) received 71. 53 million tourists and the business revenue was 6. 5 billion yuan. The sales volume of rural e – commerce was16. 5 billion yuan, up by 15. 7%.
In the whole year, thc collective economic income of 1922 administrative villages exceeded 0. 3 million yuan, and the operating income exceeded 0. 2 million yuan, accounting for 100%. The coverage rate of beautiful rural administrative villages at the city and county levels reached 54. 5%.

III. Industry and Construction

The added value of the industrial sector was 422. 1 billion yuan, up by 2. 6%. Of this total, the added value of industrial enterprises above designated size was 346. 7 billion yuan, up by 3. 8%. The added value of eight high energy consuming industries accounted for 20. 4% , decreased by 3. 2 percentage points. The added value of 17 traditional manufacturing industries decreased by 3. 1%. The total output value of industrial enterprises above designated size was 1471. 2 billion yuan, of which the export delivery value was 187. 4 billion yuan. The output value ratio of new products was 40. 0% , and the production – sales ratio of industrial products was 98. 6%. The output of integrated circuits, industrial robots, optical cables and other products included in the national "three new" statistics increased by 62. 7% , 45. 4% and 32. 1% respectively.

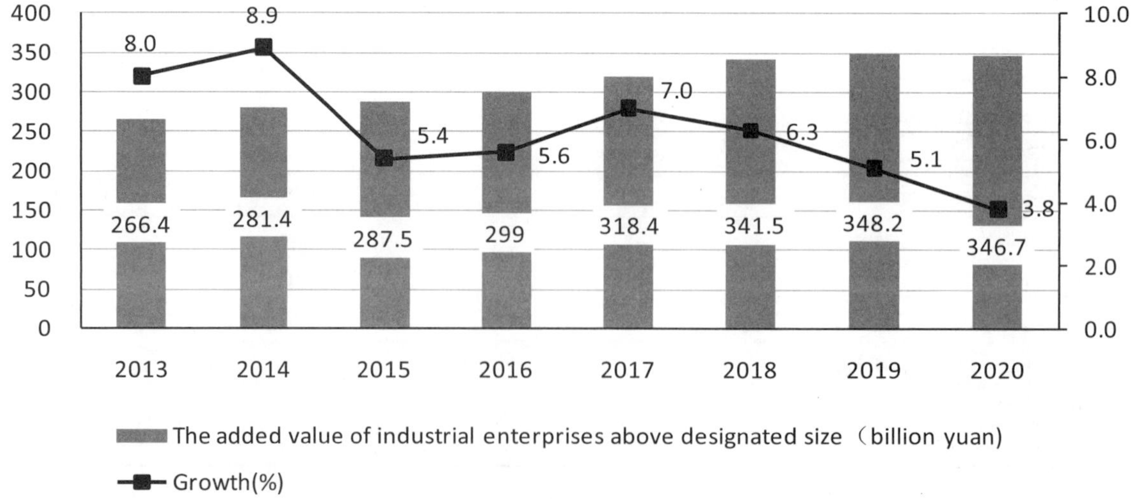

The added value of industrial enterprises above designated size from 2013 to 2020

The added value of construction industry was 60. 1 billion yuan, up by 0. 2%。

IV. Transportation, Post and Telecommunications

The added value of transportation, storage and post achieved 39. 2 billion yuan, down by 4. 4%.

The annual total freight traffic was 0. 42 billion tons, up by 9. 1%. The total passenger traffic was 0. 12 billion persons, down by 41. 7%. By the end of 2020, 336 air routes had been opened, including 69 international routes and 6 routes to Hong Kong, Macao and Taiwan. The aviation passenger throughput was 28. 22 million persons, down by 29. 6% ; and the cargo throughput was 0. 802 million tons, up by 16. 2%. The annual subway passengers were 0. 58 billion persons, down by 8. 1%.

The total possession of motor vehicles reached 3. 119 million, up by 4. 8%. The total possession of civil vehicles reached 2. 584 million, up by 4. 9% , of which private cars numbered 2. 275 million, up by 5. 2%.

The business income of postal enterprises and express delivery enterprises above designated size totaled 45. 00 billion yuan, up by 11. 9% , of which the business income of express delivery was 36. 70 billion yuan, up by 12. 3%. At the end of 2020, there were 2. 0455 million fixed – line telephone subscribers, 18. 689 million mobile phone users and 5. 4758 million broadband subscribers.

Freight and Passenger Traffic Completed by Various Transport Modes in 2020

Item	Number	Growth(%)
Total Freight Traffic(million tons)	41944	9.1
Railway (million tons)	578	7.6
Highway (million tons)	34837	3.1
Waterway (million tons)	6483	59.2
Aviation (million tons)	46	11.9
Total Passenger Traffic(million person)	12183	-41.7
Railway(million person)	5895	-33.6
Highway(million person)	4535	-51.6
Waterway(million person)	339	-44.4
Aviation(million person)	1414	-30.8

V. Financial Intermediation

The added value of financial intermediation achieved 203. 8 billion yuan, up by 10. 6%.

The saving deposits of RMB and foreign exchange from all financial institutions in Hangzhou was 5424. 65 billion yuan, up by 19. 8% ; and the loans balance was 4979. 93 billion yuan, up by 17. 9%.

Deposit and Loan Balance in RMB and Foreign Exchange from All Financial Institutions at the End of 2020

Item	Year – end Figure (100 million yuan)	Growth(%)
Total Deposit Balance	54246.5	19.8
Of which: Household Deposit	14398.1	21.0
Non – financial EnterpriseDeposit	24934.8	23.0
Total Loan Balance	49799.3	17.9
Of which: Household Loans	20428.8	23.7
Non – financial Enterprise Loans	29021.3	14.4
Of which: Short – term Loan	9012.7	11.1
Medium and Long Term Loans	17194.5	17.1
Bill financing	1849.9	13.7

There were 218 listed companies in Hangzhou at the year - end, of which 161 were listed domestically. There were 28 newly authorized listed companies in Hangzhou, and raised a total of 50. 91 billion yuan, up by 213. 6%. There were 34 companies listed on small and medium board, and 46 companies were listed on entrepreneurship board.

The premiums received by the insurance companies totaled 96. 44 billion yuan, up by 14. 0%. Of this total, the premiums of property insurance was 26. 08 billion yuan, and that of life insurance was 70. 36 billion yuan. The payments of insurance indemnity of various kinds totaled 26. 46 billion yuan, up by 8. 9%. Of this total, the payments of property insurance was 15. 52 billion yuan, and that of life insurance was 10. 95 billion yuan.

VI. Investment in Fixed Assets and Real Estate

Investment in Fixed Assets

The investment in fixed assets increased by 6. 8% over the previous year, of which the private investment increased by 3. 4%, the investment in infrastructure increased by 7. 7%, the investment in transportation increased by 6. 6%. Grouped by sectors, the investment in the secondary industry increased by 6. 2%, of which the industrial investment increased by 6. 9%; the investment in the tertiary industry increased by 6. 8%. The investment in high - tech industries increased by 10. 0%.

Investment in Real Estate

The added value of the real estate industry was 122. 6 billion yuan, up by 3. 9%.

The investment in real estate increased by 5. 3% over the previous year, of which residential investment increased by 0. 8%, the investment in office buildings increased by 11. 5%, and the investment in commercial business housing increased by 3. 5%. At the end of the year, the floor space under construction was 133. 10 million square meters, up by 11. 0%; the newly started floor space under construction was 35. 43 million square meters, up by 45. 5%; the completed floor space was 17. 99 million square meters, up by 4. 1%. The sold floor space of commercial buildings was 16. 99 million square meters, up by 12. 3%; the sales of commercial housing was 459. 5 billion yuan, up by 17. 1%.

Main Indicators of Real Estate Development and Sales in 2020

Item	Number	Growth(%)
The Floor Space Under Construction(million square meters)	13310	11.0
Of which: Residence (million square meters)	6959	11.1
The Completed Floor Space(million square meters)	1799	4.1
Of which: Residence (million square meters)	934	-3.1
The Sold Floor Space of Commercial Buildings(million square meters)	1699	12.3
Of which: Residence (million square meters)	1472	14.6

VII. Domestic Trade

The added value of wholesale and retail sale was 127. 2 billion yuan, up by 2. 3%; the added value of accommodation and catering services was 21. 3 billion yuan, down by 10. 6%.

The total retail sales of consumer goods reached 605. 5 billion yuan, down by 3. 5%. Grouped by consumption type, the retail sales of consumer goods reached 506. 0 billion yuan, down by 2. 4%; the revenue of catering services reached 99. 5 billion yuan, down by 8. 5%. Among the retail sales of wholesale and retail enterprises above quota, the retail sales of cosmetics, cultural office supplies and daily necessities increased by 10. 4% , 10. 3% and 10. 3% respectively; the consumption of upgraded commodities such as new energy vehicles, smart home appliances and audio – visual equipment increased by 24. 2% and 12. 8% respectively. Retail sales through public network of wholesale and retail units above quota increased by 15. 4%.

There were 617 commodity markets of various types throughout the year, with an annual transaction volume of 343. 1 billion yuan.

VIII. Foreign Economic Relations

International Trade

The total value of import and export of goods in 2020 was 593. 4 billion yuan, up by 5. 9%. Of this total, the export was 369. 3 billion yuan, up by 2. 1% ; the import was 224. 1 billion yuan, up by 12. 9%. The export of high – tech products was 64. 9 billion yuan, up by 14. 1% , the export of electromechanical products was 165. 9 billion yuan, up by 4. 1%. The export to the countries which along The Belt and Road was 117. 0 billion yuan, accounting for 31. 7% of the total export. Exports to the United States and the 28 EU countries increased by 5. 7% and 8. 5% respectively; exports to Japan and South Korea decreased by 4. 9% and 1. 8% respectively. The export of service trade was 13. 84 billion U. S. dollars, up by 10. 8%.

The import and export volume of cross border e – commerce was 108. 42 billion yuan, up by 13. 9% ; of this total, the export was 75. 68 billion yuan, and the import was 32. 74 billion yuan, up by 14. 9% and 11. 6% respectively.

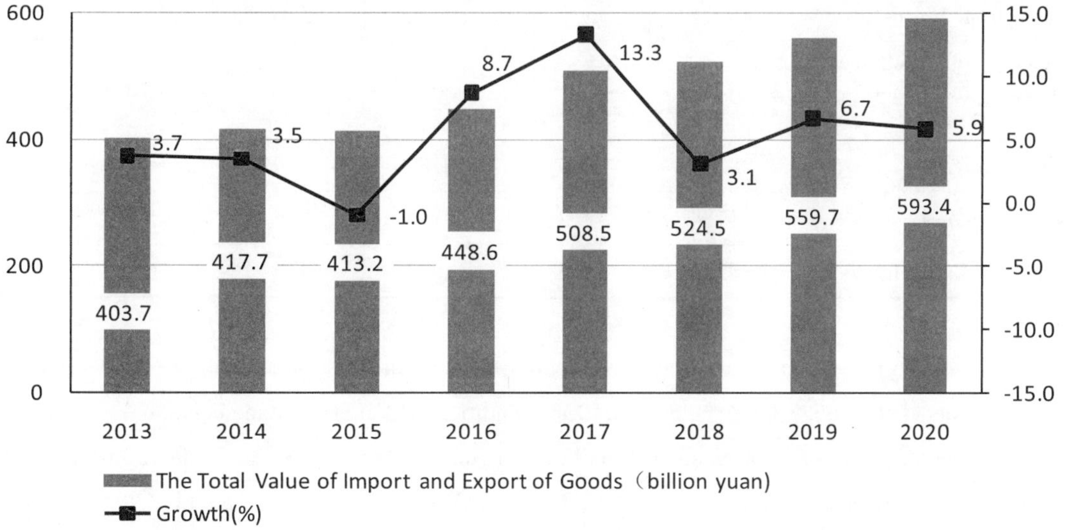

The Total Value of Import and Export of Goods from 2013 to 2020

Utilization of Foreign Capital

In the whole year, 804 foreign – invested projects were newly introduced, including 98 projects with a total investment of more than 30 million U. S. dollars. The actually utilized of foreign direct investment was 7. 20 billion U. S. dollars, up by 17. 5%. Of this total, the actually utilized of foreign direct investment in secondary industry was 2. 33 billion U. S. dollars, up by 218. 8% ; and that in tertiary industry was 4. 87 billion U. S. dollars, down by 9. 7%. By the end of 2020, 126 companies of Global Fortune 500 invested 222 projects in Hangzhou.

International Cooperation

By the end of 2020, the total number of overseas investment enterprises (Institutions) in Hangzhou was 2,445, up by 9. 3%. The accomplished business revenue through oversea contract engineering projects and labor cooperation was 1. 86

billion U. S. dollars, down by 31. 9%. The contract execution amount of offshore service outsourcing was 7. 77 billion U. S. dollars, up by 8. 1%.

IX. Living Conditions and Social Security

Living Conditions

The annual per capita disposable income in Hangzhou was 61,879 yuan, up by 4. 4% or a real increase of 2. 3% after deducting price factors. In terms of resident area, the annual per capita disposable income of urban households reached 68,666 yuan, up by 3. 9% or a real increase of 1. 8% after deducting price factors; and the annual per capita disposable income of rural households was 38, 700 yuan, up by 6. 7% or 4. 5% after deducting price factor. The per capita disposable income of low – income farmers up by 13. 7%.

The per capita consumption expenditure in Hangzhou was 38,235 yuan, down by 4. 5%. In terms of residence area, the per capita consumption expenditure of urban households was 41,916 yuan, and that of rural households was 25,664 yuan, down by 4. 9% and 2. 4% respectively.

Per Capita Disposable Income and Consumption Expenditure in Hangzhou in 2020

Item	All Residents		Urban Residents		Rural Residents	
	Absolute Number(yuan)	Growth (%)	Absolute Number(yuan)	Growth (%)	Absolute Number(yuan)	Growth (%)
Disposable Income	61879	4.4	68666	3.9	38700	6.7
1. Income from Wages	36014	5.5	39720	5.0	23359	8.1
2. Income of Staff & workers in Other – owned Units	6446	–2.1	5640	–3.6	9196	1.4
3. Property Income	8235	1.5	10182	1.4	1586	0.8
4. Transfer Income	11184	7.2	13124	6.4	4559	13.6
Consumption Expenditure	38235	–4.5	41916	–4.9	25664	–2.4

By the end of the year, the per capita floor space of residential building in urban areas reached 39. 3 square meters, and every 100 urban households had 65. 3 family cars, 252. 2 air conditioners and 90. 6 home computers, up by 4. 3% ,0. 8% and 0. 9%. The per capita floor space of residential building in rural areas reached 75. 5 square meters, and every 100 rural households had 54. 9 family cars, 211. 6 air conditioners and 61. 3 family cars, up by 4. 2% ,0. 1% and 1. 8% respectively.

Social Security

By the end of the year, a total of 7. 515 million people participated in the basic social pension insurance for employees, up by 6. 7% ; a total of 7. 135 million people participated in the basic medical insurance program for employees, up by 6. 3% ; a total of 5. 235 million people participated in the unemployment insurance, 6. 334 million people participated in the maternity insurance, up by 7. 6% and 13. 8% respectively. The minimum subsistence guarantee standard for residents in urban areas increased to 1102 yuan per person per month, up by 5. 9%. By the end of the year, 98. 8 thousand people were benefitted from the city's minimum living guarantee system, the annual payment of minimum living guarantee system reached 1. 081 billion yuan, up by 21. 8%.

Social Security Related Treatment Standards

Item	2019	2020
Minimum Unemployment Insurance Standard (Urban Residents)	1608 yuan/month	1608 yuan/month
Urban and Rural Minimum Subsistence Guarantee Standard(Urban Areas Excluding Lin'an)	1041 yuan/month	1102 yuan/month
Urban and Rural Minimum Subsistence Guarantee Standard (Tonglu, Jiande)	833 yuan/month	882 yuan/month
Urban and Rural Minimum Subsistence Guarantee Standard(Chun'an)	833 yuan/month	955 yuan/month
Urban and Rural Minimum Subsistence Guarantee Standard(Lin'an)	989 yuan/month	1102 yuan/month
Minimum wage for employees(Urban)	2010 yuan/month	2010 yuan/month

Social Welfare

By the end of the year, the number of community home care service centers reached 2,910. There were 330 welfare institutions and nursing homes for the aged, providing 75.8 thousand beds, accommodating 35.5 thousand people. There were 8 child welfare institutions with 1,040 beds.

The fund raised by all kinds of welfare lotteries issued this year reached 2.47 billion yuan, down by 18.4%.

X. Science & Technology, Education

Science & Technology

The expenditures on research and development activities (R&D) accounted for 3.59% of Hangzhou's GDP. The expenditure on science and technology was 14.43 billion yuan, accounted for 7.0% of the general public budget expenditure.

In 2020, 55,297 invention patents were applied and 17,327 were authorized, up by 27.7% and 47.5% respectively. There were a total of 817 enterprise technology centers above city level, of which 45 at national level. There were 11 national technological innovation demonstration enterprises and 11 provincial technological innovation demonstration enterprises. There were 209 technology enterprise incubators, of which 41 at national level and 107 at provincial level. There were 181 public innovation spaces in Hangzhou, of which 68 at national level and 144 at provincial level. The total number of technology contracts signed throughout the year was 16,307 and 52.03 billion yuan.

Education

At the end of 2020, there were 40 regular institutions of higher education with 551 thousand students, an increase of 32 thousand than last year, of which 85 thousand were postgraduates, with a gross enrollment rate of 70.04% for higher education; There were 91 ordinary high schools with 125 thousand students, an increase of 7 thousand ; There were 37 professional high schools and secondary technical schools with 64 thousand students, an increase of 2 thousand; There were 280 junior high schools with 249 thousand students, an increase of 5 thousand, and the proportion of junior high school graduates entering into various kinds of high schools was 99.76%; There were 496 primary schools with 645 thousand students, an increase of 28 thousand; There were1,049 kindergartens, with 375 thousand children, an increase of 25 thousand, and the enrollment rate of children who 3 years preschool was 99.15%. The number of migrant workers' children who were enrolled in the stage of compulsory education in Hangzhou was accumulated to 285 thousand. There were 74 home and abroad cooperative projects at all education levels, of which 8 projects were municipal colleges and universities, 7 projects were senior secondary schools.

XI. Culture, Tourism, Public Health and Sports

Culture and Tourism

The added value of cultural industry was 228. 5 billion yuan, up by 8. 2%. By the end of 2020, there were 15 cultural centers (including provincial level), 15 public libraries (including provincial level), 11 theaters (including provincial level), 12 concert halls (including provincial level), 78 museums and memorials, 48 national key cultural relics protection units. During the year, we produced 199 episodes of 5 TV series, and 26,733 minutes of original cartoons. There were 1. 16 million times of all kinds of films, the ticket revenue was 0. 48 billion yuan. At the end of the year, there were 3. 107 million registered cable TV users.

The added value of tourism and leisure industry in the whole year was 99. 9 billion yuan, down by 16. 3%. The total revenue of tourism reached 333. 54 billion yuan, down by 16. 7%. The total tourists were175. 731 million, down by 15. 6%, of which 0. 143 million were overseas visitors, down by 87. 4%. At the end of 2020, there were 926 travel agencies, up by 3. 5%; 119 star-rated hotels, including 23 5-star hotels. There were 111 A-level scenic spots, of which 3 were 5A-level.

Public Health

The added value of health industry in the whole year was 115. 6 billion yuan, up by 8. 3%. At the end of the year, there were 5,675 medical and health institutions in Hangzhou, including 353 hospitals. There were 134 thousand professional medical personnel, including 51 thousand licensed (assistant) doctors and 59 thousand registered nurses, up by 7. 5%, 8. 6% and 9. 1% respectively. There were 90 thousand beds, including 84 thousand hospital beds, up by 5. 3% and 5. 9% respectively. A total of 154. 04 million patients received diagnosis and treatment in medical institutions, up by 5. 2%. The city's grassroots consultation rate was 67%, and the county consultation rate was 90. 1%. The infant mortality rate and the mortality rate of children under the age of 5 were 1. 87 and 2. 88 respectively. The mortality per 100, 000 pregnant women was 1. 68 persons.

Sports

Throughout the year, Hangzhou athletes won 204 medals in national competitions, including 56 gold medals and 75 silver medals. Hangzhou successfully held more than 10 large-scale brand sports events such as Hangzhou Marathon, Crossing the Qiantang River and National Physical Fitness Finals. The upgrading project of 6 swimming pools, 8 football fields, and 23 provincial-level community multifunctional sports fields has been completed.

The annual sales of sports lottery reached 2. 95 billion yuan, down by 13. 25%.

XII. Urban Construction

The total mileage of roads in the whole year reached 16,919 km, including 801 km of expressways. At the end of the year, there were 367 public transport lines in the main urban area, of which 24 were newly opened lines, 29 were optimized lines. The total operational metro mileage reached 306. 3 km, and the metro mileage under construction was 210 kilometers.

The electricity consumption of the whole city was 80. 8 billion KWH, down by 1. 1%, of which the consumption of the tertiary industry was 66. 4 billion KWH, down by 2. 2%; the consumption of residents in urban and rural areas was 14. 4 billion KWH, up by 4. 7%.

A total of 102 thousand parking spaces were newly completed, of which 13 thousand were public parking spaces.

XIII. Environmental Protection and Production Safety

The annual average temperature in the urban area throughout the year was 18. 3℃, 0. 3℃ higher than the previous year; the total precipitation was 1,664 mm, an increase of 14 mm over the previous year.

The total days of good ambient air accumulated to 334 throughout the year, the rate of good was 91. 3%. The average concentration of PM2. 5 in the urban area was 29. 8 micrograms per cubic meter. The annual average concentration of nitrogen dioxide was 38 micrograms per cubic meter, up by 7. 3%; the annual average concentration of sulfur dioxide was 6 micrograms per cubic meter, down by 14. 3%.

The proportion of surface water national examination sections reached or exceeded class III was 100%, and the proportion of provincial examination section s reached or exceeded class III was 100%, 3. 1 percentage points higher than the previous year.

A total of 171 production safety accidents and 136 deaths occurred throughout the year, a decrease of 25. 3% and 28. 4% respectively.

Notes:

1. Some data presented in this communiqu are preliminary data for the year. There may have a difference between sub item and aggregate, because some data were half adjusted.
2. GDP and absolute added value of various industries are calculated based on current price, whereas the growth rate is calculated based on constant price; the classification on primary, secondary and tertiary industries is subjected to the 《Classification on Primary, Secondary and Tertiary Industries(2012)》 which was revised by National? Statistics? Bureau in 2018.
3. Service industry enterprises above designated size: service industry legal entities with an annual operating income of 20 million yuan or above in the jurisdiction. Including health industry category and other three categories: transportation, warehousing and postal industry; information transmission, software and information technology service industry; water conservancy, environment and public facilities management industry. Service industry legal entities with annual business income of 10 million yuan or above in the jurisdiction. Including three categories and four sub - categories: leasing and business service industry, scientific research and technical service industry, education; and property management, real estate intermediary services, real estate leasing operation and other real estate industry. Service industry legal entities with an annual business income of 5 million yuan or above in the jurisdiction. Including social work industry category and other 2 categories: Resident service, repair and other service industries; culture, sports and entertainment industries.

Source of Statistics:

Statistics on newly increased employed people in urban areas, registered urban unemployment rate and social security are from Hangzhou Municipal Bureau of Human Resources and Social Security; statistics on private enterprises, individual businesses and patents are from the Municipal Bureau of Market Supervision; fiscal statistics are from Hangzhou Bureau of Finance; statistics on agricultural park, beautiful countryside and happy farmhouse are from Municipal Bureau of Agriculture and Rural Area; statistics on education are from Hangzhou Municipal Bureau of education; statistics on import and export are from Qianjiang Custom; statistics on subsistence allowance, social services and assistance, welfare lottery are from Hangzhou Municipal Bureau of Civil Affairs; statistics on highway mileage, bus lines are from Hangzhou Transportation Bureau; statistics on air passenger throughput, freight and postal throughput, navigable routes are form Xiaoshan International Airport; statistics on passenger capacity of metro are form Hangzhou Metro Group; statistics on parking places are from Municipal Construction Commission; statistics on ecological construction and environmental monitoring are from Hangzhou Municipal Bureau of Environmental Protection; statistics on production safety are from Hangzhou Emergency Management Bureau; statistics on actually utilized foreign direct investment are from Municipal Investment Promotion Bureau; statistics on oversea contract projects and service trade are from Hangzhou Municipal Bureau of Commerce; statistics on electricity consumption are from State Grid Hangzhou Power Supply Company; statistics on household population, motor vehicle ownership are from Municipal Bureau of Public Security; statistics on post are from Postal Administration Bureau; statistics on money and finance are from Hangzhou Center Branch of People's Bank; statistics on insurance are from Zhejiang Bureau of China Insurance Regulatory Commission; statistics on museums, memorial halls are from Municipal Park and Cultural Relics Bureau; statistics on technological innovation, high - tech Enterprises, research center, public innovation spaces are from Municipal Science and Technology Bureau; statistics on tourism, art performance groups, libraries, cultural centers are from Hangzhou Municipal Bureau of Culture and Tourism; statistics on films and cartoons are from Hangzhou Municipal Party Committee Publicity Department; statistics on newly authorized listed companies are from Hangzhou Finance Office; statistics on healthcare are from Hangzhou Municipal Health Commission; statistics on medical insurance are from Hangzhou Medical Security Bureau; statistics on sports are from Hangzhou Municipal Burcau of Sports; statistics on construction land are from Municipal Bureau of Planning and Natural Resources; statistics on enterprise technology center and technological innovation demonstration are from Hangzhou Municipal Bureau of Economy and Information Technology; statistics on fixed telephone users, mobile phone users and (fixed) Internet broadband access users are from Hangzhou Municipal Information Infrastructure Construction (5G Pilot City Construction) Work Leading Group Office; statistics on price, income and expenditure of urban and rural residents, per capita floor space, durable goods per 100 households are from Hangzhou Survey Office of National Bureau of Statistics; other statistics are from Hangzhou Municipal Bureau of Statistics.

一、综合

GENERAL SURVEY

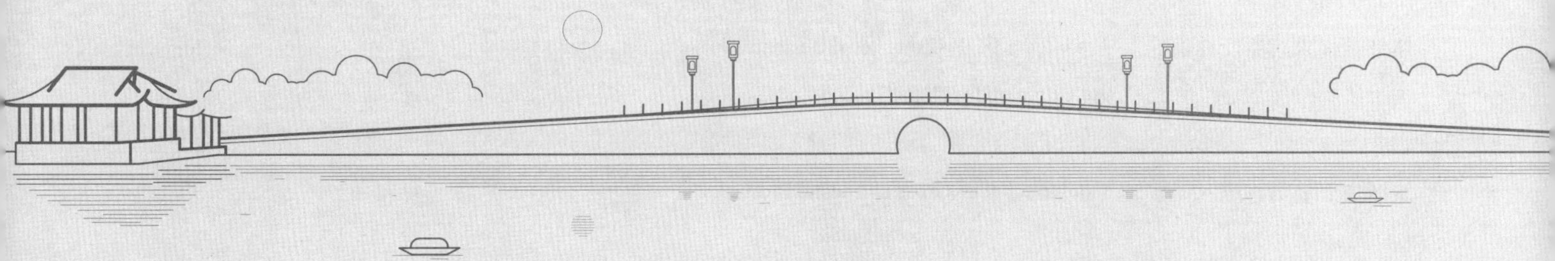

1 综　　合 General Survey

主要统计指标 Major Statistical Indicators

全市生产总值	Gross Domestic Product	16105.83	亿元	(100 million yuan)
为上年	As Compared with the Preceding Year	103.9	%	(%)
第一产业	Primary Industry	326.22	亿元	(100 million yuan)
为上年	As Compared with the Preceding Year	98.9	%	(%)
第二产业	Secondary Industry	4820.54	亿元	(100 million yuan)
为上年	As Compared with the Preceding Year	102.3	%	(%)
第三产业	Tertiary Industry	10959.07	亿元	(100 million yuan)
为上年	As Compared with the Preceding Year	105.0	%	(%)
常住居民人均生产总值	Per Capita GDP (Long-term Residents)	136617	元	(yuan)
为上年	As Compared with the Preceding Year	100.8	%	(%)
地区生产总值构成	Composition of Gross Domestic Product	100	%	(%)
第一产业	Primary Industry	2.0	%	(%)
第二产业	Secondary Industry	29.9	%	(%)
第三产业	Tertiary Industry	68.0	%	(%)

1-01 行政区划(2020年末)

Administrative Division(End of 2020)

单位:个 (unit)

地区	Region	街道 Subdistricts	乡(镇) Towns and Townships	镇 Towns	村、社区、居民区 Villages, Communities and Residential Areas	村 Villages
全市	**Whole City**	**93**	**98**	**75**	**3184**	**1922**
市区	Urban District	86	52	46	2356	1175
上城区	Shangcheng	6	–	–	54	–
下城区	Xiacheng	8	–	–	75	–
江干区	Jianggan	10	–	–	193	4
拱墅区	Gongshu	10	–	–	99	–
西湖区	Xihu	10	2	2	218	41
高新(滨江)区	Hi-Tech(Binjiang)	3	–	–	62	–
萧山区	Xiaoshan	15	12	12	621	411
余杭区	Yuhang	14	6	6	397	173
富阳区	Fuyang	5	19	13	329	276
临安区	Lin'an	5	13	13	308	270
桐庐县	Tonglu	4	10	6	203	181
淳安县	Chun'an	–	23	11	354	337
建德市	Jiande	3	13	12	271	229

注:西湖区含风景名胜区,江干、萧山含托管在钱塘新区的街道数据。

a) Figures of Xihu include the West Lake Scenic Zone, and Figures of Jianggan and Xiaoshan include subdistricts which under administered by Qiantang New Area.

1－02　土地面积和人口密度(2020 年末)
Land Area and Population Density(End of 2020)

地　区	Region	土地面积(平方千米) Land Area (sq. km)	年末总人口(万人) Population (10000 persons)	人口密度(人/平方千米) Population Density (person/sq. km)
全　市	**Whole City**	**16850**	**1196.5**	**710**
市　区	Urban District	8289	1073.9	1296
上城区	Shangcheng	26	35.8	13760
下城区	Xiacheng	29	48.6	16589
江干区	Jianggan	200	149.2	7449
拱墅区	Gongshu	69	63.6	9189
西湖区	Xihu	309	111.5	3603
高新(滨江)区	Hi－Tech(Binjiang)	72	50.6	7006
萧山区	Xiaoshan	1414	226.4	1601
余杭区	Yuhang	1228	241.4	1965
富阳区	Fuyang	1821	83.3	457
临安区	Lin'an	3119	63.5	204
桐庐县	Tonglu	1829	45.4	248
淳安县	Chun'an	4418	32.9	74
建德市	Jiande	2314	44.3	191

注:土地面积取自 2017 年土地变更调查成果数据,西湖区含风景名胜区,江干、萧山含托管在钱塘新区的街道数据。
a) Figures of Xiaoshan include Dajiangdong, Figures of Xihu include the West Lake Scenic Zone, and Figures of Jianggan and Xiaoshan include districts which under administered by Qiantang New Area.

1-03 平均每天主要社会经济活动(2012-2020年)
Selected Indicators on Average Daily Social and Economic Activities(2012-2020)

指标 Item	2012	2013	2014	2015	2016	2017	2018	2019	2020
全市生产总值 (万元) Gross Domestic Product (10,000 yuan)	217721	236710	260335	287542	319930	360568	391965	421179	440050
工业增加值 (万元) Value-Added of Industry (10,000 yuan)	85072	87282	94747	99774	101894	107739	113221	117491	115324
规模以上工业企业利税总额 (万元) Total Pre-tax Profits of Industrial Enterprises above Designated Size (10,000 yuan)	36711	39741	42139	42731	45236	48617	49322	50822	54821
农林牧渔业总产值 (万元) Gross Output Value of Farming, Forestry, Animal Husbandry and Fishery (10,000 yuan)	10530	10942	11468	12066	12268	12540	12770	13730	13679
固定资产投资 (万元) Investment in Fixed Assets (10,000 yuan)	101993	116818	135690	152228	159629	160456	-	-	-
住宅竣工面积 (平方米) Floor Space of Residential Buildings Completed (sq. m)	18466	23154	25425	29323	30419	40297	30434	28301	-
社会消费品零售总额 (万元) Total Retail Sales of Consumer Goods (10,000 yuan)	83018	99719	107540	119378	131447	145220	158046	171869	165450
住户存款新增额 (万元) The Increased Amount of Household Deposits (10,000 yuan)	14863	8729	9825	8739	23921	4858	41861	46066	68219
财政总收入 (万元) Total Financial Revenue (10,000 yuan)	44600	47534	52606	61335	69902	80036	94725	100001	105306

1－04 国民经济

Major Indicators of

指　　标		Item	
年末常住人口	（万人）	Long－term Residents(End of 2020)	(10,000 persons)
年末户籍人口	（万人）	Household Registration Population(End of 2020)	(10,000 persons)
#城镇人口	（万人）	Urban Population	(10,000 persons)
年末从业人员数	（万人）	Total Number of Employed Persons(End of 2020)	(10,000 persons)
全市生产总值	（亿元）	Gross Domestic Product	(100 million yuan)
第一产业	（亿元）	Primary Industry	(100 million yuan)
第二产业	（亿元）	Secondary Industry	(100 million yuan)
第三产业	（亿元）	Tertiary Industry	(100 million yuan)
人均生产总值(户籍)	（元）	Per Capita GDP(Household)	(yuan)
人均生产总值(常住)	（元）	Per Capita GDP(Long－term)	(yuan)
主要农产品产量		Output of Major Farm Products	
粮食	（万吨）	Grain	(10,000 tons)
棉花	（吨）	Cotton	(ton)
油菜籽	（吨）	Rapeseeds	(ton)
茶叶	（吨）	Tea	(ton)
蚕茧	（吨）	Silk－worm Cocoons	(ton)
生猪年末存栏	（万头）	Hogs in Stock at Year End	(10,000 heads)
肉类产量	（万吨）	Output of Meat	(10,000 tons)
淡水产品产量	（吨）	Freshwater Aquatic Products	(ton)
全部工业总产值	（亿元）	The Total Output Value of Industrial Enterprises	(100 million yuan)
规模以上工业总产值	（亿元）	The Output Valne of Industrial Enterprises Above Designated Size	(100 million yuan)
规模以上工业企业利税总额	（亿元）	Total Pre－tax Profits of Industrial Enterprises Above Designated Size	(100 million yuan)
客运量	（万人次）	Total Passenger Traffic	(10,000 person－times)
货运量	（万吨）	Total Freight Traffic	(10,000 tons)
固定资产投资	（亿元）	Investment in Fixed Assets	(100 million yuan)
社会消费品零售总额	（亿元）	Total Retail Sales of Consumer Goods	(100 million yuan)

注:1. 规模以上工业的计算口径,1997 年以前为乡及乡以上,1998 年－2010 年为主营业务收入 500 万元及以上,2011 年起为 2000 万元及以上的工业企业。

2. 从 2014 年起,粮食数据按粮食生产统计监测抽样调查口径。

主要指标（主要年份）
National Economy (Main Years)

1985	1990	1995	2000	2005	2010	2014	2015	2016	2017	2018	2019	2020
	583.21		701.70	771.30	870.54	1013.50	1038.00	1061.00	1092.10	1125.40	1161.30	1196.50
543.05	574.78	597.96	621.58	660.45	689.12	715.76	723.55	736.00	753.90	774.10	795.37	813.83
153.46	169.00	191.43	226.99	297.54	365.24	404.27	447.24	463.86	482.55	515.04	535.96	568.23
330.37	363.49	422.55	408.11	481.10	626.33	654.92	663.03	676.95	681.06	690.10	720.00	748.39
90.49	189.62	762.01	1395.67	2973.74	6049.56	9502.21	10495.28	11709.45	13160.72	14306.72	15418.80	16105.83
15.97	30.94	69.25	103.96	140.29	205.34	266.62	278.98	293.63	299.96	305.56	325.72	326.22
52.08	96.17	410.00	717.88	1524.25	2861.45	3953.53	4133.92	4226.87	4453.44	4694.06	4838.08	4820.54
22.44	62.51	282.76	573.83	1309.21	2982.77	5282.07	6082.38	7188.96	8407.32	9307.10	10255.00	10959.07
1675	3310	12797	22554	45327	88154	133611	145838	160453	176668	187263	196483	200171
					71007	95313	102318	111572	122249	129035	134856	136617
180.00	189.56	174.50	153.08	103.50	58.00	47.53	45.91	45.91	47.26	49.60	49.64	50.86
6704	6693	8038	2112	1038	704	426	378	300	255	240	292	243
51849	60683	61446	80436	70733	67946	50181	51186	43526	47223	55584	59503	61388
22742	26429	19824	24810	25551	30500	26548	28139	28150	30103	30091	31342	29575
7980	11085	13240	9308	16339	11700	6364	4880	3482	3013	4564	3454	–
166.10	159.00	147.58	172.16	165.28	192.53	173.46	156.82	126.91	114.03	107.02	90.34	104.51
11.16	14.93	19.21	25.24	30.74	31.78	26.98	24.31	22.19	21.27	19.11	14.97	10.98
30400	47588	63294	91626	147800	208945	186026	178880	173447	172845	166947	168042	172247
				6589.51	12810.52	15851.40	15018.77	15054.78	15688.35	16087.41	16895.32	–
128.59	292.26	1020.03	1543.57	5441.13	11081.04	12853.05	12415.68	12420.96	12963.76	14016.41	14585.45	14712.08
24.81	31.54	63.05	161.61	450.68	1224.48	1538.07	1559.68	1655.64	1774.52	1800.26	1854.99	2006.46
6724	8119	16620	18607	24124	33772	24070	23942	20541	22289	20121	20888	12183
2488	6522	10347	11459	19909	25915	29335	29384	30170	34785	35180	36384	41944
14.19	22.92	156.63	376.65	1277.80	2651.88	4952.70	5556.32	5842.42	5856.65	–	–	–
47.81	98.17	299.35	514.68	967.38	2155.37	3925.21	4357.31	4810.95	5300.52	5768.67	6273.22	6055.47

a) The standard for above designated size of industry, before 1997, it was above the sub – district level; 1998 – 2010, it was the annual sales income over 5 million yuan; since 2011, it was the annual sales income over 20 million yuan.

b) The data of grain was obtained from the sampling survey of grain production in 2014.

1－04 续表

指　　标		Item	
境外旅游者人数	（万人次）	Number of Foreign Tourists	(10,000 person－times)
财政总收入	（亿元）	Total Financial Revenue	(100 million yuan)
一般公共预算支出	（亿元）	General Public Budget Revenue	(100 million yuan)
金融机构存款余额(本外币)	（亿元）	Deposits of Financial Institutions	(100 million yuan)
住户存款余额	（亿元）	Household Deposits	(100 million yuan)
金融机构贷款余额(本外币)	（亿元）	Loans of Financial Institutions	(100 million yuan)
非私营单位就业人员工资总额	（亿元）	Total Wages of Employed Persons in Non－private Units	(100 million yuan)
非私营单位就业人员平均工资	（元）	Average Wage of Employed Persons in Non－private Units	(yuan)
市区居民消费价格指数	（以 1978 年为 100）	Consumer Price Index in Urban District	(Year of 1978＝100)
市区商品零售价格指数	（以 1978 年为 100）	Retail Price Index in Urban District	(Year of 1978＝100)
全体居民人均可支配收入	（元）	Per Capita Annual Disposable Income of Urban and Rural Residents	(yuan)
城镇居民人均可支配收入	（元）	Per Capita Annual Disposable Income of Urban Residents	(yuan)
农村居民人均可支配收入	（元）	Per Capita Annual Disposable Income of Rural Residents	(yuan)
高等学校在校学生数	（人）	Student Enrollment in Institutions of Higher Education	(person)
中等专业学校在校学生数	（人）	Student Enrollment in Secondary Specialized Schools	(person)
普通中学在校学生数	（人）	Student Enrollment in Secondary Schools	(person)
小学在校学生数	（人）	Student Enrollment in Primary Schools	(person)
卫生机构数	（个）	Number of Health Institutions	(unit)
#医院	（个）	Number of Hospitals	(unit)
卫生技术人员	（人）	Number of Medical Technical Personnel	(person)
#执业(助理)医师	（人）	Number of Lisensed(Assistant) Doctors	(person)
床位数	（张）	Number of Beds in Health Institutions	(unit)
#医院	（张）	Beds in Hospital	(unit)

continued

1985	1990	1995	2000	2005	2010	2014	2015	2016	2017	2018	2019	2020
23.84	38.83	44.13	70.71	151.36	275.71	326.13	341.56	363.23	402.23	420.51	113.31	14.31
18.65	25.25	55.13	142.85	520.79	1245.43	1920.11	2238.75	2558.41	2921.30	3457.46	3650.04	3854.19
5.77	11.82	24.91	73.43	238.33	616.58	961.18	1205.48	1404.31	1540.92	1717.08	1952.85	2069.66
48.50	133.77	707.97	2088.47	6748.72	17084.35	24450.51	29863.83	33386.04	36483.24	39810.50	45286.99	54246.47
15.96	69.75	342.34	788.56	2191.66	4990.97	6767.20	7617.75	8493.27	8670.60	10198.52	11901.30	14398.12
58.01	180.33	567.20	1686.64	5545.30	15078.73	21316.83	23327.95	26169.00	29270.94	36598.25	42245.17	49799.28
13.01	27.79	89.05	126.75	297.02	933.06	1982.27	2152.40	2417.60	2646.72	2864.69	3298.52	3676.74
1266	2382	7156	14257	31069	48772	69209	76073	85022	93891	103798	117339	128308
140.21	246.68	503.06	611.07	623.07	701.33	787.63	801.81	822.66	843.23	862.62	889.36	908.04
142.61	256.45	476.99	504.42	470.47	526.76	573.35	574.50	583.12	588.95	600.73	619.35	624.92
						39237	42642	46116	49832	54348	59261	61879
1026	1985	6301	9668	16601	30035	44632	48316	52185	56276	61172	66068	68666
624	1171	3012	4894	7655	13186	23555	25719	27908	30397	33193	36255	38700
36996	39866	63124	122386	351918	434811	474652	475558	480953	484070	496383	518325	550608
16527	23564	42784	45238	20344	3999	3974	3968	4402	4566	4448	4535	4540
244399	199940	257071	342533	362257	352997	324414	321306	326187	337851	349327	362109	373997
414839	460514	513988	485679	458942	453897	502688	524513	543038	560411	590491	616929	645302
1582	1738	1712	1599	2196	2819	4198	4428	4691	4933	5377	5925	5675
404	440	414	396	127	151	218	244	277	302	316	343	353
25593	30990	34245	35487	42353	61117	85614	93036	101194	110395	117425	126995	134258
11503	14483	16465	16317	17833	24345	31977	34832	38172	41833	44896	48962	51135
19637	24121	26684	27166	33251	42828	55779	63632	69452	75948	81215	85708	90057
15010	18879	21360	23303	25907	33611	50805	58400	63994	70187	75186	79957	84251

1-05 地区生产总值及发展指数(1949-2020年)

Gross Domestic Product and its Indices(1949-2020)

单位:万元 (10000 yuan)

年份 Year	地区生产总值(亿元) Gross Domestic Product (100 million yuan)	第一产业 Primary Industry	第二产业 Secondary Industry	第三产业 Tertiary Industry	人均地区生产总值(元)常住 Per Capita GDP(yuan) Long-term Residents	人均地区生产总值(元)户籍 Per Capita GDP(yuan) Household Registered
1949	2.55	1.43	0.38	0.74		89
1950	2.99	1.73	0.48	0.79		102
1951	3.76	1.94	0.86	0.96		125
1952	4.47	2.28	1.05	1.14		145
1953	5.02	2.32	1.32	1.37		159
1954	5.17	2.28	1.50	1.40		160
1955	5.37	2.43	1.49	1.45		161
1956	6.20	2.50	1.94	1.76		181
1957	7.04	2.33	2.61	2.10		198
1958	9.91	2.55	5.28	2.07		268
1959	12.50	2.63	7.20	2.71		330
1960	13.39	2.49	7.74	3.16		345
1961	10.70	2.70	5.16	2.84		273
1962	9.94	3.04	4.24	2.67		249
1963	10.32	3.28	4.39	2.64		252
1964	11.56	3.39	5.49	2.68		274
1965	12.77	3.56	6.38	2.83		296
1966	13.91	3.82	7.10	2.99		317
1967	13.27	3.72	6.49	3.05		298
1968	13.06	3.77	6.26	3.03		288
1969	15.13	3.81	8.09	3.23		332
1970	16.73	4.07	9.25	3.42		366
1971	19.10	4.74	10.59	3.77		412
1972	19.92	5.19	10.83	3.90		423
1973	20.75	4.99	11.72	4.04		435
1974	18.98	5.14	9.80	4.04		393
1975	18.63	4.88	9.62	4.13		381
1976	19.04	5.00	9.87	4.17		386
1977	23.06	4.91	13.59	4.56		463
1978	28.40	6.34	16.93	5.13		565
1979	33.53	8.39	19.41	5.73		659
1980	40.65	8.15	25.35	7.14		791
1981	46.82	9.10	28.76	8.96		904
1982	50.19	10.88	29.47	9.84		957
1983	55.89	10.11	33.44	12.34		1054
1984	69.47	12.64	40.55	16.27		1298
1985	90.49	15.97	52.09	22.44		1675
1986	105.36	17.76	60.13	27.47		1917
1987	126.02	20.44	71.89	33.69		2276
1988	152.54	25.68	85.53	41.33		2717
1989	166.29	28.27	89.67	48.35		2928

1－05 续表 continued

年 份 Year	地区生产总值（亿元） Gross Domestic Product (100 million yuan)	第一产业 Primary Industry	第二产业 Secondary Industry	第三产业 Tertiary Industry	人均地区生产总值（元）常住 Per Capita GDP(yuan) Long－term Residents	人均地区生产总值（元）户籍 Per Capita GDP(yuan) Household Registered
1990	189.62	30.94	96.17	62.51		3310
1991	227.95	33.40	113.11	81.44		3952
1992	290.07	34.90	148.78	106.38		4996
1993	424.71	41.94	226.44	156.33		7263
1994	585.52	57.51	314.34	213.67		9924
1995	762.01	69.25	410.00	282.75		12797
1996	906.61	84.00	477.62	344.99		15095
1997	1036.33	91.36	541.50	403.47		17113
1998	1134.89	96.06	587.96	450.88		18611
1999	1225.28	97.58	630.75	496.95		19961
2000	1395.67	103.96	717.88	573.83		22554
2001	1582.94	111.46	803.16	668.32		25313
2002	1798.96	114.64	912.78	771.53		28421
2003	2118.71	126.59	1087.74	904.38		33115
2004	2566.46	132.23	1334.99	1099.24		39653
2005	2973.74	140.29	1524.25	1309.21		45327
2006	3483.41	149.88	1763.65	1569.89	44639	52510
2007	4155.84	162.85	2085.15	1907.84	52065	62090
2008	4850.59	178.50	2419.08	2253.01	59619	71861
2009	5181.80	188.45	2404.92	2588.44	62673	76146
2010	6049.56	205.34	2861.45	2982.77	71007	88154
2011	7153.03	232.32	3326.34	3594.38	80360	103306
2012	7968.58	249.44	3553.18	4165.95	85831	114144
2013	8639.91	254.74	3649.62	4735.54	89649	122802
2014	9502.21	266.62	3953.53	5282.07	95313	133611
2015	10495.28	278.98	4133.92	6082.38	102318	145838
2016	11709.45	293.63	4226.87	7188.96	111572	160453
2017	13160.72	299.96	4453.44	8407.32	122249	176668
2018	14306.72	305.56	4694.06	9307.10	129035	187263
2019	15418.80	325.72	4838.08	10255.00	134856	196483
2020	16105.83	326.22	4820.54	10959.07	136617	200171

注：根据2020人口普查和第四次经济普查结果，对历史数据进行了修订。

a) Based on the results of the 2020 Population Census and the Fourth Economic Census, historical data have been revised.

1－06 市区生产总值及发展指数(1978－2020年)

Gross Domestic Product and its Indices of Urban District (1978－2020)

单位:万元 (10000 yuan)

年份 Year	地区生产总值(当年价格) Gross Domestic Product (Current Price)	第一产业 Primary Industry	第二产业 Secondary Industry	第三产业 Tertiary Industry	人均生产总值(元)(按户籍) Per Capita GDP (Household Registered)	人均生产总值(元)(按常住) Per Capita GDP (Long－term Residents)	地区生产总值指数(%) Indices of Gross Domestic product(%) (1978＝100)	第一产业 Primary Industry	第二产业 Secondary Industry	第三产业 Tertiary Industry
1978	141995	5215	106663	30117	1389	－	100.0	100.0	100.0	100.0
1979	167206	6527	126517	34162	1555	－	116.4	109.4	118.1	111.6
1980	208220	5943	159161	43116	1863	－	145.3	94.0	150.9	133.9
1981	229243	6165	171946	51132	2005	－	159.9	90.3	163.9	157.2
1982	248297	7327	183284	57686	2125	－	173.7	107.3	176.0	175.6
1983	282171	5938	200334	75899	2369	－	197.9	83.1	193.8	229.5
1984	353781	8469	244445	100867	2919	－	245.4	114.9	235.5	298.4
1985	448574	11233	293579	143762	3633	－	289.9	120.7	270.1	382.2
1986	513639	12245	324585	176809	4042	－	317.3	122.6	287.7	446.1
1987	605234	15408	370668	219158	4724	－	353.2	137.1	313.8	517.4
1988	708474	19602	425319	263553	5441	－	370.8	136.0	332.7	534.0
1989	772208	23869	435847	312492	5848	－	347.0	146.6	296.5	544.8
1990	896496	23919	470844	401733	6722	－	366.5	147.5	314.3	573.1
1991	1096628	25767	547949	522912	8158	－	426.0	151.3	356.0	690.6
1992	1413278	27611	712697	672970	10420	－	535.3	153.0	447.0	877.0
1993	2086571	36208	1052187	998176	15196	－	687.6	157.5	583.3	1116.5
1994	2788314	48257	1395127	1344930	19945	－	870.9	172.2	779.0	1334.2
1995	3697793	57784	1866784	1773225	25969	－	1041.7	183.4	944.9	1573.0
1996	4727377	110881	2356408	2260088	28552	－	1194.9	194.6	1102.7	1768.1
1997	5414265	130062	2630349	2653853	32227	－	1354.9	214.0	1229.3	2050.9
1998	5905726	134320	2786159	2985247	34620	－	1482.5	230.5	1336.1	2264.2
1999	6317335	145242	2915614	3256479	36394	－	1599.3	254.3	1429.9	2465.8
2000	7111585	145715	3278310	3687560	40127	－	1785.5	255.3	1595.4	2761.7
2001	12260890	582492	6026353	5652045	32607	－	2017.2	275.4	1803.8	3123.4
2002	14042278	605433	6901224	6535621	36640	－	2300.8	289.8	2036.9	3604.4
2003	16647332	665083	8343138	7639111	42675	－	2664.8	301.9	2446.4	4055.0
2004	20362738	664676	10368453	9329609	51241	－	3077.4	312.8	2871.6	4626.8
2005	23789254	682559	11800886	11305809	58659	－	3461.3	316.5	3125.6	5379.2
2006	27930116	728962	13551253	13649901	67816	51904	3950.8	320.3	3475.2	6348.1
2007	33296640	780966	15859466	16656208	79879	59911	4526.3	325.0	3933.7	7401.8
2008	38841136	838780	18288447	19713909	92062	68036	5013.2	327.9	4238.9	8442.8
2009	41615787	879676	18119189	22616921	97491	71325	5534.9	337.5	4507.0	9657.4
2010	48718469	920654	21638629	26159186	112740	80230	6195.6	342.1	4985.8	10952.7
2011	57405621	1019227	25002422	31383972	131189	89363	6814.7	348.7	5375.7	12275.2
2012	64206239	1083214	26609724	36513301	144973	94881	7425.1	355.9	5712.4	13665.1
2013	70003793	1108054	27286186	41609552	156215	98841	8004.4	353.9	6081.4	14903.3
2014	83305362	1506729	33190100	48608533	159934	102178	8658.9	357.3	6560.8	16192.3
2015	92269251	1589108	34672097	56008046	174434	109395	9556.0	362.7	6907.0	18561.2
2016	103682893	1664265	35642963	66375666	192444	119512	10492.4	362.9	7189.5	21087.3
2017	122414796	2100929	40378589	79935278	201827	128103	11355.1	367.1	7534.8	23293.0
2018	133519062	2123934	42866281	88528847	213540	135202	12125.3	372.7	7986.0	25011.0
2019	144057812	2270061	44070699	97717051	223020	141012	12951.5	378.2	8333.8	27091.5
2020	150970622	2252861	44153674	104564086	226707	142890	13481.3	370.4	8543.3	28468.4

1－07　地区生产总值指数(1949－2020年)

Indices of Gross Domestic Product (1949－2020)

(上年＝100)　　(Preceding Year＝100)

年　份 Year	地区生产总值(％) Gross Domestic Product (％)	第一产业 Primary Industry	第二产业 Secondary Industry	第三产业 Tertiary Industry	人均地区生产总值(％)常住 Per Capita GDP(％) Long－term Residents	人均地区生产总值(％)户籍 Per Capita GDP(％) Household Registered
1949	100.0	100.0	100.0	100.0		100.0
1950	116.4	119.9	116.8	105.8		113.0
1951	118.3	112.9	165.8	111.0		115.4
1952	119.0	114.7	135.3	120.4		116.1
1953	108.9	103.4	115.9	119.9		106.2
1954	101.9	99.5	111.7	100.4		99.5
1955	105.6	106.9	104.4	103.3		102.3
1956	111.2	103.1	124.0	121.9		108.4
1957	113.6	99.9	144.4	116.2		109.4
1958	132.2	105.7	204.0	99.2		127.6
1959	118.9	101.9	129.4	129.8		116.1
1960	105.4	91.8	110.1	117.2		102.8
1961	76.7	94.6	61.8	87.6		76.0
1962	91.3	104.5	77.6	94.6		89.7
1963	105.3	109.4	104.5	101.3		102.5
1964	111.5	105.4	126.0	107.6		108.4
1965	112.3	106.5	120.9	105.8		109.7
1966	107.0	103.8	110.5	101.5		105.3
1967	96.6	94.4	96.1	99.3		95.0
1968	99.2	105.5	93.9	106.4		97.6
1969	114.1	96.9	130.3	105.8		113.3
1970	109.8	110.3	114.8	110.1		109.6
1971	100.3	100.9	96.0	103.4		99.0
1972	114.4	109.1	123.1	103.6		112.5
1973	103.6	96.4	108.2	100.2		102.2
1974	92.9	103.6	84.3	100.2		91.9
1975	98.7	95.7	99.1	102.4		97.7
1976	102.4	102.9	102.7	101.0		101.2
1977	118.8	98.3	136.7	109.3		117.9
1978	120.2	119.1	123.7	111.6		119.0
1979	113.3	114.2	114.0	110.0		112.1
1980	119.7	92.5	130.2	118.8		118.4
1981	113.6	102.9	114.0	124.2		112.6
1982	107.2	119.4	103.2	108.6		105.9
1983	111.2	89.1	114.3	124.7		109.9
1984	122.7	121.2	120.8	129.0		121.6
1985	119.4	99.9	122.6	124.4		118.2
1986	111.5	103.6	111.5	116.2		110.3
1987	112.8	102.5	114.0	115.1		111.3
1988	107.4	97.8	109.8	105.4		105.8
1989	96.9	99.8	94.4	102.3		95.8

1－07 续表 continued

年 份 Year	地区生产总值(%) Gross Domestic Product (%)	第一产业 Primary Industry	第二产业 Secondary Industry	第三产业 Tertiary Industry	人均地区生产总值(%)常住 Per Capita GDP(%) Long－term Residents	人均地区生产总值(%)户籍 Per Capita GDP(%) Household Registered
1990	105.8	106.4	106.5	103.8		104.9
1991	118.1	104.4	116.6	127.0		117.3
1992	122.9	100.3	129.7	122.3		122.1
1993	130.1	105.9	138.3	125.8		129.1
1994	126.3	108.1	132.1	122.0		125.2
1995	119.9	107.1	123.1	117.6		118.8
1996	113.0	105.4	114.5	112.2		112.0
1997	113.1	106.8	112.8	114.8		112.1
1998	111.2	109.4	111.8	110.7		110.5
1999	110.2	105.5	110.1	111.1		109.4
2000	112.0	105.7	112.5	112.1		111.1
2001	112.2	107.4	112.7	112.5		111.1
2002	113.2	104.1	113.3	114.7		111.8
2003	115.2	106.0	118.6	112.6		114.0
2004	115.0	105.1	116.7	114.3		113.7
2005	113.1	103.4	111.6	116.5		111.6
2006	114.3	104.1	112.5	117.4		113.0
2007	114.7	102.8	114.4	116.3	112.2	113.7
2008	111.0	103.8	108.8	114.0	108.9	110.0
2009	110.0	103.1	106.0	114.7	108.2	109.1
2010	112.0	102.5	111.2	113.5	108.7	111.1
2011	110.1	102.5	108.5	112.2	105.4	109.1
2012	109.0	102.5	106.9	111.3	104.5	108.1
2013	108.0	101.4	106.7	109.5	104.0	107.2
2014	108.2	101.9	107.8	108.8	104.6	107.0
2015	110.2	101.8	105.5	114.6	107.1	108.9
2016	109.7	101.4	104.5	113.6	107.2	108.2
2017	108.2	101.7	104.8	110.6	105.5	106.0
2018	106.7	101.8	105.8	107.5	103.6	104.1
2019	106.8	101.9	104.7	108.1	103.5	103.9
2020	103.9	98.9	102.3	105.0	100.8	100.0

注:本表按可比价格计算。

a) The indices in this table are calculated at comparable prices.

1－08　市区生产总值指数(1978－2020年)

Indices of Gross Domestic Product of Urban District (1978－2020)

(上年＝100)　　(Preceding Year＝100)

年　份 Year	地区生产总值 Gross Domestic Product	第一产业 Primary Industry	第二产业 Secondary Industry	第三产业 Tertiary Industry	人均生产总值(元)(按户籍) Per Capita GDP(yuan)(Household Registered)	人均生产总值(元)(按常住) Per Capita GDP(yuan)(Long－term Residents)
1978	120.1	118.8	122.3	113.6	118.0	
1979	116.4	109.4	118.1	111.6	111.4	
1980	124.8	85.9	127.8	120.0	119.7	
1981	110.1	96.1	108.6	117.4	107.6	
1982	108.6	118.8	107.4	111.7	106.3	
1983	113.9	77.5	110.1	130.7	111.7	
1984	124.0	138.2	121.5	130.0	121.8	
1985	118.2	105.0	114.7	128.1	116.0	
1986	109.4	101.6	106.5	116.7	107.4	
1987	111.3	111.8	109.1	116.0	109.4	
1988	105.0	99.2	106.0	103.2	103.3	
1989	93.6	107.8	89.1	102.0	92.2	
1990	105.6	100.6	106.0	105.2	104.6	
1991	116.2	102.6	113.3	120.5	115.3	
1992	125.7	101.1	125.6	127.0	124.5	
1993	128.5	103.0	130.5	127.3	126.9	
1994	126.6	109.3	133.6	119.5	124.4	
1995	119.6	106.5	121.3	117.9	117.4	
1996	114.7	106.1	116.7	112.4	105.3	
1997	113.4	110.0	111.5	116.0	104.7	
1998	109.4	107.7	108.7	110.4	107.8	
1999	107.9	110.3	107.0	108.9	106.0	
2000	111.6	100.4	111.6	112.0	109.3	
2001	113.0	107.9	113.1	113.1	111.2	
2002	114.1	105.2	112.9	115.4	111.9	
2003	115.8	104.2	120.1	112.5	113.8	
2004	115.5	103.6	117.4	114.1	113.4	
2005	112.5	101.2	108.8	116.3	110.2	
2006	114.1	101.2	111.2	118.0	112.4	
2007	114.6	101.5	113.2	116.6	113.2	111.0
2008	110.8	100.9	107.8	114.1	109.4	107.9
2009	110.4	102.9	106.3	114.4	109.1	108.0
2010	111.9	101.4	110.6	113.4	110.6	107.6
2011	110.0	101.9	107.8	112.1	108.6	104.0
2012	109.0	102.1	106.3	111.3	107.7	103.4
2013	107.8	99.4	106.5	109.1	106.5	103.0
2014	108.2	101.0	107.9	108.6	106.7	104.0
2015	110.4	101.5	105.3	114.6	108.7	106.7
2016	109.8	100.1	104.1	113.6	107.8	106.7
2017	108.2	101.2	104.8	110.5	105.6	105.1
2018	106.8	101.5	106.0	107.4	103.6	103.3
2019	106.8	101.5	104.4	108.3	103.4	103.3
2020	104.1	98.0	102.5	105.1	101.0	100.6

1－09 分行业
Composition of

单位:万元

行　　业	Sector	全 Whole 2020	为上年(%) As Compared with the Preceding Year(%)
全市生产总值	Gross Domestic Product	161058285	103.9
按行业分	Grouped by Sector		
#农、林、牧、渔业	Farming, Forestry, Animal Husbandry & Fishery	3340124	99.1
工业	Industry	42208653	102.6
建筑业	Construction	6013081	100.2
批发和零售业	Wholesale and Retail Trade	12723536	102.3
交通运输、仓储和邮政业	Transportation, Storage and Post	3922494	98.2
住宿和餐饮业	Hotels and Catering Services	2126381	89.4
信息传输、软件和信息技术服务业	Information Transmission, Software and Information Technology Services	31702106	111.6
金融业	Financial Intermediation	20384891	110.6
房地产业	Real Estate	12256804	103.9
租赁和商务服务业	Leasing and Busyness Service	3965096	87.0
科学研究、技术服务业	Scientific Research, Technical Service	4623313	100.6
水利环境和公共设施管理业	Management of Water Conservancy, Enviroment and Public Facilities	1485246	104.6
居民服务、修理和其他服务业	Service for the Residents, Repair and Others	895006	101.0
教育	Education	5416586	100.9
卫生和社会工作	Health Care and Social Work	4528693	101.1
文化、体育和娱乐业	Culture, Sports and Entertainment	836767	72.6
公共管理、社会保障和社会组织	Public Administration, Social Security and Social Organization	4629508	103.3
第一产业	Primary Industry	3262206	98.9
第二产业	Secondary Industry	48205404	102.3
第三产业	Tertiary Industry	109590676	105.0

生产总值构成(2020 年)

Gross Domestic Product(2020)

(10000 yuan)

市 City		#市 区 Urban District			
比 重 (%) Proportion(%)		2020	为上年(%) As Compared with the Preceding Year(%)	比 重 (%) Proportion(%)	
2020	2019			2020	2019
100.0	100.0	150970622	104.1	100.0	100.0
2.1	2.2	2312149	98.2	1.5	1.6
26.2	27.6	39026755	102.7	25.9	27.2
3.7	3.8	5141945	101.2	3.4	3.4
7.9	8.2	11935212	102.1	7.9	8.2
2.4	2.7	3450787	98.6	2.3	2.5
1.3	1.5	1933630	89.9	1.3	1.5
19.7	18.3				
12.7	11.5	19752042	110.5	13.1	11.9
7.6	7.0	11330428	103.6	7.5	6.9
2.5	2.9				
2.9	3.0				
0.9	0.9				
0.6	0.6				
3.4	3.4				
2.8	2.9				
0.5	0.7				
2.9	2.9				
2.0	2.1	2252861	98.0	1.5	1.6
29.9	31.4	44153674	102.5	29.2	30.6
68.0	66.5	104564086	105.1	69.3	67.8

1－10　分地区和产业生产总值构成(2020 年)

Gross Domestic Product by Region and Industry(2020)

单位:万元　　　　(10000 yuan)

地　区	Region	地区生产总值 Gross Domestic Product	第一产业 Primary Industry	第二产业 Secondary Industry	第三产业 Tertiary Industry	工　业 Industry	建筑业 Construction	户籍人口人均 GDP(元) Per Capita GDP (yuan)(Household Registered)	常住人口人均 GDP(元) Per Capita GDP (Long－term Residents)
全　市	**Whole City**	**161058285**	**3262206**	**48205404**	**109590676**	**42208653**	**6013081**	**197902**	**136617**
市　区	Urban District	150970622	2252861	44153674	104564086	39026755	5141945	223560	142890
#上城区	Shangcheng	11920558	－	4115387	7805171	3904846	210572	371597	332976
下城区	Xiacheng	11343801	－	468521	10875280	163966	304664	262449	232217
江干区	Jianggan	10265317	－	1401452	8863865	542648	859800	197901	107942
拱墅区	Gongshu	6685983	－	1254020	5431963	956513	302066	161517	105875
西湖区	Xihu	15875779	29869	1168465	14677445	796318	373280	205128	147819
高新(滨江)区	Hi－Tech (Binjiang)	17457435	6414	8089961	9361059	7941517	148552	597144	352320
萧山区	Xiaoshan	18284700	578687	6933816	10772197	6181558	754654	150862	92324
余杭区	Yuhang	30516111	526208	6769291	23220613	6261972	509912	250329	130049
富阳区	Fuyang	8120652	495083	3450240	4175329	2967802	483805	117501	98194
临安区	Lin'an	6004051	460050	2800463	2743538	2363373	437122	111124	95076
钱塘新区	Qiantang New Area	10957389	144390	7322213	3490787	6946241	377671	343214	144652
西湖风景名胜区	The West Lake Scenic Zone	458950	9650	172	449127	－	174	237564	191229
桐庐县	Tonglu	3762737	253611	1607775	1901351	1312365	296388	89756	83339
淳安县	Chun'an	2406208	384213	624339	1397656	379155	245422	52749	73026
建德市	Jiande	3918719	371520	1819616	1727582	1490377	329326	76853	88559

注:萧山区不含托管在钱塘新区的街道数据。

a) Figures of Xiaoshan District don't include districts which under administered by Qiantang New Area.

1-11 分地区和产业生产总值指数(2020年)

Indices of Gross Domestic Product by Region and Industry(2020)

(上年=100) (Preceding Year=100)

地 区	Region	地区生产总值 Gross Domestic Product	第一产业 Primary Industry	第二产业 Secondary Industry	第三产业 Tertiary Industry	工 业 Industry	建筑业 Construction
全 市	**Whole City**	**103.9**	**98.9**	**102.3**	**105.0**	**102.6**	**100.2**
市 区	Urban District	104.1	98.0	102.5	105.1	102.7	101.2
#上城区	Shangcheng	101.8	-	103.4	100.8	103.4	104.8
下城区	Xiacheng	108.0	-	108.3	108.0	108.9	107.8
江干区	Jianggan	105.0	-	103.7	105.3	110.4	98.6
拱墅区	Gongshu	100.1	-	95.5	101.6	95.3	96.2
西湖区	Xihu	107.2	115.5	100.7	107.9	101.5	98.2
高新(滨江)区	Hi-Tech(Binjiang)	107.2	91.3	109.6	105.0	109.7	103.5
萧山区	Xiaoshan	101.0	94.5	97.4	104.8	97.1	102.5
余杭区	Yuhang	105.3	99.8	106.5	105.0	106.7	103.0
富阳区	Fuyang	101.1	100.1	97.3	105.3	96.1	111.4
临安区	Lin'an	103.5	100.1	105.3	101.8	106.0	99.3
钱塘新区	Qiantang New Area	102.7	98.5	103.5	100.8	103.6	101.4
西湖风景名胜区	The West Lake Scenic Zone	96.5	100.9	78.9	96.5	99.6	18.4
桐庐县	Tonglu	102.1	100.4	102.4	102.0	102.1	104.7
淳安县	Chun'an	95.2	100.6	86.9	99.3	87.5	85.3
建德市	Jiande	105.3	101.5	105.1	106.4	106.8	94.7

注:萧山区不含托管在钱塘新区的街道数据。

a) Figures of Xiaoshan District don't include districts which under administered by Qiantang New Area.

1－12　主要指标占全省比重(2020 年)
Proportion of Main Indicators in Whole Province(2020)

指　标 Item		全　省 Zhejiang Province	杭州市 Hangzhou City	杭州市占全省(%) Proportion of Hangzhou in Zhejiang(%)
年末常住人口 Long－term Residents(End of 2020)	(万人) (10000 persons)	6468	1196.50	18.5
年末户籍人口 Household Registration Population(End of 2020)	(万人) (10000 persons)	5069	813.83	16.1
年末就业人员数 Total Number of Employed Persons	(万人) (10000 persons)	3857	748.39	19.4
地区生产总值 Gross Domestic Product	(亿元) (100 million yuan)	64613.34	16105.83	24.9
第一产业 Primary Industry	(亿元) (100 million yuan)	2169.23	326.22	15.0
第二产业 Secondary Industry	(亿元) (100 million yuan)	26412.95	4820.54	18.3
第三产业 Tertiary Industry	(亿元) (100 million yuan)	36031.16	10959.07	30.4
常住人口人均生产总值 Per Capita GDP of Long－term Residents	(元) (yuan)	100620	136617	－
农林牧渔业总产值 Gross Output Value of Farming,Forestry,Animal Husbandry and Fishery	(亿元) (100 million yuan)	3496.94	500.65	14.3
主要农产品产量 Output of Major Farm Products				
#粮食 Grain	(万吨) (10000 tons)	605.7	50.86	8.4
生猪年末存栏 Hogs in Stock at Year End	(万头) (10000 heads)	627.58	104.51	16.7
肉类产量 Output of Meat	(万吨) (10000 tons)	－	10.98	－
淡水产品总产量 Freshwater Aquatic products	(万吨) (10000 tons)	138.61	17.22	12.4

1－12　续表1　continued 1

指　标 Item	全　省 Zhejiang Province	杭州市 Hangzhou City	杭州市占全省(%) Proportion of Hangzhou in Zhejiang(%)
规模以上工业企业总产值（亿元） Output Value of Industrial Enterprises Above Designated Size (100 million yuan)	75684.8	14712.08	19.4
规模以上工业企业利税总额（亿元） Total Pre－tax Profits of Industrial Enterprises above Designed Size (100 million yuan)	8583.44	2006.46	23.4
主要工业产品产量 Output of Major Industrial Products			
#发电量（亿千瓦时） Electricity (100 million kWh)	–	161.6	–
氢氧化钠(烧碱)(折100%)（万吨） Caustic Soda(100% discount) (10000 tons)	208.35	23.68	11.4
碳酸钠(纯碱)（万吨） Soda Ash (10000 tons)	29.59	29.59	100.0
合成氨（万吨） Synthetic Ammonia (10000 tons)	61.07	22.32	36.5
水泥（万吨） Cement (10000 tons)	13236.14	1736	13.1
钢材（万吨） Steels (10000 tons)	3806.68	498	13.1
化学纤维（万吨） Chemical Fiber (10000 tons)	2968.18	867.88	29.2
纱（万吨） Yarn (10000 tons)	136.98	33.1	24.2
自行车（万辆） Bicycles (10000 units)	304	107	35.2
电冰箱（万台） Household Refrigerator (10000 units)	593	81.9	13.8
洗衣机（万台） Washing Machine (10000 units)	907	232.3	25.6
客运量（万人次） Volume of Passenger Transport (10000 person－times)	60463	12183	20.1

1－12　续表2　continued 2

指　　标 Item		全　省 Zhejiang Province	杭州市 Hangzhou City	杭州市占全省（%） Proportion of Hangzhou in Zhejiang（%）
货运量 Volume of Goods Transport	（万吨） （10000 tons）	299919	41944	14.0
社会消费品零售总额 Total Retail Sales of Consumer Goods	（亿元） （100 million yuan）	26629.81	6055.47	22.7
出口额 Total Exports	（亿元） （100 million yuan）	25170.56	3693.23	14.7
实际利用外资 Foreign Capital Actually Used	（亿美元） （100 million USD）	157.85	72.02	45.6
财政总收入 Total Financial Revenue	（亿元） （100 million yuan）	12421.49	3854.19	31.0
#一般公共预算收入 General Public Budget Revenue	（亿元） （100 million yuan）	7248.24	2093.39	28.9
一般公共预算支出 Financial Expenditure	（亿元） （100 million yuan）	10082.01	2069.66	20.5
金融机构存款余额（本外币） Deposits of Financial Institutions	（亿元） （100 million yuan）	152233.51	45246.5	29.7
住户存款余额 Deposits of Households	（亿元） （100 million yuan）	61568.65	14398.1	23.4
金融机构贷款余额（本外币） Loans of Financial Institutions	（亿元） （100 million yuan）	143611.59	49799.3	34.7
非私营单位就业人员平均工资 Average Wage of Employed Persons of Non－private Units	（元） （yuan）	108645	128308	118.1
全体居民人均可支配收入 Per Capita Annual Disposable Income of Urban and Rural Residents	（元） （yuan）	52397	61879	118.1
城镇居民人均可支配收入 Per Capita Annual Disposable Income of Urban Residents	（元） （yuan）	62699	68666	109.5
农村居民人均可支配收入 Per Capita Annual Disposable Income of Rural Residents	（元） （yuan）	31930	38700	121.2
高等学校在校学生数 Number of Institutions of Higher Education	（万人） （10000 persons）	125.9	55.06	43.7
普通中学在校学生数 Number of Secondary Schools	（万人） （10000 persons）	244.5	37.40	15.3
小学在校学生数 Number of Primary Schools	（万人） （10000 persons）	372.7	64.53	17.3

1-13 国民经济主要指标人均水平(2015-2020年)
Major Per Capita Indicators of National Economy(2015-2020)

指标 Item	2015	2016	2017	2018	2019	2020
全市生产总值 (元) Gross Domestic Product (yuan)	102318	111572	122249	129035	134856	136617
规模以上工业总产值 (元) Gross Industrial Output Value above Designatted Size (yuan)	121040	118351	120419	126416	127568	124795
农林牧渔业总产值 (元) Gross Output Value of Farming, Forestry, Animal Husbandry and Fishery (yuan)	4294	4278	4252	4204	4383	4247
社会消费品零售总额 (元) Total Retail Sales of Consumer Goods (yuan)	42479	45840	49236	52029	54867	51365
财政总收入 (元) Financial Revenue (yuan)	21825	24377	27136	31183	31924	32693
#一般公共预算收入 (元) General Public Budget Revenue (yuan)	12029	13362	14560	16461	17195	17757
一般公共预算支出 (元) General Public Budgetary Expenditure (yuan)	11752	13381	14313	15487	17080	17556
全体居民可支配收入 (元) Annual Disposable Income of Urban and Rural Residents (yuan)	42642	46116	49832	54348	59261	61879
全体居民消费性支出 (元) Annual Living Expendituer of Urban and Ruarual Residents (yuan)	30181	31905	34146	37369	40016	38235
城镇居民可支配收入 (元) Annual Disposable Income of Urban Residents (yuan)	48316	52185	56276	61172	66068	68666
城镇居民消费性支出 (元) Annual Living Expenditure of Urban Residents (yuan)	33818	35686	38179	41615	44076	41916
农村居民可支配收入 (元) Annual Disposable Income of Rural Residents (yuan)	25719	27908	30397	33193	36255	38700
农村居民消费性支出 (元) Annual Living Expenditure of Rural Residents (yuan)	19334	20563	21983	24203	26296	25664

1－14　数字经济主要指标(2019－2020 年)
Digital Economy(2019－2020)

指　　标 Item	2019 年 营业收入(亿元) Revenue from Principal Business (100 million yuan)	增速(%) Growth (%)	增加值(亿元) Added Value (100 million yuan)	增速(%) Growth (%)	2020 年 营业收入(亿元) Revenue from Principal Business (100 million yuan)	增速(%) Growth (%)	增加值(亿元) Added Value (100 million yuan)	增速(%) Growth (%)
数字经济核心产业 Digital Economy Core Industry	**11296**	**19.4**	**3795**	**15.1**	**12937**	**15.4**	**4290**	**13.3**
相关产业 Related industries								
电子商务产业 E－commerce	3197	23.6	1847	14.6	3483	7.4	1933	3.0
云计算与大数据产业 Cloud Computing and Big Data	2948	16.0	1381	6.0	3335	11.9	1389	1.6
物联网产业 Internet of Things	2040	14.1	582	13.6	2317	8.7	600	8.1
数字内容产业 Digital Content	7576	24.5	2505	16.3	8325	16.9	3113	12.7
软件与信息服务产业 Soft－ware and Information Service	8898	21.4	2889	15.7	9889	16.1	3441	12.9
电子信息产品制造产业 Electronic Information Products Manufacturing Industry	3641	11.3	911	10.6	4460	12.8	1090	14.7
集成电路产业 Integrate Circuit Industry	282	8.8	84	7.4	330	15.7	88	10.5
机器人产业 Robot Industry	95	10.6	27	11.3	118	9.9	34	12.3

注:2018 年起采用浙江数字经济口径,之前为杭州信息经济口径。

a) Since 2018, the statistical caliber was zhejiang Digital Economy, it was Hangzhou Information Economy before.

1-15 分地区数字经济核心产业增加值(2020年)
Added Value of Core Industries of Digital Economy by Region(2020)

地　　区	Region	增加值(亿元) Added Value (100 million yuan)	比上年增长(%) Increase over the preceding year(%)	占地区生产总值(%) Proportion in Gross Domestic Product(%)
杭州市	**Hangzhou**	**4290**	**13.3**	**26.6**
#上城区	Shangcheng	27	4.2	2.2
下城区	Xiacheng	25	0.2	2.2
江干区	Jianggan	41	1.4	4.0
拱墅区	Gongshu	37	17.2	5.6
西湖区	Xihu	590	37.5	37.2
高新(滨江)区	Hi-Tech(Binjiang)	1343	16.6	76.9
萧山区	Xiaoshan	107	20.5	5.8
余杭区	Yuhang	1708	5.6	56.0
富阳区	Fuyang	80	2.5	9.9
临安区	Lin'an	64	17.5	10.6
钱塘新区	Qiantang New Area	108	2.1	9.9
西湖风景名胜区	The West Lake Scenic Zone	-	-	-
桐庐县	Tonglu	50	14.7	13.4
淳安县	Chun'an	7	-2.6	2.8
建德市	Jiande	9	9.0	2.2

注:快报未经省局核定,且萧山区不含托管在钱塘新区的街道数据。
a) The preliminary statistics has not been approved by the Provincial Bureau, Figures of Xiaoshan District don't include subdistricts which under administered by Qiantang New Area.

1-16 “1+6”产业集群主要指标(2019-2020年)
“1+6” Industrial Cluster(2019-2020)

产业分组 Industry Grouping	2019年		2020年	
	增加值(亿元) Added Value (100 million yuan)	速度(%) Growth (%)	增加值(亿元) Added Value (100 million yuan)	速度(%) Growth (%)
数字经济核心产业 Digital Economy Core Industry	3795	15.1	4290	13.3
文化创意产业 Cultural and Creative Industry	3735	15.6	2285	8.2
金融产业 Financial service Industry	1791	9.1	2041	10.6
旅游休闲产业 Tourism Leisure Industry	1191	12.1	999	-16.3
健康产业 Health Industry	975	12.5	1156	8.3
时尚产业(制造业) Fashion Industry (Manufacturing)	213	-1.5	282	16.3
高端装备产业(制造业) High-end Equipment Industry(Manufacturing)	653	1.2	791	14.3

1－17 按机构类型和登记注册类型分组的法人单位数(2020 年)

Number of Corporation Units by Types of Organization and Registration(2020)

单位:个 (unit)

指标名称	Item	法人单位数 Number of Corporation Units	单产业法人单位 Containing Single Industrial Activity	多产业法人单位 Containing Multiple Industrial Activity
总计	**Total**	**542286**	**529127**	**13159**
按机构类型分组	**By Type of Organization**			
企业	Enterprises	514688	501827	12861
事业单位	Publlic Institution	5607	5468	139
机关	Office	1231	1124	107
社会团体	Social Group	4218	4216	2
民办非企业单位	Private Non－enterprise Unit	8024	8023	1
基金会	Foundation	258	258	－
居委会	Neighborhood Committees	1177	1162	15
村委会	Villagers Committees	2007	1998	9
农民专业合作社	Specialty Cooperative of Peasants	2816	2805	11
农村集体经济组织	Rural Collective economic organization	968	959	9
其他组织机构	Other	1292	1287	5
按登记注册类型分组	**Grouped By Registered Type**	**542286**	**529127**	**13159**
内资企业	Domestic－funded	536236	523588	12648
国有企业	State－owned	8015	7693	322
集体企业	Collective－owned	3051	3010	41
股份合作企业	Cooperative	402	387	15
联营企业	Joint Ownership	44	43	1
国有联营企业	State Joint Ownership	3	3	－
集体联营企业	Collective Joint	8	8	－
国有与集体联营企业	Joint State－collective	12	12	－
其他联营企业	Other Joint Ownership	21	20	1

指标名称	Item	法人单位数 Number of Corporation Units	单产业法人单位 Containing Single Industrial Activity	多产业法人单位 Containing Multiple Industrial Activity
有限责任公司	Limited Liability Corporations	17079	15776	1303
国有独资公司	State－funded Corporations	714	610	104
其他有限责任公司	Other Limited Liability Corporations	16365	15166	1199
股份有限公司	Share－holding Corporations Ltd.	1140	810	330
私营企业	Private	490482	479885	10597
私营独资企业	Private－funded	13219	13044	175
私营合伙企业	Private Partnership	10529	10499	30
私营有限责任公司	Private Limited Liability Corporations	465828	455554	10274
私营股份有限公司	Private Share－holding Corporations Ltd.	906	788	118
其他企业	Other Domestic－funded	16023	15984	39
港、澳、台商投资企业	Enterprises With Investment from Hong Kong, Macao and Taiwan	2344	2141	203
合资经营企业(港或澳、台资)	Joint－venture Enterprises with funds from Hong Kong, Macao and Taiwan	718	650	68
合作经营企业(港或澳、台资)	Cooperative Enterprises with funds from Hong Kong, Macao and Taiwan	18	17	1
港、澳、台商独资经营企业	Enterprises With Sole Investment from Hong Kong, Macao and Taiwan	1552	1428	124
港、澳、台商投资股份有限公司	Share－holding Corporations Ltd. With Investment from Hong Kong, Macao and Taiwan	43	34	9
其他港、澳、台商投资企业	Other Enterprises With Investment from Hong Kong, Macao and Taiwan	13	12	1
外商投资企业	With Foreign Investment	3706	3398	308
中外合资经营企业	Joint－venture	1270	1179	91
中外合作经营企业	Cooperation Enterprises	39	31	8
外资企业	With Sole Foreign Investment	2272	2077	195
外商投资股份有限公司	Share－holding Corporations Ltd. With Foreign Investment	59	46	13
其他外商投资企业	Other Enterprises With Foreign Investment	66	65	1

1－18　按行业和地区分组的法人单位数(2020 年)

Number of Corporation Units by Sector and Region(2020)

单位:个　　(unit)

指标名称　Item	法人单位数 Number of Corporation Units	单产业法人单位 Containing Single Industrial Activity	多产业法人单位 Containing Multiple Industrial Activity
合计 Total	**542286**	**529127**	**13159**
一、按国民经济行业分组 Grouped by Sector			
农、林、牧、渔业 Farming, Forestry, Animal Husbandry and Fishery	6504	6467	37
农业 Agriculture	3773	3758	15
林业 Forestry	957	952	5
畜牧业 Animal Husbandry	659	652	7
渔业 Fishery	641	634	7
农、林、牧、渔、服务业 Services for Farming, Forestry, Animal Husbandry and Fishery	474	471	3
采矿业 Mining and Quarrying	143	140	3
煤炭采选业和洗选业 Coal Mining and Processing	2	2	–
黑色金属矿采选业 Ferrous Metals Mining and Processing	6	6	–
有色金属矿采选业 Nonferrous Metals Mining and Processing	10	9	1
非金属矿采选业 Nonmetal Minerals Mining and Processing	121	119	2
开采专业及辅助性活动 Supplementary Activities for Mining	2	2	–
其他采矿业 Other Minerals Mining	2	2	–
制造业 Manufacturing Industry	53918	52905	1013
农副食品加工业 Agricultural Products Processing	890	864	26
食品制造业 Food Manufacturing	814	765	49
酒、饮料和精制茶制造业 Wine, Beverage and Tea Manufacturing	607	581	26
烟草制品业 Tobacco Processing	1	–	1
纺织业 Textile Industry	4556	4482	74
纺织服装、服饰业 Textile Products and Costune Indnstry	4734	4662	72

指标名称　Item	法人单位数 Number of Corporation Units	单产业法人单位 Containing Single Industrial Activity	多产业法人单位 Containing Multiple Industrial Activity
皮革、毛皮、羽毛及其制品和制鞋业 Leather. Furs. Downand Related and Shoes Products	1019	1007	12
木材加工和木、竹、藤、棕、草制品业 Timber Processing, Bamboo, Cane, Palm Fiber and Straw Products	1072	1064	8
家具制造业 Furniture Manufacturing	1057	1036	21
造纸和纸制品业 Paper Making and Paper Products	2230	2211	19
印刷和记录媒介复制业 Printing and Record Media	1314	1297	17
文教、工美、体育和娱乐用品制造业 Cultural, Educational. Industrial Arts. Sports and Entertainment Goods	2262	2239	23
石油、煤炭及其他燃料加工业 Petroleum, Coal and other Fuel Processing	85	83	2
化学原料和化学制品制造业 Raw Chemical Materials and Chemical Products	1779	1730	49
医药制造业 Medical and Pharmaceutical Products	426	414	12
化学纤维制造业 Chemical Fiber	363	357	6
橡胶和塑料制品业 Rubber and Plastic Products	3318	3277	41
非金属矿物制品业 Nonmetal Minerals Products	2538	2491	47
黑色金属冶炼和压延加工业 Smelting and Processing of Ferrous Metal	273	269	4
有色金属冶炼和压延加工业 Smelting and Processing of Nonferrous Metals	336	329	7
金属制品业 Metals Products	5811	5745	66
通用设备制造业 Ordinary Machinery	5786	5675	111
专用设备制造业 For Special Purpose Equipment Manufacturing	3123	3051	72
汽车制造业 Automobile Manufacturing	1751	1728	23
铁路、船舶、航空航天和其他运输设备制造业 Railway. watercraft. Avigation spaceflight and other Equipment Manufacturing	468	461	7
电气机械和器材制造业 Electric Equipment and Machinery	3248	3167	81
计算机、通信和其他电子设备制造业 Computers. Telecommunications and Other Electronic Equipment Manufacturing	2002	1930	72
仪器仪表制造业 Instruments and Meters Manufacturing	1092	1043	49

单位:个　　1－18　续表2　continued 2　　(unit)

指标名称　Item	法人单位数 Number of Corporation Units	单产业法人单位 Containing Single Industrial Activity	多产业法人单位 Containing Multiple Industrial Activity
其他制造业 Other Manufacturing	403	400	3
废弃资源综合利用业 Multiple Utilization of Waste Resouces	158	153	5
金属制品、机械和设备修理业 Metal Products, Machinery and Equipment Repair	402	394	8
电力、热力、燃气及水生产和供应业 Produotion and supply of electricity, gas & water	752	720	32
电力、热力生产和供应业 Production and Supply of Electric Power and Hot Water	468	459	9
燃气生产和供应业 Production and Supply of Gas	67	59	8
水的生产和供应业 Production and Supply of Tap Water	217	202	15
建筑业 Construction	24270	23371	899
房屋建筑业 Housing	3077	2833	244
土木工程建筑业 Civil Engineering	5376	5101	275
建筑安装业 Installation	2516	2384	132
建筑装饰、装修和其他建筑业 Building Decoration and Others	13301	13053	248
批发和零售业 Wholesale and Retail Trade	174209	171064	3145
批发业 Wholesale	105881	104408	1473
零售业 Retail Trade	68328	66656	1672
交通运输、仓储和邮政业 Transportation, Storage and Post	10259	9908	351
铁路运输业 Railway Transport	11	11	–
道路运输业 Highway Transport	7453	7251	202
水上运输业 Water Transport	127	120	7
航空运输业 Air Transport	76	71	5
管道运输业 Pipeline Transport	2	2	–
多式联运和运输代理业 Multimodal Transport and Transport Agency	1415	1361	54

指标名称　Item	法人单位数 Number of Corporation Units	单产业法人单位 Containing Single Industrial Activity	多产业法人单位 Containing Multiple Industrial Activity
装卸搬运和仓储业 Carrying and Storage	728	706	22
邮政业 Postal Services	447	386	61
住宿和餐饮业 Lodging and Catering Services	12289	11523	766
住宿业 Lodging	3734	3584	150
餐饮业 Catering Services	8555	7939	616
信息传输、软件和信息技术服务业 Information Transmission，Software and Information Technology Services	60278	59376	902
电信、广播电视和卫星传输服务 Telecommunication, Radio and Television, Satellite Transmission Services	642	589	53
互联网和相关服务 Internet and Related Services	4790	4693	97
软件和信息技术服务业 Software and Information Technology Services	54846	54094	752
金融业 Banking and Insurance	3522	3244	278
货币金融服务 Monetary and Financial Services	376	291	85
资本市场服务 Capital Market Services	2330	2285	45
保险业 Insurance	247	126	121
其他金融业 Others	569	542	27
房地产业 Real Estate	19088	18158	930
房地产业 Real Estate	19088	18158	930
租赁和商务服务业 Renting and Business Service	76960	74860	2100
租赁业 Renting	4897	4765	132
商务服务业 Commercial Service	72063	70095	1968
科学研究和技术服务业 Scientific Research and Technical Service	40022	39070	952
研究和试验发展 Research and Experiment	4394	4333	61
专业技术服务业 Technical Services	19263	18540	723

单位:个　　　　1－18　续表4　continued 4　　　　(unit)

指标名称　Item	法人单位数 Number of Corporation Units	单产业法人单位 Containing Single Industrial Activity	多产业法人单位 Containing Multiple Industrial Activity
科技推广和应用服务业 Promotion and Application of Service and Technology Services	16365	16197	168
水利、环境和公共设施管理业 Water Conservancy, Environment and Public Utility	2724	2617	107
水利管理业 Water Conservancy	173	166	7
生态保护和环境治理业 Ecological Protection and Environmental Management	513	491	22
公共设施管理业 Public Facilities	1871	1808	63
土地管理业 Land Management	167	152	15
居民服务、修理和其他服务业 Service for the Residents ,Repair and Others	12699	12256	443
居民服务业 Resident Services	7048	6749	299
机动车、电子产品和日用产品修理业 Motor Vehicles , Electronics and Household Goods Repair Industry	3867	3776	91
其他服务业 Other Services	1784	1731	53
教育 Education	11406	10993	413
教育 Education	11406	10993	413
卫生和社会工作 Health Care, Sports & Social Welfare	4322	3976	346
卫生 Health Care	2188	1867	321
社会工作 Sports & Social Welfare	2134	2109	25
文化、体育和娱乐业 Culture, Sports and Entertainment	16426	16123	303
新闻和出版业 News and Publishing	250	241	9
广播、电视、电影和录音制作业 Television, Radio, Film and Television Sound Recording Production	3335	3295	40
文化艺术业 Culture and Arts	3743	3712	31
体育 Sports	1672	1568	104
娱乐业 Recreation	7426	7307	119

指标名称 Item	法人单位数 Number of Corporation Units	单产业法人单位 Containing Single Industrial Activity	多产业法人单位 Containing Multiple Industrial Activity
公共管理、社会保障和社会组织 Public Administration ,Social Security and Social Organization	12495	12356	139
中国共产党机关 Communist Party Agencies	134	134	-
国家机构 Government Agencies	2789	2676	113
人民政协、民主党派 The CPPCC, Democratic Parties	51	51	-
社会保障 Social Security	50	50	-
群众团体、社会团体和其他成员组织 Mass Organizations,Social Groups and Other Members of Organization	5225	5223	2
基层群众自治组织及其他组织 Basic Level Mass Autonomous Organization and Other Organizations	4246	4222	24
二、按地区分组			
杭州市 HangZhou	542286	529127	13159
上城区 Shangcheng	16697	15858	836
下城区 Xiacheng	33223	32063	1167
江干区 Jianggan	67855	66081	1752
拱墅区 Gongshu	39812	38608	1190
西湖区 Xihu	56534	54622	1930
滨江区 Binjiang	33520	32651	869
萧山区 Xiaoshan	103439	101698	1741
余杭区 Yuhang	95578	93623	1953
富阳区 Fuyang	32081	31552	549
临安区 Lin'an	17923	17594	328
桐庐县 Tonglu	18712	18445	265
淳安县 Chun'an	13860	13517	342
建德市 Jiande	13052	12815	237

注:建筑业单位按地区分组汇总按照注册地行政区划代码进行,因此与分机构类型、登记注册类型及行业汇总数据有差异。

a) Construction enterprises grouped by region is according to the code of administrative division of the registered area, therefore the data is different to grouped by organizations, groupe by registration types and industry aggregate.

1－19　市区分月气象概况(2020年)
Monthly Meteorological Conditions in Urban District(2020)

月　份	Month	平均气温(度) Average Temperature(℃)	日照时数(小时) Sunshine Hours(hours)	降雨天数(天) Rainfall Days (day)	降雨水量(毫米) Precipitation(mm)
全　年	**Whole Year**	**18.30**	**1619.30**	**166.00**	**1664.20**
1　月	January	7.30	73.90	18.00	227.60
2　月	February	9.90	108.50	16.00	82.40
3　月	March	13.10	109.20	19.00	155.10
4　月	April	16.40	197.50	9.00	45.70
5　月	May	23.50	155.10	15.00	152.20
6　月	June	26.10	106.40	19.00	382.90
7　月	July	26.90	102.70	21.00	236.40
8　月	August	31.00	258.00	6.00	66.10
9　月	September	23.90	122.90	16.00	222.30
10　月	October	19.20	134.00	7.00	39.90
11　月	November	15.00	131.90	10.00	32.40
12　月	December	6.90	119.20	10.00	21.20

1－20 气　　象
Meteorological

指　　标	Item	市　区 Urban District	萧山区 Xiaoshan
一、气　温	**The Atmospheric Temperature**		
全年平均气温（度）	Annual Average Temperature（℃）	18.3	18.0
极端最高气温（度）	The Highest Temperature of the Year（℃）	39.0	38.1
出现日期（日/月）	Date（d/m）	15/8	20/8
极端最低气温（度）	The Lowest Temperature of the Year（℃）	－5.8	－5.8
出现日期（日/月）	Date（d/m）	31/12	31/12
二、降　雨	**Rainfall**		
本年降雨日数（日）	Total Rainy Days（day）	166	169
全年降雨总量（毫米）	Annual Rainfall（millimeters）	1664.2	1768.8
最长连续降雨日数（日）	Longest Consecutive Days of Rain（day）	10	11
最长连续降雨总量（毫米）	Rainfall（millimeters）	193.5	29.6
最长连续降雨起止日期（日/月）	Start/End（d/m）	14/9－23/9	19－29/11
日最大降雨量（毫米）	Maximum Daily Rainfall（millimeters）	121.2	121.6
出现日期（日/月）	Date（d/m）	17/9	3/7
三、全年日照总时数（小时）	**Total Sunshine Hours（hours）**	**1619.3**	**1499.7**
四、降　霜	**Frost**		
全年降霜日数（日）	Annual Frost Days（day）	5	13
初霜日期（日/月）	Start Date（d/m）	3/12	3/12
终霜日期（日/月）	End Date（d/m）	18/2	19/2
五、降　雪	**Snow**		
全年降雪日数（日）	Annual Frost Days（day）	4	6
初雪日期（日/月）	Start Date（d/m）	16/2	16/2
终雪日期（日/月）	End Date（d/m）	16/2	16/2

概　　况(2020 年)
Conditions by Region(2020)

余杭区 Yuhang	富阳区 Fuyang	临安区 Lin'an	桐庐县 Tonglu	淳安县 Chun'an	建德市 Jiande
17.8	18.1	17.2	17.9	18.0	17.8
38.5	38.3	38.5	38.7	37.6	38.4
14/8	15/8	15/8	15/8	15/8	25/8
-6.9	-6.4	-7.3	-6.1	-5.4	-4.9
31/12	31/12	31/12	31/12	31/12	31/12
170	164	173	160	169	164
1699.7	1904.0	1821.8	2043.0	2249.3	1905.1
10	10	10	11	15	11
188.1	319.8	316.6	156.6	236.1	310.4
2/7 - 11/7	2/7 - 11/7	2/7 - 11/7	13/9 - 23/9	10/9 - 24/9	18/6 - 28/6
72.1	110.4	76.8	115	123.5	124.4
17/9	3/7	2/7	7/7	19/6	7/7
	1346.7	**1342.6**	**1381.2**	**1480.0**	**1317.7**
0	11	7	5	2	5
15/12	3/12	22/12	3/12	4/12	3/12
18/2	18/2	17/2	18/2	18/2	18/2
8	5	4	10	6	4
30/12	16/2	14/12	20/12	16/2	16/2
9/1	16/2	16/2	28/3	28/3	16/2

主要统计指标解释

地区生产总值(GDP) 指一个国家(或地区)所有常住单位在一定时期内生产活动的最终成果。地区生产总值有三种表现形态,即价值形态、收入形态和产品形态。从价值形态看,它是所有常住单位在一定时期内生产的全部货物和服务价值超过同期投入的全部非固定资产货物和服务价值的差额,即所有常住单位的增加值之和;从收入形态看,它是所有常住单位在一定时期内创造并分配给常住单位和非常住单位的初次收入分配之和;从产品形态看,它是所有常住单位在一定时期内最终使用的货物和服务价值与货物和服务净出口价值之和。在实际核算中,生产总值有三种计算方法,即生产法、收入法和支出法。三种方法分别从不同的方面反映生产总值及其构成。

三次产业 是根据社会生产活动历史发展的顺序对产业结构的划分,产品直接取自自然界的部门称为第一产业,对初级产品进行再加工的部门称为第二产业,为生产和消费提供各种服务的部门称为第三产业。它是世界上较为通用的产业结构分类,但各国的划分不尽一致。2012 年前的三次产业划分标准按照当年《统计年鉴》,从 2013 年起,三次产业划分调整为:

第一产业是指农、林、牧、渔业(不含农、林、牧、渔服务业)。

第二产业是指工业[采矿业(不含开采辅助活动),制造业(不含金属制品、机械和设备修理业),电力、热力、燃气及水生产和供应业]和建筑业。

第三产业即服务业,是指除第一产业、第二产业以外的其他行业。

可比价格 指在不同时期的价值指标对比时,扣除了价格变动的因素,以确切反映物量的变化。按可比价格计算有两种方法:一种是直接用产品产量乘每一年的不变价格计算;另一种使用价格指数换算。

不变价格 指用同类产品的年平均价格作为固定价格,来计算各年产品价值。按不变价格计算的产品价值消除了价格变动因素,不同时期对比可反映出生产的发展速度。新中国成立后,随着工农业产品价格的变化,国家统计局先后五次制定了全国统一的工业产品不变价格和农业产品不变价格,从 1949 年到 1957 年使用 1952 工(农)业产品不变价格,从 1957 年到 1971 年使用 1957 年不变价格,从 1981 年到 1990 年使用 1980 年不变价格,从 1991 年到 2000 年使用 1990 年不变价格,从 2001 年到 2005 年使用 2000 年不变价格,从 2006 年到 2010 年使用 2005 年不变价格,从 2011 年到 2015 年使用 2010 年不变价格,从 2016 年到 2020 年使用 2015 年不变价格。

数字经济 按照《国民经济行业分类(2017 版)》新的行业分类目录,界定数字经济核心产业统计分类目录,确定了计算机通信和其他电子设备制造业、电子信息机电制造业、专用电子设备制造业、电信广播电视和卫星传输服务业、互联网及其相关服务业、软件和信息技术服务业、文化数字内容及其服务业等 7 大类 128 个小类行业作为数字经济核心产业统计范围,并确定在全省组织开展数字经济核心产业定期统计监测工作。

“1 +6 产业集群” 2016 年,杭州在国民经济和社会发展第“十三个”五年规划纲要中,提出:构建以信息经济为引领、现代服务业为主导、先进制造业为支撑、都市现代农业为基础的现代产业新体系,推进产业迈向中高端。确立发展万亿信息产业集群以及文化创意、旅游休闲、金融服务、健康、时尚、高端装备制造等六大千亿产业集群的目标。

降水量 从天空降落到地面的液态或固态(经融化后)降水,未经蒸发、渗透、流失而在水平面上积聚的深度。降水量以毫米为单位。

空气的温度(简称气温) 表示空气冷热程度的物理量。

日照时数 太阳在一地实际照射地面的时数。

Explanatory Notes on Main Statistical Indicators

Gross Domestic Product (GDP) refers to the final products of all resident units in a country (or a region) during a certain period of time. Gross domestic product is expressed in three different forms, i. e. value, income, and products respectively. The form of value refers to the total value of all products and services produced by all resident units during a certain period of time minus total value of input of materials and services of the nature of non – fixed assets or the summation of the value – added of all resident units; the form of income includes all the income created by all resident units and distributed primarily to all resident and non – resident units; the form of products refers to all goods and services for final use by all resident units plus net export of goods and services during a given period of time. In the practice of national accounting, gross domestic product is calculated with three approaches, i. e. production approach, income approach, and expenditure approach, which reflect gross domestic product and its composition from different aspects.

Three Industries Industry structure has been classified according to the historical sequence of development. Primary Industry refers to extraction of natural resources; Secondary Industry involves processing of primary products; and Tertiary Industry provides services of various kinds for production and consumption. The above classification is universal although it varies to some extent from country to country. The division standard of three industries was in accordance with Hangzhou Statistical Yearbook of the year before 2012, but since 2013 it has been adjusted as follows.

Primary Industry refers to agriculture, forestry, animal husbandry and fishery industries (excluding their service industries).

Second Industry refers to industry [mining(excluding its support activities), manufacturing(excluding the repair services of metal product, machine and equipment), production and supply of electricity, heat, water and gas] and construction.

Tertiary Industry is the service industry, refers to all other industries other than Primary or Secondary industries.

Comparable Price refers to the price deducting the factor of price change when comparing value indicators of different periods to reflect accurately the changes in physical value. There are two methods to calculate comparable price: one is to multiply the output of products by their constant prices of a certain year, and the other is to converse the data by relevant price index.

Constant Price refers to the average price of a given production a certain year, which is used to calculate the product value per year. The product value calculated on constant prices eliminates the factor of price changes, so its comparison between different periods may reflect the speed of production development. Since the establishment of new China,, with the changes in general price level, the State Statistical Bureau has issued nationally unified constant prices for five times. The 1952 constant prices had been used from1949 to1957, the 1957 constant prices from1957 to1971, the 1970 constant prices from1971 to1981, the 1980 constant prices from1981 to1990, the 1990 constant prices from 1991 to 2000, the 2000 constant prices from 2001 to 2005, the 2005 constant prices from 2006 to 2010, the 2010 constant prices from 2011 to 2015, and the 2015 constant prices from 2016 to 2020.

Digital Economy According to the new industry classification catalogue of national economic industry classification (2017 Edition), define the statistical classification catalogue of core industries of digital economy. The statistical scope of the core industries of digital economy is determined as seven categories and 128 sub industries, including computer communication and other electronic equipment manufacturing industry, electronic information electromechanical manufacturing industry, special electronic equipment manufacturing industry, telecommunication, radio and television and satellite transmission service industry, Internet and its related service industry, software and information technology service industry, cultural digital content and its service industry. The regular statistical monitoring work of digital economy core industry is launched in the whole province.

"1 +6"Industrial Cluster In 2016, in the outline of the 13th five – year plan for national economic and social development, Hangzhou suggested to establish a new system of modern industry led by the information economy , dominated by the modern service industry, supported by the advanced manufacturing industry and based on the urban modern agriculture to promote industries to develop towards medium and high end. An aim is established to develop a trillion – scale information industrial cluster, and six hundred – billion – scale industrial cluster of Cultural and Creative Industry, Tourism Leisure Industry, Financial Services Industry, Health Industry, Fashion Industry and High – end Equipment Manufacturing Industry.

Precipitation refers to the depth of the water accumulated on the horizontal plane by rainwater, liquid or melt from solid, falling from the sky to the ground without evaporation, infiltration and loss.

It is calculated in the unit of millimeter (mm).

Air Temperature refers to the physical quantity indicating the degree of coldness or hotness of the air.

Duration of sunshine refers to the number of hours the sun actually shines on the ground in one place.

二、人口和就业人员

POPULATION AND EMPLOYMENT

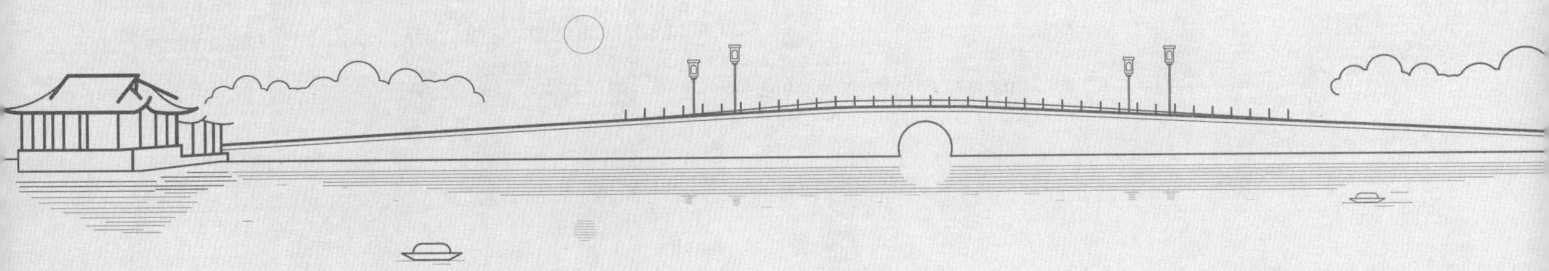

2 人口和就业人员 Population and Employment

主要统计指标
Major Statistical Indicators

年末常住人口	Long-term Residents(year-end)	1196.50	万人	(10, 000 persons)
为上年	As Compared with the Preceding Year	103.0	%	(%)
#城镇人口	Urban Population	996.64	万人	(10, 000 persons)
年末户籍登记户数	Total Registration Households(year-end)	254.75	万户	(10, 000 Subscribers)
为上年	As Compared with the Preceding Year	102.7	%	(%)
年末户籍登记人口	Total Registration Population(year-end)	813.83	万人	(10, 000 persons)
为上年	As Compared with the Preceding Year	102.3	%	(%)
#男性	Male	402.72	万人	(10, 000 persons)
为上年	As Compared with the Preceding Year	102.1	%	(%)
户籍人口自然增长率	Natural Growth Rate of Household Registered Population	4.63	‰	(‰)
年末就业人员	Number of Employed Persons(year-end)	748.39	万人	(10, 000 persons)
为上年	As Compared with the Preceding Year	103.9	%	(%)

2-01 历次普查常住人口情况

Long - term Residents in the Past Population Census

单位:万人 (10000 persons)

地 区 Region	第一次人口普查 1953.7.1 the First Population Census (1953.7.1)	第二次人口普查 1964.7.1 the Second Population Census (1964.7.1)	第三次人口普查 1982.7.1 the Third Population Census (1982.7.1)	第四次人口普查 1990.7.1 the Fourth Population Census (1990.7.1)	第五次人口普查 2000.11.1 the Fifth Population Census (2000.11.1)	第六次人口普查 2010.11.1 the Sixth Population Census (2010.11.1)	第七次人口普查 2020.11.1 the Seventh Population Census (2020.11.1)
杭州市 Hangzhou	**301.13**	**421.90**	**526.05**	**583.21**	**687.87**	**870.04**	**1193.60**
市 区 Urban District	227.49	318.88	405.55	454.38	564.52	752.64	1071.12
#上城区 Shangcheng				21.10	33.51	34.46	35.77
下城区 Xiacheng				25.66	41.24	52.61	48.58
江干区 Jianggan				36.12	56.54	99.88	148.78
拱墅区 Gongshu				29.34	42.93	55.19	63.51
西湖区 Xihu				35.40	59.33	82.00	111.30
高新(滨江)区 Hi - Tech(Binjiang)					11.59	31.90	50.38
萧山区 Xiaoshan	56.32	82.34	106.11	113.06	123.33	151.13	225.89
余杭区 Yuhang	52.28	64.96	80.50	86.08	81.77	117.03	240.25
富阳区 Fuyang	29.22	39.66	54.13	58.07	62.86	71.77	83.20
临安区 Lin'an	26.01	35.57	45.65	49.55	51.42	56.67	63.46
桐庐县 Tonglu	19.73	26.20	34.83	37.66	37.81	40.64	45.31
淳安县 Chun'an	27.49	38.66	42.03	43.55	38.23	33.68	32.90
建德市 Jiande	26.42	38.15	43.64	47.63	47.31	43.08	44.27

注:历年普查市区口径均已按现行行政辖区调整。

a) The data of the past population censuses in urban district were adjusted according to the current administrative division.

2－02　第七次人口普查基本情况
Basic Statistics on the Seventh Population Census

项　　目	Item	全市 Whole City	比重(%) Proportion(%)
总户数(万户)	**Total Households (10,000 households)**	**495.50**	
平均每户人数(人)	Average number of people per household (person)	2.41	
总人口(万人)	**Total population (10,000 people)**	**1193.60**	
按性别分	By gender	1193.60	100.00
男	Male	621.60	52.08
女	Female	572.01	47.92
按城乡分	By Urban and Rural Areas	1193.60	100.00
城镇人口	Urban Population	994.21	83.29
乡村人口	Rural Population	199.39	16.71
按年龄分	By Age	1193.60	100.00
0－14岁	0－14 years old	155.35	13.02
15－59岁	15－59 years old	836.92	70.12
60岁及以上	60 years old and above	201.33	16.87
其中:65岁及以上	Of Which: 65 Years Old and Above	139.14	11.66
按文化程度分	By Education Level	1193.60	100.00
大学	University	349.92	29.32
高中	High School	183.41	15.37
初中	Junior High School	313.04	26.23
小学	Primary School	246.39	20.64
文盲、半文盲(15岁及15岁以上)	Illiterate, semi－illiterate (15 years old and above)	21.59	1.81
按民族分	By Nationality	1193.60	100.00
汉族	The Han nationality	1165.88	97.68
少数民族	Ethnic minority	27.72	2.32
畲族	The She Nationality	1.91	0.16
苗族	The Miao Nationality	7.33	0.61
回族	The Hui Nationality	1.59	0.13
满族	The Manchu nationality	1.33	0.11
蒙古族	The Mongolian Nationality	0.71	0.06
壮族	The Zhuang nationality	2.23	0.19

2－03 户籍人口和总户数(1949－2020年)

Household Registered Population and Households(1949－2020)

单位:万人 (10000 Persons)

年份 Year	总户数 Total Households	总人口 Total Population	城镇人口 Urban Population	按性别分 By Gender 男 Male	女 Female
1949		288.08	68.67	152.99	135.09
1950		297.64	70.08	158.74	138.90
1951		304.89	73.10	163.27	141.61
1952		318.97	75.18	164.60	147.52
1953		328.63	77.17	168.69	150.28
1954		339.29	82.71	173.67	154.96
1955		346.57	85.27	179.25	160.04
1956		365.64	86.97	182.86	163.71
1957		372.75	99.49	192.46	173.18
1958		384.41	108.15	198.82	173.93
1959		391.16	117.88	204.89	179.52
1960		391.16	126.55	207.87	183.29
1961		393.79	119.23	207.15	186.64
1962		403.74	108.96	211.02	192.72
1963		416.36	108.83	217.15	199.21
1964		426.76	104.96	222.66	204.10
1965		435.66	107.29	226.56	209.10
1966		441.84	106.64	229.25	212.59
1967		449.35	107.92	233.27	216.18
1968		456.39	107.14	236.76	219.63
1969		455.58	104.49	235.77	219.81
1970		458.82	101.94	237.09	221.73
1971		467.81	105.98	241.93	225.88
1972		474.06	109.08	244.68	229.88
1973		480.62	110.10	248.06	232.56
1974		485.68	109.87	250.73	234.95
1975		491.68	110.87	253.71	237.97
1976		495.91	112.05	255.78	240.10
1977		499.96	112.14	257.75	242.20
1978	117.89	505.55	116.06	260.74	244.81
1979	116.61	511.83	124.60	263.97	247.86
1980	119.11	515.53	128.88	266.02	249.51
1981	125.96	520.73	134.56	268.69	252.04
1982	131.53	528.06	139.94	272.72	255.34
1983	135.55	533.05	143.34	275.64	257.41
1984	139.24	537.49	147.46	278.04	259.45
1985	145.23	543.05	153.46	281.11	261.94
1986	151.59	549.53	157.19	284.57	264.96
1987	157.66	557.63	161.12	288.70	268.93
1988	164.41	565.04	164.87	292.21	272.83
1989	169.09	570.98	167.28	295.15	275.83

单位:万人　　2－03　续表　continued　　(10000 Persons)

年　份 Year	总户数 Total Households	总人口 Total Population	城镇人口 Urban Population	按性别分 By Gender 男 Male	女 Female
1990	171.94	574.78	169.00	297.02	277.76
1991	174.78	578.73	171.25	298.85	279.88
1992	177.68	582.40	174.03	300.63	281.77
1993	179.17	587.10	179.11	303.03	284.07
1994	180.65	592.93	186.50	306.00	286.93
1995	182.55	597.96	191.43	308.25	289.71
1996	184.33	603.22	196.68	310.76	292.46
1997	186.28	607.96	204.39	313.02	294.94
1998	187.80	611.64	210.52	314.69	296.95
1999	191.60	616.05	219.05	316.63	299.42
2000	193.48	621.58	227.00	319.09	302.49
2001	195.56	629.14	237.77	322.78	306.36
2002	198.27	636.81	252.02	326.62	310.19
2003	201.12	642.78	263.67	329.04	313.74
2004	204.52	651.68	282.58	332.62	319.06
2005	207.42	660.45	297.54	336.12	324.33
2006	209.91	666.31	309.78	338.23	328.08
2007	211.99	672.35	323.75	340.50	331.85
2008	213.74	677.64	340.76	342.45	335.19
2009	215.28	683.38	354.48	344.51	338.87
2010	216.51	689.12	365.24	346.56	342.56
2011	218.26	695.71	376.03	349.09	346.62
2012	218.95	700.52	384.09	350.90	349.62
2013	220.66	706.61	393.88	353.32	353.29
2014	222.35	715.76	404.27	357.26	358.50
2015	225.79	723.55	447.24	360.68	362.87
2016	229.57	736.00	463.86	366.47	369.53
2017	235.26	753.88	482.55	374.75	379.12
2018	241.84	774.10	515.04	384.20	389.90
2019	248.14	795.37	535.96	394.26	401.11
2020	254.75	813.83	568.23	402.72	411.11

注:1. 按公安户籍人口统计。
2. 城镇人口 2015 年前为非农业人口。
a) Figures in this table are based on the household registered statistics which published by Public Security Bureau.
b) Since 2015, the donotation of Non－agriculture Population has been adjusted to Urban Population.

2-04 市区户籍人口和总户数(1978－2020年)

Household Registered Population and Households of Urban District(1978－2020)

年 份 Year	总户数 (万户) Total Households (10000 households)	总人口数 (万人) Total Population (10000 persons)	城镇人口(万人) Urban Population (10000 persons)	按性别分 By Gender 男(万人) Male (10000 persons)	女(万人) Female (10000 persons)
1978	25.52	104.53	78.73	53.95	50.58
1979	26.23	110.50	85.05	57.09	53.41
1980	27.23	113.08	87.93	58.56	54.52
1981	29.88	115.59	90.53	59.96	55.63
1982	31.24	118.05	92.72	61.28	56.77
1983	32.69	120.13	94.94	62.43	57.70
1984	34.07	122.29	97.34	63.63	58.66
1985	35.36	124.67	100.01	64.96	59.71
1986	37.02	127.07	102.59	66.29	60.78
1987	38.70	129.16	104.09	67.38	61.78
1988	40.05	131.26	107.30	68.46	62.80
1989	41.19	132.84	108.88	69.28	63.56
1990	42.26	133.89	109.97	69.75	64.14
1991	42.98	134.97	111.20	70.33	64.64
1992	43.63	136.30	112.70	71.08	65.22
1993	44.55	138.33	115.13	72.22	66.11
1994	45.04	141.27	118.48	73.82	67.45
1995	46.06	143.52	121.38	74.91	68.61
1996	52.39	166.73	128.76	87.15	79.58
1997	53.14	169.29	131.76	88.53	80.76
1998	53.92	171.89	134.62	89.86	82.03
1999	54.64	175.27	139.29	91.65	83.62
2000	55.34	179.18	143.69	93.64	85.54
2001	115.81	379.49	193.26	194.59	184.90
2002	117.11	387.01	205.98	198.47	188.54
2003	119.01	393.19	216.13	201.14	192.05
2004	120.56	401.59	233.08	204.43	197.16
2005	122.02	409.52	245.56	207.70	201.82
2006	123.31	414.18	256.42	209.45	204.73
2007	124.40	419.50	269.30	211.59	207.91
2008	125.56	424.30	285.11	213.54	210.76
2009	126.92	429.44	297.83	215.56	213.88
2010	128.43	434.82	307.52	217.65	217.16
2011	130.14	440.34	317.63	219.86	220.48
2012	131.48	445.43	325.50	221.99	223.43
2013	133.27	450.82	334.38	224.24	226.58
2014	157.11	525.07	358.56	261.17	263.90
2015	160.47	532.86	389.14	264.71	268.15
2016	164.22	544.68	403.20	270.31	274.38
2017	188.48	615.23	440.61	304.86	310.37
2018	194.84	635.30	469.27	314.28	321.02
2019	201.01	656.56	488.16	324.39	332.17
2020	207.43	675.30	517.09	333.05	342.25

注:城镇人口2015年前为非农业人口。

a) Before 2015, the Urban Population was Non－agriculture Population.

2-05 分地区户籍人口和总户数(2020 年末)

Household Registered Population and Households by Region(End of 2020)

地 区 Region	总户数 (户) Total Households (household)	总人口数 (人) Total Population (person)	按性别分 By Gender 男(人) Male (person)	 女(人) Female (person)
全 市 Whole City	**2547517**	**8138304**	**4027248**	**4111056**
市 区 Urban District	2074302	6753023	3330491	3422532
#上城区 Shangcheng	112134	320793	158969	161824
下城区 Xiacheng	133053	432229	211281	220948
江干区 Jianggan	208671	676382	333644	342738
拱墅区 Gongshu	145541	413949	203445	210504
西湖区 Xihu	223272	793264	394705	398559
西湖风景名胜区 The West Lake Scenic Zone	6122	19319	9113	10206
高新(滨江)区 Hi-Tech(Binjiang)	79616	292349	147170	145179
萧山区 Xiaoshan	398702	1373598	673119	700479
余杭区 Yuhang	363263	1219042	594615	624427
富阳区 Fuyang	220568	691114	345768	345346
临安区 Lin'an	189482	540303	267775	272528
桐庐县 Tonglu	150102	419220	208131	211089
淳安县 Chun'an	146913	456160	230578	225582
建德市 Jiande	176200	509901	258048	251853
钱塘新区 Qiantang	87430	319258	158295	160963

注:西湖区包含风景名胜区,江干、萧山含托管在钱塘新区的街道数据。

a) Figures of Xihu include the West Lake Scenic Zone, and Figures of Jianggan and Xiaoshan include subdistricts which under administered by Qiantang New Area.

2-06 分地区户籍人口年龄构成(2020年末)

Age Structure of Household Registered Population by Region(End of 2020)

地 区 Region	0-17岁 0~17 years old		18-34岁 18~34 years old		35-59岁 35~59 years old		60岁以上 over 60 years old	
	人数(人) Number of people (person)	占总人口% of the total population	人数(人) Number of people (person)	占总人口% of the total population	人数(人) Number of people (person)	占总人口% of the total population	人数(人) Number of people (person)	占总人口% of the total population
全 市 Whole City	**1449655**	**17.8**	**1759081**	**21.6**	**3046950**	**37.4**	**1882618**	**23.2**
市 区 Urban District	1245987	18.5	1474743	21.8	2493805	36.9	1538488	22.8
#上城区 Shangcheng	40494	12.6	60357	18.8	113804	35.5	106138	33.1
下城区 Xiacheng	56314	13.0	108064	25.1	148878	34.4	118973	27.5
江干区 Jianggan	151491	22.4	155973	23.1	243649	36.0	125269	18.5
拱墅区 Gongshu	76936	18.6	79376	19.2	153424	37.0	104213	25.2
西湖区 Xihu	160426	20.3	186721	23.5	300210	37.8	145907	18.4
高新(滨江)区 Hi-Tech(Binjiang)	67747	23.2	80715	27.6	103048	35.2	40839	14.0
萧山区 Xiaoshan	234789	17.1	291876	21.2	496909	36.2	350024	25.5
余杭区 Yuhang	267083	21.9	268326	22.0	438949	36.0	244684	20.1
富阳区 Fuyang	111799	16.2	138414	20.0	279176	40.4	161725	23.4
临安区 Lin'an	78908	14.6	104921	19.4	215758	39.9	140716	26.1
桐庐县 Tonglu	64737	15.4	86099	20.5	163821	39.2	104563	24.9
淳安县 Chun'an	66332	14.5	91552	20.1	189196	41.5	109080	23.9
建德市 Jiande	72599	14.3	106687	20.9	200128	39.2	130487	25.6

2-07 户籍人口自然变动情况(1949-2020年)
Natural Changes of Household Registered Population(1949-2020)

年份 Year	人口自然变动人数(人) Population Natural Change			人口自然变动率(‰) Population Natural Change Rate		
	出生人数 Birth Population	死亡人数 Death Population	自然增长人数 Natural Growth Population	出生率 Birth Rate	死亡率 Death Rate	自然增长率 Natural Growth Rate
1949	-	-	-	-	-	-
1950	101227	41810	59417	34.56	14.28	20.28
1951	116825	43156	73669	38.78	14.32	24.46
1952	120319	45073	75246	39.00	14.61	24.39
1953	124863	44777	80086	39.57	14.19	25.38
1954	130491	45526	84965	40.30	14.06	26.24
1955	130236	43984	86252	39.00	13.17	25.83
1956	111440	30537	80903	32.50	8.90	23.60
1957	142406	34673	107733	39.99	9.74	30.25
1958	137238	35642	101596	37.17	9.65	27.52
1959	102030	40031	61999	26.95	10.57	16.38
1960	108282	34569	73713	27.92	8.91	19.01
1961	83206	34361	48845	21.20	8.75	12.45
1962	155335	32116	123219	38.95	8.05	30.90
1963	170431	30884	139547	41.59	7.54	34.05
1964	146073	36868	109205	34.62	8.74	25.88
1965	137319	32585	104734	31.85	7.56	24.29
1966	120047	31509	88538	27.36	7.18	20.18
1967	107577	28248	79329	24.14	6.34	17.80
1968	111134	28303	82831	24.55	6.25	18.30
1969	109723	26956	82767	24.06	5.91	18.15
1970	101075	27768	73307	22.08	6.08	16.00
1971	96497	28571	67926	20.83	6.17	14.66
1972	85188	27890	57298	18.09	5.92	12.17
1973	81414	28144	53270	17.06	5.90	11.16
1974	70353	29723	40630	14.56	6.15	8.41
1975	74209	29655	44554	15.19	6.07	9.12
1976	71064	30053	41011	14.39	6.09	8.30
1977	73471	33239	40232	14.76	6.68	8.08
1978	73550	29928	43622	14.63	5.95	8.68
1979	71442	29500	41942	14.04	5.80	8.24
1980	52145	30727	21418	10.15	5.98	4.17
1981	73015	31352	41663	14.09	6.05	8.04
1982	82910	30805	52105	15.81	5.87	9.94
1983	69940	33598	36342	13.18	6.33	6.85
1984	60091	33070	27021	11.23	6.18	5.05
1985	66757	33715	33042	12.36	6.24	6.12
1986	84702	33576	51126	15.50	6.15	9.35
1987	94127	33238	60889	17.00	6.00	11.00
1988	85472	35356	50116	15.23	6.30	8.93
1989	81048	34031	47017	14.27	5.99	8.28

2-07 续表 continued

年 份 Year	人口自然变动人数(人) Population Natural Change			人口自然变动率(‰) Population Natural Change Rate		
	出生人数 Birth Population	死亡人数 Death Population	自然增长人数 Natural Growth Population	出生率 Birth Rate	死亡率 Death Rate	自然增长率 Natural Growth Rate
1990	76579	34977	41602	13.37	6.11	7.26
1991	66144	33534	32610	11.47	5.81	5.66
1992	61708	34681	27027	10.63	5.97	4.66
1993	62465	34127	28338	10.68	5.84	4.84
1994	63580	35099	28481	10.78	5.95	4.83
1995	62586	36186	26400	10.51	6.08	4.43
1996	63680	35417	28263	10.60	5.90	4.70
1997	58471	34663	23808	9.65	5.72	3.93
1998	53951	38302	15649	8.85	6.28	2.57
1999	59085	36866	22219	9.63	6.01	3.62
2000	62300	40218	22082	10.07	6.50	3.57
2001	52088	33827	18261	8.33	5.41	2.92
2002	53064	35867	17197	8.38	5.67	2.72
2003	51420	36662	14758	8.04	5.73	2.31
2004	59940	34078	25862	9.26	5.27	3.99
2005	57233	35417	21816	8.72	5.39	3.33
2006	57790	38892	18898	8.71	5.86	2.85
2007	60296	37833	22463	9.01	5.65	3.36
2008	61332	42648	18684	9.09	6.32	2.77
2009	62441	39159	23282	9.18	5.76	3.42
2010	69606	46193	23413	10.14	6.73	3.41
2011	70337	38225	32112	10.16	5.52	4.64
2012	77349	49789	27560	11.08	7.13	3.95
2013	70850	37544	33306	10.07	5.34	4.73
2014	89743	40415	49328	12.62	5.68	6.94
2015	70617	40326	30291	9.81	5.60	4.21
2016	90896	35614	55282	12.46	4.88	7.58
2017	109496	63366	46130	14.70	8.51	6.19
2018	94713	46525	48188	12.40	6.09	6.31
2019	91450	36774	54676	11.65	4.68	6.97
2020	79806	42532	37274	9.92	5.29	4.63

注:本表按公安部门统计。

a) Figures in this table are based on the Public Security Bureau.

2-08 市区户籍人口自然变动情况(1978-2020年)

Natural Changes of Household Registered Population of Urban District(1978-2020)

年份 Year	人口自然变动人数(人) Population Natural Change			人口自然变动率(‰) Population Natural Change Rate		
	出生人数 Birth Population	死亡人数 Death Population	自然增长人数 Natural Growth Population	出生率 Birth Rate	死亡率 Death Rate	自然增长率 Natural Growth Rate
1978	11923	6449	5474	11.56	6.25	5.31
1979	13184	5808	7376	12.26	5.40	6.86
1980	9708	6511	3197	8.68	5.82	2.86
1981	14938	6599	8339	13.06	5.77	7.29
1982	18092	6494	11598	15.49	5.56	9.93
1983	17107	6949	10158	14.36	5.84	8.52
1984	16257	6892	9365	13.41	5.69	7.72
1985	15824	7403	8421	12.81	6.84	6.82
1986	17120	6865	10255	13.60	5.45	8.15
1987	18701	7070	11631	14.60	5.52	9.08
1988	18503	7503	11000	14.21	5.76	8.45
1989	15868	6985	8883	12.02	5.29	6.73
1990	14085	7490	6595	10.56	5.62	4.94
1991	10195	7025	3170	7.58	5.22	2.36
1992	9994	7259	2735	7.37	5.35	2.02
1993	10099	7196	2903	7.35	5.24	2.11
1994	9918	7082	2836	7.09	5.06	2.03
1995	9806	7367	2439	6.89	5.17	1.72
1996	12098	8221	3877	7.80	5.30	2.50
1997	12304	8630	3674	7.32	5.13	2.19
1998	11714	9060	2654	6.87	5.31	1.56
1999	13694	8148	5546	7.89	4.69	3.20
2000	15058	10996	4062	8.50	6.20	2.30
2001	30902	19439	11463	8.22	5.17	3.05
2002	33156	19922	13234	8.65	5.20	3.45
2003	29019	21176	7843	7.44	5.43	2.01
2004	34858	19445	15413	8.77	4.89	3.88
2005	34056	21310	12746	8.39	5.25	3.14
2006	33260	21156	12104	8.08	5.14	2.94
2007	37029	20051	16978	8.88	4.81	4.07
2008	38703	21428	17275	9.17	5.08	4.09
2009	40293	22178	18115	9.44	5.20	4.24
2010	47052	25404	21648	10.89	5.88	5.01
2011	47256	22140	25116	10.80	5.06	5.74
2012	51892	27271	24621	11.72	6.16	5.56
2013	48107	21332	26775	10.74	4.76	5.97
2014	69577	27249	42328	13.36	5.23	8.13
2015	55275	26492	28783	10.45	5.01	5.44
2016	71427	23544	47883	13.26	4.37	8.89
2017	92571	52817	39754	15.96	9.11	6.85
2018	80238	36336	43902	12.83	5.81	7.02
2019	78168	27683	50485	12.10	4.28	7.82
2020	68661	33013	35648	10.31	4.96	5.35

2-09 分地区户籍人口自然变动情况(2020 年)
Natural Changes of Household Registered Population by Region(2020)

地　区 Region	出　生 Birth		死　亡 Death		自然增长 Natural Growth	
	人数(人) Birth Population (person)	出生率(‰) Birth Rate(‰)	人数(人) Death Population (person)	死亡率(‰) Death Rate(‰)	人数(人) Natural Growth Population (person)	自然增长率(‰) Natural Growth Rate(‰)
全　市 Whole City	**79806**	**9.92**	**42532**	**5.29**	**37274**	**4.63**
市　区 Urban District	68661	10.31	33013	4.96	35648	5.35
#上城区 Shangcheng	2078	6.50	1966	6.15	112	0.35
下城区 Xiacheng	3512	8.21	2080	4.86	1432	3.35
江干区 Jianggan	8102	12.30	2128	3.23	5974	9.07
拱墅区 Gongshu	3874	9.56	2289	5.65	1585	3.91
西湖区 Xihu	7626	9.76	2500	3.20	5126	6.56
西湖风景名胜区 The West Lake Scenic Zone						
高新(滨江)区 Hi-Tech(Binjiang)	3853	13.51	836	2.93	3017	10.58
萧山区 Xiaoshan	13265	9.75	7826	5.75	5439	4.00
余杭区 Yuhang	16183	13.60	5626	4.73	10557	8.87
富阳区 Fuyang	6094	8.84	3961	5.74	2133	3.10
临安区 Lin'an	4074	7.55	3801	7.04	273	0.51
桐庐县 Tonglu	3561	8.50	2697	6.44	864	2.06
淳安县 Chun'an	3402	7.44	3462	7.57	-60	-0.13
建德市 Jiande	4182	8.19	3360	6.58	822	1.61
钱塘新区 Qiantang						

2-10 分地区户籍人口机械变动情况(2020年)

Mechanical Changes of Household Registered Population by Region(2020)

单位:人 (person)

地 区 Region	本年迁入人数 Number of the Persons Moved in(person)		本年迁出人数 Number of the Persons Moved Out(person)		本年净迁入人数 Net Persons Moved in
	省 内 From Zhejiang Province	省 外 From Other Provinces	省 内 To Zhejiang Province	省 外 To Other Provinces	
全 市 Whole City	**71751**	**106469**	**13895**	**16752**	**147573**
市 区 Urban District	70155	103545	6568	15045	152087
#上城区 Shangcheng	2839	3827	280	748	5638
下城区 Xiacheng	7159	12757	596	1549	17771
江干区 Jianggan	14574	15911	1297	2510	26678
拱墅区 Gongshu	6000	5215	444	732	10039
西湖区 Xihu	12614	15657	1457	4235	22579
西湖风景名胜区 The West Lake Scenic Zone					
高新(滨江)区 Hi-Tech(Binjiang)	6168	7046	465	1103	11646
萧山区 Xiaoshan	5838	10829	550	1150	14967
余杭区 Yuhang	13485	28601	801	1611	39674
富阳区 Fuyang	543	1732	301	782	1192
临安区 Lin'an	935	1970	377	625	1903
桐庐县 Tonglu	719	1233	1764	630	-442
淳安县 Chun'an	313	682	2883	563	-2451
建德市 Jiande	564	1009	2680	514	-1621
钱塘新区 Qiantang					

2-11 婚姻登记情况(2019-2020年)
Marriage Registration Situations(2019-2020)

地区 Region	2019 准予登记结婚对数(对) Marriages Legally Registered(couples)	2019 再婚人数(人) Re-married (person)	2019 离婚对数(对) Divorces (couples)	2020 准予登记结婚对数(对) Marriages Legally Registered(couples)	2020 再婚人数(人) Re-married (person)	2020 离婚对数(对) Divorces (couples)
全市 Whole City	**56330**	**18471**	**23172**	**57692**	**16910**	**22699**
市区 Urban District	47793	15106	18942	50310	13914	19014
#萧山区 Xiaoshan	7977	2396	2577	9561	2406	2525
余杭区 Yuhang	7154	2773	3204	6251	2351	2147
富阳区 Fuyang	4519	1821	1878	4147	1592	1821
临安区 Lin'an	3351	1491	1789	3034	1308	1616
桐庐县 Tonglu	2611	1085	1397	2425	1007	1245
淳安县 Chun'an	2808	1058	1272	2219	835	1053
建德市 Jiande	3118	1222	1561	2738	1154	1387

2－12 规模以上单位

Number of Employed Persons of

单位：人

地区、行业	Region, Sector	就业人员合计 Number of Employed Persons	非私营单位 Non－private
全市	**Total**	**3218287**	**1480931**
市区	Urban District	3006075	1424515
#上城区	Shangcheng District	138446	73349
下城区	Xiacheng District	191072	128018
江干区	Jianggan District	192124	89332
拱墅区	Gongshu District	176038	74736
西湖区	Xihu District	392939	235357
高新（滨江）区	Hi－Tech（Binjiang）District	369264	210198
萧山区	Xiaoshan District	522469	190622
余杭区	Yuhang District	478283	158422
富阳区	Fuyang District	124681	49638
临安区	Lin'an District	114386	33734
钱塘新区	Qiantang District	294661	173242
西湖风景名胜区	The West Lake Scenic Zone	11712	7867
桐庐县	Tonglu County	110821	24222
淳安县	Chun'an County	36504	12307
建德市	Jiande City	64887	19887
按国民经济行业分组	**Grouped by Sector**		
农、林、牧、渔业	Farming, Forestry, Animal Husbandry & Fishery	－	－
采矿业	Mining	1539	368
制造业	Manufacturing	997615	502620
电力、热力、燃气及水生产和供应业	Production & Supply of Electricity, Heat, Gas & Water	17099	15397
建筑业	Construction	772781	181661
批发和零售业	Wholesale & Retail Trades	299699	141709
交通运输、仓储和邮政业	Transportation, Storage and Posts	138301	87249
住宿和餐饮业	Hotels and Catering Services	118385	65325
信息传输、软件和信息技术服务业	Information Transmission, Software and Information Technology	276563	172864
金融业	Financial Intermediation	－	－
房地产业	Real Estate	175780	113700
租赁和商务服务业	Leasing and Business Services	176635	78590
科学研究、技术服务业	Scientific Research, Technical Services	111421	59222
水利、环境和公共设施管理业	Management of Water Conservancy, Environment and Public Facilities	35072	22708
居民服务、修理和其他服务业	Service to Households, Repair and Other Services	37732	14477
教育	Education	18458	8148
卫生和社会工作业	Health Care and Social Work	25413	6435
文化、体育和娱乐业	Culture, Sports and Entertainment	15794	10458
公共管理、社会保障和社会组织	Public Management, Social Security and Social Organizations	－	－

注：2020 年数据口径范围调整为规模以上单位从业人员数。

就业人员数(2020 年末)

Units Above Designated Size(End of 2020)

(person)

女性 Female	非私营单位 Non - private	在岗职工 Staff and Workers	非私营单位 Non - private	其他就业人员 Other Employed Persons	非私营单位 Non - private
1070933	**511926**	**3087043**	**1422004**	**131244**	**58927**
1007613	492411	2880986	1366255	125089	58260
54535	29813	132355	70200	6091	3149
67356	42070	176833	115850	14239	12168
64753	29993	186064	86338	6060	2994
57285	27599	169902	71280	6136	3456
135298	85312	374265	225600	18674	9757
119165	67140	360010	207821	9254	2377
158025	59992	503786	184583	18683	6039
169307	59648	454405	156797	23878	1625
45088	16651	123060	49187	1621	451
37372	9968	112555	32923	1831	811
94341	61047	276446	158089	18215	15153
5088	3178	11305	7587	407	280
29325	9171	109164	23901	1657	321
14020	4934	34371	12097	2133	210
19975	5410	62522	19751	2365	136
–	–	–	–	–	–
322	62	1520	368	19	
372916	169160	973155	484529	24460	18091
4344	3961	16822	15132	277	265
94855	16518	723786	174151	48995	7510
158014	71583	288276	133050	11423	8659
40932	25150	135208	85471	3093	1778
66227	37542	105209	54849	13176	10476
99056	63970	273999	171067	2564	1797
–	–	–	–	–	–
78827	52375	167310	108207	8470	5493
50309	21287	165895	76898	10740	1692
35710	20333	108470	57535	2951	1687
11020	6640	34545	22495	527	213
21209	8127	35985	14426	1747	51
11457	5357	17557	7728	901	420
17595	4459	24131	6007	1282	428
8140	5402	15175	10091	619	367
–	–	–	–	–	–

a) Numbers in 2020 are employees in units above designated size.

2－13　规模以上单位

Average Number of Employed Persons of

单位:人

地区、行业	Region,Sector	就业人员年平均人数 Annual Average Number of Staff and Workers	非私营单位 Non－private
全市	**Total**	**3118256**	**1452745**
市区	Urban District	2925808	1248795
#上城区	Shangcheng District	130653	73296
下城区	Xiacheng District	188965	126268
江干区	Jianggan District	183359	84568
拱墅区	Gongshu District	173017	72866
西湖区	Xihu District	381491	228776
高新(滨江)区	Hi－Tech(Binjiang) District	361150	205368
萧山区	Xiaoshan District	506241	186508
余杭区	Yuhang District	465783	154519
富阳区	Fuyang District	121254	48096
临安区	Lin'an Districty	110782	32521
钱塘新区	Qiantang District	291621	176326
西湖风景名胜区	The West Lake Scenic Zone	11492	7934
桐庐县	Tonglu County	93402	23749
淳安县	Chun'an County	35920	12260
建德市	Jiande City	63126	19690
按国民经济行业分组	**Grouped by Sector**		
农、林、牧、渔业	Farming,Forestry,Animal Husbandry & Fishery	－	－
采矿业	Mining	1514	350
制造业	Manufacturing	999403	506287
电力、热力、燃气及水生产和供应业	Production & Supply of Electricity,Heat,Gas & Water	16984	15271
建筑业	Construction	714211	169078
批发和零售业	Wholesale & Retail Trades	300046	140986
交通运输、仓储和邮政业	Transportation,Storage and Posts	136594	85263
住宿和餐饮业	Hotels and Catering Services	110678	64089
信息传输、软件和信息技术服务业	Information Transmission, Software and Information Technology	269767	169659
金融业	Financial Intermediation	－	－
房地产业	Real Estate	169866	108909
租赁和商务服务业	Leasing and Business Services	164927	76852
科学研究、技术服务业	Scientific Research,Technical Services	108131	57678
水利、环境和公共设施管理业	Management of Water Conservancy,Environment and Public Facilities	33016	20233
居民服务、修理和其他服务业	Service to Households,Repair and Other Services	35373	13268
教育	Education	17171	7858
卫生和社会工作	Health Care and Social Work	24990	6452
文化、体育和娱乐业	Culture,Sports and Entertainment	15585	10512
公共管理、社会保障和社会组织	Public Management,Social Security and Social Organizations	－	－

注:2020 年数据口径范围调整为规模以上单位从业人员数。

平均人员数(2020 年)
Units Above Designated Size(2020)

(person)

在岗职工年平均人数 Staff and Workers	非私营单位 Non - private	其他就业人员年平均人数 Average Number of Other Employed Persons	非私营单位 Non - private
2988661	**1393373**	**129595**	**59372**
2802201	1204936	123607	43859
125004	70320	5649	2976
174386	113814	14579	12454
176909	81292	6450	3276
166756	69207	6261	3659
363097	218971	18394	9805
353551	203036	7599	2332
487993	180299	18248	6209
441145	152874	24638	1645
119520	47629	1734	467
109108	31944	1674	577
273659	161242	17962	15084
11073	7671	419	263
91814	23485	1588	264
33790	12065	2130	195
60856	19524	2270	166
–	–	–	–
1491	350	23	
974460	487825	24943	18462
16710	15010	274	261
665589	162064	48622	7014
287762	131874	12284	9112
133407	83172	3187	2091
97961	53653	12717	10436
267226	167962	2541	1697
–	–	–	–
161736	103669	8130	5240
156222	75105	8705	1747
105212	55992	2919	1686
32431	20035	585	198
33626	13218	1747	50
16240	7315	931	543
23640	5987	1350	465
14948	10142	637	370
–	–	–	–

a) Numbers in 2020 are employees in units above designated size.

2－14 分行业规模以上单位

The Education Level of Workers in

单位：人

行业	Sector	单位就业人员 The Education Level 研究生及以上 Graduate of above
总 计	**Total**	**119350**
农、林、牧、渔业	Farming, Forestry, Animal Husbandry & Fishery	－
采矿业	Mining	3
制造业	Manufacturing	30422
电力、热力、燃气及水生产和供应业	Production & Supply of Electricity, Heat, Gas & Water	602
建筑业	Construction	3244
批发和零售业	Wholesale & Retail Trades	7682
交通运输、仓储及邮政业	Transportation, Storage and Posts	1388
住宿和餐饮业	Hotels and Catering Services	496
信息传输、软件和信息技术服务业	Information Transmission, Software and Information Technology	45583
金融业	Financial Intermediation	－
房地产业	Real Estate	3437
租赁和商务服务业	Leasing and Business Services	5646
科学研究和技术服务业	Scientific Research, Technical Services	15513
水利、环境和公共设施管理业	Management of Water Conservancy, Environment and Public Facilities	516
居民服务、修理和其他服务业	Service to Households, Repair and Other Services	76
教育	Education	2081
卫生和社会工作	Health Care and Social Work	1147
文化、体育和娱乐业	Culture, Sports and Entertainment	1514
公共管理、社会保障和社会组织	Public Management, Social Security and Social Organizations	－

注：2020 年数据口径范围调整为规模以上单位从业人员数。

职工素质情况(2020 年末)

Units Above Designated Size by Sector(End of 2020)

(persons)

文化程度 of the Employed Persons in Onits				单位就业人员中专业技术人员 Professional and Technical Personnel	单位就业人员中技术工人 Skilled Workers
大学本科 Bachelor's Degree	大专 College Degree	中专及高中 Technical Secondary School and High School	初中及以下 Junior High School and Below		
690576	**606121**	**764727**	**1037513**	**673870**	**1158960**
–	–	–	–	–	–
58	172	410	896	103	476
163688	148466	253188	401851	174065	544140
6734	4614	3325	1824	3344	7919
81303	114578	228763	344893	147299	315114
81350	87732	75872	47063	38871	43190
24357	33510	44487	34559	14646	44958
15449	26281	37104	39055	4716	24138
157367	59401	11600	2612	132909	39374
–	–	–	–	–	–
33686	36875	38399	63383	21180	44628
34789	33177	42809	60214	26036	52419
55867	29029	8320	2692	77509	6869
7708	9504	4606	12738	3040	18330
2367	5437	7550	22302	1930	12582
11606	3113	1173	485	8454	1013
7020	10984	4478	1784	13733	2670
7227	3248	2643	1162	6035	1140
–	–	–	–	–	–

a) Numbers in 2020 are employees in units above designated size.

2-15 三次产业就业人员及构成(2012-2020年)
Number of Employed Persons by Three Industries(2012-2020)

单位:万人 (10000 persons)

指标名称	Item	2012	2013	2014	2015	2016	2017	2018	2019	2020
全市总计	**Total**	**644.43**	**650.51**	**654.92**	**663.03**	**676.95**	**681.06**	**696.10**	**720.00**	**748.39**
第一产业	Primary Industry	70.39	70.07	66.39	67.01	66.11	66.29	59.70	56.70	30.31
第二产业	Secondary Industry	290.01	291.51	286.99	271.90	261.78	257.60	244.30	256.60	255.40
第三产业	Tertiary Industry	284.03	288.93	301.54	324.12	349.06	357.17	392.10	406.70	462.68
全市构成(以合计为100)	**Composition (Total=100)**	**100**	**100**	**100**	**100**	**100**	**100**	**100**	**100**	**100**
第一产业	Primary Industry	10.9	10.8	10.1	10.1	9.8	9.7	8.6	7.9	4.1
第二产业	Secondary Industry	45.0	44.8	43.9	41.0	38.7	37.8	35.1	35.6	34.1
第三产业	Tertiary Industry	44.1	44.4	46.0	48.9	51.5	52.5	56.3	56.5	61.8

主要统计指标解释

人口数 指一定时点、一定地区范围内的有生命的个人的总和。

年度统计的年末人口数是指每年 12 月 31 日 24 时的人口数。

出生率(又称粗出生率) 指一定时期内(通常为一年)平均每千人所出生的人数的比率,一般用千分率表示。计算公式:

$$出生率=\frac{年出生人数}{年平均人数}\times1000‰$$

出生人数是指活产婴儿,即胎儿脱离母体时(不管怀孕月数),有过呼吸或其他生命现象。

年平均人数是年初、年底人口数的平均数,也可用年中人口数代替。

死亡率(又称粗死亡率) 指一定时期内(通常为一年)一定地区的死亡人数与同期平均人数(或期中人数)之比,一般用千分率表示。计算公式:

$$死亡率=\frac{年死亡人数}{年平均人数}\times1000‰$$

人口自然增长率 指一定时期内(通常为一年)人口自然增加数(出生人数减死亡人数)与该时期内平均人数(或期中人数)之比,一般用千分率表示。计算公式:

$$人口自然增长率=\frac{本年出生人数-本年死亡人数}{年平均人数}\times1000‰$$

人口自然增长率 = 人口出生率 - 人口死亡率

就业人员 指从事一定社会劳动并取得劳动报酬或经营收入人员,包括各级机关企事业单位就业人员、个体户主、个体就业人员、农村就业人员及其他未包括的就业人员(包括宗教职业者、现役军人等)。

单位就业人员 是指在各级国家机关、政党机关、社会团体及企业、事业单位中工作,并取得劳动报酬的全部人员。包括在岗职工、再就业的离退休人员、民办教师、在各单位中工作的外方人员和港、澳、台方人员以及聘用的外单位下岗职工、兼职人员、从事第二职业人员、使用的劳务派遣人员。各单位的就业人员反映了实际参加生产或工作的全部劳动力。

在岗职工 指在本单位工作并由单位支付劳动报酬的人员,以及在本单位有工作岗位,但由于学习、病伤产假等原因暂未工作,仍由单位支付劳动报酬的人,包括本单位临时性用工并支付劳动报酬的人员。2012 年开始在岗职工包含劳务派遣人员。

非私营单位 包括独立核算的机关、事业单位和国有、集体、股份制、港澳台投资及外商投资企业等。

规模以上单位 包括辖区内规模以上工业、有资质的建筑业、限额以上批发和零售业、限额以上住宿和餐饮业、有开发经营活动的全部房地产开发经营业、规模以上服务业法人单位。

Explanatory Notes on Main Statistical Indicators

Total Population refers to the total number of people alive at a certain point of time within a given area. The annual statistics on total population is taken at midnight on December 31.

Birth Rate (or Crude Birth Rate) refers to the ratio of the number of births to the average population during a certain period of time (usually a year) , which is often expressed in ‰. The following formula is used:

$$\text{Birth Rate} = \frac{\text{Number of Births}}{\text{Average Number of Population}} \times 1000‰$$

Number of births refers to live births, i. e. the births when babies had showed any vital phenomena regardless of the length of pregnancy.

Annual Average Number of Population is the average of the number of population at the beginning of the year and that at the end of the year. Sometimes it is substituted by the mid – year population.

Death Rate (or Crude Death Rate) refers to the ratio of the number of deaths to the average population (or mid – year population) during a certain period of time (usually a year) , which is often expressed in ‰. The following formula is used:

$$\text{Death Rate} = \frac{\text{Number of Deaths}}{\text{Annual Average Number of Population}} \times 1000‰$$

Natural Growth Rate of Population refers to the ratio of natural increase in population (number of births minus number ofdeaths) in a certain period of time (usually a year) to the average population(or mid – year population) of the same period, which is often expressed in ‰. The following formulas are applied:

$$\text{Natural Growth Rate of Population} = \frac{\text{Number of Births} - \text{Number of Deaths}}{\text{Average Number of Population}} \times 1000‰$$

Natural Growth Rate of Population = Birth Rate – Death Rate

Employed Persons refer to persons who are engaged in social labour and receive remuneration payment or earn business income, including all employees of government, enterprises and institutions, self – employed workers, employed persons in the rural areas and other employed workers(including religious professionals, servicemen, etc.).

Persons Employed in Various Units refer to all the persons working in government agencies of various levels, political and party organizations, social organizations, enterprises, institutions, and receiving wages or other forms of payment, which include fully – employed staff and workers, re – employed retirees, teachers in schools run by the local people, foreigners and Chinese compatriots from Hong Kong, Macao, and Taiwan working in various units, hired laid – off workers from other units, part – time employees, employees engaged a second job, dispatched personnels. Persons Employed in various units reflect the total laborers actually engaged in production or work.

Fully Employed Staff and Workers refer to persons who work and receive wages from their working units, as well as persons who maintain their posts, are out of commission temporarily for reasons of study, sickness, injury or maternal leave, but still receive wages from their working units, which includes persons who are temporarily employed and receive remuneration payment. After2012, fully employed staff includes dispatched personnels.

Non – private Units include independent accounting government organizations and institutions, state – owned, collective – owned and joint stock enterprises, and enterprises with funds from foreign and from Hong Kong, Macao and Taiwan.

Units above designated size include industries above designated size, qualified construction industries, wholesale and retail Industries above designated size, accommodation and catering industries above designated size, all real estate development and operation industries with development and business activities, and service industries legal entities above designated size.

三、农业

AGRICULTURE

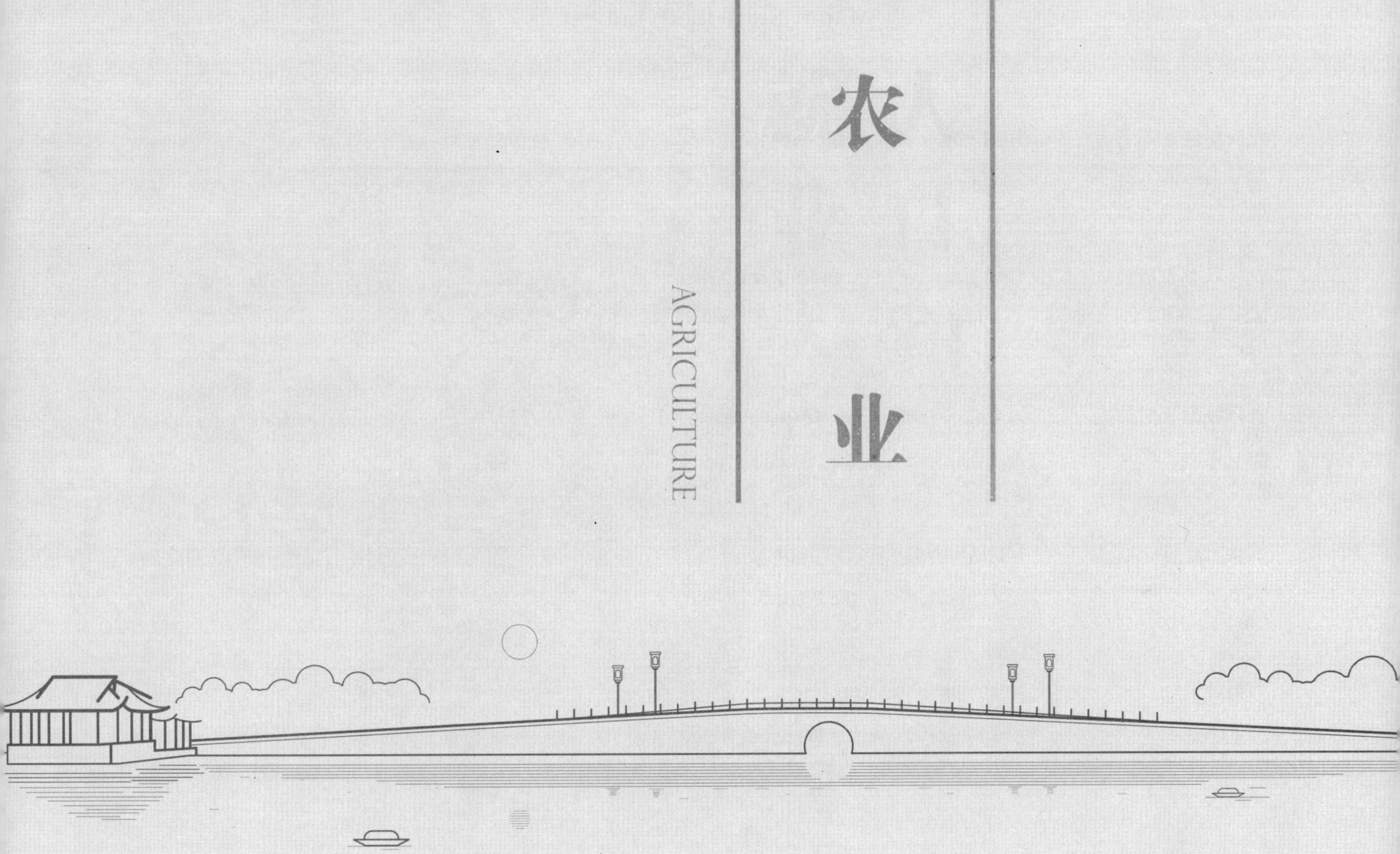

3 农　　业
Agriculture

主要统计指标
Major Statistical Indicators

农村机械总动力	Total Power of Agricultural Machinery	195.88	万千瓦	(10, 000 kW)
为上年	As Compared with the Preceding Year	91.2	%	(%)
农村从业人员数	Total Employed Persons in Rural Areas	262.77	万人	(10, 000 persons)
为上年	As Compared with the Preceding Year	99.2	%	(%)
农林牧渔业增加值	Value-added of Farming,Forestry,Animal Husbandry and Fishery	334.01	亿元	(100 million yuan)
为上年	As Compared with the Preceding Year	99.1	%	(%)
粮食总产量	Total Output of Grain Crops	50.9	万吨	(10, 000 tons)
为上年	As Compared with the Preceding Year	102.4	%	(%)
肉类产量	Total Output of Meat	10.98	万吨	(10, 000 tons)
为上年	As Compared with the Preceding Year	56.0	%	(%)

3-01 分地区农林牧渔业增加值(2020年)

The Added Value of Agriculture, Forestry, Animal Husbandry and Fishery(2020)

单位:万元 (10000 yuan)

地 区 Region	农林牧渔业合计 Total	为上年%	农、林、牧、渔专业及辅助性活动 Services for Farming, Forestry, Animal Husbandary and Fishery	为上年%
全 市 Whole City	**3340124**	**99.1**	**77918**	**108.9**
市区 Urban District	2312149	98.2	59287	109.1
#西湖区 Xihu	30909	114.8	1040	100.0
高新(滨江)区 Hi-Tech(Binjiang)	6414	91.3		
萧山区 Xiaoshan	600345	95.1	21658	110.5
余杭区 Yuhang	550004	100.2	23796	109.2
富阳区 Fuyang	498652	100.2	3569	109.6
临安区 Lin'an	465931	100.2	5881	108.5
钱塘新区 Qiantang New Area	147734	98.6	3344	105.2
西湖风景名胜区 The West Lake Scenic Zone	9650	100.9		
桐庐县 Tonglu	258325	100.5	4714	109.3
淳安县 Chun'an	390279	100.7	6066	109.6
建德市 Jiande	379372	101.6	7851	106.1

3-02 农林牧渔业总产值(1949-2020年)
Gross Output Value of Agriculture, Forestry, Animal Husbandry and Fishery (1949-2020)

单位:亿元 (100 million yuan)

年份 Year	合计 Total	为上年(%)	#农业 Agriculture	#林业 Forestry	#牧业 Husbandry	#渔业 Fishery	农、林、牧、渔专业及辅助性活动 Services for Farming, Forestry, Animal Husbandary and Fishery
1949	3.38	-	2.34	0.47	0.47	0.10	
1950	4.03	119.3	2.85	0.55	0.52	0.11	
1951	4.57	113.3	3.27	0.61	0.58	0.11	
1952	5.16	112.9	3.71	0.65	0.69	0.12	
1953	5.33	103.2	3.77	0.66	0.78	0.13	
1954	5.24	98.5	3.58	0.73	0.80	0.13	
1955	5.67	108.1	4.10	0.72	0.70	0.14	
1956	5.99	105.7	4.15	0.80	0.89	0.15	
1957	6.40	106.8	4.34	0.78	1.13	0.15	
1958	6.76	105.6	4.97	0.80	0.86	0.13	
1959	6.89	101.9	4.93	0.95	0.86	0.15	
1960	6.32	91.8	4.53	0.86	0.80	0.13	
1961	5.97	94.5	4.53	0.65	0.67	0.11	
1962	6.24	104.4	4.63	0.71	0.80	0.09	
1963	6.74	108.1	4.97	0.64	1.03	0.09	
1964	7.20	106.8	5.24	0.66	1.19	0.11	
1965	7.86	109.1	5.67	0.66	1.36	0.17	
1966	8.10	103.1	5.82	0.67	1.47	0.14	
1967	7.94	98.1	5.81	0.53	1.50	0.10	
1968	7.98	100.5	5.92	0.59	1.35	0.11	
1969	8.06	101.0	5.96	0.59	1.39	0.12	
1970	8.40	104.7	6.15	0.56	1.61	0.13	
1971	8.44	100.1	6.21	0.38	1.74	0.11	
1972	9.16	108.5	6.85	0.43	1.79	0.11	
1973	8.79	98.9	6.43	0.44	1.80	0.12	
1974	9.05	103.0	6.61	0.46	1.87	0.11	
1975	8.62	95.2	6.29	0.45	1.74	0.13	
1976	8.85	102.7	6.72	0.49	1.53	0.12	
1977	8.90	100.5	6.73	0.46	1.58	0.13	
1978	8.59	114.0	6.74	0.34	1.45	0.07	
1979	11.56	115.0	8.47	0.46	2.52	0.11	
1980	11.24	92.3	7.90	0.73	2.50	0.11	
1981	12.08	105.9	8.74	0.83	2.38	0.13	
1982	15.06	116.5	10.76	0.89	3.18	0.23	
1983	14.89	95.7	10.37	0.98	3.27	0.27	
1984	17.70	113.5	12.26	1.48	3.59	0.38	
1985	21.30	98.3	13.69	1.90	5.01	0.69	
1986	23.83	105.8	15.08	2.00	5.82	0.93	
1987	28.13	104.4	17.31	2.64	7.01	1.17	
1988	35.85	101.0	20.88	3.14	10.10	1.72	
1989	38.68	100.3	22.60	2.79	11.40	1.90	

年　份 Year	合计 Total	为上年(%)	#农业 Agriculture	#林业 Forestry	#牧业 Husbandry	#渔业 Fishery	农、林、牧、渔专业及辅助性活动 Services for Farming, Forestry, Animal Husbandary and Fishery
1990	42.10	103.3	26.00	2.70	11.34	2.06	
1991	46.36	104.4	28.43	3.78	11.75	2.41	
1992	49.79	104.7	30.08	3.56	13.39	2.76	
1993	60.08	106.7	36.51	4.75	15.48	3.34	
1994	81.25	106.6	49.64	5.86	21.72	4.02	
1995	99.64	105.2	62.01	8.13	24.41	5.10	
1996	117.33	104.7	74.02	9.57	27.17	6.57	
1997	128.77	106.2	79.78	11.45	29.42	8.12	
1998	136.76	105.2	84.51	12.12	28.91	11.22	
1999	141.47	103.4	87.67	12.60	29.35	11.86	
2000	152.65	107.9	90.33	13.68	33.16	15.48	
2001	165.00	108.1	96.50	14.93	36.23	17.34	
2002	168.50	102.1	93.30	16.22	39.19	19.80	
2003	189.01	112.2	99.16	18.26	41.78	23.26	6.56
2004	198.27	104.9	101.09	20.68	45.76	23.41	7.33
2005	219.48	110.7	113.66	23.30	49.59	27.08	5.85
2006	225.38	102.7	122.48	26.77	49.04	20.61	6.47
2007	247.14	109.7	130.80	29.47	58.55	22.26	6.05
2008	273.76	110.8	140.81	32.02	63.66	30.93	6.34
2009	289.74	105.5	149.74	36.23	64.29	32.56	6.92
2010	316.34	109.2	169.88	32.93	70.56	34.90	8.07
2011	357.07	112.9	190.79	34.85	83.65	39.00	8.78
2012	384.34	107.6	207.72	38.18	86.85	42.00	9.59
2013	399.37	103.9	216.11	40.82	91.13	40.73	10.59
2014	418.58	104.8	233.38	47.02	82.82	44.20	11.16
2015	440.41	105.2	252.42	49.81	80.70	45.23	12.26
2016	449.01	102.0	262.15	53.05	76.88	43.61	13.32
2017	457.70	101.9	273.88	54.91	68.58	45.32	15.00
2018	466.10	101.8	282.71	57.30	61.85	47.47	16.77
2019	501.15	107.5	295.34	61.89	76.77	48.57	18.58
2020	500.65	99.9	296.05	63.10	70.87	49.99	20.62

3-03 农林牧渔业总产值构成(1978-2020年)

Composition of Gross Output Value of Agriculture, Forestry, Animal Husbandry and Fishery(1978-2020)

单位:% (%)

年份 Year	农林牧渔业 Gross Output Value	#农业 Farming	种植业 Planting	林业 Forestry	畜牧业 Animal Husbandry	渔业 Fishery	农、林、牧、渔专业及辅助性活动 Services for Farming, Forestry, Animal Husbandary and Fishery
1978	100	78.4	74.9	4.0	16.8	0.8	-
1979	100	73.3	70.9	4.0	21.8	0.9	-
1980	100	70.3	67.7	6.5	22.2	1.0	-
1981	100	72.3	67.6	6.9	19.7	1.1	-
1982	100	71.4	68.6	5.9	21.1	1.6	-
1983	100	69.6	64.7	6.6	22.0	1.8	-
1984	100	69.2	65.1	8.3	20.3	2.2	-
1985	100	64.3	59.2	9.0	23.5	3.2	-
1986	100	63.3	58.0	8.4	24.4	3.9	-
1987	100	61.5	55.4	9.4	24.9	4.2	-
1988	100	58.2	52.3	8.8	28.2	4.8	-
1989	100	58.4	52.1	7.2	29.5	4.9	-
1990	100	61.8	55.4	6.4	26.9	4.9	-
1991	100	61.3	55.0	8.2	25.3	5.2	-
1992	100	60.4	51.6	7.2	26.9	5.5	-
1993	100	60.8	50.1	7.9	25.8	5.5	-
1994	100	61.1	51.1	7.2	26.7	5.0	-
1995	100	62.2	52.8	8.2	24.5	5.1	-
1996	100	63.1	52.6	8.2	23.1	5.6	-
1997	100	62.0	51.7	8.9	22.8	6.3	-
1998	100	61.8	51.3	8.9	21.1	8.2	-
1999	100	62.0	52.1	8.9	20.7	8.4	-
2000	100	59.2	49.4	9.0	21.7	10.1	-
2001	100	58.5	52.2	9.0	22.0	10.5	-
2002	100	55.4	52.6	9.6	23.3	11.7	-
2003	100	52.5	50.2	9.7	22.1	12.3	3.4
2004	100	51.0	49.1	10.4	23.1	11.8	3.7
2005	100	51.8	50.3	10.6	22.6	12.3	2.7
2006	100	54.3	52.9	11.9	21.8	9.1	2.9
2007	100	52.9	51.8	11.9	23.7	9.0	2.5
2008	100	51.4	50.2	11.7	23.3	11.3	2.3
2009	100	51.7	50.5	12.5	22.2	11.2	2.4
2010	100	53.7	52.9	10.4	22.3	11.0	2.6
2011	100	53.4	52.7	9.8	23.4	10.9	2.5
2012	100	54.0	53.1	9.9	22.6	10.9	2.6
2013	100	54.1	53.1	10.2	22.8	10.2	2.7
2014	100	55.8	54.7	11.2	19.8	10.6	2.6
2015	100	57.3	56.1	11.3	18.3	10.3	2.8
2016	100	58.4	57.0	11.8	17.1	9.7	3.0
2017	100	59.8	58.5	12.0	15.0	9.9	3.3
2018	100	60.7	59.3	12.3	13.3	10.2	3.5
2019	100	58.9	57.7	12.3	15.3	9.7	3.8
2020	100	59.1	57.9	12.6	14.2	10.0	4.1

3－04　农林牧渔业分项产值(2013－2020年)

Gross Output Value of Agriculture, Forestry, Animal Husbandry and Fishery by Branch(2013－2020)

单位:万元　　　　(10000 yuan)

指　　标	Item	2013	2014	2015	2016	2017	2018	2019	2020
农林牧渔业总产值(现价)	**Gross Output Value (Current Price)**	**3993712**	**4185804**	**4404121**	**4490065**	**4577017**	**4660989**	**5011510**	**5006463**
一、农业产值	**Farming**	**2161055**	**2333804**	**2524163**	**2621544**	**2738813**	**2827117**	**2953377**	**2960514**
1. 种植业产值	Planting	2120540	2291071	2468981	2558927	2677779	2666080	2892153	2900314
粮食	Grain	248550	224164	228341	171736	177764	175924	179017	192009
油料	Oil－bearing Crops	37649	37530	48373	34737	37332	38607	45369	47251
棉花	Cotton	1571	1152	1094	467	397	371	451	381
麻类	Fiber Crops	25	8	6	5	3	2	2	－
甘蔗	Sugarcane	18496	17347	16322	5770	5214	5102	8426	9763
烟叶	Tobacco	1	1	1	1	1	－	－	－
药材类	Crude Drugs	67623	75180	86538	98954	112902	122997	139832	151006
蔬菜	Vegetables	665429	686995	748644	834633	829020	842779	880336	875957
茶、桑、果、坚果	Tea, Mulberry & Fruits	630899	749516	802647	828571	908024	942095	985879	989268
其他	Others	450297	499178	537015	584053	607122	638203	652841	634679
2. 其他农业产值	Other Farming	40515	42733	55182	62617	61034	61037	61224	60200
二、林业产值	**Forestry**	**408170**	**470164**	**498051**	**530464**	**549138**	**572957**	**618886**	**631016**
人造林木生长	Artificial Forestry	33734	31640	32574	31490	31415	32211	32962	33162
林产品	Forest Products	227962	267839	294806	327864	349421	373384	414016	432001
竹木采伐	Lumbering	103425	130794	127670	125112	122773	121574	124431	117730
采集野生植物	Wild Plant collected	43049	39891	43001	45998	45529	45788	47477	48123
三、畜牧业产值	**Animal Husbandry**	**911324**	**828184**	**807001**	**768795**	**685811**	**618513**	**767683**	**708743**
牲畜	Livestock Raising	589952	522674	522001	572122	498108	411261	556348	514871
家禽饲养	Poultry Raising	77869	72333	72394	36208	30122	36241	43002	39813
活的畜禽产品	Livestock Products	132151	127075	112964	92066	88831	98876	98252	85921
捕猎野兽野禽	Hunting Wild Beast and Wild Fowl	5126	6260	5256	6032	6043	5534	6777	6842
其他动物饲养	Other Animals Raising	106226	99842	94386	62367	62707	66601	63304	61296
四、渔业产值	**Fishery**	**407292**	**442023**	**452309**	**436050**	**453211**	**474742**	**485734**	**499942**
五、农、林、牧、渔专业及辅助性活动	**Services for Farming, Forestry, Animal Husbandary and Fishery**	**105871**	**111629**	**122597**	**133212**	**150044**	**167660**	**185830**	**206248**

3-05 农林牧渔业分项

Composition of Gross Output Value of Agriculture, Forestry,

单位：%

指　　标	Item	2013	2014
农林牧渔业总产值(现价)	**Gross Output Value(Current Price)**	**100**	**100**
一、农业产值	**Farming**	**54.1**	**55.8**
1.种植业产值	Planting	53.1	54.7
粮食	Grain	6.2	5.4
油料	Oil Plants	0.9	0.9
棉花	Cotton	–	–
麻类	Fiber Crops	–	–
甘蔗	Sugarcane	0.5	0.4
烟叶	Tobacco	–	–
药材类	Crude Drugs	1.7	1.8
蔬菜	Vegetables	16.7	16.4
茶、桑、果、坚果	Tea, Mulberry & Fruits	15.8	17.9
其他	Others	11.3	11.9
2.其他农业产值	Other Farming	1.0	1.0
二、林业产值	**Forestry**	**10.2**	**11.2**
人造林木生长	Artificial Forestry	0.8	0.8
林产品	Forest Products	5.7	6.4
竹木采伐	Lumbering	2.6	3.1
采集野生植物	Wild Plant collected	1.1	0.9
三、畜牧业产值	**Animal Husbandry**	**22.8**	**19.8**
牲畜	Livestock Raising	14.8	12.5
家禽饲养	Poultry Raising	1.9	1.7
活的畜禽产品	Livestock Products	3.3	3.0
捕猎野兽野禽	Hunting Wild Beast and Wild Fowl	0.1	0.1
其他动物饲养	Other Animals Raising	2.7	2.4
四、渔业产值	**Fishery**	**10.2**	**10.6**
五、农、林、牧、渔专业及辅助性活动	**Services for Farming, Forestry, Animal Husbandary and Fishery**	**2.7**	**2.6**

产值构成(2013－2020 年)

Animal Husbandry and Fishery by Branch(2013－2020)

(%)

2015	2016	2017	2018	2019	2020
100	**100**	**100**	**100**	**100**	**100**
57.3	**58.4**	**59.8**	**60.7**	**58.9**	**59.1**
56.1	57.0	58.5	59.3	57.7	57.9
5.2	3.8	3.9	3.8	3.6	3.8
1.1	0.8	0.8	0.8	0.9	0.9
–	–	–	–	–	–
–	–	–	–	–	–
0.4	0.1	0.1	0.1	0.2	0.2
–	–	–	–	–	–
2.0	2.2	2.5	2.6	2.8	3.0
16.9	18.6	18.1	18.1	17.6	17.5
18.2	18.5	19.8	20.2	19.7	19.8
12.2	13.0	13.3	13.7	13.0	12.7
1.3	1.4	1.3	1.4	1.2	1.2
11.3	**11.8**	**12.0**	**12.3**	**12.3**	**12.6**
0.7	0.7	0.7	0.7	0.6	0.7
6.7	7.3	7.6	8.0	8.3	8.6
2.9	2.8	2.7	2.6	2.5	2.4
1.0	1.0	1.0	1.0	0.9	0.9
18.3	**17.1**	**15.0**	**13.3**	**15.3**	**14.2**
11.9	12.7	10.9	8.9	11.1	10.3
1.6	0.8	0.7	0.8	0.8	0.8
2.6	2.1	1.9	2.1	2.0	1.7
0.1	0.1	0.1	0.1	0.1	0.1
2.1	1.4	1.4	1.4	1.3	1.3
10.3	**9.7**	**9.9**	**10.2**	**9.7**	**10.0**
2.8	**3.0**	**3.3**	**3.5**	**3.8**	**4.1**

3－06 分地区农林牧

Gross Output Value of Agriculture, Forestry,

单位:万元

指　标	Item	全　市 Whole City	市　区 Urban District	江干区 Jianggan	西湖区 Xihu	高新(滨江)区 Hi－Tech (Binjiang)
合　计	**Gross Output Value**	**5006463**	**3490546**		**41827**	**9303**
一、农业产值	**Farming**	**2960514**	**1975502**		**29678**	**8520**
(一)种植业产值	Planting	2900314	1951807		29678	8520
#副产品产值	By－products	9893	6203		24	8
1.粮食作物	Grain	192009	132603		491	124
谷　物	Cereal	148524	108743		491	124
豆　类	Beans	14958	8405		–	–
薯　类	Tubers	28527	15455		–	–
2.油　料	Oil Plants	47251	21424		84	–
3.棉　花	Cotton	381	173		–	–
4.麻　类	Fiber Crops	–	–		–	–
5.甘　蔗	Sugarcane	9763	7973		126	–
6.烟　叶	Tobacco	–	–		–	–
7.药材类	Crude Drugs	151006	50425		–	–
8.蔬　菜	Vegetables	875957	674838		5210	2316
9.茶、桑、果、坚果	Tea, Mulberry & Fruits	989268	510872		10416	1010
10.其　他	Others	634679	553499		13398	5057
(二)其他农业产值	Other Farming	60200	23695		–	–
二、林业产值	**Forestry**	**631016**	**466389**		**–**	**–**
1.人造林木生长	Artificial Forestry	33162	24455		–	–
2.林产品	Forest Products	432001	324704		–	–
3.村及村以下竹木采伐	Lumbering	117730	87793		–	–
4.采集野生植物	Wild Plant collected	48123	29437		–	–
三、畜牧业产值	**Animal Husbandry**	**708743**	**455165**		**–**	**–**
1.牲畜	Livestock	514871	368146		–	–
2.家禽饲养	Poultry Raising	39813	25987		–	–
3.活的畜禽产品	Livestock Products	85921	26619		–	–
4.捕猎野兽野禽	Hunting Wild Beast and Wild Fowl	6842	4642		–	–
5.其他动物饲养	Other Animals Raising	61296	29770		–	–
四、渔业产值	**Fishery**	**499942**	**432242**		**10385**	**783**
五、农、林、牧、渔专业及辅助性活动	**Services for Farming, Forestry, Animal Husbandary and Fishery**	**206248**	**161248**		**1764**	**–**

渔业总产值(2020 年)

Animal Husbandry and Fishery by Region(2020)

(10000 yuan)

萧山区 Xiaoshan	余杭区 Yuhang	富阳区 Fuyang	临安区 Lin'an	钱塘新区 Qiantang New Area	西湖风景名胜区 The West Lake Scenic Zone	桐庐县 Tonglu	淳安县 Chun'an	建德市 Jiande
941763	**842439**	**697968**	**670393**	**226116**	**15289**	**379603**	**542133**	**594181**
596253	**450891**	**420593**	**316529**	**137749**	**15289**	**241309**	**373962**	**369741**
596224	447271	406711	310365	137749	15289	236357	372549	339601
1456	1838	1702	647	528	–	795	970	1925
25712	40157	38097	18816	9206	–	18989	16553	23864
22215	37275	30810	10414	7414	–	13892	7825	18064
2166	1909	2170	401	1759	–	1081	3208	2264
1331	973	5117	8001	33	–	4016	5520	3536
5601	2287	7147	4099	2240	–	6626	8407	10794
102	53	–	–	18	–	–	166	42
–	–	–	–	–	–	–	–	–
4518	700	482	32	2115	–	975	109	706
–	–	–	–	–	–	–	–	–
9467	10659	13969	16330	–	–	14285	48593	37703
246402	165505	98497	65705	91203	–	68035	65281	67803
48781	127422	143542	153617	10795	15289	100372	207331	170693
255641	100488	104977	51766	22172	–	27075	26109	27996
29	3620	13882	6164	–	–	4952	1413	30140
16233	**90189**	**136827**	**223140**	**–**	**–**	**55041**	**72959**	**36627**
3140	14123	3198	3999	–	–	2027	2561	4119
8960	58924	92039	164781	–	–	41079	46860	19358
3838	15788	25516	42651	–	–	4518	15204	10215
295	1354	16079	11709	–	–	7417	8334	2935
169651	**38964**	**89774**	**105564**	**51212**	**–**	**51396**	**55880**	**146302**
149853	23898	65216	80767	48412	–	30846	35955	79924
5618	10516	6448	2580	825	–	1709	2356	9761
7125	3185	4041	10621	1647	–	3116	5733	50453
–	254	3311	1077	–	–	1320	156	724
7055	1111	10758	10519	328	–	14405	11680	5441
98363	**197584**	**40872**	**8703**	**30104**	**–**	**18824**	**27754**	**21122**
61263	**64811**	**9902**	**16457**	**7051**	**–**	**13033**	**11578**	**20389**

3-07 主要农作物播种面积及产量(2019-2020年)
Sown Areas and Yield of Major Farm Crops(2019-2020)

指 标	Item	2019			2020		
		播种面积(千公顷) Sown Area (1000 hectares)	总产量(吨) Total Output (ton)	公顷产量(公斤) Yield per Hectare (kg/hectare)	播种面积(千公顷) Sown Area (1000 hectares)	总产量(吨) Total Output (ton)	公顷产量(公斤) Yield per Hectare (kg/hectare)
农作物总计	**Total Farm Crops**	**282.21**	**-**	**-**	**248.15**	**-**	**-**
一、粮 食	**Grain Crops**	**88.7**	**496447**	**5595**	**90.84**	**508643**	**5599**
(一)谷 物	Cereals	-	-	-	-	-	-
1.稻谷	Rice	-	-	-	-	-	-
①早稻及早中稻	Early Rice & Semi-late Rice	-	-	-	-	-	-
②晚稻及迟中稻	Late Rice & Semi-late Rice	-	-	-	-	-	-
#单季稻	#Single-crop Rice	-	-	-	-	-	-
2.小麦	Wheat	-	-	-	-	-	-
3.大麦	Barley	-	-	-	-	-	-
4.玉米	Corn	-	-	-	-	-	-
5.其他谷物	Other Cereals	-	-	-	-	-	-
(二)豆 类	Beans	-	-	-	-	-	-
1.大豆	Soybeans	-	-	-	-	-	-
2.其他小豆类	Other	-	-	-	-	-	-
(三)薯 类	Tubers	-	-	-	-	-	-
二、油料	**Oil Plants**	**26.32**	**70593**	**2682**	**26.73**	**72178**	**2700**
1.油菜籽	Rapeseeds	22.55	59503	2639	23.07	61388	2661
2.花生	Peanuts	2.34	8728	3724	2.27	8482	3733
3.芝麻	Sesame	1.42	2343	1645	1.36	2238	1648
4.其他	Others	0.01	19	3167	0.006	20	3333
三、棉花(皮棉)	**Cotton**	**0.19**	**292**	**1521**	**0.16**	**243**	**1519**
四、麻类	**Fiber Cropers**	**0.003**	**5**	**1667**	**-**	**-**	**-**
五、糖类	**Sugar Crops**	**0.84**	**49886**	**59177**	**0.96**	**56704**	**58822**
六、烟叶	**Tobacco**	**-**	**-**	**-**	**-**	**-**	**-**
七、药材	**Crude Drugs**	**8.47**	**49093**	**5799**	**8.94**	**50481**	**5644**
八、蔬菜	**Vegetables**	**98.53**	**3400525**	**34514**	**99.34**	**3476884**	**34999**
九、果用瓜	**Melon as Fruit**	**10.79**	**368848**	**34191**	**10.61**	**359751**	**33923**
#西瓜	Watermelon	7.29	276084	37877	7.13	267948	37596
草莓	Strawberry	1.6	45015	28170	1.64	45768	27856
十、花卉苗木	**Flower Gardening**	**37.53**	**-**	**-**	**-**	**-**	**-**
十一、其他作物	**Others**	**10.84**	**-**	**-**	**10.57**	**-**	**-**
#绿肥	Green Manure	1.46	-	-	-	-	-

注:2020年蔬菜产量包含食用菌。

a) Vegetable Output contains edible fungus since 2020.

3－08 分地区粮食播种面积及产量(2020年)
Sown Areas and Yield of Grain Crops by Region(2020)

地　　区	Region	播种面积总计(公顷)(Sown Area of Grain Crops (hectare))	总产量(吨) Yield of Grain Crops(ton)	公顷产量(公斤) Yield per Hectare(kg)
全　市	**Whole City**	**90840**	**508643**	**5599**
市区	Urban District	58672	351071	5984
萧山区	Xiaoshan	12701	70020	5513
余杭区	Yuhang	17301	112509	6503
富阳区	Fuyang	15301	98045	6408
临安区	Lin'an	7101	39004	5493
钱塘新区	Qiantang New Area	5901	28887	4895
其他市区	Other	367	2606	7101
桐庐县	Tonglu	8167	46553	5700
淳安县	Chun'an	11434	42513	3718
建德市	Jiande	12567	68506	5451

3－09 分地区油、菜、茶、

Statistics on Rapeseeds, Vegetables, Tea,

指标	Item	全市 Whole City	市区 Urban District	江干区 Jianggan	西湖区 Xihu	高新(滨江)区 Hi－Tech (Binjiang)
一、油料	**Oil Plants**					
播种面积 (公顷)	Sown Area (hectare)	26728	11335		104	11
每公顷产量 (公斤)	Yield per Hectare (kg)	2701	2740		1548	1546
总产量 (吨)	Total Output (ton)	72178	31057		161	17
二、蔬菜	**Vegetables**					
播种面积 (公顷)	Sown Area (hectare)	99343	73401		827	393
总产量 (吨)	Total Output (ton)	3476884	2708619		15368	13092
三、茶叶	**Tea**					
(一)茶园面积 (公顷)	Tea Garden Area (hectare)	35609	14701		1044	49
(二)总产量 (吨)	Output of Tea (ton)	29575	17947		476	19
春　茶 (吨)	Spring Tea (ton)	20037	12212		302	12
夏　茶 (吨)	Summer Tea (ton)	6635	4452		52	－
秋　茶 (吨)	Autumn Tea (ton)	2903	1283		122	7
四、桑蚕	**Silkworm Cocoons & Mulberry**					
(一)桑园总面积 (公顷)	Mulberry Garden Area (hectare)	5944	1010		2	－
(二)蚕茧总产量 (吨)	Output of Silkworm Cocoons (ton)					
春　茧 (吨)	Spring Silkworm Cocoons (ton)					
夏　茧 (吨)	Summer Silkworm Cocoons (ton)					
秋　茧 (吨)	Autumn Silkworm Cocoons (ton)					

注:1. 蔬菜产量包含食用菌

2. 萧山区不含托管在钱塘新区的街道数据

蚕、果生产情况(2020 年)

Silkworm Cocoons and Fruits Production by Region(2020)

萧山区 Xiaoshan	余杭区 Yuhang	富阳区 Fuyang	临安区 Lin'an	钱塘新区 Qiantang New Area	西湖风景名胜区 The West Lake Scenic Zone	桐庐县 Tonglu	淳安县 Chun'an	建德市 Jiande
2773	1513	3698	1828	1408	–	3044	6116	6233
2846	2416	2782	2629	3010	–	2412	1908	3546
7893	3655	10287	4806	4238	–	7342	11672	22107
20560	22528	10858	8414	9821	–	7390	9377	9175
942312	688989	412330	219495	417033	–	237490	266403	264372
1198	4338	4066	3643	–	363	4061	12582	4265
495	7187	7070	2579	–	121	3813	4710	3105
408	4408	5066	1911	–	105	1823	3786	2216
37	1911	1958	489		5	1045	501	637
50	868	46	179	–	11	945	423	252
–	144	117	747	–	–	426	4305	203

a) Vegetable Output contains edible fungus.

b) Figures of Xiaoshan District don't include subdistricts which under administered by Qiantang New Area.

3－09 续表

指标	Item	全市 Whole City	市区 Urban District	江干区 Jianggan	西湖区 Xihu	高新（滨江）区 Hi－Tech (Binjiang)
五、水果生产	**Fruits**					
（一）果园面积合计（公顷）	Area of Orchards (hectare)	29333	11351		72	70
柑桔园（公顷）	Citrus (hectare)	7232	476		10	－
梨园（公顷）	Pears (hectare)	3848	1911		7	17
桃园（公顷）	Peaches (hectare)	4389	1789		21	－
杨梅园（公顷）	Red Bayberry (hectare)	3156	1463		4	50
枇杷园（公顷）	Loquat (hectare)	2986	1396		－	－
柿子园（公顷）	Persimmons (hectare)	811	252		－	－
葡萄园（公顷）	Grapes (hectare)	1307	1008		12	3
其他果园（公顷）	Others (hectare)	4097	2446		18	－
（二）水果总产量（吨）	Yield of Fruits (ton)	831148	375905		958	565
柑桔（吨）	Citrus (ton)	192589	5806		125	－
梨（吨）	Pears (ton)	65968	35074		35	220
桃子（吨）	Peaches (ton)	81452	50302		38	－
杨梅（吨）	Red Bayberry (ton)	13328	6664		－	33
枇杷（吨）	Loquat (ton)	18722	8447		－	－
柿子（吨）	Persimmons (ton)	9582	4002		－	－
葡萄（吨）	Grapes (ton)	24291	18745		243	10
果用瓜（吨）	Melon as Fruit (ton)	359751	211483		364	302
其他水果（吨）	Others (ton)	47353	27285		153	－

continued

萧山区 Xiaoshan	余杭区 Yuhang	富阳区 Fuyang	临安区 Lin'an	钱塘新区 Qiantang New Area	西湖风景名胜区 The West Lake Scenic Zone	桐庐县 Tonglu	淳安县 Chun'an	建德市 Jiande
2039	3867	2983	2219	101	–	3650	8617	5715
37	69	222	135	3	–	128	4674	1954
111	891	547	330	8	–	1041	546	350
143	463	809	341	12	–	862	1023	715
586	261	405	157	–	–	573	426	694
8	1309	60	18	1	–	137	864	589
70	23	117	42	–	–	28	450	81
82	318	332	188	73	–	117	96	86
960	395	283	688	2	–	509	336	806
86910	58776	130312	60221	38163	–	92056	130811	232376
363	1247	2663	1342	66	–	2580	66914	117289
1350	14309	15168	3827	165	–	18759	6085	6050
1539	8146	34154	6262	163	–	10916	11463	8771
2766	1239	1635	991	–	–	2095	2005	2564
119	7838	201	270	19	–	672	6680	2923
964	706	1276	1053	3	–	279	4016	1285
1281	6637	5731	3534	1309	–	1908	1175	2463
70370	12252	64846	27007	36342	–	48476	26200	73592
7118	4097	3175	12691	51	–	3761	3422	12885

3－10　分地区畜牧业

Statistics on Animal Husbanday

指　标		Item		全市 Whole City		市区 Urban District	
				2019 年	2020 年	2019 年	2020 年
一、生猪		**Hogs**					
生猪年末存栏	（万头）	Being Raised at Year－end	（10000 heads）	90.34	104.51	72.04	
#能繁殖的母猪	（万头）	#Reproducible	（10000 heads）	7.22	7.17	5.95	
年内肥猪出栏	（万头）	Slaughtered Hogs of the Year	（10000 heads）	140.50	112.91	116.33	
全年饲养量	（万头）	Number of Hogs Raised in the year	（10000 heads）				
二、牛		**Cattle & Buffaloes**					
牛年末存栏	（头）	Being Raised at Year－end	（head）	13013	12062	8884	
#良种及改良种乳牛	（头）	#Improved Milk Cows	（head）		6410		
牛年内出栏	（头）	Slaughtered Cattle & Buffaloes of the Year	（head）	13928	7243	11613	
三、羊		**Sheep & Goats**					
羊年末存栏	（万只）	Being Raised at Year－end	（10000 heads）	18.75	20.20	16.48	
羊年内出栏	（万只）	Slaughtered Sheep & Goats of the Year	（10000 heads）	23.83	21.07	21.93	
四、兔		**Rabbits**					
兔年末存栏	（万只）	Being Raised at Year－end	（10000 heads）	6.69	8.00	6.39	
兔年内出栏	（万只）	Slaughtered Rabbits of the Year	（10000 heads）	39.62	23.74	36.48	
五、家禽		**Poultry**					
家禽年末存栏	（万只）	Being Raised at Year－end	（10000 heads）	1025.66	1016.51	451.31	
家禽年内出栏	（万只）	Slaughtered Poultry of the Year	（10000 heads）	1836.37	1546.63	1316.18	
六、年末养蜂箱数	**（箱）**	**Beehives**	**（case）**	**170845**	**170154**	**47345**	
七、畜禽产品产量		**Output of Livestock Products**					
1.肉类产量	（吨）	Output of Meat	（ton）	149691	109826	122013	
#猪　肉	（吨）	Pork	（ton）	111811	80287	93540	

注：1.2019 年起渔业生产萧山区不含托管在钱塘新区的街道数据。

2.国家统计局浙江调查总队会同浙江省统计局对 2018 年起年度的畜牧业分地区数据进行了核定。

渔业生产(2019 - 2020 年)
and Fishery by Region(2019 - 2020)

江干区 Jianggan		西湖区 Xihu		高新(滨江)区 Hi - Tech(Binjiang)		萧山区 Xiaoshan		余杭区 Yuhang	
2019 年	2020 年	2019 年	2020 年	2019 年	2020 年	2019 年	2020 年	2019 年	2020 年
		–		–		55.02	34.01	2.90	6.28
		–		–		4.51	1.98	0.25	0.28
		–		–		76.86	34.54	6.52	4.08
		–		–		3733	2463	87	128
							2444		–
		–		–		433	528	256	144
		–		–		9.27	9.71	2.46	2.13
		–		–		8.76	8.31	4.68	3.45
		–		–		0.56	0.21	1.94	1.47
		–		–		1.52	0.37	9.03	5.38
		–		–		125.72	82.59	137.34	122.25
		–		–		313.34	215.06	488.28	378.46
		–		**–**		**13965**	**5615**	**2799**	**5754**
						70525	25326	14058	9700
		–		–		63700	20500	4927	2995

a) Fishery production of Xiaoshan District don't include subdistricts which under administered by Qiantang New Area Since 2019.

b) Zhejiang Survey Team of National Bureau of Statistics and Zhejiang Provincial Bureau of Statistics approved the regional data of animal husbandry Since 2018.

3-10 续表1

指 标		Item		全市 Whole City		市区 Urban District	
				2019年	2020年	2019年	2020年
牛 肉	(吨)	Beef	(ton)	2297	1205	1915	
羊 肉	(吨)	Mutton	(ton)	4193	3681	3861	
兔 肉	(吨)	Rabbit Meat	(ton)	669	402	625	
禽 肉	(吨)	Poultry Meat	(ton)	30358	23931	21758	
2. 禽蛋产量	(吨)	Poultry Eggs	(ton)	88661	73911	20722	
3. 蜂蜜产量	(吨)	Honey	(ton)	18367	14878	6427	
4. 蜂皇浆产量	(公斤)	Honey Tonic	(kg)	542807	462309	211888	
5. 牛奶产量	(吨)	Milk	(ton)	26335	30951	22821	
6. 兔毛产量	(吨)	Rabbit Wool	(ton)	18	–	18	
八、渔业生产		**Fishery**					
(一)淡水产品产量总计	(吨)	Total Output of Freshwater Aquatic Products	(ton)	168042	172247	136508	138887
其中:养殖产量	(吨)	Artificially Cultured	(ton)	153981	157721	128919	130649
1. 鱼 类	(吨)	Fish	(ton)	94255	107398	70989	82033
#鲫 鱼	(吨)	#Crucians	(ton)	14363	15269	10829	12478
鳊 鱼	(吨)	Breams	(ton)	7071	6886	4193	5001
黑 鱼	(吨)	Snake Heads	(ton)	568	407	501	351
2. 虾蟹类	(吨)	Shrimps, Prawns & Crabs	(ton)	26931	28934	26667	22393
3. 贝 类	(吨)	Shellfish	(ton)	848	4465	232	3053
4. 其 他	(吨)	Others	(ton)	31947	31450	31031	30208
#甲 鱼	(吨)	Turtles	(ton)	30855	29775	30113	29175
(二)淡水养殖面积合计	(公顷)	Freshwater Aquiculture Area	(hectare)	51980	52413	7916	9020

continued 1

江干区 Jianggan		西湖区 Xihu		高新(滨江)区 Hi－Tech(Binjiang)		萧山区 Xiaoshan		余杭区 Yuhang	
2019 年	2020 年	2019 年	2020 年	2019 年	2020 年	2019 年	2020 年	2019 年	2020 年
		–		–		72	88	42	24
		–		–		1541	1520	824	576
		–		–		32	5	193	122
		–		–		5180	3211	8072	5983
		–		–		1980	1822	3233	2549
		–		–		1236	286	326	212
		–		–		81903	28275	6100	30177
		–		–		9264	10462	–	–
		–		–		–	–	18	–
95	93	6340	6154	748	665	36267	36823	61729	63117
		5420	5324	386	352	35411	36156	59625	60630
		5115	5457	256	472	13278	14873	31776	33983
		950	1002	10	–	55	60	3329	3634
		365	423	–	–	12	30	1841	1884
		204	213	–	100	210	–	40	–
		102	114	50	83	18578	18669	2139	2199
		–	53	–	2	–	–	–	2487
		203	530	80	110	3555	3281	25710	24448
		202	141	80	110	3456	3210	25246	23984
		432	353	60	60	2005	2525	2510	2510

指　标		Item		富阳区 Fuyang		临安区 Lin'an	
				2019 年	2020 年	2019 年	2020 年
一、生猪		**Hogs**					
生猪年末存栏	（万头）	Being Raised at Year－end	（10000 heads）	4.25	9.02	9.87	13.45
#能繁殖的母猪	（万头）	#Reproducible	（10000 heads）	0.36	0.46	0.82	0.98
年内肥猪出栏	（万头）	Slaughtered Hogs of the Year	（10000 heads）	14.98	13.73	17.98	16.23
全年饲养量	（万头）	Number of Hogs Raised in the year	（10000 heads）				
二、牛		**Cattle & Buffaloes**					
牛年末存栏	（头）	Being Raised at Year－end	（head）	2482	1007	2582	2864
#良种及改良种乳牛	（头）	#Improved Milk Cows	（head）		–		1945
牛年内出栏	（头）	Slaughtered Cattle & Buffaloes of the Year	（head）	8642	2191	2282	2113
三、羊		**Sheep & Goats**					
羊年末存栏	（万只）	Being Raised at Year－end	（10000 heads）	1.45	1.46	3.31	3.65
羊年内出栏	（万只）	Slaughtered Sheep & Goats of the Year	（10000 heads）	3.77	2.14	4.73	4.44
四、兔		**Rabbits**					
兔年末存栏	（万只）	Being Raised at Year－end	（10000 heads）	3.2	5.03	0.69	0.58
兔年内出栏	（万只）	Slaughtered Rabbits of the Year	（10000 heads）	22.84	14.70	3.09	1.81
五、家禽		**Poultry**					
家禽年末存栏	（万只）	Being Raised at Year－end	（10000 heads）	121.04	87.89	67.21	75.88
家禽年内出栏	（万只）	Slaughtered Poultry of the Year	（10000 heads）	419.45	267.88	95.12	106.27
六、年末养蜂箱数	**（箱）**	**Beehives**	**（case）**	**19134**	**13922**	**11447**	**15199**
七、畜禽产品产量		**Output of Livestock Products**					
1.肉类产量	（吨）	Output of Meat	（ton）	20722	15931	16708	16321
#猪　肉	（吨）	Pork	（ton）	11322	10781	13591	13159

continued 2

钱塘新区 Qiantang New Area		西湖风景名胜区 The West Lake Scenic Zone		桐庐县 Tonglu		淳安县 Chun'an		建德市 Jiande	
2019年	2020年	2019年	2020年	2019年	2020年	2019年	2020年	2019年	2020年
	9.17	–		3.20	8.08	10.28	9.11	4.82	15.39
	0.82	–		0.25	0.53	0.33	0.89	0.69	1.23
	14.49	–		5.74	6.22	11.03	9.30	7.40	14.34
	1378	–		1012	934	1157	530	1960	2758
	1263				–		–		758
	231	–		944	536	635	585	736	915
	0.98	–		0.58	0.43	0.45	0.34	1.24	1.50
	0.83			0.54	0.63	0.45	0.30	0.91	0.97
0.32	0.58	–		0.16	0.04	0.14	0.05	–	0.04
1.23	0.98	–		0.48	0.19	0.16	0.28	2.5	0.03
	10.78	–		53.27	78.92	57.48	49.96	463.6	508.24
	36.58	–		71.17	60.59	63.51	63.16	385.51	418.63
5600	**3957**	**–**		**67992**	**60570**	**39937**	**44954**	**15571**	**20183**
	9726			5819	6362	9579	7451	12280	19010
	9000	–		4340	5264	8340	6385	5591	12203

3－10　续表3

指　标		Item		富阳区 Fuyang 2019年	富阳区 Fuyang 2020年	临安区 Lin'an 2019年	临安区 Lin'an 2020年
牛　肉	(吨)	Beef	(ton)	1425	367	376	373
羊　肉	(吨)	Mutton	(ton)	663	339	833	834
兔　肉	(吨)	Rabbit Meat	(ton)	344	221	56	27
禽　肉	(吨)	Poultry Meat	(ton)	6934	4222	1572	1645
2. 禽蛋产量	(吨)	Poultry Eggs	(ton)	10010	3463	5499	5739
3. 蜂蜜产量	(吨)	Honey	(ton)	3064	359	1801	1783
4. 蜂皇浆产量	(公斤)	Honey Tonic	(kg)	79549	25570	44336	46939
5. 牛奶产量	(吨)	Milk	(ton)	–	–	8650	9196
6. 兔毛产量	(吨)	Rabbit Wool	(ton)	–	–	–	–
八、渔业生产		**Fishery**					
(一)淡水产品产量总计	(吨)	Total Output of Freshwater Aquatic Products	(ton)	17780	18752	5246	5207
其中:养殖产量	(吨)	Artificially Cultured	(ton)	16860	17671	2984	2860
1. 鱼　类	(吨)	Fish	(ton)	15609	15901	2402	4321
#鲫　鱼	(吨)	#Crucians	(ton)	5597	5620	547	552
鳊　鱼	(吨)	Breams	(ton)	1735	1600	240	241
黑　鱼	(吨)	Snake Heads	(ton)	47	27	–	–
2. 虾蟹类	(吨)	Shrimps, Prawns & Crabs	(ton)	354	1009	69	153
3. 贝　类	(吨)	Shellfish	(ton)	232	303	–	208
4. 其　他	(吨)	Others	(ton)	665	1314	513	525
#甲　鱼	(吨)	Turtles	(ton)	426	855	398	411
(二)淡水养殖面积合计	(公顷)	Freshwater Aquiculture Area	(hectare)	1503	1503	734	729

continued 3

钱塘新区 Qiantang New Area		西湖风景名胜区 The West Lake Scenic Zone		桐庐县 Tonglu		淳安县 Chun'an		建德市 Jiande	
2019 年	2020 年	2019 年	2020 年	2019 年	2020 年	2019 年	2020 年	2019 年	2020 年
–	37	–		156	89	105	98	121	129
–	109	–		94	104	79	41	159	158
19	15	–		9	3	5	8	30	1
–	565	–		1177	870	1050	919	6373	6516
–	98	–		2610	2793	5120	4624	60209	52823
243	137	–		5856	5750	4012	4381	2072	1970
27707	13658	–		266166	249041	49985	52786	14768	15865
4907	6723	–		–	–	–	–	3514	4570
–	–	–		–	–	–	–	–	–
8303	9418	–		8720	9045	13345	13443	9469	9755
8233	9365	–		7980	8125	10625	10564	6457	6675
2553	2916	–		7283	8429	10442	12636	5541	8317
341	309	–		1640	1700	1259	1750	635	642
–	–	–		906	945	1042	838	930	925
–	–	–		11	11	–	–	56	26
5375	6140	–		160	153	–	169	104	245
–	–	–		–		–	417	616	997
305	362	–		537	463	183	221	196	196
305	362	–		483	440	183	211	76	51
672	672	–		1340	1340	41041	41041	1683	1680

3－11 分地区林业
Statistics on Forestry

指　标	Item	全市 Whole City	市区 Urban District
一、营林情况	**Afforestation**		
1. 当年造林面积　（公顷）	Afforested Areas　(hectare)	3421	1584
2. 迹地更新面积　（公顷）	Area of Forest Updating　(hectare)	1443	375
3. 封山育林面积　（公顷）	Area of Afforestation in Enclosed Mountain　(hectare)	267	–
4. 零星（四旁）植树　（万株）	Planting Trees　(10000 plant)	120	66
5. 中、幼龄林抚育面积（公顷）	Area of Grown Forest Cultivated　(hectare)	8005	4472
二、林产品产量	**Output of Forest Products**		
1. 油茶籽　（吨）	Camellia Seeds　(ton)	11670	250
2. 竹笋干　（吨）	Dried Bamboo Shoots　(ton)	73733	55548
3. 核　桃　（吨）	Walnuts　(ton)	26747	15891
4. 板　栗　（吨）	Chestnuts　(ton)	10649	–
三、竹木采伐量	**Lumbering**		
1. 木　材　（万立方米）	Timber Cut　(10000 cu. m)	240358.00	55661.00
2. 竹　材　（万支）	Bamboo Cut　(10000 pieces)	3487.16	2694.00

注：1. 萧山区不含托管在钱塘新区的街道数据。

2. 2019 年起封山育林面积为当年新增封山育林面积。

生产(2020 年)
by Region(2020)

萧山区 Xiaoshan	余杭区 Yuhang	富阳区 Fuyang	临安区 Lin'an	桐庐县 Tonglu	淳安县 Chun'an	建德市 Jiande
175	247	552	490	488	816	533
–	23	73	279	71	464	533
–	–	–	–	–	–	267
30	–	14	22	20	14	20
861	667	666	2130	667	1333	1533
–	–	80	170	420	8800	2200
2180	12320	14300	26748	7611	7776	2798
–	10	280	15601	1790	8915	151
410	142	40	789	3000	3492	2776
–	6533.00	22066.00	26565.00	19651.00	85623.00	79423.00
130.00	891.00	1036.15	636.85	104.60	461.21	227.35

a) Figures of Xiaoshan District don't include subdistricts which under administered by Qiantang New Area.
b) Area of Afforestation in Enclosed Mountain was newly added in the cument year since 2019.

3－12 分地区主要农
Possession of Major Agricultural

指　标		Item		全市 Whole City	余杭区 Yuhang
一、农业机械总动力	**（千瓦）**	**Total Power of Agricultural Machinery**	**(kW)**	**1958761**	**311926**
耕作机械动力	（千瓦）	Cultivation Machinery	(kW)	200937	45833
收获机械动力	（千瓦）	Harvest Machinery	(kW)	50473	10597
植保机械动力	（千瓦）	Plant Protection Machinery	(kW)	50430	3506
排灌机械动力	（千瓦）	Drainage & Irrigation Machinery	(kW)	337963	66383
农副产品加工机械动力	（千瓦）	Processing Machinery of Agricultural Products	(kW)	133915	12130
运输机械动力	（千瓦）	Transport Machinery	(kW)	7072	183
渔业机械动力	（千瓦）	Fishery Machinery	(kW)	121578	7415
其他机械动力	（千瓦）	Other Machinery	(kW)	1056393	165879
二、主要农机具		**Agricultural Machinery and Machinery For Processing Farm Products**			
大中型拖拉机	（台）	Large & Medium Tractors	(unit)	95	9
机引农具	（台）	Mechanized Farm Implement	(unit)		
农用小型拖拉机	（台）	Mini－tractors	(unit)	5260	1537
联合收获机	（台）	Combine Harvesters	(unit)	1347	231
机动割晒机	（台）	Motorized Harvesters	(unit)	6	4
机动脱粒机	（台）	Motorized Thresher	(unit)	7149	
谷物烘干机	（台）	Cereal Dryer	(unit)	798	199
机动喷雾(粉)器	（架）	Motorized Sprayer	(unit)	26131	645
农用水泵	（台）	Water Pump for Agricultural Use	(unit)	118733	14564
节水喷灌机械	（套）	Saving Water and Sprinkling Machinery	(set)	4223	339
粮食加工机械	（台）	Grain Processing Machinery	(unit)	15687	744
棉花加工机械	（台）	Cotton Processing Machinery	(unit)	189	8
油料加工机械	（台）	Oil Processing Machinery	(unit)	1459	37
农用运输机械	（台）	Vehicles for Agricultural Use	(unit)	541	44

注：萧山区不含托管在钱塘新区的街道数据。

机具年末拥有量(2020 年)
Machinery at the Year – end by Region(2020)

萧山区 Xiaoshan	富阳区 Fuyang	建德市 Jiande	西湖区 Xihu	滨江区 Binjiang	桐庐县 Tonglu	淳安县 Chun'an	临安区 Lin'an	钱塘区 Qiantang
366370	**263050**	**154766**	**65740**	**4045**	**125432**	**286902**	**290205**	**90323**
40111	27564	23019	754	73	14509	12156	22811	14105
8970	12526	4644	255		6861	1812	1643	3164
4319	4229	4793	1583	16	1592	4276	25517	598
75845	42308	42598	7389	1580	29081	21791	40178	10809
21174	10897	16581	151	1550	11539	44716	11364	3813
7	76	5640	98		126	708	234	
75429	1954	2196	386	332	1657	16967	137	15103
140515	163496	55295	55124	494	60067	184476	188321	42731
32	23				5		4	22
679	1601	626	35		424	68	227	63
313	251	111	6		151	174	46	64
	2							
2	4133	31		35	1533	1365		50
80	128	124	1		102	65	46	53
2723	1594	2243	3213		159	828	14462	264
15341	18347	22672	2036	56	11136	4985	28813	783
196	10	2947	18	2	50	570	69	22
1105	1074	1446	16	6	1163	7310	2661	162
49	43	16			13	55		5
75	83	271	2	4	224	515	178	70
2	11	279	2		7	125	71	

a) Figures of Xiaoshan District don't include subdistricts which under administered by Qiantang New Area.

3-13 农业物资
Agricultural Material

指　标	Item	全市 Whole City	市区 Urban District
一、农村用电量　（万千瓦时）	**Electricity Consumed in Rural Area (10000 kWh)**	**1080575**	**970749**
二、农业化肥施用量	**Consumption of Chemical Fertilizer**		
（一）按实物量计算　（吨）	Physical Quantity Consumption (ton)	380414	259937
1. 氮　肥　（吨）	Nitrogenous Fertilizer (ton)	142593	88315
2. 磷　肥　（吨）	Phosphate Fertilizer (ton)	56696	40050
3. 钾　肥　（吨）	Potash Fertilizer (ton)	33372	21221
4. 复合肥　（吨）	Compound Fertilizer (ton)	147753	110351
（二）按折纯法计算　（吨）	Pure Consumption (ton)	80640	48160
1. 氮　肥　（吨）	Nitrogenous Fertilizer (ton)	32251	18706
2. 磷　肥　（吨）	Phosphate Fertilizer (ton)	8462	4736
3. 钾　肥　（吨）	Potash Fertilizer (ton)	7087	3735
4. 复合肥　（吨）	Compound Fertilizer (ton)	32840	20983
三、农用塑料薄膜使用量　（吨）	**Use of Plastic Film (ton)**	**7640**	**3805**
四、农用柴油使用量　（吨）	**Consumption of Diesel Oil (ton)**	**22865**	**13872**
五、农药使用量　（吨）	**Consumption of Pesticide (ton)**	**5459**	**3673**

注：萧山区不含托管在钱塘新区的街道数据。

消耗情况（2020 年）
Consumption（2020）

萧山区 Xiaoshan	余杭区 Yuhang	富阳区 Fuyang	临安区 Lin'an	桐庐县 Tonglu	淳安县 Chun'an	建德市 Jiande
145739	**190788**	**467243**	**133364**	**70909**	**15979**	**22938**
123466	39393	17050	50797	32417	43645	44415
43977	11264	6968	14160	14935	20997	18346
23116	6644	722	4214	6638	4567	5441
10378	5163	421	4094	3599	3502	5050
45995	16322	8939	28329	7245	14579	15578
15182	10668	7331	10448	9318	6679	16483
6597	2518	2928	4360	4030	2308	7207
2217	1015	260	706	1217	599	1910
1256	1143	210	858	1222	463	1667
5112	5992	3933	4524	2849	3309	5699
1661	**365**	**273**	**1187**	**776**	**1303**	**1756**
4240	**1305**	**465**	**6802**	**4471**	**1377**	**3145**
1084	**832**	**640**	**855**	**562**	**480**	**744**

a) Figures of Xiaoshan District don't include subdistricts which under administered by Qiantang New Area.

3－14　乡（镇）

Statistics on Towns

乡镇名称 Town		社区（居民委员会） Number of communities (residents committees)	村民委员会（个） Number of Villagers' Committees (unit)	乡镇户籍户数（户） Resident Households in Towns (household)
全　市	**Whole City**	**754**	**1918**	**1798558**
西湖区	**Xihu District**	**100**	**32**	**92015**
留下街道	Liuxia Subdistrict	12	1	9230
转塘街道	Zhuantang Subdistrict	36	8	20976
三墩镇	Sandun	43	2	45256
双浦镇	Shuangpu	9	21	16553
高新（滨江）区	**Hi－Tech（Bingjiang） District**	**59**	**－**	**78209**
西兴街道	Xixing Subdistrict	17	－	24048
长河街道	Changhe Subdistrict	20	－	25942
浦沿街道	Puyan Subdistrict	22	－	28219
西湖风景名胜区	**The West Lake Scenic Zone**	**6**	**9**	**6600**
西湖街道	West Lake Subdistrict	6	9	6600
萧山区	**Xiaoshan District**	**190**	**352**	**337971**
城厢街道	Chengxiang Subdistrict	35	－	39596
北干街道	Beigan Subdistrict	33	6	27657
蜀山街道	Shushan Subdistrict	22	8	11913
新塘街道	Xintang Subdistrict	27	17	20327
靖江街道	Jingjiang Subdistrict	7	10	10420
南阳街道	Nanyang Subdistrict	3	13	11139
闻堰街道	Wenyan Subdistrict	7	6	10935
宁围街道	Ningwei Subdistrict	7	6	10795

基本情况(2020 年)
and Townships(2020)

乡镇户籍人口数 (人) Resident Population in Towns (person)	乡镇常用耕地面积 (公顷) Commonly used cultivated area of township (hectare)	一般公共预算收入 (万元) General public budget income (10000 yuan)	一般公共预算支出 (万元) General public budget expenditure (10000 yuan)
5781085	**158880**	**3164294.3**	**2026563.3**
332432	**4172.4**	**300205.3**	**93536.3**
33752	–	24804	18561
76080	405	175236.3	27095.8
156311	1163.4	59665	33418.2
66289	2604	40500	14461.3
272029	**607.8**	**161305**	**77486**
75307	151.8	50292	20642
89950	291	67300	30500
106772	165	43713	26344
19140	**–**	**18123.7**	**17893.6**
19140	–	18123.7	17893.6
1169986	**27818.3**	**725257.5**	**429644.1**
113837	–	19009.5	19462.3
82826	192	19726.5	19476.7
46978	449.9	172449	30291.2
74912	682	17028	17011.6
37217	1147	11438	11437
41441	1243	9876	1372
37751	295	57385	14422
36879	873	17794	18072

3－14 续表1

乡镇名称	Town	社区(居民委员会) Number of Communities (residents committees)	村民委员会(个) Number of Villagers´ Committees (unit)	乡镇户籍户数(户) Resident Households in Towns (household)
新街街道	Xinjie Subdistrict	5	15	17693
盈丰街道	Yingfeng Subdistrict	4	9	8166
楼塔镇	Louta	1	12	7710
河上镇	Heshang	1	15	8671
戴村镇	Daicun	1	22	11050
浦阳镇	Puyang	1	18	9723
进化镇	Jinhua	1	25	14281
临浦镇	Linpu	14	20	16676
义桥镇	Yiqiao	3	21	12042
所前镇	Suoqian	2	19	10734
衙前镇	Yaqian	2	11	6776
瓜沥镇	Guali	12	63	47025
益农镇	Yinong	1	19	12301
党湾镇	Dangwan	1	17	12341
余杭区	**Yuhang District**	**214**	**173**	**361887**
临平街道	Linping Subdistrict	15	–	16715
南苑街道	Nanyuan Subdistrict	29	–	29342
东湖街道	Donghu Subdistrict	40	3	31300
星桥街道	Xingqiao Subdistrict	17	–	14793
五常街道	Wuchang Subdistrict	18	–	16787
乔司街道	Qiaosi Subdistrict	4	11	16562

continued 1

乡镇户籍人口数（人）Resident Population in Towns (person)	乡镇常用耕地面积（公顷）Commonly used cultivated area of township (hectare)	一般公共预算收入（万元）General public budget income (10000 yuan)	一般公共预算支出（万元）General public budget expenditure (10000 yuan)
61982	1897	19622	19254
39436	642	–	0
26687	861	6755.4	6822.5
28006	1074.2	26419	21200
38649	1100	14228.7	14049.7
32591	1220.3	52618	32948
48366	1237	10879.1	26125.5
56607	1021	43800	43573
45329	1255.6	59522	17000
40905	803.6	21500	13400
27023	520	12476	29760
165292	6213	99848	42486
43772	2793	13668	12399
43500	2298.7	19215.3	19081.6
1216016	**24738.4**	**1266876.5**	**716695.9**
46139	60.7	19412.3	18249.6
96142	457.7	19000	18705.1
115043	728	122800	123908
43797	835.5	7574	1399
53682	21.6	177179	38574
62288	805.3	37377.4	32840.8

3－14 续表2

乡镇名称	Town	社区(居民委员会) Number of Communities (residents committees)	村民委员会(个) Number of Villagers' Committees (unit)	乡镇户籍户数(户) Resident Households in Towns (household)
运河街道	Yunhe Subdistrict	5	14	11507
崇贤街道	Chongxian Subdistrict	5	11	16478
仁和街道	Renhe Subdistrict	2	18	18131
良渚街道	Liangzhu Subdistrict	23	20	44629
闲林街道	Xianlin Subdistrict	8	8	21662
仓前街道	Cangqian Subdistrict	7	6	15254
余杭街道	Yuhang Subdistrict	16	11	29978
中泰街道	Zhongtai Subdistrict	4	10	11773
塘栖镇	Tangqi	10	18	23207
径山镇	Jingshan	2	13	12785
瓶窑镇	Pingyao	6	13	18752
鸬鸟镇	Luniao	1	6	4192
百丈镇	Baizhang	1	6	3156
黄湖镇	Huanghu	1	5	4884
富阳区	**Fuyang District**	**53**	**276**	**220575**
富春街道	Fuchun Subdistrict	35	12	49800
春江街道	Chunjiang Subdistrict	–	9	8397
鹿山街道	Lushan Subdistrict	2	9	8292
东洲街道	Dongzhou Subdistrict	4	15	12446
银湖街道	Yinghu Subdistrict	5	22	16738
万市镇	Wanshi	1	15	7153

continued 2

乡镇户籍人口数 (人) Resident Population in Towns (person)	乡镇常用耕地面积 (公顷) Commonly used cultivated area of township (hectare)	一般公共预算收入 (万元) General public budget income (10000 yuan)	一般公共预算支出 (万元) General public budget expenditure (10000 yuan)
43704	1284.5	32830	30784
60609	881	64593	32588
76212	2530	32927	29809
153023	2605	207820	118227
62435	262	93519.2	34994
56254	1357.4	152470	37265
90305	2747.5	93459.2	43754.9
35937	1246.6	29259.1	15521.3
82442	1813	52855	45702
39073	3175	38152	37805
62779	2187	77010	35000
12031	555.3	906.7	5236.4
10598	250.9	3589	5977
13523	934.4	4143.6	10355.8
692371	**18472.2**	**231583.7**	**170324**
135734	972	52633	22560
31927	380	21648	6256
25838	752	6400	6421
47905	1054	9857	9855
56841	1632	7568.2	6961.6
22030	1184	6508	6483

3－14　续表3

乡镇名称 Town		社区(居民委员会) Number of Communities (residents committees)	村民委员会(个) Number of Villagers´ Committees (unit)	乡镇户籍户数(户) Resident Households in Towns (household)
洞桥镇	Dongqiao	–	11	6093
渌渚镇	Luzhu	–	13	5694
永昌镇	Yongchang	–	5	3454
里山镇	Lishan	–	5	2997
常绿镇	Changlu	–	8	5166
场口镇	Changkou	1	24	13462
常安镇	Chang´an	–	16	7660
龙门镇	Longmen	–	4	2485
新登镇	Xindeng	4	28	23489
胥口镇	Xukou	–	13	6326
大源镇	Dayuan	1	15	10831
灵桥镇	Lingqiao	–	13	7567
新桐乡	Xintong	–	7	4935
上官乡	Shangguan	–	5	2667
环山乡	Huanshan	–	7	3851
湖源乡	Huyuan	–	10	4378
春建乡	Chunjian	–	6	2948
渔山乡	Yushan	–	4	3746
临安区	**Lin´an City**	**42**	**270**	**186916**
玲珑街道	Linlong Subdistrict	2	14	8396
锦南街道	Jinnan Subdistrict	3	7	3516
锦城街道	Jincheng Subdistrict	15	4	34079
锦北街道	Jinbei Subdistrict	9	5	14402
青山湖街道	Qingshanghu Subdistrict	7	14	13851

continued 3

乡镇户籍人口数（人）Resident Population in Towns (person)	乡镇常用耕地面积（公顷）Commonly used cultivated area of township (hectare)	一般公共预算收入（万元）General public budget income (10000 yuan)	一般公共预算支出（万元）General public budget expenditure (10000 yuan)
19025	1110	6259	6107
17047	921	24730	15609
11319	493	10748	10629
10204	397.8	2429	3264.3
15614	198.2	2636	1799
43516	1522	14144.5	9316.2
25250	874	4400.5	4306.5
7138	240	852.6	2750.3
68256	2258	20074	19394
18258	885	4431.7	4950.2
37111	483	8965.3	8938.4
26682	637	10843.9	5792.6
14119	705	2318	2209
8028	257.6	3204	3197
12809	355.2	4060	4113
15212	268	2156.8	3915.7
9282	704	3368	3427
13226	189.4	1348.2	2069.2
534822	**18712.4**	**194467.8**	**146575.1**
25233	614.5	16815	5620
10733	114	5460.3	5192.7
88897	333	23252	7985
41173	300	15502	6889
41591	701	72060	31548

3－14　续表4

乡镇名称	Town	社区(居民委员会) Number of Communities (residents committees)	村民委员会(个) Number of Villagers' Committees (unit)	乡镇户籍户数(户) Resident Households in Towns (household)
高虹镇	Gaohong	–	9	4766
太湖源镇	Taihuyuan	–	20	11132
於潜镇	Yuqian	1	30	17350
太阳镇	Taiyang	2	18	8845
潜川镇	Qianchuan	–	16	8357
昌化镇	Changhua	1	14	7353
河桥镇	Heqiao	–	11	5728
湍口镇	Tuankou	–	13	4173
清凉峰镇	Qingliangfeng	–	17	9631
岛石镇	Daoshi	–	16	8188
板桥镇	Banqiao	2	15	8243
天目山镇	Tianmushan	–	23	12130
龙岗镇	Longgang	–	24	6776
桐庐县	**Tonglu County**	**22**	**181**	**155311**
旧县街道	Jiuxian Subdistrict	–	5	2867
桐君街道	Tongjun Subdistrict	7	6	19051
城南街道	Chengnan Subdistrict	7	13	27892
凤川街道	Fengchuan Subdistrict	1	13	10364
富春江镇	Fuchunjiang	2	15	9397
横村镇	Hengcun	2	24	16882
分水镇	Fenshui	2	26	19099
瑶琳镇	Yaolin	–	16	12050
百江镇	Baijiang	–	15	6181
江南镇	Jiangnan	1	19	16864

continued 4

乡镇户籍人口数（人）Resident Population in Towns (person)	乡镇常用耕地面积（公顷）Commonly used cultivated area of township (hectare)	一般公共预算收入（万元）General public budget income (10000 yuan)	一般公共预算支出（万元）General public budget expenditure (10000 yuan)
14282	595	5149	11003
31296	2019.1	8267	8677.1
48845	2128.8	500	300
26512	1346.4	2942	7095
23916	1080	2684	5930
21324	941.4	4004	8739
16691	2170	4382	4839
12552	564.4	396	7579
27811	1282.6	1695	6483
24562	598.1	10230	6088
25239	914.6	10561	7463
33659	1903	3158	7531
20506	1106.5	7410.5	7613.3
427537	**15051.5**	**87338.2**	**25556.3**
8286	428	1390	927
43118	345.5	13688	3032
75623	895.3	15826	2210
30068	628	1243	661.8
24756	851	10221	1456
41311	2738	8560	1314
52739	1835.6	12393	3745.7
34674	1838.5	1985.2	1986.7
19585	911	1646	1565
51729	1522.2	7212	3102

3－14　续表5

乡镇名称	Town	社区(居民委员会) Number of Communities (residents committees)	村民委员会(个) Number of Villagers' Committees (unit)	乡镇户籍户数(户) Resident Households in Towns (household)
莪山畲族乡	Eshan	–	7	2902
钟山乡	Zhongshan	–	11	6939
新合乡	Xinghe	–	5	1650
合村乡	Hecun	–	6	3173
淳安县	**Chun'an County**	**17**	**337**	**146929**
千岛湖镇	Qiandaohu	12	16	30983
文昌镇	Wenchang	–	14	4262
石林镇	Shilin	–	7	1438
临歧镇	Linqi	1	16	5965
威坪镇	Weiping	1	35	16013
姜家镇	Jiangjia	1	17	8453
梓桐镇	Zitong	–	18	5997
汾口镇	Fenkou	1	42	16428
中洲镇	Zhongzhou	–	15	5984
大墅镇	Dashu	1	13	4415
枫树岭镇	Fengshuling	–	18	5726
里商乡	Lishang	–	13	3420
金峰乡	Jinfeng	–	9	2048
富文乡	Fuwen	–	8	2466
左口乡	Zuokou	–	9	3305
屏门乡	Pingmen	–	11	3881
瑶山乡	Yaoshan	–	10	2813
王阜乡	Wangfu	–	15	5835
宋村乡	Songcun	–	6	2105
鸠坑乡	Jiukeng	–	8	2551

continued 5

乡镇户籍人口数（人）Resident Population in Towns (person)	乡镇常用耕地面积（公顷）Commonly used cultivated area of township (hectare)	一般公共预算收入（万元）General public budget income (10000 yuan)	一般公共预算支出（万元）General public budget expenditure (10000 yuan)
9261	903.4	1179	1538
21243	1196	8991	1785.4
5187	255	1659	742.7
9957	704	1345	1490
456189	**15304.6**	**25130.8**	**194487.6**
84878	528.3	9550.6	17555
14544	551.5	2142.4	9468.3
4989	154.1	120.6	2855.1
20444	961.7	2070.7	14495.4
46832	1398.5	2301.6	18510.3
26211	1204.3	1537.1	15123.1
18651	684.4	706.3	8082.5
55012	2325	1339.8	20856.2
20140	1036.4	95.4	7464.8
13917	939.1	523	7794.8
18338	1084.4	709.5	11632.2
11305	251.6	775.9	6474.8
6045	319.6	514.4	2525.8
8324	192.6	204.1	4037.4
11605	437.9	391.3	5088.6
12344	305.8	460.4	5555.1
9592	261	345.8	3979.4
17475	342	175.9	6953.1
6930	55.1	285.3	2945.2
7508	183.8	90.5	4410.8

3－14 续表6

乡镇名称	Town	社区(居民委员会) Number of Communities (residents committees)	村民委员会(个) Number of Villagers' Committees (unit)	乡镇户籍户数(户) Resident Households in Towns (household)
浪川乡	Langchuan	–	17	6135
界首乡	Jieshou	–	8	3057
安阳乡	Anyang	–	12	3649
钱塘新区	**Qiantang New Area**	**10**	**59**	**42293**
义蓬街道	Yipeng Subdistrict	4	22	18146
河庄街道	Hezhuang Subdistrict	3	20	13732
新湾街道	Xinwan Subdistrict	1	12	7105
临江街道	Linjiang Subdistrict	1	2	1195
前进街道	Qianjin Subdistrict	1	3	2115
建德市	**Jiande City**	**41**	**229**	**169852**
新安江街道	Xin'anjiang Subdistrict	11	4	31644
洋溪街道	Yangxi Subdistrict	4	2	5714
更楼街道	Genglou Subdistrict	2	14	7676
莲花镇	Lianhua	1	6	3306
乾潭镇	Qiantan	1	24	14721
梅城镇	Meicheng	5	13	14948
杨村桥镇	Yangcunqiao	1	13	6906
下涯镇	Xiaya	1	11	8517
大洋镇	Dayang	3	19	10467
三都镇	Sandu	1	19	8654
寿昌镇	Shouchang	4	23	11923
航头镇	Hangtou	1	18	12115
大慈岩镇	Daciyan	1	12	6629
大同镇	Datong	3	34	17339
李家镇	Lijia	1	10	6548
钦堂乡	Qintang	1	7	2745

continued 6

乡镇户籍人口数（人） Resident Population in Towns (person)	乡镇常用耕地面积（公顷） Commonly used cultivated area of township (hectare)	一般公共预算收入（万元） General public budget income (10000 yuan)	一般公共预算支出（万元） General public budget expenditure (10000 yuan)
20106	914.5	241.1	8416.9
9481	443.7	182.6	4460
11518	729.3	366.5	5802.8
159196	**7914.5**	**59958**	**59000**
65824	3006.	17077	15000
54897	2345.4	20105	14000
25179	1185.1	13253	11000
4768	406	4959	10000
8528	972	4564	9000
501367	**26087.9**	**94047.8**	**95364.4**
83630	216.5	20878	5216.8
16022	179	6849	6365
23519	726.4	5215.2	5855.4
10646	367	653	1677
44555	1662	10344	10031
40680	992.7	7666	8005
20931	10216.2	3169	5625.8
27486	1012.7	9960	9296
33702	1468	2700	2447.5
24783	1101	832	5154.5
36406	1701.8	7891.6	9414.8
35301	1726	2477	5303
20582	1126.5	1867	3300.5
54109	2243.7	6171	9090.2
20417	726.8	6885	5209
8598	621.6	490	3372.9

3－15 农村基本

Basic Statistics on

指　　标		Item	
一、农村人口与从业人员		**Rural Population and Employed Persons**	
农村户数	（万户）	Rural Household	（10000 households）
农村人口	（万人）	Rural Population	（10000 persons）
男		Male	
女		Female	
农村劳动力资源数	（万人）	Rural Laboar Resources	（10000 persons）
男		Male	
女		Female	
农村从业人员	（万人）	Jobholders in Rural Areas	（10000 persons）
男		Male	
#从事农业人员		Persons Involved in Agriculture	
女		Female	
#从事农业人员		Persons Involved in Agriculture	
二、农村基础设施		**Public Facilities in Rural Areas**	
自来水受益村数		Number of Villages with Access to Tap Water	
通有线电视村数		Number of Villages Connecting to Cable TV	
通宽带村数		Number of Villages Connecting to Prroadband	
三、农林牧渔业增加值		**Value－added of Agriculture,Forestry,Animal Husbandry and Fishery**	
农业		Farming	
林业		Forestry	
畜牧业		Animal Husbandry	
渔业		Fishery	
农、林、牧、渔专业及辅助性活动		Services for Farming,Forestry, Animal Husbandary and Fishery	

情况(2012－2020年)

Rural Areas(2012－2020)

2012	2013	2014	2015	2016	2017	2018	2019	2020
129.29	132.18	131.96	132.15	132.00	131.53	127.60	126.39	133.70
425.49	469.90	480.04	482.63	482.94	488.22	471.97	467.92	461.72
213.81	236.03	241.82	243.47	244.08	247.31	238.49	236.23	233.97
211.68	233.87	238.22	239.16	238.86	240.91	233.48	231.69	227.75
276.62	304.14	314.45	313.79	314.83	317.03	304.16	300.01	301.08
143.66	157.27	163.98	163.94	164.54	165.88	159.27	157.35	157.45
132.96	146.87	150.47	149.85	150.29	151.15	144.89	142.66	143.63
257.30	279.91	286.01	284.73	281.76	282.19	270.84	264.83	262.77
134.85	145.70	151.05	151.21	149.68	149.66	143.83	140.47	139.57
		36.50	37.58	37.49	37.12	35.60	34.75	32.86
122.45	134.21	134.96	133.52	132.08	132.53	127.01	124.36	123.20
		29.75	30.22	29.74	29.17	28.51	27.84	26.69
2078	2058	2054	2054	2053	2046	2033	2021	1935
2078	2058	2054	2054	2053	2046	2033	2021	1935
2078	2058	2054	2054	2053	2046	2033	2021	1935
2551127	**2654059**	**2783252**	**2924013**	**2985617**	**3056039**	**3118849**	**3327369**	**3340124**
1510382	1571300	1685668	1806178	1866383	1951535	2009741	2101139	–
302796	324240	371932	393332	415918	428898	446920	483405	–
435191	458201	405348	395476	377688	334289	301445	369504	–
270629	262233	280544	284506	276270	284845	297480	303120	–
32129	38085	39760	44521	49358	56472	63263	70201	77918

3－16 分地区农村

Basic Statistics on

指标	Item	全市 Whole City	市区 Urban District	江干区 Jianggan	西湖区 Xihu
一、农村人口与从业人员	**Rural Population and Employed Persons**				
农村户数 （万户）	Rural Household （10000 households）	133.7	100.3		3.52
农村人口 （万人）	Rural Population （10000 persons）	461.72	368.01		14.22
男	Male	233.97	186.36		7.02
女	Female	227.75	181.65		7.2
农村劳动力资源数 （万人）	Rural Laboar Resources （10000 persons）	301.08	240.98		8.48
男	Male	157.45	125.86		4.46
女	Female	143.63	115.12		4.02
农村从业人员 （万人）	Jobholders in Rural Areas （10000 persons）	262.77	209.47		7.65
男	Male	139.57	111.26		4.11
#从事农业人员	Persons Involved in Agriculture	32.86	21.06		0.56
女	Female	123.2	98.21		3.54
#从事农业人员	Persons Involved in Agriculture	26.69	16.68		0.46
二、农村基础设施	**Public Facilities in Rural Areas**				
自来水受益村数	Number of Villages with Access to Tap Water	1935	1188		32
通有线电视村数	Number of Villages Connecting to Cable TV	1935	1188		32
通宽带村数	Number of Villages Connecting to Broadband	1935	1188		32
三、农林牧渔业增加值	**Value－added of Agriculture, Forestry, Animal Husbandry and Fishery**	**3340124**	**2312149**		**30909**
农、林、牧、渔专业及辅助性活动	Services for Farming, Forestry, Animal Husbandary and Fishery	77918	59287		1040

注：萧山区不含托管在钱塘新区的街道数据。

基本情况(2020 年末)
Rural Areas by Region(End of 2020)

高新(滨江)区 Hi - Tech (Binjiang)	萧山区 Xiaoshan	余杭区 Yuhang	富阳区 Fuyang	临安区 Lin'an	钱塘新区 Qiantang New Area	西湖风景名胜区 The West Lake Scenic Zone	桐庐县 Tonglu	淳安县 Chun'an	建德市 Jiande
2.6	28.74	29.45	17.42	13.56	4.74	0.27	11.09	9.3	13.01
10.8	107.55	117.27	58.41	40.41	18.8	0.55	33.18	19.87	40.66
5.2	53.42	60.93	29.76	20.22	9.57	0.24	16.73	10.14	20.74
5.6	54.13	56.34	28.65	20.19	9.23	0.31	16.45	9.73	19.92
6.9	68.07	78.78	38.45	27.46	12.55	0.29	21.8	12.87	25.43
3.4	34.63	42.14	20.13	14.38	6.58	0.14	11.29	6.75	13.55
3.5	33.44	36.64	18.32	13.08	5.97	0.15	10.51	6.12	11.88
5.8	58.8	68.2	33.76	23.79	11.19	0.28	19.59	12.02	21.69
3.0	30.16	37.3	18.03	12.57	5.95	0.14	10.26	6.26	11.79
0.02	4.79	3.9	6.55	4.35	0.83	0.06	2.69	4.11	5.0
2.8	28.64	30.9	15.73	11.22	5.24	0.14	9.33	5.76	9.9
0.01	3.8	2.94	5.13	3.63	0.64	0.07	2.2	3.72	4.09
–	352	187	279	270	59	9	181	337	229
–	352	187	279	270	59	9	181	337	229
–	352	187	279	270	59	9	181	337	229
6414	**600345**	**550004**	**498652**	**465931**	**147734**	**9650**	**258325**	**390279**	**379372**
–	21658	23796	3569	5881	3344	–	4714	6066	7851

a) Figures of Xiaoshan District don't include subdistricts which under administered by Qiantang New Area.

主要统计指标解释

农林牧渔业总产值　是以货币表现的农、林、牧、渔业全部产品的总量和对农林牧渔生产活动进行的各种支持性服务活动的价值。它反映一定时期内农林牧渔业生产的总规模和总成果。

农林牧渔业的统计范围是:

(1)农业　包括农作物种植业和其他农业。

农作物种植业　包括谷类、豆类、薯类、棉花、麻类、烟叶、蔬菜、药材、瓜类和其他农作物的种植以及茶园、桑园、果园的生产经营。

其他农业　包括采集野生植物的果实、纤维、树脂、油料以及柴草、野生药材、菌类等。

(2)林业　包括林木的栽培(不包括茶园、桑园和果园的栽培、管理和收获等活动)、林产品的采集、村及村以下合作经济组织和农户的竹木砍伐。

(3)牧业　包括除渔业养殖以外的一切动物饲养和放牧以及野生动物的捕猎和饲养。

(4)渔业　包括水生动物和海藻类植物的养殖和捕捞。

(5)农林牧渔服务业　包括对农林牧渔生产活动进行的各种支持性服务活动。

粮食产量　指全社会的产量,包括国营农场等全民所有制经营、集体统一经营和农民家庭经营的产量,还包括工矿企业家属办的农场和其他生产单位的产量。粮食除包括稻谷、小麦、大麦、玉米、高粱、谷子及其他杂粮外,还包括薯类和豆类。其产量计算方法,豆类按去豆荚后的干豆计算,薯类按5公斤鲜薯折1公斤粮食计算,其他粮食一律按脱粒后的原粮计算。

猪、牛、羊肉产量　指当年出栏并已屠宰的猪、牛、羊的肉产量,即屠宰后除去头蹄下水后带骨的(即胴体重)重量。

水产品产量　指人工养殖的水产品和天然生长的水产品的捕捞量。包括海水的鱼类、虾蟹类、贝类和藻类以及内陆水域的鱼类、虾蟹类和贝类,不包括淡水生植物。

有效灌溉面积　指具有一定水源,地块比较平整、灌溉工程或设备已经配套,在一般年景下当年能够进行正常灌溉的耕地面积。

农业机械总动力　指主要用于农、林、牧、渔业的各种动力机械的动力总和。包括耕作机械、排灌机械、收获机械、农用运输机械、植物保护机械、牧业机械、林业机械和其他农业机械[内燃机按引擎马力折成瓦(特)计算,电动机按功率折成瓦(特)计算]。不包括专门用于乡、镇、村、组办工业、基本建设、非农业运输、科学试验和教学等非农业方面的动力机械与作业机械。

农村用电量　指本年度内扣除在农村中的全民所有制工业、交通、基建单位的用电量以后的农村生产上和生活上的全年用电总度数(全年累计数),包括国家电网的供电量,也包括农村自办电站的供电量。

农用化肥施用量　指本年内实际用于农业生产的化肥数量。包括氮肥、磷肥、钾肥及复合肥。化肥施用量要求按折纯量计算数量。折纯量是指氮肥、磷肥、钾肥分别按含氮、含五氧化二磷、含氧化钾的百分之百成分进行折算后的数量。复合肥按其所含主要成分折算。

Explanatory Notes on Main Statistical Indicators

Gross Output Value of Farming, Forestry, Animal Husbandry and Fishery refers to the total volume of products of farming, forestry, animal husbandry and fishery in value terms and output value of all kinds of service activities that support farming, forestry, animal husbandry and fishery production. It reflects the total scale and total result of agricultural production during a given period of time.

The statistical scopes for Farming, Forestry, Animal Husbandry and Fishery are as follows:

(1) **Farming** includes crop cultivation and other farming.

Crop cultivation includes planting of cereals, beans, tubers, cotton, fiber crops, tobacco, vegetables, crude drugs, melons and others, as well as production and management of tea, mulberry and fruit plantation.

Other farming includes gathering of wild plant fruits, fiber, gum, oil, firewood, wild crude drugs, fungus.

(2) **Forestry** includes planting of trees (not including planting, management and harvest of tea, mulberry and fruit plantation), collection of forest products, and felling of bamboos and trees by villagers and cooperative organizations of villages and under villages.

(3) **Animal Husbandry** includes raising and grazing of any kind of animals and hunting and raising of wild animals, other than fish breeding.

(4) **Fishery** includes cultivation and catches of aquatic animals and seaweed.

(5) **Service Industry for Farming, Forestry, Animal Husbandry and Fishery** refers to all kinds of service activities that support farming, forestry, animal husbandry and fishery production.

Grain Yield refers to the total yield including grains produced by state – owned, collectively operated and family farms as well as grains produced by farms run by family members of industrial and mining enterprises. Grain includes rice, wheat, corn, sorghum, millet and other miscellaneous grains as well as tubers and beans. For the yield of beans, it is to calculated by beans without pods, for tubers is to convert the yield of fresh tubers into that of grain at the ratio 5:1, and for others are all the husked grain.

Output of Pork, Beef, and Mutton refers to the meat weight of slaughtered hogs, cattle, sheep and goats, which are full grown, without heads, feets and offal but with bones.

Output of Aquatic Products refers to catches of both artificially cultured and naturally grown aquatic products, including fish, shrimps, crabs and shellfish in sea and inland water as well as seaweed. Freshwater plants are not included.

Irrigated Area refers to cultivated areas that are flat with water source and complete irrigation projects or equipments to be effectively irrigated under normal conditions. ,

Total Power of Farm Machinery refers to total mechanical power of machinery used in farming, forestry, animal husbandry, and fishery, including the machinery of ploughing, irrigation and drainage, harvesting, transport, plant protection, stock breeding, forestry and others. For internal combustion engine is to calculate its engine power in watts and for electric motor is to calculate its power in watts. Machinery employed for non – agricultural purposes, such as the machines used in town and village run industries, capital construction, non – agricultural transport, scientific experiments and teaching, is excluded.

Electricity Consumption in Rural Areas refers to annual total degree (annual aggregate) of electricity consumption of rural production and living discounting the consumption of industries owned by the whole people, transport and infrastructure units in the rural areas, including the power supply of State Grid and rural run power stations.

Consumption of Chemical Fertilizers in Agriculture refers to the quantity of chemical fertilizers applied in agriculture in the year, including nitrogen, phosphorus, potassium and compound fertilizers. The consumption of chemical fertilizers is required to calculate by the purity, i. e. by 100% nitrogen content in nitrogenous fertilizer, 100% phosphorous pent oxide content in phosphorus fertilizer, 100% potassium oxide contents in potassium fertilizer. Compound fertilizer is calculated by its major component.

四、工业、能源

INDUSTRY AND ENERGY

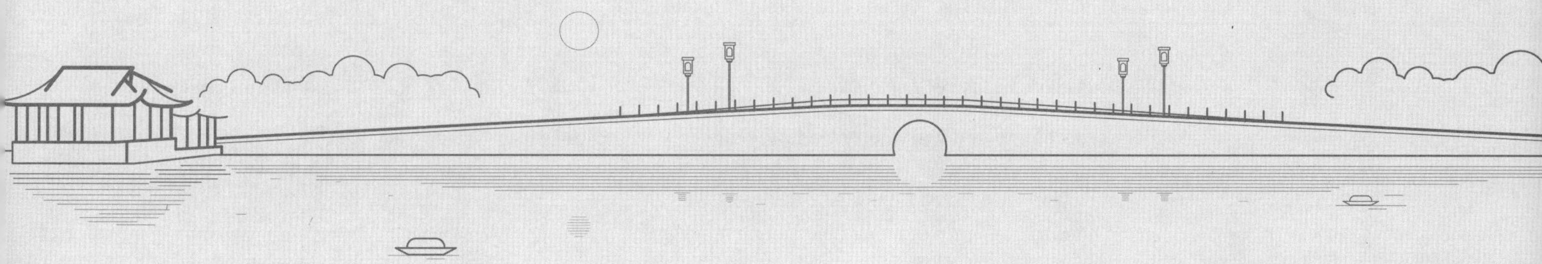

4 工业、能源
Industry and Energy

主要统计指标
Major Statistical Indicators

规模以上工业企业单位数	Number of Industrial Enterprises above Designated Size	5992	个	(unit)
为上年	As Compared with the Preceding Year	105.16	%	(%)
规模以上工业增加值	Value-added of Industrial Enterprises above Designated Size	3467	亿元	(100 million yuan)
为上年	As Compared with the Preceding Year	103.8	%	(%)
规模以上工业总产值	Gross Output Value of Industrial Enterprises above Designated Size	14712	亿元	(100 million yuan)
为上年	As Compared with the Preceding Year	99.26	%	(%)
轻工业	Light Industry	4839	亿元	(100 million yuan)
为上年	As Compared with the Preceding Year	89.41	%	(%)
重工业	Heavy Industry	9872	亿元	(100 million yuan)
为上年	As Compared with the Preceding Year	104.80	%	(%)

4-01 工业企业单位数(主要年份)

Number of Industrial Enterprises(Main Years)

单位:个 (unit)

年 份 Year	规模以上工业合计 Industry above Designated Size Total	国有经济 State - owned Enterprises	集体经济 Collective - owned Enterprises	其他各种经济类型 Enterprises of Other Types of Ownership
1978	2868	680	2188	-
1980	3519	691	-	-
1985	5800	823	-	-
1990	6183	921	4966	11
1991	6234	933	5219	82
1992	6235	941	5162	132
1995	6744	1086	4722	936
1996	6148	1011	4268	869
1997	4980	760	3250	970
1998	2559	464	815	1280
1999	2474	396	689	1389
2000	2715	282	598	1835
2001	3580	237	252	3091
2002	4015	172	232	3611
2003	4689	144	219	4326
2004	7738	185	192	7361
2005	7359	124	169	7066
2006	7826	110	162	7554
2007	8674	71	131	8472
2008	9907	73	101	9733
2009	10032	71	84	9877
2010	10370	74	68	10228
2011	5868	52	25	5791
2012	5927	56	20	5851
2013	6284	25	11	6248
2014	6169	22	9	6138
2015	6073	17	5	6051
2016	5684	15	4	5665
2017	5533	10	2	5521
2018	5431	9	1	5421
2019	5698	7	-	5691
2020	5992	14	3	5975

注:规模以上工业口径:1997 年及以前为乡及以上工业;1998 -2010 年为主营业务收入 500 万及以上;2011 年为主营业务收入 2000 万及以上(后同)。

a) Industry above Designated Size: Data after 2011 refer to all the industrial enterprises with annual Sales income of over 20 million yuan, data in 1998 - 2010 refer to all the industrial enterprises with annual sales income of over 5 million yuan, data in 1997 and before refer to enterprises at township and above level.

4-02 市区工业企业单位数(主要年份)

Number of Industrial Enterprises in Urban District(Main Years)

单位:个 (unit)

年份 Year	规模以上工业合计 Industry above Designated Size Total	国有经济 State-owned Enterprises	集体经济 Collective-owned Enterprises	其他各种经济类型 Enterprises of Other Types of Ownership
1978	787	313	414	-
1980	894	315	579	-
1985	1250	345	859	7
1990	1360	361	971	28
1991	1411	382	990	39
1992	1490	395	1024	71
1995	1998	440	1102	456
1996	2043	458	1109	476
1997	1733	372	951	410
1998	1019	315	315	389
1999	959	255	284	420
2000	1005	182	253	570
2001	2645	195	200	2250
2002	2838	140	178	2520
2003	3230	115	158	2957
2004	5527	156	122	5249
2005	4995	98	104	4793
2006	5195	85	91	5019
2007	5726	54	77	5595
2008	6530	55	64	6411
2009	6477	52	49	6376
2010	6478	51	37	6390
2011	3867	36	10	3821
2012	3862	37	7	3818
2013	4145	18	5	4122
2014	4716	17	5	4694
2015	4584	12	3	4569
2016	4235	11	2	4222
2017	4726	8	1	4717
2018	4746	8	1	4737
2019	4984	6	-	4978
2020	5188	13	2	5173

4－03　工业总产值(1949－2020年)

Gross Industrial Output Value(1949－2020)

单位:亿元　　(100 million yuan)

年　份 Year	工业总产值 Gross Industrial Output Value	轻工业 Light Industry	重工业 Heavy Industry	#国有经济 State－owned	#集体经济 Collective－owned
1949	1.41				
1950	1.60				
1951	2.46				
1952	3.00				
1953	3.80				
1954	4.26				
1955	4.38				
1956	5.42				
1957	6.08				
1958	11.73				
1959	16.16				
1960	18.48				
1961	12.65				
1962	10.30				
1963	10.76				
1964	12.82				
1965	15.12				
1966	14.81				
1967	16.73				
1968	15.90				
1969	20.74				
1970	24.08				
1971	27.04				
1972	28.32				
1973	31.38				
1974	26.24				
1975	25.10				
1976	26.24				
1977	35.92				
1978	43.96				
1979	51.00				
1980	63.45				
1981	71.00				
1982	75.08				
1983	84.44				
1984	106.21				
1985	146.55				
1986	177.96				
1987	226.30				
1988	297.62				
1989	331.56				
1990	359.47				
1991	435.79				
1992	568.33				
1993	828.92				
1994	1181.50				
1995	1509.71				
1996	1479.22				
1997	1654.70				

单位:亿元　　　　4－03　续表　continued　　　　(100 million yuan)

年　份 Year	工业总产值 Gross Industrial Output Value	轻工业 Light Industry	重工业 Heavy Industry	#国有经济 State－owned	#集体经济 Collective－owned
1998	1109.94	572.64	537.30	342.23	282.48
1999	1200.08	613.00	587.08	316.46	254.40
2000	1543.57	762.33	781.24	186.03	269.84
2001	1919.51	995.70	923.81	178.88	191.13
2002	2400.30	1243.55	1156.75	214.71	215.15
2003	3202.52	1565.25	1637.28	248.42	244.40
2004	4486.58	1976.19	2510.38	342.00	55.89
2005	5441.13	2405.97	3035.16	605.43	60.34
2006	6975.46	2909.35	4066.11	677.68	66.76
2007	8351.40	3587.84	4763.56	768.89	51.79
2008	9379.58	3873.53	5506.05	744.07	38.61
2009	9390.73	4011.60	5379.14	757.65	35.47
2010	11081.04	4576.47	6504.57	905.05	30.03
2011	12352.92	4866.08	7486.84	1022.05	17.19
2012	12959.68	5137.76	7821.92	1150.72	16.73
2013	12418.00	4866.38	7551.63	714.09	3.98
2014	12853.05	4997.92	7855.13	692.22	3.22
2015	12415.68	4820.80	7594.88	230.94	1.41
2016	12420.96	4693.99	7726.97	553.41	1.23
2017	12963.76	4711.50	8252.27	187.04	0.59
2018	14106.41	4882.08	9134.33	169.11	0.24
2019	14585.45	5221.27	9364.18	177.62	–
2020	14712.08	4839.21	9872.87	355.79	4.37

注:从1998年以来为规模以上工业。

a) It was industry above designated size since 1998.

4-04 市区工业总产值(主要年份)

Gross Industrial Output Value in Urban District(Main Years)

单位:万元 (10000 yuan)

年 份 Year	工业总产值 Gross Industrial Output Value	轻 工 业 Light Industry	重 工 业 Heavy Industry	国有经济 State-owned	集体经济 Collective-owned	其他经济 Other Types of Ownership
1978	305224	190668	114556			
1980	434328	281545	152783			
1985	872030	546050	325980			
1990	1661400	1067000	594400			
1991	1986800	1262400	724400			
1992	2530300	1534100	996200			
1995	5832200	3326700	2505500			
1996	6176899	3445918	2730981			
1997	6706012	3673146	3032866			
1998	6110192	3068600	3041592	2989467	1123013	1997712
1999	6280838	3178286	3102552	2668519	979070	2633249
2000	7804302	3635578	4168724	1498595	968509	5337198
2001	16156245	8377563	7778681	1695132	1792228	12668885
2002	20252484	10431428	9821056	2036097	2045450	16170937
2003	26945006	13080771	13864235	2390424	2305431	22249151
2004	37564968	16361706	21203262	3097656	419720	34047592
2005	44775260	19601053	25174207	5592419	390555	38792286
2006	57255453	23722868	33532585	6305071	347788	50602594
2007	67565456	29452269	38113187	7123810	323842	60117804
2008	74564803	31236743	43328060	6812616	219140	67533047
2009	74059755	32178951	41880805	6880470	148937	67030348
2010	86653885	36440816	50213069	8155395	156026	78342464
2011	97800625	39467105	58333520	9253445	70299	88476881
2012	101396009	41428864	59967145	10452692	72743	90870574
2013	94197123	38407906	55789218	6332681	22398	87842044
2014	110230328	42840596	67389732	6463681	22354	103744292
2015	105641721	40775608	64866113	1841145	8633	103791944
2016	105688299	39331082	66357217	5061048	6629	100620622
2017	119823690	42792636	77031054	1689177	2846	118131668
2018	131259285	45433816	85825469	1570111	2375	129686799
2019	135952373	48734026	87218347	1649607	-	134302766
2020	136802990	44921301	91881690	3437846	41400	133323745

注:从1998年以来为规模以上工业。

a) It was industry above designated size since 1998.

4－05 规模以上工业企业

Main Economic Indicators of Industrial

单位:亿元

年份 Year	规模以上工业总产值 Output Value of Industrial Enterprises Above Designated Size	规模以上工业增加值 Added Value of Industrial Enterprises Above Designated Size	资产总计 Total Assets	流动资产合计 Total Current Assets	主营业务收入 Revenue from Principal Business	利润总额 Total Profits
2001	1919.51	444.91	2148.96	1122.07	1828.28	107.56
2002	2400.30	597.01	2514.19	1313.92	2288.21	145.48
2003	3202.52	783.51	3258.93	1783.50	3117.46	194.16
2004	4486.58	1019.47	4118.31	2300.84	4363.27	226.74
2005	5441.13	1126.54	4781.34	2692.73	5282.80	234.99
2006	6975.46	1363.17	5564.68	3215.19	6807.64	314.49
2007	8351.40	1717.65	6573.12	3880.23	8057.03	414.55
2008	9379.58	1743.20	7506.26	4437.50	8976.46	453.92
2009	9390.73	1792.00	8405.62	4968.21	9026.32	510.97
2010	11081.04	2153.83	9937.41	6011.68	10843.24	764.47
2011	12352.92	2369.00	10968.69	6709.76	12022.57	795.53
2012	12959.68	2492.00	11983.52	7215.40	12525.39	771.68
2013	12418.00	2664.13	12680.28	7609.51	12424.15	853.60
2014	12853.05	2813.51	13376.72	7938.51	12833.70	904.60
2015	12415.68	2875.05	14015.54	8306.78	12237.39	891.12
2016	12420.96	2990.34	14467.36	8502.92	12367.54	946.06
2017	12963.76	3184.05	15403.30	9009.58	13209.59	998.56
2018	14016.41	3415.45	16662.89	9885.42	14432.89	1015.16
2019	14585.45	3481.89	18290.37	10971.46	15212.51	1126.17
2020	14712.08	3467.16	20502.77	12384.26	15712.46	1302.40

主要经济效益指标(2001－2020年)
Enterprises Above Designated Size(2001－2020)

(100 million yuan)

利税总额 Total Profits and Tax	资产负债率(%) Ratio of Debts to Assets(%)	流动资产周转次数(次) Turnover of Current Assets(times)	成本费用利润率(%) Ratio of Profits to Costs(%)	全员劳动生产率(元/人) Overall Labor Productivity (Yuan/Person)	产品销售率(%) Rate of Production Sold (%)
208.54	57.20	1.70	6.26	59518	97.40
274.98	56.82	1.82	6.84	76402	97.76
359.54	58.70	1.87	6.69	91284	97.68
427.23	59.80	2.00	5.50	98809	98.10
450.68	60.12	2.06	4.69	105786	98.25
576.51	59.83	2.23	4.87	120289	98.36
730.50	60.43	2.21	5.44	138016	98.17
802.13	60.42	2.10	5.34	152070	98.14
882.62	59.07	1.86	5.86	151002	98.63
1224.48	58.34	1.96	7.60	166516	98.83
1330.48	59.12	1.91	6.96	190110	98.61
1339.94	49.57	1.74	6.60	232587	98.63
1450.55	58.09	1.63	7.39	222570	99.18
1538.07	56.83	1.62	7.61	245726	98.48
1559.68	55.69	1.54	7.91	257020	98.50
1655.64	54.29	1.53	7.97	278384	99.43
1772.81	54.66	1.55	7.77	301608	98.45
1800.26	55.00	1.54	7.19	330206	98.28
1854.99	55.02	1.46	7.85	339577	-
2006.46	54.26	1.34	8.51	340083	-

4-06 分地区工业

Number of Industrial Enterprises

单位:个

项　目	Item	全市 Whole City	市区 Urban District	上城区 Shangcheng	下城区 Xiacheng	江干区 Jianggan	拱墅区 Gongshu	西湖区 Xihu
规模以上工业合计	**Industrial above Designated Size**	**5992**	**5188**	**37**	**25**	**50**	**78**	**133**
一、按轻重工业分	**Grouped by Light & Heavy Industry**							
轻工业	Light Industry	2781	2396	5	7	16	23	33
重工业	Heavy Industry	3211	2792	32	18	34	55	100
二、按所有制分	**Grouped by Ownership**							
国有企业	State - owned Enterprises	14	13				2	
集体企业	Collective - owned Enterprises	3	2					
股份合作企业	Cooperative Enterprises	8	7		1		1	
联营企业	Joint Ownership Enterprises							
有限责任公司	Limited Liability Corporations	525	453	6	8	6	11	27
股份有限公司	Share - holding Corporations Ltd.	245	223	6	1	6	11	17
私营企业	Private Enterprises	4453	3792	21	12	33	43	73
外商及港澳台投资企业	Enterprises with Investment from Foreign、Hong Kong、Macao and Taiwan	744	698	4	3	5	10	16
其他企业	Other Enterprises	-	-	-	-	-	-	-
合计中:国有控股企业	Of the Total:Controlling Share Hold Enterprises	206	177	4	3	1	9	11
三、按企业规模分	**Grouped by Size of Enterprises**							
大型企业	Large	119	112	1	1	2	2	2
中型企业	Medium - sized	561	517	3	1	8	6	14
小微企业	Small	5312	4559	33	23	40	70	117

企业单位数(2020 年末)
by Region(End of 2020)

(unit)

	高新(滨江)区 Hi - Tech (Binjiang)	萧山区 Xiaoshan	余杭区 Yuhang	富阳区 Fuyang	临安区 Lin'an	钱塘新区 Qiantang New Area	西湖风景名胜区 The West Lake Scenic Zone	桐庐县 Tonglu	淳安县 Chun'an	建德市 Jiande
	218	**1480**	**1277**	**616**	**656**	**617**	**1**	**355**	**83**	**366**
	50	904	605	214	285	254		198	39	148
	168	576	672	402	371	363	1	157	44	218
	1	2	3		2	3		1		
		1				1				1
		2	3					1		
	32	53	85	66	60	99		30	14	28
	31	31	58	22	21	18	1	8	3	11
	112	1201	987	490	547	273		283	60	318
	42	190	141	38	26	223	–	32	6	8
	18	20	31	17	23	39	1	11	5	13
	16	21	17	4	7	39		5		2
	36	138	123	45	39	104		17	8	19
	166	1321	1137	567	610	474	1	333	75	345

单位：万元

项 目	Item	全 市 Total	市 区 Urban District	上城区 Shangcheng
规模以上工业合计	**Industrial above Designated Size**	**147120822**	**136802990**	**7349208**
一、按轻重工业分	**Grouped by Light & Heavy Industry**			
轻工业	Light Industry	48392106	44921301	3583981
重工业	Heavy Industry	98728716	91881690	3765227
二、按所有制分	**Grouped by Ownership**			
国有企业	State－owned Enterprises	3557859	3437846	
集体企业	Collective－owned Enterprises	43654	41400	
股份合作企业	Cooperative Enterprises	33771	30113	
联营企业	Joint Ownership Enterprises			
有限责任公司	Limited Liability Corporations	36941134	34004321	6725953
股份有限公司	Share－holding Corporations Ltd.	19656908	18640851	328534
私营企业	Private Enterprises	49546283	44203241	241137
外商及港澳台投资企业	Enterprises with Investment from Foreign、Hong Kong、Macao and Taiwan	37341214	36445219	53584
其他企业	Other Enterprises			
合计中：国有控股企业	Of the Total：Controlling Share Hold Enterprises	26049114	24155484	6716599
三、按企业规模分	**Grouped by Size of Enterprises**			
大型企业	Large	44084177	41963764	107123
中型企业	Medium－sized	43064000	40484384	386588
小微企业	Small	59972645	54354842	6855498

总产值(2020 年)
Output Value by Region(2020)

(10000 yuan)

下城区 Xiacheng	江干区 Jianggan	拱墅区 Gongshu	西湖区 Xihu	高新(滨江)区 Hi－Tech(Binjiang)	萧山区 Xiaoshan
487618	**1625945**	**2598867**	**2973406**	**24731954**	**25042895**
64702	318402	1145458	794466	2405006	13147321
422916	1307544	1453409	2178940	22326947	11895574
		13057		1663229	900790
					22032
5476		3			12040
113556	124504	469372	640567	3978914	3334276
16634	74277	417711	397916	4647014	2156139
55512	479879	1526676	953595	1909185	13747713
296441	947285	172048	981328	12533611	4869906
55844	60540	455677	538477	4610076	2270497
254107	913600	1054453	449280	11700613	4382660
26440	261619	559649	1039231	9033284	8565333
207070	450727	984765	1484895	3998057	12094902

项　目	Item	余杭区 Yuhang	富阳区 Fuyang
规模以上工业合计	**Industrial above Designated Size**	**20935233**	**11554518**
一、按轻重工业分	**Grouped by Light & Heavy Industry**		
轻工业	Light Industry	7464864	2199919
重工业	Heavy Industry	13470369	9354599
二、按所有制分	**Grouped by Ownership**		
国有企业	State－owned Enterprises	711021	
集体企业	Collective－owned Enterprises		
股份合作企业	Cooperative Enterprises	12594	
联营企业	Joint Ownership Enterprises		
有限责任公司	Limited Liability Corporations	2050048	4321294
股份有限公司	Share－holding Corporations Ltd.	4834787	1546505
私营企业	Private Enterprises	10201767	4818464
外商及港澳台投资企业	Enterprises with Investment from Foreign、Hong Kong、Macao and Taiwan	3125015	868255
其他企业	Other Enterprises		
合计中:国有控股企业	Of the Total:Controlling Share Hold Enterprises	3093840	1169223
三、按企业规模分	**Grouped by Size of Enterprises**		
大型企业	Large	4779204	2123751
中型企业	Medium－sized	6355259	3324146
小微企业	Small	9800769	6106621

continued (10000 yuan)

临安区 Lin'an	钱塘新区 Qiantang New Area	西湖风景名胜区 The West Lake Scenic Zone	桐庐县 Tonglu	淳安县 Chun'an	建德市 Jiande
9961411	**29538660**	**3276**	**4393675**	**850108**	**5074049**
2855914	10941268		1473980	508428	1488397
7105497	18597392	3276	2919695	341680	3585652
102507	47242		120012		
	19368				2254
			3658		
1513708	10732128		1438620	162409	1335785
3113179	1104880	3276	138370	24180	853508
4672888	5596426		2206796	599892	2536355
559129	12038616		486219	63628	346147
1401113	3780322		1292854	100649	500127
3077997	13120976		1387757		732656
2343429	8589407		739642	163825	1676149
4539986	7828277	3276	2266276	686283	2665244

4-08 规模以上工业
Main Economic Indicators of Industrial

单位:万元

项 目	Item	企业单位数（个）Number of Enterprises (unit)	亏损企业(个) Loss Making Enterprises (unit)	工业总产值（当年价格）Gross Industrial Output Value (current price)	新产品产值 Output of New Products
总 计	**Total**	**5992**	**1209**	**147120822**	**58822356**
按隶属关系分	**Grouped by Subordination**				
中央	Central	40	3	10098448	354821
地方	Local	76	7	3989952	1444427
其他	Other	5876	1199	133032422	57023108
按所有制分	**Grouped by Ownership**				
国有企业	State - owned Enterprises	14	1	3557859	85142
集体企业	Collective - owned Enterprises	3	-	43654	35577
股份合作企业	Cooperative Enterprises	8	3	33771	3854
联营企业	Joint Ownership Enterprises	-	-	-	-
有限责任公司	Limited Liability Corporations	525	97	36941134	14789061
股份有限公司	Share - holding Corporations Ltd.	245	33	19656908	13008612
私营企业	Private Enterprises	4453	897	49546283	17685584
外商及港澳台投资企业	Enterprises with Investment from Foreign、Hong Kong、Macao and Taiwan	744	178	37341214	13214525
其他企业	Other Enterprises	-	-	-	-
按企业规模分	**Grouped by Size of Enterprises**				
大型企业	Large	119	11	44084177	25115018
中型企业	Medium - sized	561	86	43064000	18615025
小微企业	Small	5312	1112	59972645	15092313
按轻重工业分	**Grouped by Light & Heavy Industry**				
轻工业	Light Industry	2781	669	48392106	15631628
重工业	Heavy Industry	3211	540	98728716	43190728

企业主要经济指标(2020 年)(一)
Enterprises Above Designated Size(2020)(Ⅰ)

(10000 yuan)

实收资本 Total Capital Hold	国家资本 State Capital	个人资本 Personal Capital	港澳台资本 Hongkong, Macau and TaiWan Capital	外商资本 Foreign Capital	就业人员年平均人数(人) Annual Average Number of Staff and Workers (person)
35491703	**2897766**	**7816597**	**2087000**	**3345828**	**1019505**
1483738	442451	6457	177178	1582	13845
1838983	563730	106450	33484	124271	32339
32168981	1891585	7703689	1876338	3219975	973321
889319	539032	252	–	–	3931
11763	–	–	–	–	702
11783	7650	4133	–	–	629
–	–	–	–	–	–
8422572	1794597	269461	4684	77517	156986
7168593	312747	2282903	7621	799	139094
10487584	43802	5007464	3960	8033	495589
8500089	199939	252384	2070736	3259478	222574
–	–	–	–	–	–
8936253	842034	1064016	279022	705802	265338
9709098	666433	1817879	480427	1089553	286453
16846352	1389299	4934702	1327551	1550473	467714
12290473	320975	3214263	935380	1616604	446775
23201230	2576791	4602334	1151620	1729224	572730

项　目	Item	企业单位数(个) Number of Enterprises (unit)	亏损企业(个) Loss Making Enterprises (unit)	工业总产值(当年价格) Gross Industrial Output Value (current price)	新产品产值 Output of New Products
按市、县分	**Grouped by County**				
市　区	Urban District	5188	1058	136802990	54444062
#萧山区	Xiaoshan	1480	297	25042895	8820020
余杭区	Yuhang	1277	279	20935233	10372185
富阳区	Fuyang	616	121	11554518	4356471
临安区	Lin'an	656	123	9961411	4372694
桐庐县	Tonglu	355	74	4393675	2093291
淳安县	Chun'an	83	29	850108	138763
建德市	Jiande	366	48	5074049	2146241
按国民经济行业分	**Grouped by Economic Sector**				
采矿业	Mining and Quarrying	24	2	261869	23542
煤炭开采和洗选业	Coal Mining and Dressing	1	–	4881	2206
黑色金属矿采选业	Ferrous Metals Mining and Dressing	–	–	–	–
有色金属矿采选业	Nonferrous Metals Mining and Dressing	4	–	31649	–
非金属矿采选业	Nonmetal Minerals Mining and Dressing	19	2	225338	21337
制造业	Manufacturing Industry	5865	1198	136796044	58626702
农副食品加工业	Agricultural Products Processing	117	32	1262847	152295
食品制造业	Food Manufacturing	116	33	2064633	317591
酒、饮料和精制茶制造业	Wine, Beverage and Tea Manufacturing	53	3	1666283	448603
烟草制品业	Tobacco Processing	1	–	3450003	–
纺织业	Textile Industry	668	179	6384383	2176103
纺织服装、服饰业	Textile Products and Costune Indnstry	241	96	1780116	744384
皮革、毛皮、羽毛及其制品和制鞋业	Leather. Furs. Downand Related and Shoes Products	103	38	1007087	319187
木材加工和木、竹、藤、棕、草制品业	Timber Processing, Bamboo, Cane, Palm Fiber and Straw Products	36	6	204072	47477
家具制造业	Furniture Manufacturing	103	26	1310387	561850

continued 1　　(10000 yuan)

实收资本 Total Capital Hold	国家资本 State Capital	个人资本 Personal Capital	港澳台资本 Hongkong, Macau and TaiWan Capital	外商资本 Foreign Capital	就业人员年平均人数(人) Annual Average Number of Staff and Workers (person)
32797805	4704854	7144481	1987426	3167495	923486
7603917	110065	2055241	510591	873100	223851
4456513	365244	1440880	371695	297610	191918
3131173	281590	779969	17575	162644	79821
1996579	168446	702433	57299	49601	72889
1333907	26817	258432	63722	94253	45922
331529	90791	117760	4657	3057	12288
1028462	75304	295924	31194	81023	37809
67466	1000	10116	–	–	1508
98	–	98	–	–	20
–	–	–	–	–	–
6068	–	5568	–	–	499
61300	1000	4450	–	–	989
32048599	1332227	7775649	1987649	3313208	998075
224761	–	80308	25442	20961	8154
634902	28687	104470	43793	270919	22677
562014	20919	60822	121371	129578	11362
60512	–	–	–	–	2438
1507986	9844	770261	63663	190848	91831
617893	11906	119057	293043	56059	38750
239880	179	65126	26385	13266	14565
47015	–	23389	–	–	3150
389968	440	82440	20439	57952	23346

单位:万元 4-08 续表2

项　目	Item	企业单位数(个) Number of Enterprises (unit)	亏损企业(个) Loss Making Enterprises (unit)	工业总产值(当年价格) Gross Industrial Output Value (current price)	新产品产值 Output of New Products
造纸和纸制品业	Paper Making and Paper Products	207	45	2842579	1071304
印刷和记录媒介复制业	Printing and Record Media	94	24	700932	124700
文教、工美、体育和娱乐用品制造业	Cultural, Educational. Industrial Arts. Sports and Entertainment Goods	90	23	1206397	434302
石油、煤炭及其他燃料加工业	Petroleum, Coal and Other Fuel Processing	16	4	154751	16707
化学原料和化学制品制造业	Raw Chemical Materials and Chemical Products	298	41	7399164	3223389
医药制造业	Medical and Pharmaceutical Products	125	24	6838634	2058672
化学纤维制造业	Chemical Fiber	132	30	6565496	2467169
橡胶和塑料制品业	Rubber and Plastic Products	336	49	6039650	1984982
非金属矿物制品业	Nonmetal Minerals Products	361	54	8029454	1537716
黑色金属冶炼和压延加工业	Ferrous Metals Smelting and Processing	47	10	936226	363872
有色金属冶炼和压延加工业	Nonferrous Metals Smelting and Processing	42	6	3675505	764129
金属制品业	Metals Products	413	63	5700899	2299558
通用设备制造业	Ordinary Machinery	573	70	12032063	6466119
专用设备制造业	For Special Purpose Equipment Manufacturing	304	56	3450453	1344293
汽车制造业	Automobile Manufacturing	211	54	6740543	4719085
铁路、船舶、航空航天和其他运输设备制造业	Railway. watercraft. Avigation spaceflight and other Equipment Manufacturing	50	12	900868	403935
电气机械和器材制造业	Electric Equipment and Machinery	487	95	14180833	8347546
计算机、通信和其他电子设备制造业	Computers. Telecommunications and Other Electronic Equipment Manufacturing	385	90	25296636	13906807
仪器仪表制造业	Instruments and Meters Manufacturing	208	24	4198428	2033464
其他制造业	Other Manufacturing	22	4	220298	86872
废弃资源综合利用业	Multiple Utilization of Waste Resouces	23	7	522832	204380
金属制品、机械和设备修理业	Metal Products, Machinery and Equipment Repair	3	–	33593	211
电力、燃气及水的生产和供应业	Produotion and supply of electricity, gas & water	103	9	10062909	172112
电力、热力生产和供应业	Production and Supply of Electric Power and Hot Water	57	4	6679494	171785
燃气生产和供应业	Production and Supply of Gas	16	3	2841355	–
水的生产和供应业	Production and Supply of Tap Water	30	2	542060	327

continued 2 (10000 yuan)

实收资本 Total Capital Hold	国家资本 State Capital	个人资本 Personal Capital	港澳台资本 Hongkong, Macau and TaiWan Capital	外商资本 Foreign Capital	就业人员年平均人数(人) Annual Average Number of Staff and Workers (person)
800480	2235	183843	65755	17162	23862
247098	23558	74347	58500	2965	10497
215484	–	61706	7801	91123	13755
172760	–	19431	353	4200	919
1829382	11290	407605	37410	199651	37374
1352732	119886	191560	20343	257553	41853
2310482	–	546773	12931	82316	31519
1154146	39700	345932	31453	230299	53780
1078653	60237	344509	70198	93016	35465
159429	–	64861	–	4715	3251
430585	–	18884	7236	26152	6464
1006750	53086	382948	146658	35676	46965
2540835	122990	794476	131839	299542	103940
1189240	37954	304585	153431	169346	38511
2880196	437796	322077	223137	280271	40994
174297	650	44384	–	24223	7493
4163943	183040	843331	143414	359172	90090
5012506	159899	1082811	261726	306903	146576
929570	7932	397256	21326	78634	42619
29283	–	16624	–	4138	3066
84118	–	20533	–	6570	2619
1700	–	1300	–	–	190
3375637	1564539	30832	99351	32620	19922
1607068	556423	19745	55984	8150	11490
756740	678624	1225	40868	24470	2530
1011830	329492	9862	2500	–	5902

4-09 规模以上工业

Main Economic Indicators of Industrial

单位:万元

项　目	Item	资产合计 Total Assets	流动资产合计 Total Circulating Funds	应收账款 Receivables	存　货 Stock
总　计	**Total**	**205027678**	**123842635**	**41337002**	**22224177**
按隶属关系分	**Grouped by Subordination**				
中央	Central	9182425	4141059	584076	2038214
地方	Local	10293445	4522566	872550	769521
其他	Other	185551808	115179010	39880376	19416442
按所有制分	**Grouped by Ownership**				
国有企业	State - owned Enterprises	2277957	549005	164339	15916
集体企业	Collective - owned Enterprises	5425746	149473	40191	9879
股份合作企业	Cooperative Enterprises	59815	42817	10059	3876
联营企业	Joint Ownership Enterprises	-	-	-	-
有限责任公司	Limited Liability Corporations	52621361	28607492	11662675	5965772
股份有限公司	Share - holding Corporations Ltd.	49990865	28412188	7233752	3566533
私营企业	Private Enterprises	54659273	37080869	11582026	7151837
外商及港澳台投资企业	Enterprises with Investment from Foreign、Hong Kong、Macao and Taiwan	39992663	29000791	10643960	5510364
其他企业	Other Enterprises	-	-	-	-
按企业规模分	**Grouped by Size of Enterprises**				
大型企业	Large	69615804	43426105	17243673	5628713
中型企业	Medium - sized	69615804	43426105	17243673	5628713
小微企业	Small	73104782	45006619	13833371	9773058
按轻重工业分	**Grouped by Light & Heavy Industry**				
轻工业	Light Industry	66815425	38512663	8537292	8819756
重工业	Heavy Industry	138212253	85329972	32799710	13404421

企业主要经济指标(2020年)(二)
Enterprises Above Designated Size(2020)(Ⅱ)

(10000 yuan)

产成品 Finished Products	固定资产净额 Fixed Assets	累计折旧 Accumulated Depreciation	本年折旧 Depreciation of the year	负债合计 Total Liabilities	流动负债合计 Total Current Liabilities	非流动负债合计 Total Non－current Liabilities	所有者权益合计 Creditors´Equity
8796188	**32541053**	**30811600**	**3847286**	**111244673**	**97435810**	**13808863**	**93328571**
124913	3957454	5412900	480176	5214975	4314089	900887	3967449
357270	2559462	2093009	208219	5405034	3226827	2178207	4830892
8314005	26024137	23305691	3158891	100624663	89894894	10729769	84530230
10594	1462957	1133348	150481	1112127	557804	554324	1146652
316	104967	12106	1704	4117441	2695042	1422399	1308305
2697	13962	23421	1485	19367	14299	5068	39881
–	–	–	–	–	–	–	–
1991284	12282562	11528433	1332956	34068893	28853272	5215620	18539309
1481628	3544280	2685684	383861	18425187	15544490	2880697	31308298
3094820	9413847	8378411	1238669	31160703	28820670	2340034	23391856
2214848	5718479	7050197	738131	22340955	20950234	1390721	17594270
–	–	–	–	–	–	–	–
2453047	8131547	7058353	923445	38161261	34170393	3990868	31454544
3055691	9366955	9586157	1196115	33029310	28477319	4551991	29277781
3287449	15042551	14167091	1727727	40054102	34788098	5266004	32596247
3435950	10987846	10658176	1347711	33646467	30945939	2700529	32864117
5360237	21553207	20153424	2499575	77598205	66489871	11108334	60464455

单位:万元　　　　4－09　续表1

项　目	Item	资产合计 Total Assets	流动资产合　计 Total Circulating Funds	应收账款 Receivables	存　货 Stock
按区域分	**Grouped by County**				
市　区	Urban District	192878049	117738005	39496814	21122096
#萧山区	Xiaoshan	44937371	20299454	4877348	3746369
余杭区	Yuhang	25524876	17240434	5271405	3247473
富阳区	Fuyang	16676466	9165955	2835450	1878298
临安区	Lin'an	12566434	7889856	2373045	1301205
桐庐县	Tonglu	4755764	2760771	841813	565617
淳安县	Chun'an	1424579	702179	234993	116455
建德市	Jiande	5969286	2641680	763382	420009
按国民经济行业分	**Grouped by Economic Sector**				
采矿业	Mining and Quarrying	637404	317590	45863	10104
煤炭开采和洗选业	Coal Mining and Dressing	4266	1174	394	406
黑色金属矿采选业	Ferrous Metals Mining and Dressing	–	–	–	–
有色金属矿采选业	Nonferrous Metals Mining and Dressing	59053	31760	3046	3222
非金属矿采选业	Nonmetal Minerals Mining and Dressing	574086	284655	42423	6476
制造业	Manufacturing Industry	190140997	120456919	40836419	22088629
农副食品加工业	Agricultural Products Processing	1202446	815072	209036	264252
食品制造业	Food Manufacturing	2702311	1785394	499032	245987
酒、饮料和精制茶制造业	Wine, Beverage and Tea Manufacturing	1994382	1068452	271637	202433
烟草制品业	Tobacco Processing	3772950	2978531	89437	1881921
纺织业	Textile Industry	7871116	4723748	1076807	1176475
纺织服装、服饰业	Textile Products and Costune Indnstry	2541885	1685787	349628	454754
皮革、毛皮、羽毛及其制品和制鞋业	Leather. Furs. Downand Related and Shoes Products	1229332	893493	276617	266867
木材加工和木、竹、藤、棕、草制品业	Timber Processing, Bamboo, Cane, Palm Fiber and Straw Products	321026	181682	58040	27027
家具制造业	Furniture Manufacturing	2487377	1462215	481171	171704

continued 1 (10000 yuan)

产成品 Finished Products	固定资产净额 Fixed Assets	累计折旧 Accumulated Depreciation	本年折旧 Depreciation of the year	负债合计 Total Liabilities	流动负债合计 Total Current Liabilities	非流动负债合计 Total Non－current Liabilities	所有者权益合计 Creditors´Equity
8317543	29362887	28177777	3475902	104700471	91678195	13022276	87923490
1703552	5880927	6759913	774389	24988019	21386502	3601517	19900124
1296286	4199124	3586800	500776	13396672	12017426	1379246	12111110
858468	3041291	2243405	342956	9923326	7929890	1993436	6721161
503546	1925206	1467804	203848	6355528	5602106	753421	6196806
224391	1148811	953051	137368	2789846	2551128	238717	1966132
66815	347517	418850	46698	687078	463017	224061	537026
187439	1681839	1262522	187318	3067278	2743470	323808	2901924
7154	57484	57051	13697	237173	193219	43953	400231
216	1065	949	202	3593	3593	–	673
–	–	–	–	–	–	–	–
2246	12262	7294	1022	16133	13112	3021	42920
4692	44157	48808	12473	217447	176515	40932	356638
8745790	24608677	22897144	3080651	102074463	92020410	10054053	87612101
70362	215440	139341	21193	810440	781062	29378	391923
88834	580676	582383	72026	1123663	1091324	32339	1567097
80209	660784	829341	86698	1053050	979968	73082	941331
89227	382897	533554	62428	1064474	1062653	1822	2708476
662575	1853006	2121452	254752	4374445	4072155	302290	3484841
266327	413006	345198	37299	1298387	1160889	137498	1242212
79969	157819	112860	14184	849708	825543	24166	379525
14402	28899	19249	3719	211266	204937	6330	109759
47342	234682	173312	25160	1401131	1311572	89559	1086247

项　目	Item	资产合计 Total Assets	流动资产合　计 Total Circulating Funds	应收账款 Receivables	存　货 Stock
造纸和纸制品业	Paper Making and Paper Products	3368878	2211826	477582	323335
印刷和记录媒介复制业	Printing and Record Media	902546	576352	191922	87277
文教、工美、体育和娱乐用品制造业	Cultural, Educational. Industrial Arts. Sports and Entertainment Goods	806956	546912	91522	232302
石油、煤炭及其他燃料加工业	Petroleum, Coal and Other Fuel Processing	433506	188116	75577	18516
化学原料和化学制品制造业	Raw Chemical Materials and Chemical Products	10911742	5369271	1084458	894252
医药制造业	Medical and Pharmaceutical Products	7930071	4724707	898817	1148527
化学纤维制造业	Chemical Fiber	14257063	5097297	922848	832171
橡胶和塑料制品业	Rubber and Plastic Products	5900818	3547039	1234683	799629
非金属矿物制品业	Nonmetal Minerals Products	7933229	5440220	3138107	654041
黑色金属冶炼和压延加工业	Ferrous Metals Smelting and Processing	669623	452981	64592	93060
有色金属冶炼和压延加工业	Nonferrous Metals Smelting and Processing	2299009	1419917	255553	413010
金属制品业	Metals Products	4552060	3172347	912444	808395
通用设备制造业	Ordinary Machinery	17127218	11487878	3287800	2053607
专用设备制造业	For Special Purpose Equipment Manufacturing	5039494	3734711	970836	790279
汽车制造业	Automobile Manufacturing	19005009	9548475	5811330	917795
铁路、船舶、航空航天和其他运输设备制造业	Railway. watercraft. Avigation spaceflight and other Equipment Manufacturing	988324	685884	210602	149168
电气机械和器材制造业	Electric Equipment and Machinery	22551115	14657948	4698090	2642650
计算机、通信和其他电子设备制造业	Computers. Telecommunications and Other Electronic Equipment Manufacturing	32801159	25451735	11510016	3325282
仪器仪表制造业	Instruments and Meters Manufacturing	7506258	5784958	1563926	1070572
其他制造业	Other Manufacturing	341890	261540	27736	46171
废弃资源综合利用业	Multiple Utilization of Waste Resouces	675830	488439	92521	96822
金属制品、机械和设备修理业	Metal Products, Machinery and Equipment Repair	16377	13995	4056	351
电力、燃气及水的生产和供应业	Produotion and supply of electricity, gas & water	14249277	3068127	454720	125445
电力、热力生产和供应业	Production and Supply of Electric Power and Hot Water	6616624	1102778	256206	30018
燃气生产和供应业	Production and Supply of Gas	2673151	466159	134086	25352
水的生产和供应业	Production and Supply of Tap Water	4959502	1499190	64427	70075

continued 2 (10000 yuan)

产成品 Finished Products	固定资产净额 Fixed Assets	累计折旧 Accumulated Depreciation	本年折旧 Depreciation of the year	负债合计 Total Liabilities	流动负债合计 Total Current Liabilities	非流动负债合计 Total Non－current Liabilities	所有者权益合计 Creditors′Equity
140262	664618	534731	83657	1839027	1547245	291782	1506241
38727	240322	347117	32701	489623	449251	40373	412922
66925	163018	192365	21249	418906	392230	26675	386746
11382	26607	18594	4380	208475	178350	30125	224463
433757	1864562	1589009	225260	4780849	3838970	941879	6049327
574516	1503316	960794	166050	3250227	2966077	284150	4679843
487963	1586250	1718018	185341	8571685	7813647	758038	5649747
483480	1463237	1919700	183154	3212263	2878372	333891	2684076
298695	1175593	1033441	163107	5421743	5055134	366610	2511479
38053	105884	179508	17596	464828	425733	39096	190702
142941	329654	303779	40589	1568598	1523895	44703	730410
335206	829966	793995	100625	2425149	2196336	228813	2115300
783220	1929481	1787791	232790	8915526	8134285	781241	8209374
228273	603537	600374	72859	2096583	1936556	160028	2920162
438074	2328606	1880017	304743	13684440	11556246	2128194	5320570
60232	135253	97851	14693	633990	595835	38156	354334
1225695	2237526	1891053	267922	11460144	9765318	1694827	10876862
1159813	2200402	1633251	297162	16681989	15742860	939129	16103684
345200	541603	466715	73236	3182807	3013735	169072	4323448
8810	38328	32328	3166	147872	138381	9491	191969
45313	113104	59396	12690	420618	370799	49819	255212
6	603	628	224	12554	11054	1500	3823
43244	7874892	7857405	752938	8933037	5222181	3710857	5316239
225	4443431	5813483	517656	4043051	2941561	1101489	2573574
17907	1850046	745836	108441	1895846	1048199	847647	777305
25112	1581415	1298086	126840	2994141	1232421	1761720	1965361

单位:万元

项 目	Item	主营业务收入 Revenues in Main Business	销售费用 Sales Expenses	管理费用 Management Expenses
总 计	**Total**	**157124601**	**8037214**	**5799711**
按隶属关系分	**Grouped by Subordination**			
中央	Central	10094192	110984	205143
地方	Local	4203068	215514	245140
其他	Other	142827341	7710715	5349428
按所有制分	**Grouped by Ownership**			
国有企业	State－owned Enterprises	3565934	20743	12969
集体企业	Collective－owned Enterprises	44231	647	4430
股份合作企业	Cooperative Enterprises	33883	621	2303
联营企业	Joint Ownership Enterprises	－	－	－
有限责任公司	Limited Liability Corporations	41760378	993068	1155365
股份有限公司	Share－holding Corporations Ltd.	20730027	1619470	853783
私营企业	Private Enterprises	50903192	2352519	2188615
外商及港澳台投资企业	Enterprises with Investment from Foreign、Hong Kong、Macao and Taiwan	40086956	3050146	1582248
其他企业	Other Enterprises	－	－	－
按企业规模分	**Grouped by Size of Enterprises**			
大型企业	Large	48880615	3498988	1262282
中型企业	Medium－sized	45627975	2431117	1590576
小微企业	Small	62616011	2107109	2946853
按轻重工业分	**Grouped by Light & Heavy Industry**			
轻工业	Light Industry	52718781	3929007	2382137
重工业	Heavy Industry	104405821	4108206	3417575

企业主要经济指标(2020年)(三)

Enterprises Above Designated Size(2020)(Ⅲ)

(10000 yuan)

财务费用 Financial Expenses	利息支出 Interest Expenditure	营业利润 Business Profits	利润总额 Total Profits	利税总额 Total Pre - tax Profits	本年应交增值税 Value Added Tax Payable
1310054	**1387219**	**12354840**	**13023992**	**20064577**	**4032699**
12267	30023	447936	464625	3181492	485947
57974	85203	517065	529557	679884	123437
1239813	1271992	11389839	12029809	16203201	3423315
22079	21843	57105	65907	123351	51140
2307	8975	30371	30316	32087	1145
538	752	2894	2995	4269	1114
–	–	–	–	–	–
377748	411577	2322638	2414348	5978164	1087144
188712	284985	4341576	4441755	5276323	708183
492116	489694	3187624	3455488	5110737	1421419
226554	169394	2412633	2613183	3539646	762556
–	–	–	–	–	–
277123	346443	5192135	5280352	6892068	1271338
373165	397556	3736294	3944062	5128662	988305
659766	643220	3426411	3799577	8043848	1773056
507001	530897	4115057	4476303	8611777	1679591
803053	856322	8239784	8547688	11452800	2353109

项　目	Item	主营业务收　入 Revenues in Main Business	销售费用 Sales Expenses	管理费用 Management Expenses
按市、县分	**Grouped by County**			
市　区	Urban District	146912628	7596909	5356205
#萧山区	Xiaoshan	28507600	663436	924674
余杭区	Yuhang	21671654	1277300	957629
富阳区	Fuyang	13652733	351095	450889
临安区	Lin'an	10252739	374823	354235
桐庐县	Tonglu	4252029	136427	186848
淳安县	Chun'an	907914	54211	44438
建德市	Jiande	5052031	249668	212220
按国民经济行业分	**Grouped by Economic Sector**			
采矿业	Mining and Quarrying	255208	13846	28418
煤炭开采和洗选业	Coal Mining and Dressing	4835	11	288
黑色金属矿采选业	Ferrous Metals Mining and Dressing	–	–	–
有色金属矿采选业	Nonferrous Metals Mining and Dressing	32492	917	6489
非金属矿采选业	Nonmetal Minerals Mining and Dressing	217882	12919	21641
制造业	Manufacturing Industry	146648804	7971718	5611673
农副食品加工业	Agricultural Products Processing	1371696	47892	36078
食品制造业	Food Manufacturing	2194892	233586	115861
酒、饮料和精制茶制造业	Wine, Beverage and Tea Manufacturing	1872237	246867	62134
烟草制品业	Tobacco Processing	3453115	74066	125539
纺织业	Textile Industry	6347375	156188	284063
纺织服装、服饰业	Textile Products and Costune Indnstry	1934809	117790	194116
皮革、毛皮、羽毛及其制品和制鞋业	Leather. Furs. Downand Related and Shoes Products	1003464	31340	39183
木材加工和木、竹、藤、棕、草制品业	Timber Processing, Bamboo, Cane, Palm Fiber and Straw Products	236636	8210	17811
家具制造业	Furniture Manufacturing	1301528	128247	84047

continued 1 (10000 yuan)

财务费用 Financial Expenses	利息支出 Interest Expenditure	营业利润 Business Profits	利润总额 Total Profits	利税总额 Total Pre - tax Profits	本年应交增值税 Value Added Tax Payable
1200674	1289739	11437932	12047784	18731746	3733424
383591	404903	1475964	1596685	2265208	561281
139499	153778	1751755	1855334	2512955	553227
239325	232294	632811	693335	1161935	419222
77965	86270	826019	864861	1125814	217131
49864	44170	279702	311920	453649	123654
10383	9040	79664	87124	128742	32807
49133	44269	557543	577165	750440	142814
4729	4570	67908	65465	88419	14773
32	–	218	184	670	376
–	–	–	–	–	–
132	132	4286	4272	8535	3319
4565	4437	63405	61009	79214	11078
1181799	1241674	11850164	12496904	19307842	3844674
14278	15615	41050	44795	65776	17948
-4860	13324	187020	225948	312117	77094
9034	11472	276115	291766	404313	72651
-19606	1117	420776	419028	2975446	347108
86897	74738	340657	425661	614734	162099
22607	15560	30238	56888	137274	69330
24445	15252	427	11554	44187	28972
4429	4302	14337	15186	22634	6209
22932	7337	153852	164900	200087	28366

单位:万元 4-10 续表2

项 目	Item	主营业务收入 Revenues in Main Business	销售费用 Sales Expenses	管理费用 Management Expenses
造纸和纸制品业	Paper Making and Paper Products	2789762	81237	117082
印刷和记录媒介复制业	Printing and Record Media	732051	19193	47627
文教、工美、体育和娱乐用品制造业	Cultural, Educational. Industrial Arts. Sports and Entertainment Goods	1173050	29414	41615
石油、煤炭及其他燃料加工业	Petroleum, Coal and Other Fuel Processing	221039	11775	10438
化学原料和化学制品制造业	Raw Chemical Materials and Chemical Products	7811856	481629	444138
医药制造业	Medical and Pharmaceutical Products	6257850	1631630	414299
化学纤维制造业	Chemical Fiber	9476874	38601	81843
橡胶和塑料制品业	Rubber and Plastic Products	6095190	305486	228909
非金属矿物制品业	Nonmetal Minerals Products	8039846	412527	273846
黑色金属冶炼和压延加工业	Ferrous Metals Smelting and Processing	1019572	6795	18288
有色金属冶炼和压延加工业	Nonferrous Metals Smelting and Processing	4494725	21579	37906
金属制品业	Metals Products	5779713	95137	180700
通用设备制造业	Ordinary Machinery	12730276	446816	583421
专用设备制造业	For Special Purpose Equipment Manufacturing	3515661	192351	278626
汽车制造业	Automobile Manufacturing	7145944	132434	317621
铁路、船舶、航空航天和其他运输设备制造业	Railway. watercraft. Avigation spaceflight and other Equipment Manufacturing	961194	45161	42058
电气机械和器材制造业	Electric Equipment and Machinery	16648380	1046970	567827
计算机、通信和其他电子设备制造业	Computers. Telecommunications and Other Electronic Equipment Manufacturing	26806614	1576681	675877
仪器仪表制造业	Instruments and Meters Manufacturing	4294069	331940	265623
其他制造业	Other Manufacturing	354171	14202	12683
废弃资源综合利用业	Multiple Utilization of Waste Resouces	550655	4662	10740
金属制品、机械和设备修理业	Metal Products, Machinery and Equipment Repair	34560	1316	1676
电力、燃气及水的生产和供应业	Produotion and supply of electricity, gas & water	10220589	51650	159621
电力、热力生产和供应业	Production and Supply of Electric Power and Hot Water	6680128	496	73249
燃气生产和供应业	Production and Supply of Gas	2957189	26829	36591
水的生产和供应业	Production and Supply of Tap Water	583272	24325	49781

continued 2 (10000 yuan)

财务费用 Financial Expenses	利息支出 Interest Expenditure	营业利润 Business Profits	利润总额 Total Profits	利税总额 Total Pre - tax Profits	本年应交增值税 Value Added Tax Payable
33714	30194	226849	292003	409930	103446
6522	6098	36663	39751	66957	23481
11009	9527	24441	28781	48302	16516
1518	4196	13118	13488	19721	5352
80707	98489	715067	750396	966620	184649
44948	44502	1040995	1050643	1403919	304390
180110	202274	220564	231528	310786	68611
51667	50022	307869	322971	469476	122536
71458	66713	771690	738873	1051216	271167
9174	13034	15151	16954	28120	9559
25316	22422	63284	69319	217218	141502
47542	40715	217961	231690	366246	116303
50529	78239	1231054	1318076	1693889	319525
33338	21538	534072	567404	706126	118117
35540	49023	211378	218479	505951	109894
9825	3569	64425	67180	89194	11771
148488	186123	1069975	1128590	1488448	297519
146473	115124	2900598	2974541	3710555	641447
21039	30310	640043	681288	852950	146712
1147	594	20898	21395	23940	1301
11460	10199	58230	76390	99971	20852
120	54	1369	1440	1744	246
123526	140976	436768	461622	668316	173253
44838	48997	233981	259138	428649	146712
43974	45171	126309	125669	142052	11168
34714	46808	76478	76815	97614	15373

4－11　分行业规模以上工业
Main Economic Beneficial Indicators of Industrial

行　业	Sector
总　　计	**Total**
煤炭开采和洗选业	Coal Mining and Dressing
黑色金属矿采选业	Ferrous Metals Mining and Dressing
有色金属矿采选业	Nonferrous Metals Mining and Dressing
非金属矿采选业	Nonmetal Minerals Mining and Dressing
农副食品加工业	Agricultural Products Processing
食品制造业	Food Manufacturing
酒、饮料和精制茶制造业	Wine, Beverage and Tea Manufacturing
烟草制品业	Tobacco Processing
纺织业	Textile Industry
纺织服装、服饰业	Textile Products and Costune Indnstry
皮革、毛皮、羽毛及其制品和制鞋业	Leather. Furs. Downand Related and Shoes Products
木材加工和木、竹、藤、棕、草制品业	Timber Processing, Bamboo, Cane, Palm Fiber and Straw Products
家具制造业	Furniture Manufacturing
造纸和纸制品业	Paper Making and Paper Products
印刷和记录媒介复制业	Printing and Record Media
文教、工美、体育和娱乐用品制造业	Cultural, Educational. Industrial Arts. Sports and Entertainment Goods
石油、煤炭及其他燃料加工业	Petroleum, Coal and Other Fuel Processing
化学原料和化学制品制造业	Raw Chemical Materials and Chemical Products
医药制造业	Medical and Pharmaceutical Products

企业主要经济效益指标(2020 年)
Enterprises Above Designated Size by Sector(2020)

每百元固定资产原值实现利税 (元) Pre tax Profits per 100 Yuan Original Value of Fixed Assets (yuan)	每百元主营业务收入实现利税 (元) Pre tax Profits per 100 yuan Revenues in Main Business (yuan)	新产品产值率 (%) New Product ratio (%)
31.23	**12.77**	**39.98**
33.29	13.86	45.19
43.38	26.27	–
18.31	4.80	12.06
26.67	14.22	15.38
26.68	21.60	26.92
324.67	86.17	–
15.18	9.68	34.08
17.99	7.09	41.82
16.27	4.40	31.69
47.01	9.56	23.26
48.59	15.37	42.88
31.17	14.69	37.69
11.37	9.15	17.79
13.53	4.12	36.00
43.41	8.92	10.80
27.41	12.37	43.56
56.87	22.43	30.10

4-11 续表

行 业	Sector
化学纤维制造业	Chemical Fiber
橡胶和塑料制品业	Rubber and Plastic Products
非金属矿物制品业	Nonmetal Minerals Products
黑色金属冶炼和压延加工业	Ferrous Metals Smelting and Processing
有色金属冶炼和压延加工业	Nonferrous Metals Smelting and Processing
金属制品业	Metals Products
通用设备制造业	Ordinary Machinery
专用设备制造业	For Special Purpose Equipment Manufacturing
汽车制造业	Automobile Manufacturing
铁路、船舶、航空航天和其他运输设备制造业	Railway. watercraft. Avigation spaceflight and other Equipment Manufacturing
电气机械和器材制造业	Electric Equipment and Machinery
计算机、通信和其他电子设备制造业	Computers. Telecommunications and Other Electronic Equipment Manufacturing
仪器仪表制造业	Instruments and Meters Manufacturing
其他制造业	Other Manufacturing
废弃资源综合利用业	Multiple Utilization of Waste Resouces
金属制品、机械和设备修理业	Metal Products, Machinery and Equipment Repair
电力、热力生产和供应业	Production and Supply of Electric Power and Hot Water
燃气生产和供应业	Production and Supply of Gas
水的生产和供应业	Production and Supply of Tap Water

continued

每百元固定资产原值实现利税（元） Pre tax Profits per 100 Yuan Original Value of Fixed Assets (yuan)	每百元主营业务收入实现利税（元） Pre tax Profits per 100 yuan Revenues in Main Business (yuan)	新产品产值率（%） New Product ratio (%)
9.17	3.28	37.58
13.76	7.70	32.87
46.31	13.08	19.15
9.62	2.76	38.87
34.29	4.83	20.79
22.06	6.34	40.34
44.54	13.31	53.74
57.50	20.09	38.96
11.73	7.08	70.01
38.26	9.28	44.84
35.33	8.94	58.86
95.60	13.84	54.97
84.23	19.86	48.43
33.78	6.76	39.43
57.95	18.15	39.09
95.07	5.04	0.63
4.18	6.42	2.57
5.47	4.80	-
3.39	16.74	0.06

4－12　市区规模以上工业

Main Economic Indicators of Industrial Enterprises

单位:万元

项　目	Item	企业单位数(个) Number of Enterprises (unit)	亏损企业(个) Loss Making Enterprises (unit)	工业总产值(当年价格) Gross Industrial Output Value (current price)	新产品产值 Output of New Products
总　　计	**Total**	**5188**	**1058**	**136802990**	**54444062**
按隶属关系分	**Grouped by Subordination**				
中央	Central	32	3	9715816	344546
地方	Local	69	6	3989952	1444427
其他	Other	5087	1049	123237464	52678907
按所有制分	**Grouped by Ownership**				
国有企业	State－owned Enterprises	13	1	3437846	85142
集体企业	Collective－owned Enterprises	2	－	41400	35577
股份合作企业	Cooperative Enterprises	7	3	30113	3854
联营企业	Joint Ownership Enterprises	－	－	－	－
有限责任公司	Limited Liability Corporations	453	79	34004321	13206980
股份有限公司	Share－holding Corporations Ltd.	223	29	18640851	12529438
私营企业	Private Enterprises	3792	784	44203241	15720753
外商及港澳台投资企业	Enterprises with Investment from Foreign、Hong Kong、Macao and Taiwan	698	162	36445219	12862317
其他企业	Other Enterprises	－	－	－	－
按企业规模分	**Grouped by Size of Enterprises**				
大型企业	Large	112	10	41963764	23691255
中型企业	Medium－sized	517	80	40484384	17354657
小微企业	Small	4559	968	54354842	13398150
按轻重工业分	**Grouped by Light & Heavy Industry**				
轻工业	Light Industry	2396	590	44921301	14271517
重工业	Heavy Industry	2792	468	91881690	40172544

企业主要经济指标(2020 年)(一)
Above Designated Size in Urban District(2020)(Ⅰ)

(10000 yuan)

实收资本 Total Capital Hold	国家资本 State Capital	个人资本 Personal Capital	港澳台资本 Hongkong, Macau and TaiWan Capital	外商资本 Foreign Capital	就业人员年平均人数(人) Annual Average Number of Staff and Workers (person)
32797805	**2704854**	**7144481**	**1987426**	**3167495**	**923486**
1396241	438484	5967	177178	1582	12111
1838983	563730	106450	33484	124271	31322
29663605	1785464	7032063	1778294	3041992	880053
848191	539032	252	–	–	3877
11733	–	–	–	–	699
4133	–	4133	–	–	626
–	–	–	–	–	–
7901549	1633894	259165	4684	77517	154992
6931351	309366	2162544	7621	799	138313
9009265	25402	4478076	3960	8033	489701
8091582	197160	240310	1971162	3081145	221695
–	–	–	–	–	–
8723896	842034	1056815	279022	683327	263477
9124163	643053	1696892	430427	1052334	284098
14949745	1219767	4390773	1277977	1431834	462329
11188120	296079	2896036	862320	1521189	442793
21609685	2408775	4248445	1125106	1646306	567110

项　目	Item	企业单位数(个) Number of Enterprises (unit)	亏损企业(个) Loss Making Enterprises (unit)	工业总产值(当年价格) Gross Industrial Output Value (current price)	新产品产值 Output of New Products
按国民经济行业分	**Grouped by Economic Sector**				
采矿业	Mining and Quarrying	12	2	173559	21337
煤炭开采和洗选业	Coal Mining and Dressing	–	–	–	–
黑色金属矿采选业	Ferrous Metals Mining and Dressing	–	–	–	–
有色金属矿采选业	Nonferrous Minerals Mining and Dressing	3	–	18977	–
非金属矿采选业	Nonmetal Minerals Mining and Dressing	9	2	154583	21337
制造业	Manufacturing Industry	5099	1050	127092713	54250614
农副食品加工业	Agricultural Products Processing	102	27	1125683	133808
食品制造业	Food Manufacturing	100	26	2000705	287205
酒、饮料和精制茶制造业	Wine, Beverage and Tea Manufacturing	34	1	924822	150041
烟草制品业	Tobacco Processing	1	–	3450003	–
纺织业	Textile Industry	590	154	5953610	2010259
纺织服装、服饰业	Textile Products and Costume Industry	180	82	1560123	685995
皮革、毛皮、羽毛及其制品和制鞋业	Leather. Furs. Downand Related and Shoes Products	93	36	961276	309058
木材加工和木、竹、藤、棕、草制品业	Timber Processing, Bamboo, Cane, Palm Fiber and Straw Products	33	5	194611	43013
家具制造业	Furniture Manufacturing	85	22	1157845	493533
造纸和纸制品业	Paper Making and Paper Products	195	41	2557253	926169
印刷和记录媒介复制业	Printing and Record Media	85	23	641136	116207
文教、工美、体育和娱乐用品制造业	Cultural, Educational. Industrial Arts. Sports and Entertainment Goods	63	18	1069441	362184
石油、煤炭及其他燃料加工业	Petroleum, Coal and Other Fuel Processing	12	4	141692	12594
化学原料和化学制品制造业	Raw Chemical Materials and Chemical Products	249	35	5920885	2639043

continued 1 (10000 yuan)

实收资本 Total Capital Hold	国家资本 State Capital	个人资本 Personal Capital	港澳台资本 Hongkong, Macau and TaiWan Capital	外商资本 Foreign Capital	就业人员年平均人数(人) Annual Average Number of Staff and Workers (person)
47868	–	6368	–	–	1455
–	–	–	–	–	18
–	–	–	–	–	–
3868	–	3368	–	–	474
44000	–	3000	–	–	963
29655327	1280335	7110641	1890702	3134875	988825
196148	–	67608	25442	20928	8062
592719	27937	81447	42982	270919	22547
433434	2519	27664	121371	128328	10990
60512	–	–	–	–	2438
1444609	9844	739390	62741	182404	91236
562257	11906	93285	292893	52414	38360
231561	179	61435	26385	13266	14449
42903	–	21927	–	–	3132
334403	440	67734	15053	35477	22987
455189	2235	157593	65755	5171	23686
235560	23558	69789	58500	2965	10437
202561	–	52577	7636	91123	13505
169048	–	17131	–	4200	912
1470878	5131	328449	12460	116821	36634

项　目	Item	企业单位数（个）Number of Enterprises (unit)	亏损企业(个) Loss Making Enterprises (unit)	工业总产值(当年价格) Gross Industrial Output Value (current price)	新产品产值 Output of New Products
医药制造业	Medical and Pharmaceutical Products	111	23	6551840	1931516
化学纤维制造业	Chemical Fiber	131	30	6563350	2466118
橡胶和塑料制品业	Rubber and Plastic Products	282	41	5270524	1620827
非金属矿物制品业	Nonmetal Mineral Products	252	37	6588481	1092484
黑色金属冶炼和压延加工业	Ferrous Metals Smelting and Processing	40	9	896814	349549
有色金属冶炼和压延加工业	Nonferrous Metals Smelting and Processing	35	5	3601664	734215
金属制品业	Metal Products	362	60	5366003	2188793
通用设备制造业	Ordinary Machinery	516	62	11532161	6196578
专用设备制造业	For Special Purpose Equipment Manufacturing	276	54	3271588	1246099
汽车制造业	Automobile Manufacturing	199	51	6644019	4686781
铁路、船舶、航空航天和其他运输设备制造业	Railway. watercraft. Avigation spaceflight and other Equipment Manufacturing	44	11	840673	371602
电气机械和器材制造业	Electric Equipment and Machinery	443	85	13824611	8246519
计算机、通信和其他电子设备制造业	Computers. Telecommunications and Other Electronic Equipment Manufacturing	347	78	23715747	12690705
仪器仪表制造业	Instruments and Meters Manufacturing	206	24	4188683	2028387
其他制造业	Other Manufacturing	17	3	201617	79075
废弃资源综合利用业	Multiple Utilization of Waste Resouces	13	3	342260	152047
金属制品、机械和设备修理业	Metal Products, Machinery and Equipment Repair	3	–	33593	211
电力、燃气及水的生产和供应业	Produotion and supply of electricity, gas & water	77	6	9536718	172112
电力、热力生产和供应业	Production and Supply of Electric Power and Hot Water	40	3	6204198	171785
燃气生产和供应业	Production and Supply of Gas	12	2	2811458	–
水的生产和供应业	Production and Supply of Tap Water	25	1	521061	327

continued 2 (10000 yuan)

实收资本 Total Capital Hold	国家资本 State Capital	个人资本 Personal Capital	港澳台资本 Hongkong, Macau and TaiWan Capital	外商资本 Foreign Capital	就业人员年平均人数(人) Annual Average Number of Staff and Workers (person)
1291093	116919	176139	20343	257553	41578
2310186	–	546773	12931	82316	31516
1038103	39700	314340	23773	229949	52574
800526	36622	269801	67232	93016	34712
148258	–	57920	–	4715	3227
425925	–	17224	7236	26152	6422
931384	53086	353173	145712	35676	46490
2336557	122990	728193	131032	295122	103317
1104569	37954	280205	103431	169159	38221
2858090	437796	313675	223137	280271	40866
164838	650	39382	–	24223	7374
4015937	183040	763283	143414	323203	89636
4809484	159899	1048783	259915	306736	145157
928070	7932	395756	21326	78634	42614
26725	–	16066	–	4138	3039
32101	–	2600	–	–	2519
1700	–	1300	–	–	190
3094610	1424519	27472	96724	32620	19623
1392320	468732	16385	55984	8150	11250
732112	657584	1225	38240	24470	2509
970178	298203	9862	2500	–	5864

4－13 市区规模以上工业
Main Economic Indicators of Industrial

单位:万元

项 目	Item	资产合计 Total Assets	流动资产合计 Total Circulating Funds	应收账款 Receivables	存货 Stock
总计	**Total**	**192878049**	**117738005**	**39496814**	**21122096**
按隶属关系分	**Grouped by Subordination**				
中央	Central	8798364	4096740	555160	2034768
地方	Local	10293445	4522566	872550	769521
其他	Other	174024447	109164980	38078837	18330114
按所有制分	**Grouped by Ownership**				
国有企业	State－owned Enterprises	2173333	541606	160264	15629
集体企业	Collective－owned Enterprises	5424211	148379	39300	9692
股份合作企业	Cooperative Enterprises	45294	38514	10059	3875
联营企业	Joint Ownership Enterprises	－	－	－	－
有限责任公司	Limited Liability Corporations	49672002	27756830	11383322	5818274
股份有限公司	Share－holding Corporations Ltd.	47993231	27426581	7045460	3415825
私营企业	Private Enterprises	49023376	33538091	10412981	6485110
外商及港澳台投资企业	Enterprises with Investment from Foreign、Hong Kong、Macao and Taiwan	38546603	28288006	10445428	5373692
其他企业	Other Enterprises	－	－	－	－
按企业规模分	**Grouped by Size of Enterprises**				
大型企业	Large	67994912	42890626	17097845	5524356
中型企业	Medium－sized	58505774	33602315	9834072	6524319
小微企业	Small	66377364	41245065	12564897	9073421
按轻重工业分	**Grouped by Light & Heavy Industry**				
轻工业	Light Industry	62780961	36240319	7905466	8318985
重工业	Heavy Industry	130097089	81497686	31591348	12803111

企业主要经济指标(2020 年)(二)

Enterprises Above Designated Size in Urban District(2020)(Ⅱ)

(10000 yuan)

产成品 Finished Products	固定资产净额 Fixed Assets	累计折旧 Accumulated Depreciation	本年折旧 Depreciation of the year	负债合计 Total Liabilities	流动负债合计 Total Current Liabilities	非流动负债合计 Total Non-current Liabilities	所有者权益合计 Creditors´Equity
8317543	**29362887**	**28177177**	**3475902**	**104700471**	**91678195**	**13022276**	**87923490**
123924	3677143	4981263	443902	4977811	4147497	830314	3820553
357270	2559462	2093009	208219	5405034	3226827	2178207	4830892
7843207	23277697	21232665	2841622	94412065	84365864	10046201	79415812
10594	1372751	1030927	138680	1070208	529061	541147	1083947
183	104527	11721	1604	4116310	2693911	1422399	1307901
2697	3771	7546	874	13856	13788	68	30871
–	–	–	–	–	–	–	–
1943451	11010413	10494358	1196174	32239352	27282594	4956757	17419493
1393331	3288250	2479623	353757	17682895	14991937	2690959	30252816
2799151	8206913	7358379	1079284	27963293	25851116	2112177	20953855
2168136	5376264	6794625	705530	21614557	20315788	1298769	16874608
–	–	–	–	–	–	–	–
2404315	7555394	6708637	866958	37394215	33481017	3913198	30600698
2922632	8487820	8754628	1089144	30935211	26582036	4353176	27570562
2990596	13319673	12713912	1519800	36371045	31615143	4755903	29752231
3201476	9974569	9876545	1222048	31362341	28919922	2442420	31314117
5116068	19388318	18300632	2253854	73338130	62758273	10579856	56609373

项　目	Item	资产合计 Total Assets	流动资产合　计 Total Circulating Funds	应收账款 Receivables	存　货 Stock
按国民经济行业分	**Grouped by Economic Sector**				
采矿业	Mining and Quarrying	284084	218122	35901	7896
煤炭开采和洗选业	Coal Mining and Dressing	–	–	–	–
黑色金属矿采选业	Ferrous Metals Mining and Dressing	–	–	–	–
有色金属矿采选业	Nonferrous Minerals Mining and Dressing	12420	3552	－40	2695
非金属矿采选业	Nonmetal Minerals Mining and Dressing	271664	214570	35941	5201
制造业	Manufacturing Industry	179196831	114646644	39052780	20992878
农副食品加工业	Agricultural Products Processing	1059919	722928	176051	236995
食品制造业	Food Manufacturing	2583529	1722295	480104	231230
酒、饮料和精制茶制造业	Wine, Beverage and Tea Manufacturing	1250244	806447	181450	137399
烟草制品业	Tobacco Processing	3772950	2978531	89437	1881921
纺织业	Textile Industry	7457389	4439081	996766	1107402
纺织服装、服饰业	Textile Products and Costume Industry	2308206	1545179	308950	426652
皮革、毛皮、羽毛及其制品和制鞋业	Leather. Furs. Downand Related and Shoes Products	1144529	854842	271886	255150
木材加工和木、竹、藤、棕、草制品业	Timber Processing, Bamboo, Cane, Palm Fiber and Straw Products	297930	161632	52965	25960
家具制造业	Furniture Manufacturing	2331241	1371186	447007	147596
造纸和纸制品业	Paper Making and Paper Products	2966047	1917894	455460	280807
印刷和记录媒介复制业	Printing and Record Media	852194	536569	177022	77839
文教、工美、体育和娱乐用品制造业	Cultural, Educational. Industrial Arts. Sports and Entertainment Goods	697432	464244	75141	216106
石油、煤炭及其他燃料加工业	Petroleum, Coal and Other Fuel Processing	420370	178511	71884	16919
化学原料和化学制品制造业	Raw Chemical Materials and Chemical Products	8554439	4258242	865286	738789

continued 1 (10000 yuan)

产成品 Finished Products	固定资产净额 Fixed Assets	累计折旧 Accumulated Depreciation	本年折旧 Depreciation of the year	负债合计 Total Liabilities	流动负债合计 Total Current Liabilities	非流动负债合计 Total Non - current Liabilities	所有者权益合计 Creditors´Equity
5425	37417	47554	11092	126557	119329	7228	157526
–	–	–	–	–	–	–	–
–	–	–	–	–	–	–	–
1977	7941	3823	541	8355	8355	–	4066
3448	29476	43731	10551	118203	110975	7228	153461
8269766	21990307	20932197	2773599	96101373	86615129	9486245	82841370
58742	186689	122122	18032	708535	681415	27120	351383
82699	553526	563543	69882	1055667	1033120	22547	1516312
60927	332277	522212	37573	522071	502035	20035	728173
89227	382897	533554	62428	1064474	1062653	1822	2708476
620897	1761330	2022366	243170	4094847	3807584	287262	3350712
258962	379507	301055	32605	1159706	1027680	132026	1147214
74317	143108	101849	12907	789659	765658	24002	354772
14236	25853	18054	3557	193526	187196	6330	104404
42506	200841	149610	21562	1325377	1239551	85826	1005864
112691	592340	485999	74503	1570474	1287456	283019	1371963
33989	230284	331960	31012	463445	423087	40358	388748
58864	144494	174134	17946	347812	322898	24915	348317
10991	23423	16301	3973	200166	170041	30125	219637
351416	1412843	1295508	174117	3870742	3058543	812199	4602132

单位:万元　　4－13　续表2

项　目	Item	资产合计 Total Assets	流动资产合　计 Total Circulating Funds	应收账款 Receivables	存　货 Stock
医药制造业	Medical and Pharmaceutical Products	7625738	4560522	846926	1095598
化学纤维制造业	Chemical Fiber	14254562	5096035	922272	831991
橡胶和塑料制品业	Rubber and Plastic Products	5318058	3340098	1164945	767126
非金属矿物制品业	Nonmetal Mineral Products	6172289	4635229	2818870	553166
黑色金属冶炼和压延加工业	Ferrous Metals Smelting and Processing	636721	427650	56177	89033
有色金属冶炼和压延加工业	Nonferrous Metals Smelting and Processing	2262103	1392897	238814	407270
金属制品业	Metal Products	4245344	2987500	827763	766169
通用设备制造业	Ordinary Machinery	16417637	10971025	3047489	1993468
专用设备制造业	For Special Purpose Equipment Manufacturing	4771293	3525935	929526	755677
汽车制造业	Automobile Manufacturing	18874407	9479236	5787752	906372
铁路、船舶、航空航天和其他运输设备制造业	Railway. watercraft. Avigation spaceflight and other Equipment Manufacturing	924920	642427	199821	137432
电气机械和器材制造业	Electric Equipment and Machinery	21813960	14236703	4557748	2542475
计算机、通信和其他电子设备制造业	Computers. Telecommunications and Other Electronic Equipment Manufacturing	31938557	25048149	11331825	3205005
仪器仪表制造业	Instruments and Meters Manufacturing	7501578	5781307	1562980	1069708
其他制造业	Other Manufacturing	327127	252849	24269	45577
废弃资源综合利用业	Multiple Utilization of Waste Resouces	399746	297507	82139	45695
金属制品、机械和设备修理业	Metal Products, Machinery and Equipment Repair	16377	13995	4056	351
电力、燃气及水的生产和供应业	Produotion and supply of electricity, gas & water	13397134	2873239	408133	121322
电力、热力生产和供应业	Production and Supply of Electric Power and Hot Water	5934936	983173	217865	27089
燃气生产和供应业	Production and Supply of Gas	2619977	451624	130067	24401
水的生产和供应业	Production and Supply of Tap Water	4842222	1438443	60201	69832

continued 2 (10000 yuan)

产成品 Finished Products	固定资产净额 Fixed Assets	累计折旧 Accumulated Depreciation	本年折旧 Depreciation of the year	负债合计 Total Liabilities	流动负债合计 Total Current Liabilities	非流动负债合计 Total Non－current Liabilities	所有者权益合计 Creditors′Equity
551080	1399152	928461	155775	3120624	2856132	264492	4505112
487844	1585036	1717715	185237	8569900	7811862	758038	5649032
469054	1169401	1687707	160258	2887053	2559885	327168	2426921
256142	790817	721587	118012	4370040	4096174	273866	1802247
36344	100166	174990	17030	444964	405868	39096	177664
141484	322730	295931	39797	1531702	1487046	44656	730400
315846	751716	734400	91783	2257464	2035682	221782	1976270
764212	1816607	1698661	221410	8617575	7845510	772065	7797744
209090	567873	570960	68544	2003222	1843904	159319	2745323
430981	2290233	1846937	299712	13643534	11519517	2124016	5230875
55777	124707	86389	13101	588006	551890	36116	336914
1188873	2175133	1796634	259403	11093251	9499992	1593259	10706460
1117564	1887497	1511179	256752	16090931	15220768	870163	15832140
345021	540767	466587	73172	3179794	3010722	169072	4321780
8620	32681	30601	2858	139123	130632	8491	185954
21364	65778	24565	7265	185136	159575	25561	214610
6	603	628	224	12554	11054	1500	3823
42352	7335163	7197426	691212	8472540	4943737	3528803	4924594
210	3963315	5197251	460666	3673394	2715145	958249	2261541
17038	1823523	734116	106641	1862722	1018523	844199	757255
25104	1548325	1266060	123905	2936424	1210069	1726354	1905798

4-14 市区规模以上工业

Main Economic Indicators of Industrial

单位:万元

项目	Item	主营业务收入 Revenues in Main Business	销售费用 Sales Expenses	管理费用 Management Expenses
总计	**Total**	**146912628**	**7596909**	**5356205**
按隶属关系分	**Grouped by Subordination**			
中央	Central	9707438	109740	193722
地方	Local	4203068	215514	245140
其他	Other	133134199	7272989	4923207
按所有制分	**Grouped by Ownership**			
国有企业	State - owned Enterprises	3445921	20733	12890
集体企业	Collective - owned Enterprises	42065	364	4355
股份合作企业	Cooperative Enterprises	30519	618	2213
联营企业	Joint Ownership Enterprises	-	-	-
有限责任公司	Limited Liability Corporations	38873892	912279	1050186
股份有限公司	Share - holding Corporations Ltd.	19629349	1570002	798735
私营企业	Private Enterprises	45689687	2086676	1949162
外商及港澳台投资企业	Enterprises with Investment from Foreign、Hong Kong、Macao and Taiwan	39201194	3006237	1538664
其他企业	Other Enterprises	-	-	-
按企业规模分	**Grouped by Size of Enterprises**			
大型企业	Large	46761812	3394332	1198034
中型企业	Medium - sized	43143487	2356242	1477509
小微企业	Small	57007328	1846336	2680663
按轻重工业分	**Grouped by Light & Heavy Industry**			
轻工业	Light Industry	49351657	3733127	2221564
重工业	Heavy Industry	97560971	3863782	3134642

企业主要经济指标(2020 年)(三)
Enterprises Above Designated Size in Urban District(2020)(Ⅲ)

(10000 yuan)

财务费用 Financial Expenses	利息支出 Interest Expenditure	营业利润 Business Profits	利润总额 Total Profits	利税总额 Total Pre – tax Profits	本年应交增值税 Value Added Tax Payable
1200674	**1289739**	**11437932**	**12047784**	**18731746**	**3733424**
7869	29053	399032	414584	3109775	467075
57974	85203	517065	529557	679884	123437
1136991	1177154	10539814	11122407	14964420	3145875
21151	21843	57318	65599	118342	46948
2307	8975	30366	30280	31973	1080
340	429	1360	1190	2441	1103
–	–	–	–	–	–
360068	394467	1978220	2062206	5527455	1003180
179599	274958	4251336	4348602	5162928	691767
432648	434000	2744026	2971184	4422111	1247539
204560	155067	2375306	2568722	3466497	741807
–	–	–	–	–	–
272538	339300	5121518	5208489	6779521	1235834
342129	370272	3328264	3520299	4595565	898924
586007	580167	2988149	3318996	7356660	1598666
459215	496997	3731400	4061394	8067604	1574581
741459	792742	7706531	7986390	10664143	2158843

单位:万元 4－14 续表1

项 目	Item	主营业务收入 Revenues in Main Business	销售费用 Sales Expenses	管理费用 Management Expenses
按国民经济行业分	**Grouped by Economic Sector**			
采矿业	Mining and Quarrying	–	–	–
煤炭开采和洗选业	Coal Mining and Dressing	–	–	–
黑色金属矿采选业	Ferrous Metals Mining and Dressing	–	–	–
有色金属矿采选业	Nonferrous Minerals Mining and Dressing	19405	761	2161
非金属矿采选业	Nonmetal Minerals Mining and Dressing	146913	11479	18825
制造业	Manufacturing Industry	–	–	–
农副食品加工业	Agricultural Products Processing	1230317	42998	31623
食品制造业	Food Manufacturing	2132705	230155	110649
酒、饮料和精制茶制造业	Wine, Beverage and Tea Manufacturing	1138158	197540	41934
烟草制品业	Tobacco Processing	3453115	74066	125539
纺织业	Textile Industry	5949279	138803	265574*
纺织服装、服饰业	Textile Products and Costume Industry	1719001	112083	182259
皮革、毛皮、羽毛及其制品和制鞋业	Leather. Furs. Downand Related and Shoes Products	966306	30509	36122
木材加工和木、竹、藤、棕、草制品业	Timber Processing, Bamboo, Cane, Palm Fiber and Straw Products	227807	7900	17417
家具制造业	Furniture Manufacturing	1151911	120549	73999
造纸和纸制品业	Paper Making and Paper Products	2535477	75394	109080
印刷和记录媒介复制业	Printing and Record Media	655793	17054	45274
文教、工美、体育和娱乐用品制造业	Cultural, Educational. Industrial Arts. Sports and Entertainment Goods	1047341	19784	35597
石油、煤炭及其他燃料加工业	Petroleum, Coal and Other Fuel Processing	207480	10729	9787
化学原料和化学制品制造业	Raw Chemical Materials and Chemical Products	6233909	411851	380095

continued 1 (10000 yuan)

财务费用 Financial Expenses	利息支出 Interest Expenditure	营业利润 Business Profits	利润总额 Total Profits	利税总额 Total Pre - tax Profits	本年应交增值税 Value Added Tax Payable
–	–	–	–	–	–
–	–	–	–	–	–
–	–	–	–	–	–
68	68	1096	1066	3490	2034
1995	1903	37951	35623	45373	5776
–	–	–	–	–	–
12365	13764	40371	43536	63104	16787
-6700	11748	189117	227141	312120	76077
4402	7075	106472	120170	191374	43618
-19606	1117	420776	419028	2975446	347108
79149	68426	310371	390864	568898	152545
18474	12364	29497	53198	127095	63627
22390	13686	1896	9903	41578	28188
4433	4271	13927	14712	21906	5980
19360	5853	153416	163202	193059	23705
31095	28068	165317	227648	336896	96276
6381	5875	33823	36763	62416	22103
8781	7422	21105	23888	38201	11910
1450	4118	12622	12969	18880	5147
65752	84741	592889	627465	816531	161990

项　目	Item	主营业务收　入 Revenues in Main Business	销售费用 Sales Expenses	管理费用 Management Expenses
医药制造业	Medical and Pharmaceutical Products	5998774	1579743	398229
化学纤维制造业	Chemical Fiber	9474866	38525	81738
橡胶和塑料制品业	Rubber and Plastic Products	5311688	246036	199982
非金属矿物制品业	Nonmetal Mineral Products	6662960	350515	206953
黑色金属冶炼和压延加工业	Ferrous Metals Smelting and Processing	978416	5199	17143
有色金属冶炼和压延加工业	Nonferrous Metals Smelting and Processing	4420633	20546	36498
金属制品业	Metal Products	5451035	85557	165426
通用设备制造业	Ordinary Machinery	12246686	421879	555731
专用设备制造业	For Special Purpose Equipment Manufacturing	3345349	182390	265930
汽车制造业	Automobile Manufacturing	7053911	130380	311987
铁路、船舶、航空航天和其他运输设备制造业	Railway. watercraft. Avigation spaceflight and other Equipment Manufacturing	901720	41498	34767
电气机械和器材制造业	Electric Equipment and Machinery	16300583	1033568	538955
计算机、通信和其他电子设备制造业	Computers. Telecommunications and Other Electronic Equipment Manufacturing	25254340	1563264	629339
仪器仪表制造业	Instruments and Meters Manufacturing	4284719	331445	265047
其他制造业	Other Manufacturing	335695	13463	11742
废弃资源综合利用业	Multiple Utilization of Waste Resouces	342957	1290	7440
金属制品、机械和设备修理业	Metal Products, Machinery and Equipment Repair	34560	1316	1676
电力、燃气及水的生产和供应业	Produotion and supply of electricity, gas & water	－	－	－
电力、热力生产和供应业	Production and Supply of Electric Power and Hot Water	6207313	479	60027
燃气生产和供应业	Production and Supply of Gas	2927024	24998	34540
水的生产和供应业	Production and Supply of Tap Water	564483	23163	47122

continued 2 (10000 yuan)

财务费用 Financial Expenses	利息支出 Interest Expenditure	营业利润 Business Profits	利润总额 Total Profits	利税总额 Total Pre - tax Profits	本年应交增值税 Value Added Tax Payable
42076	42017	1005571	1013016	1353367	293324
180101	202266	220532	231428	310662	68589
46468	45566	290170	302007	425827	103109
56831	50416	520930	485001	723200	206837
8849	12710	13520	15268	25716	8913
24184	21293	63606	69404	216263	140574
42743	37244	203629	215757	340627	107865
45378	73509	1200193	1283208	1641970	304662
29742	19819	488806	516557	643588	107783
35591	48624	210012	216814	501683	107658
9116	2919	62188	64296	83767	9508
142449	181383	1085190	1141591	1492840	290607
145990	112146	2845309	2915602	3619995	613004
21045	30310	640042	681216	852709	146554
927	471	20469	20671	22769	905
4168	2526	56586	69016	80249	10096
120	54	1369	1440	1744	246
–	–	–	–	–	–
36853	44359	178435	200115	344659	125102
43539	44805	125862	125164	140910	10627
34717	46808	74870	73039	92838	14589

4－15 规模以上工业企业

Main Economic Indicators of Industrial Enterprises

单位：万元

项　目	Item	企业单位数（个）Number of Enterprises（unit）	亏损企业（个）Loss Making Enterprises（unit）	工业总产值（当年价格）Gross Industrial Output Value（current price）	新产品产值 Output of New Products
按登记注册类型分组	**Grouped by Status of Registration**				
内资企业	Domestic－funded Enterprises	5248	1031	109779608	45607831
国有企业	State－owned Enterprises	14	1	3557859	85142
中央企业	Central Enterprises	4	－	1680554	－
地方企业	Local Enterprises	10	1	1877305	85142
集体企业	Collective－owned Enterprises	3	－	43654	35577
股份合作企业	Cooperative Enterprises	8	3	33771	3854
联营企业	Joint Ownership Enterprises	－	－	－	－
集体联营企业	Collective Joint Ownership Enterprises	－	－	－	－
有限责任公司	Limited Liability Corporations	525	97	36941134	14789061
国有独资公司	State－funded Corporations	31	10	7703888	159918
其他有限责任公司	Other Limited Liability Corporations	494	87	29237246	14629142
股份有限公司	Share－holding Corporations Ltd.	245	33	19656908	13008612
私营企业	Private Enterprises	4453	897	49546283	17685584
私营独资企业	Private－funded Enterprises	97	16	429780	53181
私营合伙企业	Private Partnership Enterprises	11	3	41883	2691
私营有限责任公司	Private Limited Liability Corporations	4225	850	46406132	16224527
私营股份有限公司	Private Share－holding Corporations Ltd.	120	28	2668488	1405186
港、澳、台商投资公司	Enterprises with Investment from Hong Kong, Macao and Taiwan	284	84	10945527	3070501
内地与港澳台合资经营企业	Joint－venture Enterprises with funds from Hong Kong, Macao and Taiwan	139	35	3794118	1707415
内地与港澳台合作经营企业	Cooperative Enterprises with funds from Hong Kong, Macao and Taiwan	－	－	－	－
港澳台商独资经营企业	Enterprises with Sole Investment from Hong Kong, Macao and Taiwan	127	40	6100583	773063
港澳台商投资股份有限公司	Share－holding Corporations Ltd. with Investment from Hong Kong, Macao and Taiwan	17	8	1048330	589126
其他港澳台商投资	Other Enterprises with Investment from Hong Kong, Macao and Taiwan	1	1	2497	898
外商投资企业公司	Enterprises with Foreign Investment	460	94	26395687	10144024
中外合资经营企业	Joint－venture Enterprises	177	41	6947775	2404782
中外合作经营企业	Cooperation Enterprises	5	1	1196905	35327
外商独资经营企业	Enterprises with Sole Foreign Investment	262	48	17212575	7087199
外商投资股份有限公司	Share－holding Corporations Ltd. with Foreign Investment	16	4	1038431	616715
其他外商投资企业		－	－	－	－

主要经济指标按登记注册类型分(2020 年)
Above Designated Size by Status of Registration(2020)

(10000 yuan)

实收资本 Total Capital Hold	国家资本 State Capital	个人资本 Personal Capital	港澳台资本 Hongkong, Macau and TaiWan Capital	外商资本 Foreign Capital	就业人员年平均人数(人) Annual Average Number of Staff and Workers (person)
26991613	2697827	7564213	16265	86349	796931
889319	539032	252	–	–	3931
576937	261528	–	–	–	2060
312382	277504	252	–	–	1871
11763	–	–	–	–	702
11783	7650	4133	–	–	629
–	–	–	–	–	–
–	–	–	–	–	–
8422572	1794597	269461	4684	77517	156986
848254	214251	–	–	–	12428
7574318	1580346	269461	4684	77517	144558
7168593	312747	2282903	7621	799	139094
10487584	43802	5007464	3960	8033	495589
34158	–	21473	–	–	5486
8875	–	8510	–	–	619
9459338	39401	4368103	3960	4029	462604
985213	4401	609378	–	4004	26880
3081839	48083	86016	1911708	126874	77205
1433626	100	59120	578615	110739	31590
–	–	–	–	–	–
1332280	–	–	1249976	9283	37905
312516	47983	26896	80000	6551	7605
3417	–	–	3117	300	105
5418250	151856	166368	159028	3132604	145369
1888398	146856	77728	92846	854423	56583
104420	–	1800	–	12566	1690
3132948	5000	1766	57616	2236141	81195
292484	–	85074	8565	29476	5901
–	–	–	–	–	–

4－16 分地区规上

Added Value of Industrial Enterprises Above

单位:亿元

年 份 Year	全 市 Whole City	市 区					
		上城区 Shangcheng	下城区 Xiacheng	江干区 Jianggan	拱墅区 Gongshu	西湖区 Xihu	高新(滨江)区 Hi－Tech (Binjiang)
2000	360.97						
2001	444.91						
2002	597.01						
2003	783.51						
2004	1019.47						
2005	1126.54						
2006	1363.17						
2007	1717.65						
2008	1743.20						
2009	1792.00						
2010	2153.83						
2011	2369.00	215.48	20.83	47.25	119.11	49.03	162.30
2012	2492.00	296.64	22.05	48.00	117.08	49.07	210.02
2013	2664.13	318.89	23.33	53.33	104.34	49.62	278.48
2014	2813.51	328.06	15.16	57.60	78.34	50.45	324.69
2015	2875.05	329.70	7.13	53.79	60.64	52.30	365.67
2016	2990.34	349.57	9.64	47.37	65.80	57.06	374.24
2017	3184.05	362.41	8.16	42.98	74.76	61.04	502.19
2018	3415.45	364.56	13.36	38.46	81.84	65.07	574.95
2019	3481.89	374.72	14.03	42.13	93.95	68.23	623.97
2020	3467.16	374.34	13.65	48.93	95.82	80.99	600.18

注:2019 年起萧山区不含托管在钱塘新区的街道数据。

工业增加值(2000－2020年)
Designated Size by Region (2000－2020)

(100 million yuan)

Urban District						桐庐县 Tonglu	淳安县 Chun'an	建德市 Jiande
萧山区 Xiaoshan	余杭区 Yuhang	富阳区 Fuyang	临安区 Lin'an	钱塘新区 Qiantang New Area	西湖风景名胜区 The West Lake Scenic Zone			
77.95	31.54	22.05	11.83			9.29	2.24	10.13
106.28	38.50	31.69	14.71			11.98	2.99	8.86
145.26	40.29	38.87	18.55			14.08	3.40	13.05
199.34	69.17	52.52	25.09			18.98	5.46	16.82
245.57	86.96	63.65	32.25			29.73	6.59	27.62
311.61	129.16	80.22	37.84			31.60	9.29	28.54
385.34	150.85	103.73	47.54			42.10	12.70	37.88
401.88	195.17	136.42	62.53			57.06	17.35	50.54
482.29	212.97	160.31	74.51			68.41	20.56	61.38
538.91	225.60	167.30	80.02			62.17	23.48	60.03
606.90	297.10	182.30	98.91			76.63	29.18	76.13
721.27	243.41	162.41	98.20			71.74	32.66	68.09
727.65	250.64	165.25	106.67			80.02	38.69	76.19
704.46	275.99	198.03	115.18	380.51	0.06	81.63	43.44	81.74
712.21	301.62	200.53	123.24	405.16	0.12	94.92	47.53	85.18
706.49	334.30	200.89	127.85	457.66	0.76	102.26	52.06	83.67
742.23	349.74	201.89	136.80	541.62	-1.77	99.78	49.96	85.75
745.62	386.71	234.29	138.50	417.58	-0.26	83.38	40.35	86.33
790.64	428.65	248.45	145.71	439.27	0.06	83.09	30.36	110.96
531.95	462.74	231.69	168.86	632.06	0.16	86.57	34.24	116.60
479.12	493.96	215.10	184.97	630.21	0.43	92.78	27.79	128.90

a) Figures of Xiaoshan District don't include subdistricts which under administered by Qiantang New Area Since 2019.

4-17 分地区规上

Index of Added Value of Industrial

（上年=100）

年 份 Year	全 市 Whole City	市 区					
		上城区 Shangcheng	下城区 Xiacheng	江干区 Jianggan	拱墅区 Gongshu	西湖区 Xihu	高新（滨江）区 Hi-Tech (Binjiang)
2010	114.9	110.0	121.1	112.2	110.5	109.1	119.6
2011	112.7	112.1	104.0	109.4	112.3	111.8	118.2
2012	110.9	106.6	103.5	105.5	112.2	108.8	113.7
2013	108.0	106.3	107.7	109.4	104.5	109.6	115.1
2014	108.9	108.9	91.6	115.1	105.5	104.9	118.3
2015	105.4	106.0	90.1	100.5	95.2	101.0	117.8
2016	105.6	98.5	102.0	87.5	105.0	105.0	114.9
2017	107.0	108.7	105.5	95.2	111.3	105.1	118.1
2018	106.3	101.7	118.9	101.3	111.2	99.2	117.3
2019	105.1	103.0	91.5	91.9	117.7	114.4	110.7
2020	103.8	103.4	112.5	110.8	93.0	100.4	110.8

注:2019 年起萧山区不含托管在钱塘新区的街道数据。

工业增加值发展指数(2010－2020年)

Enterprises Above Designated Size by Region(2010－2020)

(Preceding Year＝100)

Urban District						桐庐县 Tonglu	淳安县 Chun'an	建德市 Jiande
萧山区 Xiaoshan	余杭区 Yuhang	富阳区 Fuyang	临安区 Lin'an	钱塘新区 Qiantang New Area	西湖风景名胜区 The West Lake Scenic Zone			
114.3	115.0	113.1	122.7	118.5		114.0	114.9	115.5
112.9	109.2	113.3	113.1	111.2		109.1	115.1	113.0
113.5	107.2	112.1	112.4	102.4		109.0	119.6	110.8
108.1	108.0	109.3	105.5	107.3		105.6	112.7	106.1
108.1	107.0	106.2	107.2	109.3		109.0	103.2	108.1
106.2	102.6	104.1	105.1	106.9	90.9	106.9	103.4	108.2
106.3	105.0	103.0	109.0	110.2	100.3	108.6	110.6	107.0
101.3	107.6	106.0	106.7	106.5	117.5	106.3	104.1	106.7
102.6	107.0	104.5	104.5	107.0		104.6	88.2	107.6
105.1	105.3	101.1	108.8	99.7		111.1	103.5	108.6
96.5	108.3	95.9	109.5	104.2		103.1	82.9	108.5

a) Figures of Xiaoshan District don't include subdistricts which under administered by Qiantang New Area Since 2019.

4－18 规上工业三大新兴产业发展情况(2013－2020年)

Statistics on the Three Emerging Industries Above Designated Size(2013－2020)

指标 Item	高新技术产业 High－tech Industries		战略性新兴产业 Strategic Emerging Industries		装备制造业 Equipment Manufacturing Industries	
	增加值(亿元) Value－added (100 million yuan)	为上年(%) As Compared with the Preceding Year (%)	增加值(亿元) Value－added (100 million yuan)	为上年(%) As Compared with the Preceding Year (%)	增加值(亿元) Value－added (100 million yuan)	为上年(%) As Compared with the Preceding Year (%)
2013	785.4	108.9	636.6	107.1	900.5	108.6
2014	1096.6	110.5	813.1	113.0	921.4	109.3
2015	1212.6	109.8	877.3	109.4	1086.1	113.5
2016	1372.9	112.5	812.1	111.6	1249.6	114.6
2017	1605.5	113.6	979.5	115.0	1384.2	111.0
2018	1948.4	110.8	1135.3	113.1	1531.0	109.3
2019	2178.4	108.5	1328.6	113.1	1640.5	107.9
2020	2448.3	108.6	1415.1	108.1	1837.0	111.8

4－19 主要工业产品生产量(2020 年)

Output of Major Industrial Products(2020)

产品名称		Item		全市 Whole City 2020 年	全市 Whole City 为上年(%) As Compared with the Preceding Year(%)	市区 Urban District
发电量	(亿千瓦时)	Electricity	(100 million kWh)	162	100.4	116
#水力发电	(亿千瓦时)	of which:Hydropower	(100 million kWh)	42	97.5	4
垃圾发电	(亿千瓦时)	Garbage Power	(100 million kWh)	11	84.5	11
罐头	(万吨)	Canned Food	(10000 tons)	3	95.2	3
乳制品	(吨)	Dairy Products	(ton)	174137	96.7	174137
啤酒	(千升)	Beer	(1000 litres)	1056752	106.0	789335
软饮料	(万吨)	Soft Drinks	(10000 tons)			
精制茶	(吨)	Tea	(ton)	17282	77.3	11867
卷烟	(亿支)	Cigarettes	(100 million)	506	98.5	506
方便面	(吨)	Instant Noodle	(ton)	238059	113.0	238059
化学纤维	(吨)	Chemical Fiber	(ton)	8678819	91.6	8678819
#合成纤维	(吨)	Synthetic Fibre	(ton)	8677129	91.8	8677129
纱	(万吨)	Yarn	(10000 tons)	33	82.2	33
布	(万米)	Cloth	(10000 m)	200862	75.5	197834
印染布	(万米)	Printed Fabric	(10000 m)	488930	86.1	488895
蚕丝及交织机织物(含蚕丝≥50%)	(万米)	Silk and Woven Fabrics (Containing Greater than or Equal 50% silk)	(10000 m)	1051	86.4	1051
服装	(万件)	Garment	(10000 units)	19054	80.8	17485
皮革鞋靴	(万双)	Leather Footwear	(10000 units)	556	50.8	556
家具	(万件)	Furniture	(10000 units)	1900	92.1	1668
塑料制品	(万吨)	Plastic Membrane	(10000 tons)	351	100.1	328
机制纸及纸板	(万吨)	Machine Made Paper and Paperboard	(10000 tons)	182	44.0	177

4－19 续表1 continued 1

产品名称	Item	全市 Whole City 2020年	全市 Whole City 为上年(%) As Compared with the Preceding Year(%)	市区 Urban District
盐酸(含量31%以上)(吨)	Mariatic Acid(above 31% percent) (ton)	72737	96.6	72737
氢氧化钠(烧碱)(折100%)(吨)	Caustic Soda (ton)	236767	96.2	236767
碳酸钠(纯碱)(吨)	Soda ash (ton)	295876	93.2	295876
初级形态的塑料(塑料树脂及共聚物)(吨)	Plastics in Primary Form(Plastic Resins and Copolymers) (ton)	432081	104.5	432081
合成氨(吨)	Synthetic Ammonia (ton)	223180	94.9	223180
农用氮、磷、钾化学肥料总计(折纯)(吨)	Chemical Fertilizer (ton)	467415	127.8	467415
化学农药原药(折有效成分100%)(吨)	Chemical Pesticide (ton)	88495	105.1	25665
涂料(油漆)(吨)	Paint (ton)	339761	126.6	182981
合成洗涤剂(吨)	Synthetic Detergent (ton)	154580	92.7	118903
化学药品原药(化学原料药)(吨)	Original Drug Chemicals (ton)	1578	84.7	1508
中成药(吨)	Traditional Chinese Medicine (ton)	7521	88.0	5323
橡胶轮胎外胎(轮胎外胎)(万条)	Rubber Tires (10000 units)	6466	104.2	5751
水泥(万吨)	Cement (10000 tons)	1736	101.7	832
铁合金(万吨)	Iron Alloy (10000 tons)			
钢材(万吨)	Steel Products (10000 tons)	498	108.1	497
精炼铜(电解铜)(吨)	Refined Copper (ton)	393337	90.5	393337
工业锅炉(蒸发量吨)	Industry Boiler (ton)	7973	113.0	7973
金属切削机床(台)	Metal－cutting Machine Tools (unit)	9735	98.6	9735

4－19 续表2 continued 2

产品名称	Item	全市 Whole City 2020年	全市 Whole City 为上年(%) As Compared with the Preceding Year(%)	市区 Urban District
金属成形机床(锻压设备)(台)	Metal Forming Machine(Forge Equipment) (Tai)	5447	90.9	5447
泵(液体泵) (万台)	Pump (10000 sets)			
滚动轴承(轴承) (万套)	Bearings (10000 units)	12331	91.1	12331
汽车 (辆)	Motor Vehicles (unit)	98018	87.2	98018
叉车 (台)	Forklift (unit)			
两轮自行车(自行车) (万辆)	Bicycles (10000 units)	107	112.9	107
交流电动机 (万千瓦)	AC Motor (10000 kW)	317	107.6	317
钢绞线 (吨)	Strand (ton)	54094	82.6	54094
通信及电子网络用电缆 (万对千米)	Communication Cable (10000 km)	240	89.4	239
光缆(光纤通讯电缆) (万芯千米)	Electric Power Cable (10000 km)	2834	132.1	2834
家用电冰箱 (万台)	Household Refrigerators (10000 units)	82	106.7	82
家用洗衣机 (万台)	Household Washing Machines (10000 units)	232	95.1	232
吸排油烟机 (万台)	Smoke Absorbers (10000 units)	356	101.3	356
移动通信手持机(手机) (万部)	Mobile Telephone Sets (10000 units)	1363	29.5	1363
电工仪器仪表 (万台)	Electric Instrument and Apparatus (10000 units)	4078	89.3	4078
工业自动调节仪表与控制系统 (万台)	Industrial Automatic Adjustment Meter and Control System (10000 units)	546	134.9	546
电光源(灯泡) (亿只)	Light Bulbs (100 million units)	5	98.8	5
彩色电视机 (万部)	Color－Television Sets (10000 units)	－	16.1	－
微型计算机设备 (万台)	Micro－computer Equipment (10000 units)	138	81.3	138

4－20　分地区单位 GDP 能耗降低情况(2020 年)
Energy Efficency and Energy Consumption Reduction by Region(2020)

地　区	Region	单位 GDP 能耗降低率(%) Decrease Rate of Energy Consumption Per Unit of GDP (±%)	单位 GDP 电耗降低率(%) Decrease Rate of Energy Consumption Per Unit of GDP (±%)	单位工业增加值能耗降低率(%) Decrease Rate of Energy Consumption Per Unit of Industriul Value－Added (±%)
杭州市	Hangzhou	5.1	4.8	5.6
上城区	Shangcheng	–	17.9	55.5
下城区	Xiacheng	–	17.8	19.8
江干区	Jianggan	–	5.1	4.8
拱墅区	Gongshu	–	4.6	－13.0
西湖区	Xihu	–	9.5	4.2
滨江区	Binjiang	–	9.6	4.9
萧山区	Xiaoshan	1.0	3.2	－2.8
余杭区	Yuhang	0.5	－2.9	－0.8
富阳区	Fuyang	11.0	12.8	18.4
临安区	Lin'an	－2.2	－5.3	－2.3
钱塘新区	Qiantang New Area	–	1.7	3.2
桐庐县	Tonglu	－1.8	0.3	－6.5
淳安县	Chun'an	－0.7	2.7	－6.7
建德市	Jiande	－0.6	－0.4	0.5

注:1. 若降低率为负数,说明本期的指标值与去年同期相比没有降低,反而上升。
　2. 萧山区不含托管在钱塘新区的街道数据。

a) If the Decrease Rate was a negative number, it means the indicator was increased compared to last year.
b) Figures of Xiaoshan District don't include subdistricts which under administered by Qiantang New Area.

4-21 规模以上工业企业主要能源品种购进与消费(2020年)

Purchasing and Consuming of Major Energy in Industrial Enterprises Above Designated Size(2020)

能源名称		Item		购进量 Purchasing	工业生产消费 Industry Consumption
原煤	(吨)	Raw Coal	(Ton)	9236734	9288315
洗精煤	(吨)	Washing Coal	(Ton)	-	-
煤制品	(吨)	Coal Puoducts	(Ton)	676608	677928
焦炭	(吨)	Coke	(Ton)	35533	36069
天然气(气态)	(万立方米)	Natural Gas(Gas)	(10000 cu. m)	207893	206114
液化天然气(液态)	(吨)	Liquefied Natural Gas(Liquid)	(Ton)	162014	161947
汽油	(吨)	Gasoline	(Ton)	34925	13459
煤油	(吨)	Kerosene	(Ton)	580	545
柴油	(吨)	Diesel Oil	(Ton)	146754	141282
燃料油	(吨)	Fuel Oil	(Ton)	20311	20666
液化石油气	(吨)	Liquefied Petroleum Gas	(Ton)	9355	9210
润滑油	(吨)	Lubricating Oil	(Ton)	3891	3868
溶剂油	(吨)	Solvent Oil	(Ton)	360	361
石油沥青	(吨)	Petroleum Asphalt	(Ton)	112837	103741
其他石油制品	(吨)	Other Petroleum Products	(Ton)	6487	6474
热力	(百万千焦)	Heat	(Million kilo-joule)	60330057	78076761
电力	(万千瓦时)	Electricity	(10000 kWh)	3328482	3421053
煤矸石用于燃料	(吨)	Coal Gangue For Fuel	(Ton)	1211	1211
城市垃圾用于燃料	(吨)	Waste For Fuel	(Ton)	1738312	1748107
生物质废料用于燃料	(吨标准煤)	Biomass Waste For Fuel	(Ton)	125016	124769
余热余压	(百万千焦)	Residual Heat and Pressure	(Million kilo-joule)	2012041	10000885
其它工业废料用于燃料	(吨)	Other Industrial Wastes Are Used For Fuel	(Ton)	32671	825097
其它燃料	(吨标准煤)	Other Fuel		38060	38995

4-22 规模以上工业企业主要能源

Energy Consumption of Industrial

行 业 Sector	原煤(吨) Raw Coal(Ton)	洗精煤(吨) Washing Coal(Ton)	焦炭(吨) Coke(Ton)	汽油(吨) Gasoline(Ton)	煤油(吨) Kerosene(Ton)
总 计 Total	**9288315**	**-**	**36069**	**13459**	**545**
煤炭开采和洗选业 Coal Mining and Dressing	-	-	-	-	-
有色金属矿采选业 Nonferrous Minerals Mining and Dressing	-	-	-	-	-
非金属矿采选业 Nonmetal Minerals Mining and Dressing	33423	-	-	2	-
农副食品加工业 Agricultural Products Processing	-	-	-	102	-
食品制造业 Food Manufacturing	1669	-	-	167	-
酒、饮料和精制茶制造业 Wine,Beverage and Tea Manufacturing	-	-	-	-	-
烟草制品业 Tobacco Processing	-	-	-	-	-
纺织业 Textile Processing	155892	-	-	973	-
纺织服装、服饰业 Textile Products and Costume Industry	-	-	-	358	-
皮革、毛皮、羽毛及其制品和制鞋业 Leather. Furs. Downand Related and Shoes Products	-	-	-	308	-
木材加工和木、竹、藤、棕、草制品业 Timber Processing,Bamboo,Cane,Plam Fiber and Straw Products	-	-	-	15	-
家具制造业 Furniture Manufacturing	-	-	-	210	-
造纸和纸制品业 Paper Making and Paper Products	1872	-	-	278	-
印刷和记录媒介复制业 Printing	-	-	-	315	-
文教、工美、体育和娱乐用品制造业 Cultural,Educational. Industrial Arts. Sports and Entertainment Goods	-	-	129	222	-
石油、煤炭和其他燃料加工业 Petroleum,Coal and Other Fuel Processing	146447	-	-	2	-

消费量按行业分(2020 年)
Enterprises above Designated Size by Sector(2020)

柴油(吨) Diesel oil(Ton)	燃料油(吨) Fuel Oil(Ton)	液化石油气(吨) Liquefied Petroleum Gas(Ton)	天然气(万立方米) Natural Gas (10000 cu. m)	其他石油制品(吨) Other Petroleum Products(Ton)	热力(百万千焦) Heat(Million kilo - joule)	电力(万千瓦时) Electricity (10000 kWh)
141282	**20666**	**9210**	**206114**	**6474**	**78076761**	**3421053**
–	–	–	–	–	–	274
21	–	–	–	–	–	2197
4646	–	–	–	–	–	8307
1643	–	122	1799	–	240860	14483
1402	765	373	1742	–	1525913	30384
304	417	–	2509	–	1343385	60951
–	–	–	499	–	–	5035
2372	–	744	10874	–	25562641	398653
348	–	12	475	–	361201	15122
352	–	–	766	–	23984	10208
202	–	–	60	–	26222	4428
575	–	–	494	–	37484	13237
1978	–	949	3495	–	8158719	110655
733	–	–	272	–	79135	19090
211	–	–	121	–	98293	13359
592	–	–	145	–	27954	1731

4－22 续表

行　业　Sector	原煤(吨) Raw Coal(Ton)	洗精煤(吨) Washing Coal(Ton)	焦炭(吨) Coke(Ton)	汽油(吨) Gasoline(Ton)	煤油(吨) Kerosene(Ton)
化学原料和化学制品制造业 Raw Chemical Materials and Chemical Products	1687137	–	–	632	–
医药制造业 Medical and Pharmaceutical Products	24602	–	–	264	–
化学纤维制造业 Chemical Fiber	273925	–	–	80	–
橡胶和塑料制品业 Rubber and Plastic Products	160120	–	–	842	19
非金属矿物制品业 Nonmetal Minerals Products	2908989	–	–	321	–
黑色金属冶炼和压延加工业 Smelting and Processing of Ferrous Metals	–	–	–	72	–
有色金属冶炼和压延加工业 Smelting and Processing of Nonferrous Metals	–	–	35887	12	–
金属制品业 Metal Products	235	–	52	680	3
通用设备制造业 Ordinary Machinery	–	–	–	1955	269
专用设备制造业 Special Purpose Equipment	–	–	–	460	–
汽车制造业 Automobile Manufacturing	–	–	–	542	242
铁路、船舶、航空航天和其他运输设备制造业 Railway. watercraft. Avigation spaceflight and other Equipment Manufacturing	–	–	–	237	–
电气机械和器材制造业 Electric Equipment and Machinery	–	–	–	1014	8
计算机、通信和其他电子设备制造业 Computers. Telecommunications and Other Electronic Equipment Manufacturing	–	–	–	954	–
仪器仪表制造业 Instruments and Meters Manufacturing	–	–	–	518	4
其他制造业 Other Manufacturing	–	–	–	62	–
废弃资源综合利用业 Multiple Utilization of Waste Resouces	–	–	–	–	–
电力、热力生产和供应业 Production and Supply of Electric Power and Hot Water	3793571	–	–	1536	–
燃气生产和供应业 Production and Supply of Gas	–	–	–	205	–
水的生产和供应业 Production and Supply of Tap Water	100433	–	–	121	–

continued

柴油(吨) Diesel oil(Ton)	燃料油(吨) Fuel Oil(Ton)	液化石油气(吨) Liquefied Petroleum Gas(Ton)	天然气(万立方米) Natural Gas (10000 cu. m)	其他石油制品(吨) Other Petroleum Products(Ton)	热力(百万千焦) Heat(Million kilo－joule)	电力(万千瓦时) Electricity (10000 kWh)
3993	9545	100	3711	5520	27697503	381887
1134	–	–	2396	–	1483923	75493
1594	7264	–	1697	106	4640365	525017
1276	1735	3576	1066	70	2948114	226508
94512	295	526	6765	–	326282	240603
395	–	45	1417	174	227180	21655
877	–	171	3125	–	75417	78433
2809	645	319	10502	2	306881	141269
7105	–	177	3513	517	79591	117099
613	–	928	598	–	204381	28938
3976	–	94	1822	61	67668	99756
128	–	325	558	25	28063	11047
1925	–	188	2182	–	1271371	146856
1332	–	561	1065	–	277327	149837
377	–	–	55	–	3110	23614
569	–	1	129	–	15195	1703
985	–	–	141	–	51311	27634
1988	–	–	142100	–	887287	328512
89	–	–	21	–	–	952
225	–	–	–	–	–	86126

4－23 全社会用电情况(2020年)

Electricity Consumption In the Whole Society(2020)

单位:万千瓦时 (10000 kWh)

项 目	Item	2020年	增长(%) Inctease(%)
总 计	**Total**	**8079690**	**－1.1**
#线路损失电量	#Losses in Transmission	231033	2.9
全行业用电合计	**Total Electricity Consumption for the whole industries**	**6639975**	**－2.2**
第一产业	Primary Industry	34766	－1.0
第二产业	Secondary Industry	4348701	－4.5
第三产业	Tertiary Industry	2256508	2.4
全行业用电按行业分	**Electricity Consumption by Sector**		
农林牧渔业	Farming,Forestry,Animal Husbandry and Fishery Conservancy	47534	－4.5
工业	Industry	4091902	－5.5
#采矿业	#Mining and Quarrying	25135	－7.2
制造业	Manufacturing Industry	3636627	－5.6
电力、热力、燃气及水的生产和供应业	Produotion and supply of electricity,gas & water	430140	－4.3
建筑业	Construction	257363	15.7
批发和零售业	Wholesale and Retail Trade	397637	－0.6
交通运输、仓储及邮政业	Transportation,Storage,Post & Telecommunications	212371	9.7
住宿和餐饮业	Lodging and Catering Services	130882	－12.4
信息传输、软件和信息技术服务业	Information Transmission,Computer Services and Software	288005	13.4
金融业	Finance	39119	－1.1
房地产业	Real Estate	292809	6.3
租赁和商务服务业	Renting and Business Service	295970	6.6
科学研究、技术服务业	Scientific Researoh and Fechnicla Senice	34703	－8.1
水利环境和公共设施管理业	Water Conservancy,Environment and Public Utility	121246	7.0
居民服务、修理和其他服务业	Service for the Residents,Repair and others	58015	－4.3
教育	Education	140322	－10.5
卫生和社会工作	Health Care,Sports Social Welfare	97592	4.1
文化、体育和娱乐业	Culture,Sports and Entertainment	30263	－5.0
公共管理、社会保障和社会组织	Public Administration,Social Security and Social Organization	104243	－1.1
城乡居民生活用电	**Residential Consumption**	**1439716**	**4.7**
#城市	#Cities	923032	3.8
乡村	Rural Areas	516683	6.3

4－24　水资源量和总用水量(2018－2020 年)
Total Water Resources and Water Consumption(2018－2020)

单位:亿立方米　　(100 million Cubic Meters)

地区	Region	水资源量 Water Resources			用水量 Water Consumption		
		2018 年	2019 年	2020 年	2018 年	2019 年	2020 年
全市	Whole City	146.24	188.11	218.89	32.47	30.96	29.76
市区	Urban District	74.39	82.76	91.53	27.29	25.94	24.86
萧山区	Xiaoshan	10.94	11.06	11.94	7.72	7.45	7.28
余杭区	Yuhang	12.22	11.54	12.35	5.08	5.30	5.31
富阳区	Fuyang	15.61	18.37	20.67	3.78	3.59	3.19
临安区	Lin'an	28.71	35.50	39.67	2.82	2.42	2.13
桐庐县	Tonglu	14.05	20.55	23.05	1.89	1.73	1.65
淳安县	Chan'an	42.42	58.30	76.26	1.26	1.96	1.33
建德市	Jiangde	15.38	26.50	28.05	2.03	1.32	1.93

4-25 规模以下工业主要指标

Main Indicators of Industrial Enterprises Below Designated Size

指标名称		Item		2020 年
企业数	(万家)	Number of Enterprises	(10,000 Units)	2.37
年末从业人数	(万人)	Total Number of Employed Persons at Year End	(10,000 persons)	22.46
资产总计	(亿元)	Total Assets	(100 million yuan)	1368.23
负债合计	(亿元)	Total Liabilitiess	(100 million yuan)	966.57
营业收入	(亿元)	Business Revenues	(100 million yuan)	855.33
营业成本	(亿元)	Operating Costs	(100 million yuan)	658.20
税金总额	(亿元)	Total taxes	(100 million yuan)	24.87
利润总额	(亿元)	Total Profits	(100 million yuan)	8.14
应付职工薪酬	(亿元)	Employee benefits Payable	(100 million yuan)	97.67

主要统计指标解释

工业总产值 是以货币表现的工业企业在报告期内生产的已出售或可供出售工业产品总量，它反映一定时间内工业生产的总规模和总水平，它包括：在本企业内不再进行加工，经检验、包装入库（规定不需包装的产品除外）的成品价值，对外加工费收入，自制半成品，在产品期末初差额价值。工业总产值采用“工厂法”计算，即以工业企业作为一个整体，按企业工业生产活动的最终成果来计算，企业内部不允许重复计算，不能把企业内部各个车间（分厂）生产的成果相加。

工业增加值 是指工业行业在报告期内以货币表现的工业生产活动的最终成果。

固定资产原价 固定资产原值指企业在建造、购置、安装、改建、扩建、技术改造某项固定资产时所支出的全部货币总额。它一般包括买价、包装费、运杂费和安装费等。

固定资产净值 是指固定资产原价减去历年已提折旧额后的净额。

利税总额 指企业利润总额、产品销售税金及附加和应交增值税之和。

主营业务收入 指企业销售产品的销售收入和提供劳务等主要经营业务取得的收入总额。

主营业务利润 指企业销售产品和提供工业性劳务等主要经营业务收入和除其成本、费用、税金后的利润。

利润总额 指企业实现的利润。

应交增值税 指企业在报告期内应交纳的增值税额。

总资产 指企业拥有或控制的全部资产。包括流动资产、长期投资、固定资产、无形及递延资产、其他长期资产、递延税项等，即为企业资产负债表的资产总计项。

（1）流动资产指企业可以在一年内或者超过一年的一个生产周期内变现或耗用的资产合计。包括现金及各种存款、短期投资、应收及预付款项、存货等。

（2）固定资产指企业固定资产净值、固定资产清理、在建工程、待处理固定资产损失所占用的资金合计。

（3）无形资产指企业长期使用而没有实物形态的资产。包括专利权、非专利技术、商标权、著作权、土地使用权、商誉等。

总负债 指企业承担并需要偿还的全部债务。包括流动负债和长期负债、递延税项等，即为企业资产负债表的负债合计项。

（1）流动负债指企业在一年内或者超过一年的一个营业周期内需要偿还的债务合计，其中包括短期借款、应付及预收款项、应付工资、应交税金和应交利润等。

（2）长期负债指企业在一年以上或者超过一年的一个生产周期以上需要偿还的债务合计，其中包括长期借款、应付债务、长期应付款项等。

所有者权益 指企业投资人对企业净资产的所有权。企业净资产等于企业全部资产减去全部负债后的余额。其中包括投资者对企业的最初投入，以及资本公积金、盈余公积金和未分配利润，对股份制企业即为股东权益。

Explanatory Notes on Main Statistical Indicators

Gross Industrial Output Value is the total volume of industrial products sold or available for sale in value terms which reflects the total achievements and overall scale of industrial production during a given period. It includes the value of the finished products, which are not to be further processed in the enterprises and have been inspected, packed and put in storage, the income from external processing, and the difference of the value of semi – finished products between the beginning and end of the period. The gross industrial output value is calculated with "factory method", which is to consider an industrial enterprise as a whole and calculate by final results of its industrial production activities. It is not allowed to double count or to add up the production results of each workshop (or branch factory) within the enterprise.

Value Added of Industry refers to the final results of industrial production in money terms during the reference period.

Original Value of Fixed Assets refers to the total amount of the expenditure of industrial enterprises in building, purchasing, installing, reconstructing, expanding or technically transforming a fixed asset, which includes expenses on purchase, package, transportation, and installation, etc.

Net Value of Fixed Assets is obtained by deducting depreciation over years from the original value of fixed assets.

Total Pre – tax Profits refers to the sum of total profits, products sales tax and surcharges and the value added tax payable.

Main Business Revenue refers to the revenue of enterprises from selling products, providing labor services and etc.

Main Business Profit refers to the profit gained by the enterprises from the main business income of selling products and providing industrial services after deducting cost, charges and taxes.

Total Profits refer to the profits gained by the enterprises.

Value added Tax Payable refers to the amount of the value added tax which should be paid by the enterprises in the reporting period.

Total Assets refer to all assets which are owned or controlled by enterprises, including circulating assets, long term investment, fixed assets, intangible assets and deferred assets, other long term assets, and deferred taxes, etc. The summation of above items is equal to total assets shown in the balance sheets of the enterprises.

(1) Circulating assets refer to assets which can be cashed in or consumed in an operating cycle of one year or over one year, including cash, all kinds of deposits, short term investment, receivables, advance payment, stock, etc.

(2) Fixed assets refer to the sum of funds occupied by the net value of fixed assets, clearance of fixed assets, project under construction, losses of fixed assets to be processed..

(3) Intangible assets refer to assets without material form used by enterprises over a lone time, such as patents, non – patent technologies, trademarks, copyright, land use right, business reputation, etc.

Total Liabilities refer to the debts that enterprises are responsible for repayment, including liquid liabilities, long – term liabilities and deferred taxes, etc. Total liabilities correspond to the summation item of liabilities shown in the balance sheets of the enterprises.

(1) Liquid liabilities refer to enterprises´total debt payable within an operating cycle of one year or over one year, including short term loans, payables and advance payments, payable wages, taxes and profit, etc.

(2) Long term liabilities refers to total debt payable within an operating cycle of over one year, including long – term loans, payable liabilities, long – term payables, etc.

Creditors´Equity refers to investors´ownership of net assets of the enterprise. It is equal to the total assets of the enterprise minus its total liabilities, including the primary input from investors, capital accumulation fund, surplus accumulation fund and undistributed profit. It is the shareholder's equity in share – holding companies.

五、建筑业

CONSTRUCTION

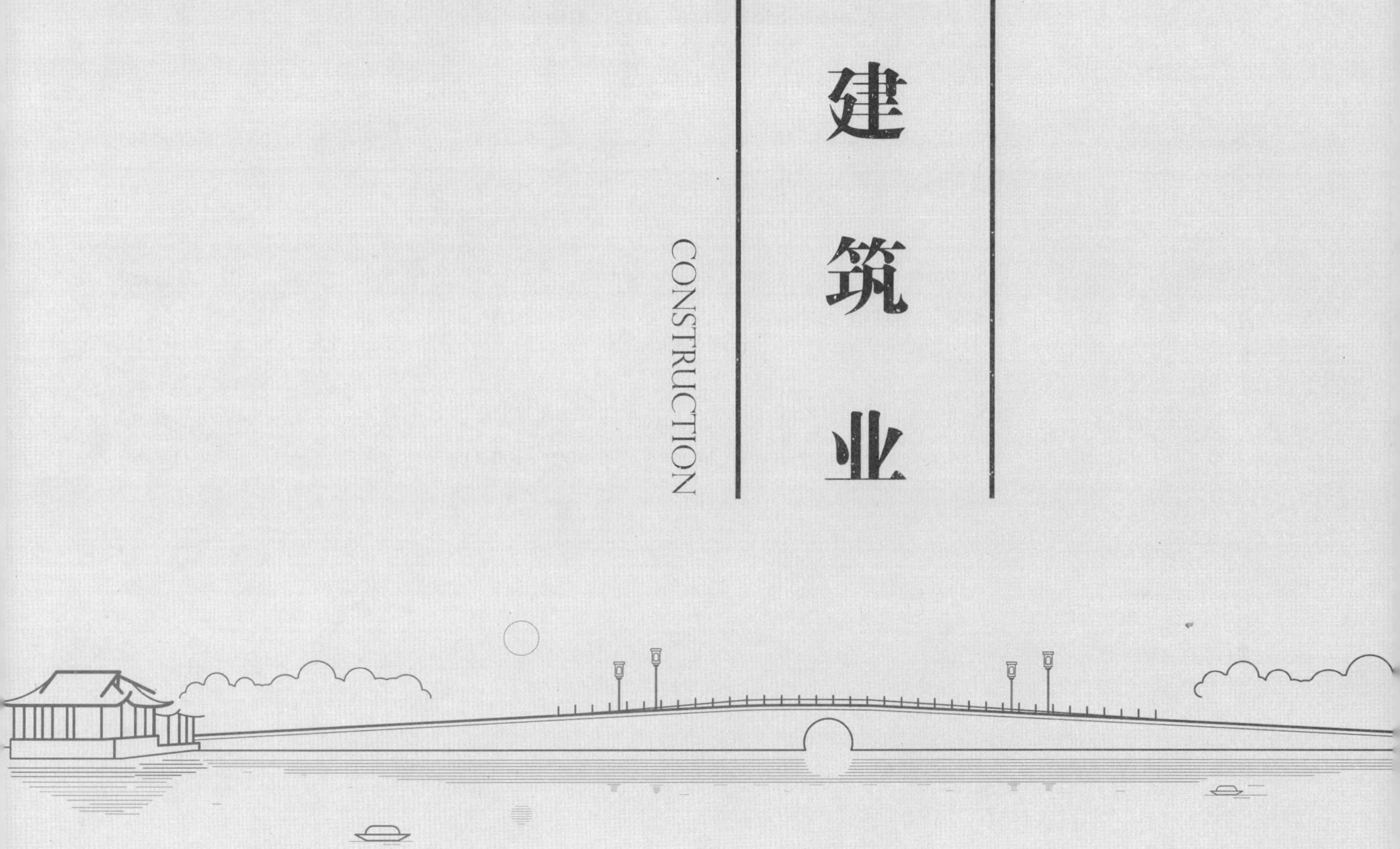

5 建 筑 业
Construction

主 要 统 计 指 标
Major Statistical Indicators

建筑业总产值	Gross Output Value of Construction	4923.98	亿元	(100 million yuan)
为上年	As Compared with the Preceding Year	107.6	%	(%)
房屋建筑施工面积	Floor Space of Buildings Under Construction	32203.78	万平方米	(10, 000 sq.m)
为上年	As Compared with the Preceding Year	109.3	%	(%)
房屋建筑竣工面积	Floor Space of Buildings Completed	6418.65	万平方米	(10, 000 sq.m)
为上年	As Compared with the Preceding Year	100.0	%	(%)

5-01 分地区建筑业总产值(2020年)
Gross Output Value of Construction by Region(2020)

单位:万元 (10000 yuan)

地 区	Region	建筑企业单位数(个) Number of Construction Enterprises (unit)	建筑业总产值 Gross Output Value of Construction	建筑工程产值 Output Value of Construction Projects	安装工程产值 Output value of Installation Projects	其他产值 Other Output Values
全 市	**Total**	**1728**	**49239845**	**43023525**	**5240694**	**975626**
市 区	Urban District	1538	47211754	41147295	5118636	945824
#上城区	Shangcheng	67	3324382	2056947	1233556	33879
下城区	Xiacheng	73	2755237	2534603	189172	31462
江干区	Jianggan	120	4325100	3709766	436577	178758
拱墅区	Gongshu	141	3769641	2763716	937053	68872
西湖区	Xihu	132	10271246	9708689	439866	122691
高新(滨江)区	Hi-Tech (Binjiang)	60	6298094	6049195	214673	34226
萧山区	Xiaoshan	323	7951802	6758053	883138	310611
余杭区	Yuhang	305	4528603	4124370	362175	42058
富阳区	Fuyang	153	1784126	1565379	182326	36421
临安区	Lin'an	86	1143714	954501	163060	26153
钱塘新区	Qiantang New Area	77	1059491	921758	77040	60693
西湖风景名胜区	The West Lake Scenic Zone	1	318	318	-	-
桐庐县	Tonglu	71	1158426	1084312	71833	2281
淳安县	Chun'an	70	326650	282932	16197	27522
建德市	Jiande	49	543015	508986	34029	-

5-02 建筑总专包

Financial Indicators on Construction Enterprises of

单位:万元

指标名称	Item	年末资产 Asset and Liabilities		
		流动资产合计 Circulating Funds	固定资产原价 Fixed Assets	资产合计 Total Assets
总　计	**Total**	**37520298**	**3457257**	**45717133**
#特、一、二级企业	of Which: Special Grade, First Grade, Second Grade	34824206	3011170	42574517
#国有及国有控股企业	of Which: State - owned and State Holding Enterprises	12596477	729371	15732959
一、按登记注册类型分组	**Grouped by Registration Status**			
内资企业	Domestic Funded	37394374	3437087	45567003
国有企业	State - owned	188461	13909	233618
集体企业	Collective - owned	2569	1481	3179
股份合作企业	Share - holding Cooperative Enterprises	32780	15088	45518
联营企业	Joint Venture			
有限责任公司	Limited Liability Corporations	16188167	994181	19299942
股份有限公司	Share - holding Corporations Ltd.	4216627	362707	5907475
私营企业	Private Enterprises	16765771	2049722	20077272
其他企业	Other Enterprises			
港、澳、台商投资企业	Funded from Hong Kong, Macao and Taiwan	92914	18577	115207
外商投资企业	Foreign Funded	33011	1592	34923
二、按国民经济行业分组	**Grouped by Sector**			
房屋建筑业	Housing Construction	18226907	1170074	22678415
土木工程建筑业	Civil Engineering Construction	13767035	1620255	16755465
建筑安装业	Installation of Lines, Pipelines and Equipment	2171792	259016	2479229
建筑装饰和其他建筑业	Fitting、Decoration of Building and Others Construction	3354565	407912	3804024

企业财务指标(2020 年)

General Contractors and Specialist Contractors(2020)

(10000 yuan)

负债 at Year - end		所有者权益合计 Owners´Equity		
流动负债合计 Current Liabilities	负债合计 Total Liabilities		实收资本 Paid - in Capitals	个人资本 State Capital
31351636	**33070346**	**12646788**	**7159307**	**2646035**
29483443	31121903	11452614	6196066	2206214
12127602	13062878	2670081	1292167	7284
31220697	32939401	12627603	7133722	2640527
176402	178402	55216	48930	-
1767	1767	1412	1218	-
31340	31340	14177	10000	10000
14776527	15693170	3606772	1685535	97952
3745483	4009316	1898159	602850	90324
12489179	13025405	7051867	4785189	2442251
106698	106704	8503	20095	3508
24242	24242	10681	5490	2000
15422787	16384315	6294100	3405628	1327010
11476198	12114469	4640996	2773654	879265
1693731	1723889	755340	402558	156971
2758920	2847672	956352	577468	282789

指标名称	Item	损益 Expenditure, Income	
		工程结算收入 Revenue of Project Settlement Accounts	工程结算成本 Costs of Project Settlement Accounts
总　计	**Total**	**47678310**	**43911621**
#特、一、二级企业	of Which: Special Grade, First Grade, Second Grade	44297172	40833081
#国有及国有控股企业	of Which: State－owned and State Holding Enterprises	13942849	13072596
一、按登记注册类型分组	**Grouped by Registration Status**		
内资企业	Domestic Funded	47586104	43826215
国有企业	State－owned	247364	230147
集体企业	Collective－owned	4678	3383
股份合作企业	Share－holding Cooperative Enterprises	17814	14252
联营企业	Joint Venture		
有限责任公司	Limited Liability Corporations	18344490	16440550
股份有限公司	Share－holding Corporations Ltd.	3594821	3248292
私营企业	Private Enterprises	25376938	23889590
其他企业	Other Enterprises		
港、澳、台商投资企业	Funded from Hong Kong, Macao and Taiwan	42618	38370
外商投资企业	Foreign Funded	49588	47035
二、按国民经济行业分组	**Grouped by Sector**		
房屋建筑业	Housing Construction	24174879	22268693
土木工程建筑业	Civil Engineering Construction	15918923	14746274
建筑安装业	Installation of Lines, Pipelines and Equipment	2886911	2623695
建筑装饰和其他建筑业	Fitting Decoration of Building and Others Construction	4697597	4272959

continued (10000 yuan)

及分配 and Distribution					
工程结算税金及附加 Taxes and Extra Charges Project Settlement Accounts	销售费用 Sales Expenses	管理费用 Management Expenditure	财务费用 Financial Expenditure	利润总额 Total Profits	应交所得税 Income Taxes Payable
136933	**142105**	**1509282**	**260854**	**1059324**	**205335**
124642	130257	1294732	245992	1002946	189675
27158	16072	373581	73622	416872	81571
136561	140876	1505218	260381	1062230	205010
864	842	8999	343	7295	1931
28	804	430		42	3
84	757	1873	785	399	100
44109	23269	487748	84049	444512	92433
6405	7851	130266	27237	180697	28347
85072	107353	875903	147975	429285	82197
253	1167	2388	371	-3516	172
119	62	1676	101	609	152
72465	16029	487152	158489	481104	86860
42624	31027	646838	69593	410350	83990
8484	14956	148917	15233	68698	12916
13361	80093	226374	17539	99172	21569

5-03 建筑业企业生产情况(2017-2020年)
Statistics on Production of Construction Enterprises(2017-2020)

指标名称	Item	2017	2018	2019	2020
一、建筑业合同情况	**Contract of Construction**				
签订的合同额 (万元)	Total Value of Contracts (10000 yuan)	80872710	87772266	100912299	113433283
上年结转合同额 (万元)	Value from Contracts Signed in 2016 (10000 yuan)	30503869	33731635	43492461	53861878
本年新签合同额 (万元)	Value from New Contracts Signed in 2017 (10000 yuan)	50368841	54040631	57419838	59571405
二、承包工程完成情况	**Completion of Contracted Projects**				
直接从建设单位承揽工程完成的产值 (万元)	Complete Output Value of Projects Contacted Directly from Investors (10000 yuan)	42804635	43606124	43690527	47053000
自行完成施工产值 (万元)	Own-completed Output Value (10000 yuan)	41202046	41057696	40837087	43764817
分包出去工程的产值 (万元)	Output Value of Out-sourced Projects (10000 yuan)	1602590	2548428	2853440	3288183
从建设单位以外承揽工程完成的产值 (万元)	Completed Output Value of Projects Contacted from Non-investors (10000 yuan)	2035210	3269828	4944966	5475028
建筑业总产值 (万元)	Gross Output Value (10000 yuan)	43237256	44327525	45782053	49239845
#装饰装修产值 (万元)	of Which: Output Value of Fitting and Decoration of Buildings (10000 yuan)	4800059	4199587	4394782	4395669
#在外省完成的产值 (万元)	of Which: Completed Output Value outside of Zhejiang Province (10000 yuan)	12005017	12095931	12442013	12008609
按构成分	by Structure				
建筑工程产值 (万元)	Output Value of Construction Projects (10000 yuan)	37584752	38230682	39495688	43023525
安装工程产值 (万元)	Output value of Installation Projects (10000 yuan)	4599347	4919966	4916534	5240694
其他产值 (万元)	Other Output Values (10000 yuan)	1053157	1176877	1369831	975626
竣工产值 (万元)	Output Value of Buildings Completed (10000 yuan)	21888828	21893653	20586072	21696056
房屋建筑施工面积 (万平方米)	Floor Space of Buildings Under Construction (10000 sq. m)	25617	26842	29470	32204
#本年新开工面积 (万平方米)	of Which: Beginning Projects in this Year (10000 sq. m)	8869	10946	10214	9444
房屋建筑竣工面积 (万平方米)	Floor space of Buildings Completed (10000 sq. m)	8108	6764	6417	6419
三、年末自有施工机械设备	**Machinery and Equipment Owned (year-end)**				
年末自有施工机械设备净值 (万元)	Net Value of Machinery and Equipment Owned (10000 yuan)	822402	742142	669716	645089
年末自有施工机械设备总台数 (台)	Number of Machinery and Equipment Owned (set)	162507	149125	147904	145649
年末自有施工机械设备总功率 (千瓦)	Total Power of Machinery and Equipment Owned (1000 kW)	3264229	3046124	2706236	3345274
四、就业人员情况	**Number of Employed Persons**				
计算劳动生产率的平均人数 (人)	Average Employed Persons Overall Labor Productivity (person)	1239143	1221420	1230569	1246941
年末就业人员数 (人)	Employed Persons (year-end) (person)	1224693	1167509	1150807	1174958

5-04 具有资质等级建筑业企业主要生产经营指标(2014-2020年)
Major Economic Indicators of Qualified Construction Enterprises(2014-2020)

单位:万元 (10000 yuan)

指标名称 Item	2014	2015	2016	2017	2018	2019	2020
企业个数(个) Nomber of Enterprises (unit)	1476	1480	1474	1410	1541	1606	1728
亏损企业个数(个) Loss Making Enterprises (unit)	224	236	256	253	329	351	482
建筑业总产值 Gross Output Value of Construction	39713876	40975734	41052972	43237256	44327525	45782053	49239845
竣工产值 Output Value of Buildings Completed	21665909	25994238	23746502	21888828	21893653	20586072	21696056
房屋建筑施工面积(万平方米) Floor Space of Buildings Under Construction (10,000 sq. m)	29581	28124	27221	25617	26842	29470	32204
房屋建筑竣工面积(万平方米) Floor Space of Buildings Completed (10,000 sq. m)	9514	10137	9754	8108	6764	6417	6419
固定资产原价 Orginal Value of Fixed Assets	3393624	3488088	3239557	3552611	3352353	3429694	3457257
实收资本合计 Total Capital Hold	5493120	5799067	5932301	6364527	6756936	6792046	7159307
流动资产合计 Circulating Funds	22168981	23867659	25412440	27695056	30371728	10116084	37520298
其中:存货 Stock	5900549	6360774	6751318	7530374	7823812	7414341	6720337
在建工程 Projects wnder Construction	313490	211195	175075	216619	262751	259028	279576
固定资产合计 Fixed Assets	2826312	2829483	2067226	2292476	1678207	-	-
年末负债合计 Total Liabilities at Year-end	18186469	19365824	20274680	22067498	25107296	29000375	33070346
流动负债合计 Circulating Funds	16894050	17964478	18752593	20579766	23735159	27570766	31351636
所有者权益合计 Crediors´Equity	9656533	10453107	10883382	12196061	12658441	12210275	12646788
营业收入 Revenue of Business	34704862	35568492	36069232	36965857	40293678	44677368	48165053
营业成本 Operating Costs	31501139	32365477	33270805	34248463	37687072	41764885	45156343
营业税金及附加 Main Sales Tax and Extra Charges	1029405	1020437	541967	199457	157132	146939	157582
管理费用 Management Expenditure	918904	965161	1042943	1163505	1263222	1399064	1509282
财务费用 Financial Expenditure	330680	301313	258903	271466	243248	298729	260854
营业利润 Management Profits	888932	883320	917779	1043476	912880	944590	1025402
利润总额 Total Profits	913117	895484	950047	1075458	983741	977498	1059324

主要统计指标解释

建筑业总产值　建筑业总产值是以货币表现的建筑业企业在一定时期内生产的建筑业产品和服务的总和。建筑业总产值包括建筑工程产值、安装工程产值和其他产值三部分内容。

房屋建筑施工面积　指报告期内施过工的全部房屋建筑面积，它包括本期新开工的面积、上期跨入本期继续施工的房屋面积、上期停缓建在本期恢复施工的房屋面积、本期竣工的房屋面积以及本期施工后又停缓建的房屋面积。

房屋建筑竣工面积　指在报告期内房屋建筑按照设计要求已全部完工，达到了使用条件，经检查验收鉴定合格的房屋建筑面积。

工程结算收入（主营业务收入）　指本企业承包工程实现的工程价款结算收入以及向发包单位收取的除工程价款以外按规定列作营业收入的各种款项，如临时设施费、劳动保险费、施工机构调迁费等以及向发包单位收取的各种索赔款。

工程结算成本（主营业务成本）　指在报告期内与发包单位办理工程价款结算的已完工程实际成本。

Explanatory Notes on Main Statistical Indicators

Gross Output Value of Construction refers to the total of construction products and services, expressed in money terms, produced or rendered by construction enterprises in a given period. It includes the output value of construction projects, installation projects and others.

Floor Space of Buildings Under Construction refers to the floor space of all buildings under construction during the reference period, including the floor space of buildings those are newly started construction, those were started earlier and continues construction; those were suspended in the previous period but resumed construction in this period, those are completed in this period, and those are under construction but suspended in this period.

Floor Space of Buildings Completed refers to the floor space of buildings that are completed in the reference period in accordance with the design requirements, up to the service standard, and qualified after inspection and acceptance.

Project Settlement Income refers to the income received by the construction enterprise from the contracted project through settlement procedures, and other charges to the contractee listed as operational costs, such as temporary facility fee, labor insurance premium, moving cost of construction equipment, as well as various types of claims to the contractee.

Project Settlement Cost refers to the actual cost of completed projects that have been settled prices with the contractee during the reporting period.

六、交通运输 邮电

TRANSPORTATION, POST AND TELECOMMUNICATIONS

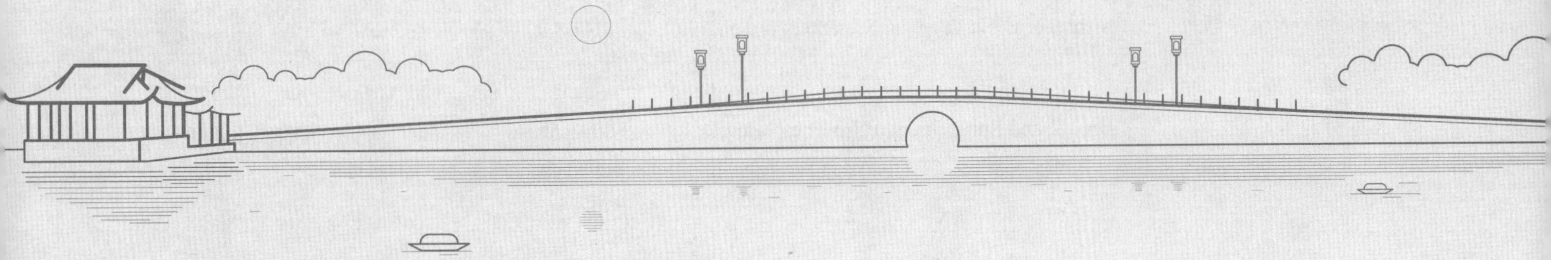

6 交通运输、邮电
Transportation, Post and Telecommunications

主要统计指标
Major Statistical Indicators

客运量	Passenger Traffic	12183	万人次	(10, 000 person-times)
为上年	As Compared with the Preceding Year	58.3	%	(%)
货运量	Freight Traffic	41944	万吨	(10, 000 tons)
为上年	As Compared with the Preceding Year	109.1	%	(%)
邮电业务收入	Business Income of Post & Telecommunication Service	662.09	亿元	(100 million yuan)
为上年	As Compared with the Preceding Year	108.9	%	(%)
年末固定电话用户数	Number of Local Telephone Subscribers(year-end)	204.55	万户	(10, 000 subscribers)
年末移动电话用户数	Number of Mobile Telephone Subscribers(year-end)	1868.9	万户	(10, 000 subscribers)
年末宽带业务户数	Broadband Subscribers of Internet(year-end)	547.58	万户	(10, 000 subscribers)

6－01 客货运输量(2014－2020年)

Total Passenger and Freight Traffic(2014－2020)

项 目 Item	2014	2015	2016	2017	2018	2019	2020
一、客运量合计(万人次) Passenger Traffic(10000 person－times)	**24070**	**23942**	**20541**	**22289**	**20121**	**20888**	**12183**
铁路客运量 Passenger Railways	4689	5282	6053	6807	7535	8874	5895
民航客运量 Passenger Civil Aviation	1334	1472	1622	1825	1956	2044	1414
公路客运量 Passenger Highways	17431	16591	12282	13019	10027	9360	4535
水路客运量 Passenger Waterways	616	597	584	638	603	610	339
二、旅客周转量合计(万人公里) Total Passenger－kilometers(10000 passenger－km)	**1151642**	**1085769**	**943874**	**905008**	**829027**	**700446**	**387013**
公路旅客周转量 Passenger－kilometers Highways	1143750	1078054	936574	897116	821267	689970	381790
水路旅客周转量 Passenger－kilometers Waterways	7892	7715	7300	7892	7760	10476	5223
三、货运量合计(万吨) Total Freight Traffic(10000 tons)	**29335**	**29384**	**30170**	**34785**	**35180**	**36384**	**41944**
铁路货运量 Freight Railways	312	307	274	328	306	537	578
民航货运量 Freight Civil Aviation	24	25	29	35	38	41	46
公路货运量 Freight Highways	23202	23800	25194	29378	30593	31732	34837
水路货运量 Freight Waterways	5797	5251	4673	5044	4244	4073	6483
四、货运周转量合计(万吨公里) Total Freight Ton－kilometers(10000 ton－km)	**4550550**	**4629814**	**4796677**	**5304007**	**5440793**	**5534460**	**10070617**
公路货物周转量 Freight Ton－kilometers Highways	2760873	3003728	3217983	3615581	3875561	3928822	4599433
水路货物周转量 Freight Ton－kilometers Waterways	1789677	1626086	1578694	1688426	1565232	1605638	5471184

6-02 货运量(1978-2020年)

Total Freight Traffic (1978-2020)

单位:万吨 (10000 tons)

年份 Year	合计 Total	铁路 Railways	公路 Highways	水路 Waterways	民航 Civil Aviation
1978	1706	418	633	655	
1979	1983	440	771	772	
1980	2070	444	762	864	
1981	1972	449	886	637	
1982	2261	485	795	981	
1983	2299	488	838	973	
1984	2385	510	888	987	
1985	2488	524	890	1074	
1986	2558	551	874	1133	
1987	2515	574	899	1041	1
1988	2416	555	823	1037	1
1989	7377	539	5095	1743	
1990	6522	449	4479	1594	
1991	7017	451	4891	1675	
1992	8434	534	6063	1836	1
1993	9082	580	6353	2148	1
1994	8962	491	6563	1907	1
1995	10347	482	7021	2842	2
1996	10962	445	7735	2780	2
1997	11015	406	7932	2676	1
1998	11329	418	8196	2713	2
1999	11684	403	8037	3241	3
2000	11459	417	7865	3173	4
2001	12443	452	8588	3398	5
2002	14347	446	10391	3504	6
2003	16815	438	12118	4253	6
2004	18895	480	13117	5289	9
2005	19909	525	13539	5833	12
2006	20924	569	14588	5754	13
2007	22569	573	16484	5500	12
2008	22550	483	16822	5232	13
2009	22372	427	16536	5396	13
2010	25915	379	19148	6371	17
2011	28831	331	21755	6727	18
2012	30089	322	23243	6503	20
2013	30734	284	23884	6545	22
2014	29335	312	23202	5797	24
2015	29384	307	23800	5251	25
2016	30170	274	25194	4673	29
2017	34785	328	29378	5044	35
2018	35180	306	30593	4244	38
2019	36384	537	31732	4073	41
2020	41944	578	34837	6483	46

6－03　客运量(1978－2020年)

Total Passenger Traffic (1978－2020)

单位:万人次　　　　(10,000 person－times)

年　份 Year	合　计 Total	铁　路 Railways	公　路 Highways	水　路 Waterways	民　航 Civil Aviation
1978	2878	485	–	–	3
1979	3122	560	1829	729	4
1980	3905	672	2358	870	5
1981	4484	769	2857	850	8
1982	5263	813	3377	1064	9
1983	5451	878	3530	1035	8
1984	6056	983	3912	1151	10
1985	6724	1004	4595	1111	14
1986	6765	1034	4768	941	22
1987	6905	1127	4852	896	30
1988	6593	1237	4445	877	34
1989	7493	1182	5488	801	22
1990	8119	1056	6350	691	22
1991	10701	1062	8876	710	53
1992	13358	1083	11538	670	67
1993	13070	1139	11403	454	74
1994	13373	1230	11669	390	84
1995	16620	1242	14921	339	118
1996	16714	1112	15184	273	145
1997	17034	1040	15623	260	111
1998	17395	1120	15925	235	115
1999	17882	1168	16369	235	110
2000	18607	1202	17102	179	124
2001	20342	1342	18707	148	145
2002	21089	1574	19213	108	194
2003	21348	1534	19510	89	215
2004	22833	1908	20372	237	316
2005	24124	2011	21431	304	378
2006	25810	2124	22961	267	458
2007	28026	2255	24836	306	629
2008	29084	2498	25630	277	679
2009	30116	2494	26454	372	796
2010	33772	2741	29671	456	904
2011	34778	2962	30305	595	916
2012	35819	3112	31126	592	989
2013	36409	3717	30994	547	1151
2014	24070	4689	17431	616	1334
2015	23942	5282	16591	597	1472
2016	20541	6053	12282	584	1622
2017	22289	6807	13019	638	1825
2018	20121	7535	10027	603	1956
2019	20888	8874	9360	610	2044
2020	12183	5895	4535	339	1414

注:1990年以前为交通系统数,1990年起为全社会数(后同)。2014年起运输量统计方法调整。

a) The data in the table only included transportation department before 1990, while extended to the whole society after 1990 (the same below). The statistical method has been adjusted since 2014.

6－04 分地区交通

Statistics on Traffic and

项 目	Item	全市 Whole City	市区 Urban District
铁路旅客运量 （万人）	Passenger Railways (10,000 Persons)	5895	5646
铁路货物运量 （万吨）	Freight Railways (10,000 tons)	578	306
公路客运量 （万人）	Passenger Highways (10,000 Persons)	4535	2935
公路货运量 （万吨）	Freight Highways (10,000 tons)	34837	22130
民用航空客运量 （万人）	Passenger Civil Aviation (10,000 Persons)	1414	1414
民用航空货邮运量（万吨）	Freight Civil Aviation (10,000 tons)	46	46
水路客运量 （万人）	Passenger Waterways (10,000 Persons)	339	160
水路货运量 （万吨）	Freight Waterways (10,000 tons)	6483	–
非营运汽车拥有量 （辆）	Possession of Non – Business Vehicles(year – end) (Unit)	2858459	2597085
#私人汽车拥有量 （辆）	in which:Possession of Private Vehicles (Unit)	2546018	2301539

运输情况(2020年)
Transport by Region(2020)

萧山区 Xiaoshan	余杭区 Yuhang	富阳区 Fuyang	临安区 Lin'an	桐庐县 Tonglu	淳安县 Chun'an	建德市 Jiande
–	83	75	–	102	85	62
197	108	–	–	–	86	186
166	72	58	106	393	310	897
2865	1749	1842	1384	10895	573	1239
1414	–	–	–	–	–	–
46	–	–	–	–	–	–
13	–	–	7	18	139	21
–	–	–	–	–	–	–
542624	459552	172545	150344	97942	69883	93549
483991	418630	158841	138239	89752	67043	87684

6-05 运输线路长度(2014-2020年)

Length of Transportation Routes(2014-2020)

单位:公里 (km)

项 目 Item	2014	2015	2016	2017	2018	2019	2020
公路通车里程 (公里) Length of Highways (km)	16024	16210	16306	16424	16520	16667	16919
#高速公路 (公里) Expressway (km)	582	615	632	632	632	632	801
一级公路 (公里) First Class Highways (km)	803	836	832	835	840	877	912
二级公路 (公里) Second Class Highways (km)	1570	1616	1615	1631	1634	1759	1700
内河通航里程 (公里) Length of Navigable Inland Waterways (km)	2006	2006	2006	2006	2006	2006	2006
民用航空航线 (条) Number of Civil Aviation Routes (line)	222	235	240	286	292	301	336
国内航线 (条) Domestic Routes (line)	186	196	195	229	234	232	261
国际航线 (条) International Routes (line)	28	32	38	49	51	63	69
地区航线 (条) Regional Routes (line)	8	7	7	8	7	6	6
民用航空通航城市 (个) Number of Cities Can Arrive by Civil Aviation	119	129	138	160	172	183	187
国内城市 (个) Domestic Cities	92	99	103	117	123	126	132
港澳台城市 (个) Hongkong, Macau and Taiwan	6	5	5	5	5	5	5
国际城市 (个) International Cities	27	30	35	43	44	52	50

6-06 民用机动车辆年末拥有量(2014-2020年末)
Total Number of Motor Vehicles End of the Year(End of 2014-2020)

单位:辆 (unit)

项目	Item	2014	2015	2016	2017	2018	2019	2020
全市合计	**Total**	**2696340**	**2733537**	**2633541**	**2793595**	**2880804**	**2975762**	**3118978**
一、汽车	Vehicles	2184000	2244767	2341536	2451226	2571230	2671807	2813576
1.载客汽车	Passenger Vehicles	1992112	2056143	2127393	2210376	2310070	2399022	2497100
其中:大型	Large	17485	18657	20017	20880	21546	20907	20470
中型	Medium	14411	10797	10035	9365	8499	7628	7394
小型	Small	1936836	2002730	2076098	2157089	2258635	2351862	2451908
微型	Mini	23380	23959	21243	23042	21390	18625	17328
其中:轿车	Car	1799442	1773864	1483128	1530805	1548328	1610070	1641979
2.载货汽车	Trucks	180475	177674	202775	229038	248614	259746	302251
其中:重型	Heavy	39998	41999	49480	57794	64289	71102	92122
中型	Medium	14444	8851	9422	9213	8147	6611	7065
轻型	Light	125508	126321	143441	161703	175945	181872	202969
微型	Mini	525	503	432	328	233	161	95
3.其他汽车	Vehicles	11413	10950	11368	11812	12546	13039	14225
其中:三轮汽车	Vehicles	182	179	139	102	69	44	26
低速货车	Low Speed Trucks	416	549	806	792	779	724	680
二、摩托车	Motorcycles	505360	481230	282477	329905	292662	281403	273133
1.普通	Genera	481027	463722	277238	324469	288562	276568	267062
2.轻便	Light	24333	17508	5239	5436	4100	4835	6071
三、挂车	Trailer	6939	7464	9457	12396	16846	22493	32220
四、其他类型	Other	41	76	71	68	66	59	49

6－07 邮政、电信主要指标(2014－2020年)
Main Indicators of Post and Telecommunications(2014－2020)

项目 Item	2014	2015	2016	2017	2018	2019	2020
邮政业务总收入(万元) Total Business Income of Postal Service (10,000 yuan)	1176704	1596884	2151732	2750911	3646724	4023039	4500008
#快递业务收入(万元) Business Income of Express Mail Service (10,000 yuan)	1022279	1437542	1956944	2510479	2966169	3267926	3669946
电信业务收入(亿元) Total Business Income of Telecommunications Services (100 million yuan)	170.08	173.66	190.83	192.68	199.70	205.48	212.09
函件(万件) Number of Letters (10,000 pcs)	17412	13256	9634	11656	8768	5508	4910
订销报纸累计份额(万份) Number of Newspapers (10,000 pcs)	29214	29304	24067	24273	23497	22342	21382
订销杂志累计份额(万份) Number of Publications (10,000 pcs)	1437	1310	1061	1010	1047	895	786
包裹(万件) Number of Parcels (10,000 pcs)	113	81	49	51	50	63	44
快递(万份) Pieces of Express Mail Service (10,000 copies)	84563	125707	180473	232630	258910	265666	300081
#国际及港澳台快递(万份) Pieces of Express to overseas and HongKong,macao,Taiwan (10,000 copies)	1731	2046	2495	4065	11005	13741	30034
纪特邮票(万枚) Stamps for Colletion (10,000 pcs)	1151	1231	1295	969	210	92860 (套)	281
年末固定电话用户数(万户) Number of Local Telephone Subscribers(year－end) (10,000 subscribers)	311.14	293.44	265.70	259.37	241.84	233.08	204.55
年末移动电话用户数(万户) Number of Subscribers of Mobile Telephone(year－end) (10,000 subscribers)	1561.71	1726.76	1734.41	1724.17	1913.91	1817.85	1868.9
年末宽带业务户数(万户) Number of Wide Band Subscribers (10,000 subscribers)	278.78	294.96	443.57	508.69	537.73	554.51	547.58

注:邮政业务总收入含规模以上快递企业。

a)The total business income of postal services included the express enterprises above designated sice.

主要统计指标解释

货(客)运量 指在一定时期内,各种运输工具实际运送的货物(旅客)数量。是反映运输业为国民经济和人民生活服务的数量指标,也是制定和检查运输生产计划、研究运输发展规模和速度的重要指标。货运按吨计算,客运按人计算。货物不论运输距离长短、货物类别,均按实际重量统计。旅客不论行程远近或票价多少,均按一人一次作为客运量统计;半价票、小孩票也按一人统计。

货物(旅客)周转量 指在一定时期内,由各种运输工具运送的货物(旅客)数量与其相应运输距离的乘积之总和。是反映运输业生产总成果的重要指标,也是编制和检查运输生产计划,计算运输效率、劳动生产率以及核算运输单位成本的主要基础资料。通常以吨公里和人公里为计算单位。计算货物周转量通常按发出站与到达站之间的最短距离,也就是计费距离计算。

邮政、电信业务总量 指以货币形式表示的邮政、电信通信企业为社会提供各类邮政、电信通信服务的总数量。计算方法为各类业务的实物量分别乘以相应的不变单价,求出各类业务的货币量加总求得。没有不变单价的业务按其业务收入直接相加。

移动电话用户 指在电信运营企业营业网点办理开户登记手续,通过移动电话交换机进入移动电话网,占用移动电话号码的各类电话用户。包括各类签约用户、智能网预付费用户、无线上网卡用户。

Explanatory Notes on Main Statistical Indicators

Freight(passenger) Transport refers to the volume of freight (passenger) transported with various means in a certain period. It provides a quantitative measure to show how the transport industry serves the national economy and people, and is also an important indicator for working out and checking the transportation plan and studying its development scale and speed. Freight transport is calculated in tons and passenger transport is d in the number of persons. Despite the type of freight and traveling distance, the freight transport is calculated in the actual weight of the goods. Despite the traveling distance and ticket price, the passenger transport is calculated by the principle that one person is counted only once in one travel. The passenger with a half – price ticket or a child ticket is also calculated as one person.

Freight Ton – kilometers(Passenger – kilometers) refers to the sum of the products of the volume of transported cargo (passengers) multiplying by the transport distance. It is an important indicator to show the total results of the transport industry, to prepare and examine the transport plan and to measure the efficiency, the labour productivity and the unit cost of transport. Normally, it is calculated using ton – kilometer and passenger – kilometer as calculation units, and by the shortest distance between the departure station and the terminal station (i. e. , the payable distance).

Business Volume of Post and Telecommunication refers to the total amount of postal and telecommunication services, expressed in value terms, provided by the post and telecommunications departments for society. Business volume of post and telecommunication is the sum of each service in kind multiplying with its correspondent unit price(constant price). Businesses without constant unit price are added directly according to their business income.

Mobile Telephone Subscribers refers to persons who have gone through registration procedures in the operation points of enterprises engaged in telecommunications and are hence connected with the mobile telephone communication network through the mobile telephone switchboards and occupy mobile phone numbers. Included are various types of subscriber, prepaid users for intelligent network and wireless network card users.

七、固定资产投资

INVESTMENT IN FIXED ASSETS

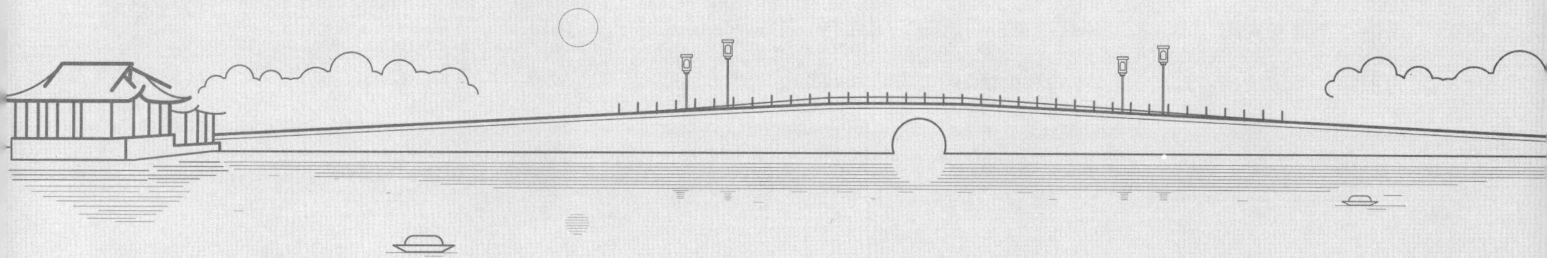

7 固定资产投资
Investment in Fixed Assets

主要统计指标
Major Statistical Indicators

固定资产投资额为上年	Investment in Fixed Assets As Compared with the Preceding Year	106.8	%	(%)
第一产业为上年	Primary Industry As Compared with the Preceding Year	260.9	%	(%)
第二产业为上年	Secondary Industry As Compared with the Preceding Year	106.2	%	(%)
第三产业为上年	Tertiary Industry As Compared with the Preceding Year	106.8	%	(%)
房地产企业营业收入	Operating Revenue of Real Estate Enterprise	3842	亿元	(100 million yuan)
为上年	As Compared with the Preceding Year	126.7	%	(%)
房地产企业单位数	Number of Enterprises for Real Estate Developement	1613	个	(unit)
为上年	As Compared with the Preceding Year	98.9	%	(%)

7－01　固定资产投资总额(1979－2020 年)

Investment in Fixed Assets (1979－2020)

单位:万元　　　　(10000 yuan)

年　份 Year	固定资产投资 Investment in Fixed Assets	房地产开发投资 Investment in Real Estate Development	项目投资 Projects Investment	基础设施投资 Investment in Infrastructure	工业投资 Industrial Investment	民间投资 Nongovernment Investment
1979	34407					
1980	45752					
1981	51538					
1982	66123					
1983	68306					
1984	93244					
1985	141889					
1986	182398					
1987	200516					
1988	205967					
1989	202131					
1990	229214	20409				
1991	255696	25247				
1992	384136	41886				
1993	825382	218006				
1994	1059437	320532				
1995	1566280	527985				
1996	1819333	572749				
1997	2139012	572686				
1998	2681740	666244				
1999	3233609	848441				
2000	3766473	1015347				
2001	4634929	1409132				
2002	5623366	1982517				
2003	8952090	2588452	6363638	2907234	3194960	4192567
2004	11081993	3285409	7796584	3254648	4357950	5761350
2005	12777972	4105706	8672266	3715525	4438723	6723758
2006	13734482	4426534	9307948	3871462	4640261	7551249
2007	15837775	5187904	10649871	4056241	5271141	8215570
2008	18822936	6154060	12668876	5410313	5693385	9450542
2009	21951706	7046752	14904954	6018416	6091653	11127373
2010	26518839	9561970	16956869	6452236	6855587	13680327
2011	31000218	13027234	17972984	6437025	7474806	17507040
2012	37227544	15973611	21253933	7785196	8518653	20595909
2013	42638732	18532841	24105891	8524663	9104614	22536325
2014	49527010	23010823	26516187	10055306	9133973	28438054
2015	55563183	24720743	30842440	13551793	9300133	29768831
2016	58424194	26064090	32360104	16305335	8839451	30067802
2017	58566453	27340047	31226406	15970399	8614761	33005389
2018 比上年增长 Increased over the Previous year in 2018	10.8	12.2	9.3	26.9	－11.3	10.1
2019	11.6	10.7	12.6	5.2	5.6	4.8
2020	6.8	5.3	8.5	7.7	6.9	3.4

注:1. 2011 年起固定资产投资口径由计划总投资 500 万元以上项目投资及房地产开发投资构成。

2. 项目投资统计口径调整,计划投资 500－5000 万项目,由原先形象进度法改为财务支出法统计。2018 年起比上年增长按可比口径计算。

3. 2018 年起基础设施投资口径调整,教育、卫生等剔除并单独设为公共服务投资。

a) Since 2011, the date of investment in fixed Assets was composed by investment projects and investment in Real Estate development of which each is over 5 million yuan.

b) The statistical caliber of project investment was adjusted, the projects which planned to invest 5 million－50 million, it was changed fron progress method to financial expenditure method. The gronth was calculated at comparable caliber Since 2018.

c) Since 2018, The statistical caliber of infrastructure investment was adjusted, education and health were excluded, and set them as public service investment.

7-02 市区固定资产投资总额(1990-2020年)

Investment in Fixed Assets of Urban District (1990-2020)

单位:万元 (10000 yuan)

年份 Year	固定资产投资 Investment in Fixed Assets	房地产开发投资 Investment in Real Estate Development	项目投资 Projects Investment	基础设施投资 Investment in Infrastructure	工业投资 Industrial Investment	民间投资 Nongovernment Investment
1990		12750				
1991		16509				
1992		29784				
1993		115116				
1994		189357				
1995		375816				
1996		439245				
1997		445316				
1998		538499				
1999		636705				
2000		737950				
2001		1255605				
2002		1724128				
2003	7409538	2176433	5233105	2535843	2424383	3316886
2004	8963515	3088508	6153009	2624214	3299235	5238005
2005	10358519	3485810	6872709	3071506	3247399	5802542
2006	10944075	3653393	7290682	3150192	3289532	5559199
2007	12630099	4298687	8331412	3396807	3617512	6218211
2008	15184281	5269947	9914334	4726734	3676567	7076219
2009	17797778	6261562	11536216	5070500	3821313	8632900
2010	21437496	8486495	12951001	5438685	4293707	10332997
2011	25202394	11409566	13792828	5451654	4801419	13302115
2012	30160782	13749412	16411370	6495070	5554286	15669790
2013	34029665	15978470	18051195	6728552	5787728	16735292
2014	42572154	21128840	21443314	8010162	7100359	24220917
2015	47507571	22981761	24525810	10960519	6835700	25114041
2016	49572744	24325359	25247385	13229143	6173050	24924679
2017	52395657	26449190	25946467	13447972	6718135	29402238
2018 比上年增长 Increased over the Previous year in 2018	11.5	11.7	11.4	31.1	-12.6	10.2
2019	11.8	11.0	12.7	5.6	5.5	5.1
2020	7.3	5.7	9.0	9.2	4.3	3.5

7-03 固定资产投资总额发展指数(2011-2020年)

Indices of Investment in Fixed Assets(2011-2020)

(上年=100) (Preceding Year=100)

年份 Year	固定资产投资 Investment in Fixed Assets	第一产业 Primary Industry	第二产业 Secondary Industry	第三产业 Primary Industry	民间投资 Nongovernment Investment	房地产开发投资 Investment in Real Estate Development	基础设施投资 Investment in Infrastructure	工业投资 Industrial Investment	高新技术产业投资 High tech industry investment
2011	116.9	183.3	108.9	119.6	128.0	136.2	99.8	109.0	-
2012	120.1	55.5	114.0	122.3	117.6	122.6	120.9	114.0	-
2013	114.5	196.9	107.0	116.7	109.4	116.0	109.5	106.9	-
2014	116.2	227.0	100.3	120.2	126.2	124.2	118.0	100.3	-
2015	112.2	165.0	101.8	114.3	104.7	107.4	134.8	101.8	-
2016	105.1	125.1	95.2	107.0	101.0	105.4	120.3	95.0	-
2017	101.4	111.2	100.9	101.5	110.4	104.9	100.1	100.5	-
2018	110.8	28.7	88.1	114.2	110.1	112.2	126.9	88.7	-
2019	111.6	61.3	106.2	112.2	104.8	110.7	105.2	105.6	108.4
2020	106.8	260.9	106.2	106.8	103.4	105.3	107.7	106.9	110.0

7－04 分地区固定资产投资发展指数(2011－2020年)

Indices of Investment in Fixed Assets by Region(2011－2020)

(上年=100)　　(Preceding Year=100)

年份 Year	全市 Whole City	上城区 Shangcheng	下城区 Xiacheng	江干区 Jianggan	拱墅区 Gongshu	西湖区 Xihu	高新(滨江)区 Hi－Tech (Binjiang)	萧山区 Xiaoshan
2011	116.9	67.8	101.3	119.1	135.3	120.6	115.9	115.0
2012	120.1	109.4	116.6	129.8	120.7	121.5	118.9	118.9
2013	114.5	107.2	125.6	92.2	125.1	124.5	111.7	118.4
2014	116.2	121.6	66.5	118.7	124.6	118.4	118.9	116.4
2015	112.2	114.1	112.5	118.5	118.9	107.2	76.5	113.2
2016	105.1	123.1	129.3	101.3	97.8	80.1	126.5	112.0
2017	101.4	111.3	102.0	87.4	75.2	120.5	79.8	104.3
2018	110.8	114.3	76.9	102.1	121.2	100.0	116.8	111.7
2019	111.6	101.1	130.2	120.5	125.8	94.9	112.1	113.8
2020	106.8	93.2	133.2	108.1	87.4	102.5	90.4	108.0

(上年=100)　　7－04 续表 continued　　(Preceding Year=100)

年份 Year	余杭区 Yuhang	富阳区 Fuyang	临安区 Lin'an	钱塘新区 Qiantang New Area	西湖风景名胜区 The West Lake Scenic Zone	桐庐县 Tonglu	淳安县 Chun'an	建德市 Jiande
2011	118.8	106.5	118.6	116.5	46.7	115.7	118.9	120.9
2012	123.9	122.5	121.6	120.7	74.2	121.9	122.0	120.8
2013	123.3	122.4	119.2	118.7	712.7	122.2	123.1	122.3
2014	124.5	122.0	120.1	106.3	125.3	121.5	121.5	121.8
2015	117.0	115.3	117.1	68.2	136.9	117.9	104.3	122.7
2016	113.1	100.2	115.0	101.2	176.4	102.5	106.0	116.7
2017	108.0	87.4	109.2	111.2	28.8	89.5	108.8	115.1
2018	110.0	100.5	111.2	110.6	36.2	89.3	85.4	118.6
2019	107.4	122.0	130.2	100.1	39.1	118.7	92.2	112.7
2020	107.6	130.7	124.5	115.0	39.9	123.4	92.6	90.1

7-05 三次产业固定资产投资(1978-2020年)

Investment in Fixed Assets Grouped by Three Industries (1978-2020)

单位:万元 (10000 yuan)

年份 Year	绝对数(万元) Absolute Figure(10000 yuan)				比重(以投资总额为100) Proportion(%)		
	合计 Total	第一产业 Primary Industry	第二产业 Secondary Industry	第三产业 Tertiary Industry	第一产业 Primary Industry	第二产业 Secondary Industry	第三产业 Tertiary Industry
1978	23941	2174	14455	7312	9.1	60.4	30.5
1979	34407	2454	19927	12026	7.1	57.9	35.0
1980	45752	1608	26211	17933	3.5	57.3	39.2
1981	51538	850	29176	21512	1.6	56.6	41.8
1982	66123	1352	37648	27123	2.0	57.0	41.0
1983	68306	1297	37823	29186	1.9	55.4	42.7
1984	93244	2831	46619	43794	3.0	50.0	47.0
1985	141889	3207	71608	67074	2.3	50.5	47.2
1986	182398	2265	94394	85739	1.2	51.8	47.0
1987	200516	2994	106600	90922	1.5	53.2	45.3
1988	205967	4746	118736	82485	2.3	57.6	40.1
1989	202131	3038	117651	81442	1.5	58.2	40.3
1990	229214	2181	126263	100770	1.0	55.1	43.9
1991	255696	3204	132303	120189	1.3	51.7	47.0
1992	384136	4424	206659	173053	1.2	53.8	45.0
1993	825382	5650	346416	473316	0.7	42.0	57.3
1994	1059437	3905	354672	700860	0.4	33.5	66.1
1995	1566280	5821	534687	1025772	0.4	34.1	65.5
1996	1819333	3100	640273	1175960	0.2	35.2	64.6
1997	2139012	1712	595966	1541334	-	27.9	72.1
1998	2681740	4053	706948	1970739	0.2	26.4	73.4
1999	3233609	23546	764309	2445754	0.7	23.6	75.7
2000	3766473	774	844334	2921365	-	22.4	77.6
2001	4634929	595	953494	3680840	-	20.6	79.4
2002	5623366	6514	1104212	4512640	0.1	19.6	80.3
2003	8952090	10489	3208885	5732716	0.1	35.9	64.0
2004	11081993	15992	4369015	6696986	0.1	39.4	60.5
2005	12777972	13982	4451936	8312054	0.1	34.8	65.1
2006	13734482	17892	4651420	9065170	0.1	33.9	66.0
2007	15837775	23278	5286340	10528157	0.1	33.4	66.5
2008	18822936	30810	5705736	13086390	0.2	30.3	69.5
2009	21951706	31335	6115482	15804889	0.1	27.9	72.0
2010	26518839	41959	6875840	19601040	0.2	25.9	73.9
2011	31000218	76931	7486832	23436455	0.2	24.2	75.6
2012	37227544	42668	8531598	28653278	0.1	22.9	77.0
2013	42638732	84018	9125316	33429398	0.2	21.4	78.4
2014	49527010	190748	9152477	40183785	0.4	18.5	81.1
2015	55563183	314688	9317825	45930670	0.6	16.8	82.6
2016	58424194	393625	8869013	49161556	0.7	15.2	84.1
2017	58566453	336686	8665510	49564257	0.6	14.8	84.6
2018 比上年增长 Increased over the Previous year in 2018	10.8	-71.3	-11.9	14.2	0.1	9.6	90.3
2019	11.6	-38.7	6.2	12.2	0.0	9.2	90.8
2020	6.8	160.9	6.2	6.8	0.1	9.1	90.8

7－06 分地区

Investment in Fixed Assets

单位:万元

年　份 Year	全　市 Whole City	上城区 Shangcheng	下城区 Xiacheng	江干区 Jianggan	拱墅区 Gongshu	西湖区 Xihu	高新(滨江)区 Hi－Tech (Binjiang)
2003	8952090						
2004	11081993						
2005	12777972						
2006	13734482						
2007	15837775						
2008	18822936						
2009	21951706						
2010	26518839	802793	1030077	2901447	1508325	2188293	1609857
2011	31000218	544686	1043891	3456831	2041130	2638752	1866605
2012	37227544	595996	1217244	4486541	2463963	3205079	2220183
2013	42638732	638625	1528423	4138372	3081999	3991415	2480827
2014	49527010	776441	1017029	4914073	3838785	4723858	2948885
2015	55563183	885811	1144348	5823773	4565672	5064510	2254688
2016	58424194	1090808	1479399	5899757	4467059	4058658	2851746
2017	58566453	1214556	1509493	5158741	3327270	4889773	2274389
2018 比上年增长 Increased over the Previous year in 2018	10.8	14.3	－23.1	2.1	21.2	0.0	16.8
2019	11.6	1.1	30.2	20.5	25.8	－5.1	12.1
2020	6.8	－6.8	33.2	8.1	－12.6	2.5	－9.6

固定资产投资(2003－2020年)
by Region(2003－2020)

(10000 yuan)

萧山区 Xiaoshan	余杭区 Yuhang	富阳区 Fuyang	临安区 Lin'an	钱塘新区 Qiantang New Area	西湖风景名胜区 The West Lake Scenic Zone	桐庐县 Tonglu	淳安县 Chun'an	建德市 Jiande
1835889	1162453	563603	346980			250100	135275	246594
2246807	1478151	767880	479669			352987	218730	299212
2161067	1718028	896329	525840			424962	275543	316779
2424763	1758656	1017368	600270			470450	324444	377875
2745133	1929019	1155871	673495			542615	403119	432576
3184947	2317510	1334619	665978			653234	475340	509484
3769557	2823192	1534401	763725			738391	542037	575374
4515095	3480147	1796500	956408	1732557	18393	1001737	668168	658530
5190805	4134743	1913712	1134746	2018316	8594	1158682	794383	796301
6169275	5121242	2343812	1379851	2436859	6378	1412038	969471	961590
7307304	6312261	2868320	1644498	2891767	45458	1725986	1193796	1176467
8508518	7861506	3500717	1975132	3074966	56971	2096371	1450503	1432850
9631238	9200016	4037889	2312053	2098220	77986	2472662	1512184	1758713
10783163	10403247	4043949	2659669	2123585	137576	2534994	1603624	2053163
11042552	11232991	3406491	2904328	2162102	39564	2133136	1744157	2293503
11.7	10.0	0.5	11.2	10.6	－63.8	－10.7	－14.6	18.6
13.8	7.4	22.0	30.2	0.1	－60.9	18.7	－7.8	12.7
8.0	7.6	30.7	24.5	15.0	－60.1	23.4	－7.4	－9.9

7-07 分地区分类型固定
Investment in Fixed Assets

单位:%

指　　标	Item	全　　市 Total	市　　区 Urban District
固定资产投资额	**Investment in Fixed Assets**	**6.8**	**7.3**
#民间投资	#Private Investment	3.4	3.5
#工业投资	Industrial Investment	6.9	4.3
#基础设施投资	Investment in Infrastructure	7.7	9.2
一、按投资类型分	**Grouped by Sector**		
投资项目完成额	Investment Projects	8.5	9.0
房地产开发投资完成额	Real Estate	5.3	5.7
二、按登记注册类型分	**Grouped by Status of Registration**		
内资	Domestic - funded	6.5	7.0
国有	State - owned	-18.5	-18.8
集体	Collective - owned	-28.1	-27.7
股份合作	Cooperative	131.3	153.5
联营企业	State Joint Ownership	-39.9	-39.9
国有独资公司	State - owned Corporations	4.8	5.2
其他有限责任公司	Other Limited Liability Corporations	19.0	20.2
股份有限公司	Share - holding Corporations Ltd.	-26.4	-26.1
私营	Private	-2.3	-2.2
其他	Other	99.1	93.8
港、澳、台商投资	Investment from Hong Kong, Macao and Taiwan	22.4	20.6
外商投资	Foreign Investment	-14.4	-13.1
个体经营	Individual	-50.5	-

资产投资(2020年)
by Region(2020)

萧山区 Xiaoshan	余杭区 Yuhang	富阳区 Fuyang	临安区 Lin'an	桐庐县 Tonglu	淳安县 Chun'an	建德市 Jiande
8.0	**7.6**	**30.7**	**24.5**	**23.4**	**-7.4**	**-9.9**
3.1	-5.4	29.4	33.2	-4.3	30.9	-2.7
-11.4	16.1	31.8	9.3	49.3	-21.3	17.1
26.2	16.3	17.3	-37.7	109.4	-35.8	-32.7
9.3	21.7	23.6	-9.7	58.8	-25.2	-7.5
7.1	-4.4	40.7	45.2	-22.4	41.3	-18.1
8.5	10.0	25.5	21.8	11.5	-6.8	-6.8
-29.9	3.8	38.2	92.5	70.6	5.3	-52.0
-33.2	-63.0	284.9	-66.7	23.4	-57.2	-45.8
-	-	-	-	-70.2	-	-83.5
-	-	-	-	-	-	-
3.6	-42.4	4.8	-44.7	17.4	-43.8	336.0
18.0	14.9	53.9	111.5	113.7	-24.0	-4.6
-46.9	28.7	-10.4	-7.2	-79.0	114.7	-19.8
8.0	17.2	13.6	-12.6	-24.3	66.3	-3.8
43.0	8.7	26.7	-68.2	500.2	-45.0	-
10.3	4.8	309.5	29.9	187.2	-23.9	-73.6
-7.4	-38.4	93.4	512.7	-24.5	-56.8	-51.7
-	-	-	-	-	-	-97.5

指　标	Item	全　市 Total	市　区 Urban District
三、按行业分	**Grouped by Sector**		
农林牧渔业	Agricultare, Forestry, Animal Husbandry and Fishery	32.8	27.7
采矿业	Mining	-7.3	72.5
制造业	Manufacturing	1.0	-2.1
电力、热力、燃气及水的生产和供应业	Production and Supply of Electric Power, Heat Power, Gas and Tap Water	30.0	24.4
建筑业	Construction	-35.9	-34.5
批发和零售业	Wholesale & Retail Trades	121.5	143.4
交通运输、仓储和邮政业	Transportation, Storage and Post	6.4	8.7
住宿和餐饮业	Hotels and Catering Services	51.9	63.1
信息传输、软件和信息技术服务业	Information Transmission, Software and Information Technology	17.6	16.2
金融业	Financial Intertnediation	-29.2	-27.0
房地产业	Real Estate	5.8	6.2
租赁和商务服务业	Leasing and Business Services	56.2	59.8
科学研究和技术服务业	Scientific Research and Technical Service	30.8	31.9
水利、环境和公共设施管理业	Management of Water Conservancy, Environment and Public Facilities	4.0	6.3
居民服务、修理和其他服务业	Residentid Service, Repairs and Other Service	23.6	34.0
教育	Education	-8.5	-8.0
卫生和社会工作	Health Care and Social Welfare	31.1	40.3
文化、体育和娱乐业	Culture, Sports and Entertainment	4.3	6.1
公共管理、社会保障和社会组织	Public Management, Social Security and Social Organizations	-8.0	-7.1

注:2018 年起采用 2017 版行业代码。

continued

萧山区 Xiaoshan	余杭区 Yuhang	富阳区 Fuyang	临安区 Lin'an	桐庐县 Tonglu	淳安县 Chun'an	建德市 Jiande
–	–	–	-76.7	-10.2	166.4	25.0
–	–	113.9	-27.5	–	-19.7	-11.6
-13.8	1.0	-2.2	2.9	21.0	-32.6	20.7
6.1	143.4	776.5	69.0	1350.9	3.4	95.9
62.3	–	–	–	–	–	–
143.7	-15.2	986.3	-2.6	-55.5	72.6	74.2
29.3	39.5	-30.2	-31.7	108.8	-39.8	-47.5
10.3	199.4	–	651.2	50.0	288.4	0.8
-16.2	10.2	131.9	25.0	99.3	223.0	-89.6
-47.8	–	–	-75.3	–	-62.1	-95.3
7.2	2.3	44.7	40.7	-20.6	34.0	-12.0
118.3	-7.2	9363.9	–	81.8	-73.3	150.0
75.5	86.5	302.0	99.4	197.5	-64.0	-81.8
30.2	2.6	21.9	-55.3	52.4	-30.6	-32.7
–	13.4	418.3	214.5	–	–	–
-10.1	-11.0	-0.3	17.9	27.3	-45.2	-52.1
15.2	74.1	302.9	677.5	193.8	-59.8	-47.7
-3.8	90.7	-46.6	-38.4	-11.8	-49.0	34.5
-16.2	-29.5	-4.9	-19.2	74.4	-29.4	-35.9

a) Note: The" classification of National Economic Industries 2017" was applied Since 2018.

7－08 分地区分类型

Investment in Industrial

单位:%

指　　标	Item	全　市 Total	市区 Urban District 合计 Total
总计	**Total**	**6.9**	**4.3**
#技术改造投资	Investment in Technique Innovation	－2.7	－6.1
一、按登记注册类型分	**Grouped by Status of Registration**		
内资	Domestic－funded	10.0	6.0
国有	State－owned	－64.4	－65.9
集体	Collective－owned	－15.8	－15.6
股份合作	Cooperative	－	－
联营企业	State Joint Ownership	－	－
国有独资公司	State－funded Corporations	494.1	523.2
其他有限责任公司	Other Limited Liability Corporations	－1.9	－11.7
股份有限公司	Share－holding Corporations Ltd.	4.5	1.7
私营	Private	12.7	11.6
其他	Other	270.2	626.6
港、澳、台商投资	Investment from Hong Kong, Macao and Taiwan	3.4	13.9
外商投资	Foreign Investment	－16.9	－13.9
个体经营	Individual	－48.0	－
二、按行业分	**Grouped by Sector**		
采矿业	Mining	－7.3	72.5
制造业	Manufacturing	1.0	－2.1
#农副食品加工业	Processing of Food from Agricultural Products Processing	31.9	69.6
食品制造业	Food Manufacturing	0.1	40.5
酒、饮料和精制茶制造业	Wine, Beverage and Tea Manufacturing	－1.0	28.7
烟草制品业	Tobacco Processing	6.3	6.3
纺织业	Textile Processing	62.0	57.2
纺织服装、服饰业	Textile Products and Costume Industry	7.4	－1.6

工业投资(2020 年)
Sector by Region(2020)

				桐庐县 Tonglu	淳安县 Chun'an	建德市 Jiande
萧山区 Xiaoshan	余杭区 Yuhang	富阳区 Fuyang	临安区 Lin'an			
-11.4	**16.1**	**31.8**	**9.3**	**49.3**	**-21.3**	**17.1**
-22.4	13.4	-14.1	-7.9	6.2	-42.9	29.9
-6.5	26.1	8.7	10.2	50.8	-34.5	32.6
-84.7	462.5	-	-36.5	-	-55.4	-1.2
-16.5	-48.6	-81.4	-	-34.9	-	-
-	-	-	-	-	-	-
-	-	-	-	-	-	-
95.8	288.2	64.2	46.5	1713.0	8.2	-
-21.1	2.9	18.4	38.0	90.4	-79.5	42.8
-52.8	17.6	34.0	7.0	587.4	-96.6	34.5
22.8	14.7	-3.7	-8.6	8.1	-5.3	22.9
-	217.9	-	-	-	-	-
-31.3	-33.2	1094.8	-15.9	49.8	361.4	-93.2
-22.3	-26.4	54.2	9.1	-24.0	-	-57.4
-	-	-	-	-	-	-97.5
-	-	113.9	-27.5	-	-19.7	-11.6
-13.8	1.0	-2.2	2.9	21.0	-32.6	20.7
-54.3	105.1	-63.6	103.5	-31.8	-	-41.2
21.4	248.4	620.3	-46.9	-57.4	-	-41.8
197.8	-51.6	-34.9	-	-77.6	-44.4	7.2
-	-	-	-	-	-	-
41.5	40.5	726.6	1313.5	20.0	4.1	148.0
74.9	-1.3	-	-	-2.5	-	274.9

指　标	Item	全　市 Total	市　区 Urban District 合　计 Total
皮革、毛皮、羽毛及其制品和制造业	Leather, Furs, Down and Related Products	12.9	8.7
木材加工和木、竹、藤、棕、草制品业	Timber Processing, Bamboo, Cane, Palm Fiber and Straw Products	-53.3	-65.3
家具制造业	Furniture Manufacturing	2.9	13.0
造纸和纸制品业	Paper Making and Paper Products	24.0	26.9
印刷业和记录媒介复制业	Printing and Reproduction of Recording media	3.9	4.4
文教、工美、体育和娱乐用品制造业	Cultural, Educational and Sports Goods	-44.7	-44.6
石油加工、炼焦和核燃料加工业	Petroleum and Nuclear Fuel Processing	-40.6	-33.2
化学原料和化学制品制造业	Raw Chemical Material and Chemical Products	-33.7	-46.1
医药制造业	Medical and Pharmaceutical Products	3.3	9.5
化学纤维制造业	Chemical Fiber	21.9	8.1
橡胶和塑料制品业	Rubber and Plastic Products	47.2	-15.7
非金属矿物制品业	Nonmetal Mineral Products	18.5	-17.1
黑色金属冶炼和压延加工业	Ferrous Metals Smelting and Pressing	-37.1	-53.4
有色金属冶炼和压延加工业	Nonferrous Metal Smelting and Pressing	38.2	-21.6
金属制品业	Metal Products	16.0	11.8
通用设备制造业	General Purpose Machinery	0.8	3.9
专业设备制造业	Special Purpose Machinery	21.6	20.0
汽车制造业	Automobile Manufacturing	-28.6	-29.5
铁路、船舶、航空航天和其他运输设备制造业	Railway, Watercraft, Avigation Spaceflight and other Equipment Manufacturing	-12.2	-23.2
电气机械和器材制造业	Electric Equipment and Machinery	-25.0	-28.1
计算机、通信和其他电子设备制造业	Computers, Telecommunications and other Electronic Equipment Manufacturing	15.5	12.0
仪器仪表制造业	Instruments and Meters Manufacturing	31.2	27.4
其他制造业	Other Manufacturing	-69.0	-50.1
废弃资源综合利用业	Multiple Utilization of Waste Resouces	20.2	-26.4
金属制品、机械和设备修理业	Metal Products, Machinery and Equipment Repair	186.3	199.8
电力、燃气及水的生产和供应业	Production and Supply of Electric Power, Heat Power, Gas and Tap Water	30.0	24.4

continued

				桐庐县 Tonglu	淳安县 Chun'an	建德市 Jiande
萧山区 Xiaoshan	余杭区 Yuhang	富阳区 Fuyang	临安区 Lin'an			
16.1	447.0	-45.5	-	553.3	-	-
-88.1	-	-	34.9	-	107.9	-66.7
33.5	-57.1	-55.9	-93.4	-55.7	-89.8	10.2
6.6	98.7	4.4	6.1	16.4	-	1.9
40.0	-26.1	33.8	-19.9	-10.6	-	-
-37.4	-62.3	312.4	-	-57.6	-	39.4
-	-	-	-	-	-	-59.4
-64.5	-7.3	29.7	-16.6	2487.2	121.8	-19.8
-34.8	25.4	32.4	-20.9	-79.3	164.9	1.1
7.9	14.9	-	-	-	-	24173.3
97.0	72.6	-48.0	5.6	584.5	-	181.0
39.5	-28.7	-22.6	-40.3	39.5	77.9	184.9
-93.2	1944.4	127.8	-	-	-	-
-5.7	-40.9	16.9	168.0	-	-	228.0
32.1	-25.0	-1.2	-27.8	1094.3	0.4	-5.4
-11.6	15.5	-9.2	-4.7	12.8	-	-43.7
-9.2	-23.2	73.5	-67.3	90.6	-	-22.3
-39.5	-32.1	43.8	-20.1	281.1	430.6	-49.9
-53.6	3.0	-65.1	-	-	-	-
-53.4	-13.5	-8.7	-20.5	88.5	-87.6	55.3
22.2	14.1	-32.2	160.9	94.4	-40.5	-90.9
81.5	-0.7	200.0	-33.1	-	-	-
-12.0	-32.0	-81.4	-	-58.2	-18.4	-91.6
-84.6	-40.8	909.0	-	-	-	80.8
597.4	-62.6	-	-	-	-	-
6.1	143.4	776.5	69.0	1350.9	3.4	95.9

7－09 分地区房地产
Investment in Real Estate

指标		Item	全市 Total	市区 Urban District 合计 Total
房地产开发投资额	**（万元）**	**Investment in Real Estate Development (10000 yuan)**	**35753272**	**34649351**
住宅	（万元）	Residential Buildings (10000 yuan)	22156019	21383188
办公楼	（万元）	Office Buildings (10000 yuan)	3114466	3098583
商业营业用房	（万元）	Buildings for Business Use (10000 yuan)	2978052	2862779
其他	（万元）	Others (10000 yuan)	7504735	7304801
房屋建筑面积		**Floor space of Buildings**		
施工面积	（万平方米）	Under Construction (10000 sq. m)	13310	12458
#住宅	（万平方米）	#Residential Buildings (10000 sq. m)	6959	6406
新开工面积	（万平方米）	Started This Year (10000 sq. m)	3543	3304
#住宅	（万平方米）	#Residential Buildings (10000 sq. m)	2110	1969
竣工面积	（万平方米）	Construction Completed (10000 sq. m)	1799	1641
#住宅	（万平方米）	#Residential Buildings (10000 sq. m)	934	829
竣工造价	（元/平方米）	Completion Cost Housing (yuan/sq. m)	5002	5249
#住宅	（元/平方米）	#Residential Buildings (yuan/sq. m)	5735	6146
商品房销售情况		**Selling of Commercialized Buildings**		
销售金额	（万元）	Total Sales of Buildings (10000 yuan)	45954860	44184187
#住宅	（万元）	#Residential Buildings (10000 yuan)	40392669	38743852
现房销售额	（万元）	Sales of Completed Buildings (10000 yuan)	2472238	2297686
#住宅	（万元）	#Residential Buildings (10000 yuan)	1601302	1470214
期房销售金额	（万元）	Sales of Future Buildings (10000 yuan)	43482622	41886501
#住宅	（万元）	#Residential Buildings (10000 yuan)	38791367	37273638
销售面积	（万平方米）	Floor Space of Buildings Sold (10000 sq. m)	1699	1574
#住宅	（万平方米）	#Residential Buildings (10000 sq. m)	1472	1357
现房销售面积	（万平方米）	Floor Space of Completed Buildings Sold (10000 sq. m)	109	93
#住宅	（万平方米）	#Residential Buildings (10000 sq. m)	58	48
期房销售面积	（万平方米）	Floor Space of Futures Buildings Sold (10000 sq. m)	1591	1481
#住宅	（万平方米）	#Residential Buildings (10000 sq. m)	1413	1309

开发投资(2020 年)
Development by Region(2020)

萧山区 Xiaoshan	余杭区 Yuhang	富阳区 Fuyang	临安区 Lin'an	桐庐县 Tonglu	淳安县 Chun'an	建德市 Jiande
8281111	**6602523**	**1845175**	**2780110**	**369779**	**364540**	**369602**
5231166	4326164	1532519	2066303	273311	268986	230534
689230	521240	55975	78445	7050	1012	7821
613926	397537	94012	134346	33434	30493	51346
1746789	1357582	162669	501016	55984	64049	79901
2953	3045	797	1307	241	286	326
1529	1818	518	839	172	176	206
674	804	303	394	84	111	44
403	522	195	281	55	64	22
513	492	54	160	37	24	97
242	317	21	106	17	21	67
4983	5410	3403	3317			
5997	6345	4182	3713			
11091787	10589695	3398082	5204528	670734	434258	665681
9875163	9848541	3121765	5008523	626227	410132	612458
233504	568651	110603	210302	74698	52343	47511
80082	392537	37294	180840	49975	43221	37892
10858283	10021044	3287479	4994226	596036	381915	618170
9795081	9456004	3084471	4827683	576252	366911	574566
382	407	163	269	40	32	54
339	370	146	254	35	29	50
14	24	8	15	7	4	5
3	15	2	12	4	3	3
368	383	156	254	32	28	50
336	355	144	242	31	27	47

7－10 分注册类型和资质等级

Financial Statistics on Enterprises for Real Estate Development

单位:万元

项 目	Item	法人企业数(个) Number of Enterprises (unit)	年末 Asset and		
			流动资产合计 Circulating Funds	应收账款 Account Receivable	固定资产合计 Fixed Assets
总计	**Total**	**1613**	**245977650**	**3070780**	**4041798**
一、按登记注册类型分组	**Grouped by Registration Status**				
内资企业	Domestic Funded	1483	215648203	2797812	2729682
国有企业	State－owned	4	902479	1122	367
集体企业	Collective－owned				
股份合作企业	Share－holding Cooperative Enterprises				
联营企业	Joint Venture	1	117811	209	356
国有独资公司	Wholly State－owned Company	31	14671877	27290	625112
有限责任公司	Limited Liability Corporations	550	92133931	1316316	862076
股份有限公司	Share－holding Corporations Ltd.	7	6494172	11169	20744
私营企业	Private Enterprises	889	101327934	1441706	1221027
其他企业	Other Enterprises	1			
港澳台商投资企业	Funded from Hong Kong, Macao and Taiwan	86	16028479	43760	820508
外商投资企业	Foreign Funded	44	14300967	229208	491608
二、按企业资质等级分	**Grouped by Qualification Grade**	1613	245977650	3070780	4041798
一级	Grade Ⅰ	34	21216790	110376	80588
二级	Grade Ⅱ	75	8538681	132675	824980
三级	Grade Ⅲ	102	11094188	120211	408169
四级	Grade Ⅳ	34	1787356	6441	14364
暂定	Tentative	831	125028576	1601795	1746623
其他	Others	537	78312059	1099282	967075

房地产开发企业财务状况(2020 年)

Grouped by Registration Status and Qualification Grade(2020)

(10000 yuan)

资产负债 Liabilities at Year－end						所有者权益合计 Creditors′ Equity	
固定资产原价 Orginal Value of Fixed Assets	累计折旧 Accumulated Depreciation	#本年折旧 Depreciation This Year	在建工程 Projects wnder Construction	资产合计 Total Assets	负债合计 Total Liabilities		实收资本 Capital Hold
5038793	**996995**	**197271**	**7914807**	**295098309**	**227138261**	**67960048**	**46297583**
3445454	715772	129333	7889749	251267928	201081651	50186277	33676823
1069	702	27	8466	983037	896436	86601	13715
1405	1050	62		149953	81969	67984	1800
734133	109021	17976	2274286	20511319	14791402	5719917	1933000
1060112	198036	41390	5178895	109981750	89211330	20770420	15408650
40694	19951	2206		8973853	6065067	2908787	776920
1608040	387013	67673	428102	110668016	90035448	20632568	15542736
1012146	191638	42820	4726	20701117	9219270	11481847	10159859
581193	89585	25118	20332	23129264	16837340	6291924	2460902
5038793	996995	197271	7914807	295098309	227138261	67960048	46297583
157433	76846	7986	4246	35596796	24668446	10928350	2656674
1012017	187037	29857	1267139	14878884	9017375	5861508	1988800
539243	131074	20301	4252861	17802940	13976535	3826406	1556368
29880	15516	1288	587154	2797199	2490268	306931	122721
2118495	371872	95866	342093	136573665	110013140	26560525	22511208
1181725	214650	41973	1461316	87448826	66972497	20476329	17461812

项　目	Item	营业收入 Revenue of Business	#主营业务收入 Main Revenue of Business	营业成本 Operating Costs	#主营业务成本 Main Cost of Business
总计	**Total**	**38421323**	**36793614**	**29215298**	**28565191**
一、按登记注册类型分组	**Grouped by Registration Status**				
内资企业	Domestic Funded	34396040	33337607	26576251	26146232
国有企业	State - owned	490	437	191	43
集体企业	Collective - owned				
股份合作企业	Share - holding Cooperative Enterprises				
联营企业	Joint Venture	8998	8878	2298	2297
国有独资公司	Wholly State - owned Company	714098	587830	626317	613885
有限责任公司	Limited Liability Corporations	11382862	11241640	8707808	8619151
股份有限公司	Share - holding Corporations Ltd.	81758	47095	51400	51045
私营企业	Private Enterprises	22207834	21451727	17188236	16859812
其他企业	Other Enterprises				
港澳台商投资企业	Funded from Hong Kong, Macao and Taiwan	2154214	1779261	1341596	1140254
外商投资企业	Foreign Funded	1871069	1676747	1297451	1278705
二、按企业资质等级分	**Grouped by Qualification Grade**	38421323	36793614	29215298	28565191
一级	Grade Ⅰ	1091353	861239	638464	627390
二级	Grade Ⅱ	799011	770874	527515	517853
三级	Grade Ⅲ	1318575	1249659	678960	633789
四级	Grade Ⅳ	52594	51817	36223	35927
暂定	Tentative	22779308	21986674	17740754	17486309
其他	Others	12380482	11873351	9593383	9263925

continued (10000 yuan)

营业税金及附加 Main Sales Tax and Extra Charges	销售费用 Cost of Sales	管理费用 Administration Cost	财务费用 Financial Cost	#利息支出 Interest Expenditure	营业利润 Management Profits	利润总额 Total Profits	应交所得税 Income Tax
1738461	**1622944**	**1553652**	**663184**	**1196993**	**5226713**	**5173018**	**1190205**
1402360	1478144	1353851	611042	738760	4321876	4233272	1005462
196	346	1629	351	1141			
720	105	946		73	7164	25721	1567
16265	12346	39275	48101	62484		3849	9604
575490	639343	535545	200760	382402	1487831	1408982	280372
3324	4837	17789	46183	73467	158547	157282	20831
806364	821167	758666	317883	219194	2699128	2639143	693326
187523	84242	114220	80433	74850	393376	405890	122584
148578	60558	85582		383383	511461	533856	62159
1738461	1622944	1553652	663184	1196993	5226713	5173018	1190205
64674	47714	164671	41245	585118	970689	963183	52465
29471	32523	75031	39183	96964	449265	437967	35981
223934	42091	89906	12664	27905	335851	355883	76085
1876	3600	6299	24340	24882		6448	1307
968862	1039497	812128	373024	361982	2142854	2074894	659493
449644	457518	405617	172728	100142	1345713	1334644	364874

7-11 分行业基础设施投资(2010-2020年)
Investment in Infrastructure by Sector(2010-2020)

单位:亿元 (100 million yuan)

年份 Year	基础设施投资 Investment in Infrastructure	水利、环境和公共设施 Water, Environment and Public Facilities	电力、热力、燃气及水的生产供应业 Produotion and supply of Electricity, heat Gas and Water	交通运输、邮政业 Transportation and Post	电信和其他信息传输服务业 Telecommunications and Other Information Transmission Services	教育设施 Education Facilities	卫生设施 Sanitary Facilities
2010	6452236	2593603	682482	2415265	162166	339381	165668
2011	6437025	2529677	809813	2193350	142099	382672	167024
2012	7785196	2725934	1275603	2572604	162947	572350	201913
2013	8524663	3486809	1167072	2375342	199444	643681	261722
2014	10055306	3940406	1131323	3129697	180788	959814	241614
2015	13551793	5899889	1616380	3892605	201924	1234331	231015
2016	16305335	8101751	1696715	3887608	231813	1587853	358314
2017	15970399	6596611	1502546	5058477	229410	1627072	396390
2018 比上年增长 Increased over the Previous year in 2018	26.9	4.0	-12.9	63.3	19.9	11.5	-24.4
2019	5.2	-8.7	9.5	16.9	-11.6	5.3	16.5
2020	7.7	4.0	30.0	6.3	8.5	-8.5	13.3

注:2018年起基础设施投资口径调整,教育、卫生等剔除并单独设为公共服务投资。

a) Since 2018, The statistical caliber of infrastructure investment was adjusted, education and health were excluded, and set them as public service investment.

7-12 分地区房地产开发企业商品房屋销售面积和销售额(2017-2020年)

Sales Area and Sales Volume of Commercial Housing of Real Estate Development Enterprises by Region(2017-2020)

城　市	City	销售面积(万平方米) Sales Area(10,000 sq. m)				销售额(亿元) Sales Volume(100 million yuan)			
		2017年	2018年	2019年	2020年	2017年	2018年	2019年	2020年
全　市	**Total**	**2053.67**	**1675.50**	**1513.62**	**1699.34**	**4180**	**4008**	**3924**	**4595**
#上城区	Shangcheng	4.17	22.40	20.70	10.41	21	152	125	73
下城区	Xiacheng	30.62	18.00	4.54	11.51	102	86	22	50
江干区	Jianggan	214.76	130.23	128.40	141.75	615	437	483	547
拱墅区	Gongshu	163.69	79.65	97.59	71.91	509	287	361	296
西湖区	Xihu	143.74	102.66	54.66	58.41	365	294	183	205
高新(滨江)区	Hi-Tech (Binjiang)	52.37	42.76	35.55	38.79	153	174	153	159
萧山区	Xiaoshan	438.70	400.85	270.90	382.19	992	988	801	1109
余杭区	Yuhang	525.23	443.92	373.52	406.91	895	949	882	1059
富阳区	Fuyang	110.69	129.66	131.03	163.41	147	225	245	340
临安区	Lin'an	139.37	141.81	218.00	268.87	162	201	372	520
钱塘新区	Qiantang New Area	51.06	11.65	78.23	64.86	70	26	160	145
西湖风景名胜区	The West Lake Scenic Zone	-	-	-	-	-	-	-	-
桐庐县	Tonglu	81.80	40.76	36.30	39.88	61	49	58	67
淳安县	Chun'an	44.22	52.66	25.33	31.79	38	73	37	43
建德市	Jiande	53.26	58.51	38.86	54.09	49	69	43	67

7-13 分地区房地产开发企业住宅销售面积和销售额(2017-2020年)

Sales Area and Sales Volume of Residence of Real Estate Development Enterprises by Region(2017-2020)

城 市	City	销售面积(万平方米) Sales Area(10,000 sq. m)				销售额(亿元) Sales Volume(100 million yuan)			
		2017年	2018年	2019年	2020年	2017年	2018年	2019年	2020年
全 市	**Total**	**1519.73**	**1328.92**	**1284.27**	**1471.62**	**3226**	**3238**	**3406**	**4039**
#上城区	Shangcheng	2.42	22.11	15.21	10.08	15	150	107	71
下城区	Xiacheng	13.71	12.27	2.02	7.94	62	71	15	40
江干区	Jianggan	146.19	76.04	93.97	108.97	447	288	376	456
拱墅区	Gongshu	99.10	46.61	68.71	58.67	371	201	290	261
西湖区	Xihu	84.56	62.48	29.68	20.41	249	202	109	88
高新(滨江)区	Hi-Tech (Binjiang)	17.86	19.64	29.48	25.70	70	96	130	120
萧山区	Xiaoshan	351.62	320.32	238.79	339.15	834	796	728	988
余杭区	Yuhang	402.05	394.17	336.73	370.44	743	869	820	985
富阳区	Fuyang	83.71	110.92	113.65	146.13	111	198	216	312
临安区	Lin'an	128.08	130.82	206.31	253.92	151	188	356	501
钱塘新区	Qiantang New Area	28.27	4.40	63.25	57.36	41	11	134	131
西湖风景名胜区	The West Lake Scenic Zone	-	-	-	-	-	-	-	-
桐庐县	Tonglu	72.41	24.77	27.68	35.27	52	33	51	63
淳安县	Chun'an	41.20	50.54	24.48	29.37	35	71	35	41
建德市	Jiande	48.55	53.82	34.30	49.89	44	63	40	61

主要统计指标解释

固定资产投资额　固定资产投资完成额是以货币表现的建造和购置固定资产的工作量以及与此有关的费用的总称。它是反映固定资产投资规模、速度、比例关系和使用方向的综合性指标。

房地产开发投资　包括各种经济类型的房地产开发公司、商品房建设公司及其他房地产开发单位统一开发的包括统代建、拆迁还建的住宅、厂房、仓库、饭店、宾馆、度假村、写字楼、办公楼等房屋建筑物和配套的服务设施、土地开发工程,如道路、给水、排水、供电、供热、通讯、平整场地等基础设施工程的投资。不包括单纯的土地交易活动。

施工和竣工房屋建筑面积　房屋建筑面积是从房屋外墙线算起的各层平面面积的总和,包括房屋结构(如柱、墙)占用的面积和地下室面积。多层建筑按各自然层面积总和计算,包括房屋内的楼隔层,突出墙面的眺望间、门斗、有柱雨罩的面积。不包括突出墙面结构的构件、艺术装饰等所占的面积,如台阶等。凹阳台、挑阳台按其水平投影面积一半计算建筑面积。

房屋新开工面积　指在报告期内新开工建设的房屋面积。不包括上期跨入报告期继续施工的房屋面积和上期停缓建而在本期恢复施工的房屋面积。房屋的开工应以房屋正式开始破土刨槽(地基处理或打永久桩)的日期为准。

商品房销售面积　指报告期内出售商品房屋的合同总面积(即双方签署的正式买卖合同中所确定的建筑面积)。由现房销售建筑面积和期房销售建筑面积两部分组成。

(1)现房销售面积:是指在报告期内正式签订买卖合同、已经竣工达到入住条件的商品房屋建筑面积。包括以一次性付款方式和分期付款方式销售的现房建筑面积。

(2)期房销售面积:是指在报告期内正式签订买卖合同、正在建设尚未竣工交付使用的商品房屋建筑面积。包括以一次性付款方式和分期付款方式销售的商品房屋建筑面积。期房销售建筑面积竣工后不再转为现房销售建筑面积。

新增固定资产　指通过投资活动所形成的新的固定资产价值。包括已经建成投入生产或交付使用的工程价值和达到固定资产标准的设备、工具、器具的价值及有关应摊入的费用。它是以价值形式表示的固定资产投资成果的综合性指标,可以综合反映不同时期、不同部门、不同地区的固定资产投资成果。

Explanatory Notes on Main Statistical Indicators

Investment in Fixed Assets refer to the volume of activities in construction and purchases of fixed assets in monetary terms and other relative expenses. It is a comprehensive indicator which shows the size, pace, proportional relations and use orientation of investment in fixed assets.

Investment in Real Estate Development include the investment by the real estate development companies, commercial buildings construction companies and other real estate development units of various types of ownership on the construction of house buildings, such as residential buildings, factory buildings, warehouses, hotels, guesthouses, Resorts and office buildings, and supporting service facilities and land development projects, and infrastructure projects like roads, water supply, water drainage, power supply, heating, telecommunications and land leveling. The simple activities of land transaction are excluded.

Floor space of Building Under Construction and Completed refer to total floor space of each story of buildings calculated from the exterior wall line of buildings, including the area occupied by construction like pillars or walls and basement area. The floor space of multi – story building includes the total floor space of each story, including area occupied by separating walls inside the house, watching rooms protruding from walls, anterooms, and rain covers with pillars, but excluding protruding wall structures, artistic decoration, etc. (for example, steps) . The floor space of recessed veranda and cantilevered balcony is counted by half of the projection area.

New Construction Floor Space of Building refer to the area space which constructed in report period, not including the floor whose construction lasted to report period and which stopped in the last period to continue construction in the report period. The new construction should be subjected to the date of breaking the earth(foundation treatment or permanent pile driving).

Sales Area of the Commercial Building refer to the total area in contracts for sale of commercial housing(i. e. the floor space confirmed in contracts signed by two parties), which is composed by the floor area of existing house sales and that of future house sales.

(1) Floor Space of Existing House: refer to the floor area of commercial houses that have been completed and reached the condition of living, and whose formal sale contracts have been signed in report period, including houses sold in one – off payment and installment payment.

(2) Floor Space of Future House: refer to the floor area of commercial houses still under constructing but whose formal sale contracts have been signed in report period, including houses sold in one – off payment and installment payment. It cannot be turned into the floor space of existing house when these houses are completed.

Newly Increased Fixed Assets refer to the value of new fixed assets through investment, including the value of projects completed and put into production, the value of equipment, tools, and vessels considered as fixed assets, as well as the relevant expenses. It is a comprehensive indicator of investment in fixed assets, reflecting the achievements of investment in fixed assets in different periods, sectors and regions.

八、批发、零售贸易和住宿餐饮业

WHOLESALE AND RETAIL TRADE AND HOTEL AND CATERING TRADE

8 批发、零售贸易和住宿餐饮业
Wholesale and Retail Trade and Hotel and Catering Trade

主要统计指标
Major Statistical Indicators

社会消费品零售总额	Total Retail Sales of Consumer Goods	6055	亿元	(100 million yuan)
为上年	As Compared with the Preceding Year	96.5	%	(%)
商品零售	Commodity Retail	5060	亿元	(100 million yuan)
为上年	As Compared with the Preceding Year	97.6	%	(%)
餐饮收入	Catering Revenue	995	亿元	(100 million yuan)
为上年	As Compared with the Preceding Year	91.5	%	(%)

8-01 社会消费品零售总额(2001-2020年)
Total Retail Sale of Consumer Goods(2001-2020)

单位:万元 (10,000 yuan)

年份 Year	全市 Total	为上年(%) As Compared with the Preceding Year(%)
2001年	5743625	113.6
2002年	6553477	114.1
2003年	7366108	112.4
2004年	8485756	115.2
2005年	9673762	114.0
2006年	11028088	114.0
2007年	12847723	116.5
2008年	15442963	120.2
2009年	17666750	114.4
2010年	21553743	122.0
2011年	26225593	121.7
2012年	30384753	115.9
2013年	36397616	119.9
2014年	39252082	107.8
2015年	43573055	111.0
2016年	48109537	110.4
2017年	53005190	110.2
2018年	57686712	108.8
2019年	62732150	108.8
2020年	60554683	96.5

注:根据国家统计制度规定,2018年经济普查后对各年度数据作了相应调整。

a) According to the national statistical regulations, the annual data of previous years has been adjusted accordingly after the Economic Census in 2018.

8－02　分地区社会消费品零售总额(2019－2020年)

Total Retail Sale of Consumer Goods by Region(2019－2020)

单位:万元　　(10000 yuan)

地　区	Region	2019年	为上年(%) As Compared with the Preceding Year (%)	2020年	为上年(%) As Compared with the Preceding Year (%)
全　市	**Total**	**62732150**	**108.8**	**60554683**	**96.5**
市　区	Urban District	59285784	108.8	57202258	96.5
#上城区	Shangcheng	3319582	108.5	3334299	100.4
下城区	Xiacheng	5348700	108.5	5380450	100.6
江干区	Jianggan	5820579	108.7	5501008	94.5
拱墅区	Gongshu	6282339	108.3	6165637	98.1
西湖区	Xihu	7117271	108.6	6896776	96.9
高新(滨江)区	Hi－Tech(Binjiang)	4260913	110.0	4288514	100.6
萧山区	Xiaoshan	8371880	109.9	7857787	93.9
余杭区	Yuhang	7877778	109.4	8550510	108.5
富阳区	Fuyang	3797291	108.8	3721013	98.0
临安区	Lin'an	2052324	109.0	1909155	93.0
钱塘新区	Qiantang New Area	3116726	108.5	3017068	96.8
西湖风景名胜区	The West Lake Scenic Zone	452035	108.5	411691	91.1
桐庐县	Tonglu	1457817	109.0	1374378	94.3
淳安县	Chun'an	839928	108.2	837355	99.7
建德市	Jiande	1148620	108.6	1140692	99.3

8-03 按登记注册类型分限额以上批发零售贸易企业商品销售总额(2020年)

Sales of Wholesale and Retail Trades Above Designated Size by Status of Registration(2020)

单位:万元 (10000 yuan)

项目	Item	法人企业(个) Number of Enterprises (unit)	销售总额 Total Sales	批发额 Wholesale	零售额 Retail
总计	**Total**	**5776**	**303955685**	**271337446**	**32618240**
1.内资企业	**Domestic - funded Enterprises**	**5523**	**278372133**	**255448568**	**22923564**
国有企业	State - owned Enterprises	28	6088604	6005653	82951
集体企业	Collective - owned Enterprises	3	22302	7513	14789
股份合作企业	Cooperative Enterprises	-	-	-	-
联营企业	Joint Ownership Enterprises	5	39887	5274	34613
国有联营企业	State Joint Ownership Enterprises	-	-	-	-
国有与集体联营企业	Joint State - collective Enterprises	3	25365	3443	21922
有限责任公司	Limited Liability Corporations	869	120211665	109266666	10944999
国有独资公司	State - funded Corporations	46	9049480	8806538	242942
其他有限责任公司	Other Limited Liability Corporations	823	111162185	100460128	10702058
股份有限公司	Share - holding Corporations Ltd.	76	25415190	24679163	736027
私营企业	Private Enterprises	4531	126564838	115461481	11103358
私营独资企业	Private - funded Enterprises	25	546631	522764	23868
私营合伙企业	Private Partnership Enterprises	-	-	-	-
私营有限责任公司	Private Limited Liability Corporations	4475	124769210	113813817	10955393
私营股份有限公司	Private Share - holding Corporations Ltd.	30	1245405	1124900	120505
其他企业	Other Enterprises	10	27994	22541	5454
2.港、澳、台商投资企业	**Enterprises With Investment from Hong Kong, Macao and Taiwan**	**84**	**9172409**	**5447312**	**3725097**
合资经营企业(港或澳、台资)	Joint - venture Enterprises (With Funds from Hong Kong, Macao and Taiwan)	22	1153663	226145	927518
合作经营企业(港或澳、台资)	Coorperative Enterprises (With Funds from Hong Kong, Macao and Taiwan)	2	55342	34356	20986
港、澳、台商独资经营企业	Enterprises With Sole Investment from Hong Kong, Macao and Taiwan	54	5035593	2699909	2335684
港、澳、台商投资股份有限公司	Share - holding Corporations Ltd. With Investment from Hong Kong, Macao and Taiwan	4	2297528	2170986	126542
其他港澳台投资企业	Other Enterprises With Investment from Hong Kong, Macao and Taiwan	2	630283	315917	314367
3.外商投资企业	**Enterprises With Foreign Investment**	**169**	**16411144**	**10441565**	**5969579**
中外合资经营企业	Joint - venture Enterprises	45	3244803	1699541	1545262
中外合作经营企业	Cooperation Enterprises	4	103303	39976	63327
外资企业	Enterprises With Sole Foreign Investment	116	12324658	7963668	4360990
外商投资股份有限公司	Share - holding Corporations Ltd. With Foreign Investment	3	383333	383333	-

8-04 按国民经济行业分限额以上批发零售

Total Sales of Wholesale and Retail Trades

单位:万元

项　　目	Item
总　　计	**Total**
一、批发业	**Wholesale**
农、林、牧产品批发	Wholesale of Farm, Forestry and Animal Husbandry Products
食品、饮料及烟草制品批发	Wholesale of Food, Beverages and Tobaccos
纺织、服装及家庭用品批发	Wholesale of Textile Products, Garments and Household Articles
文化、体育用品及器材批发	Wholesale of Cultural and Sports Goods
医药及医疗器材批发	Wholesale of Medicines and Medical Appliances
矿产品、建材及化工产品批发	Wholesale of Mineral Products, Building and Chemical Materials
机械设备、五金产品及电子产品批发	Wholesale of Machinery, Hardware and Electronic Products
#汽车、摩托车及零配件批发	Wholesale of Automobiles, Motorcycle and Parts
贸易经纪与代理	Trade Broker and agent
其他批发业	Other
二、零售业	**Retail Trade**
综合零售	Comprehensive Retail Trade
食品、饮料及烟草制品专门零售	Specialism Retail of Food, Beverages and Tobaccos
纺织、服装及日用品专门零售	Specialism Retail of Textile Products, Garments, Shoes and Caps
文化、体育用品及器材专门零售	Specialism Retail of Cultural and Sports Goods
医药及医疗器材专门零售	Specialism Retail of Medicines and Medical Appliances
汽车、摩托车、燃料及零配件专门零售	Specialism Retail of Automobiles, Motorcycle, Fuels and Parts
#汽车零售	Specialism Retail of Automobiles
家用电器及电子产品专门零售	Specialism Retail of Household Electric Applianes, and Electronic Products
五金、家具及室内装饰材料专门零售	Specialism Retail of Hardware and Upholstery Materials
货摊、无店铺及其他零售业	Stall, Non - shop and Other Retails

贸易企业商品销售总额(2020 年)
Above Designated Size by Sector(2020)

(10000 yuan)

法人企业(个) Number of Enterprises(unit)	销售总额 Total Sales	批发额 Wholesale	零售额 Retail
5776	**303955685**	**271337446**	**32618240**
4330	**267687546**	**264997492**	**2690053**
51	1562753	1560730	2023
354	17897782	17659985	237797
935	28796868	28302879	493989
187	4938793	4836093	102700
286	11797098	11749976	47121
1669	166612490	166135387	477103
734	30776671	30114121	662550
170	12085333	11653168	432164
3	8470	1702	6767
111	5296621	4636619	660002
1446	**36268140**	**6339953**	**29928187**
123	6279127	865036	5414091
112	531485	58836	472649
84	838660	263894	574766
47	293090	41866	251224
83	920969	142334	778635
563	15341619	2917701	12423918
386	10813259	1600247	9213012
104	1332877	447461	885416
27	230075	30418	199656
303	10500238	1572406	8927832

8－05 按登记注册类型分限额以上

Main Financial Indicators of Enterprises Above Designated Size of

单位：万元

项　目	Item	法人企业数(个) Number of Enterprises (unit)	年末资产负债 Assets and Liabilities 流动资产合计 Circulating Funds	存　货 Inventory	固定资产原价 Orginal Value of Fixed Assets
批发零售贸易业企业合计	**Total**	**5776**	**98038447**	**14174282**	**6879628**
1. 内资企业	**Domestic－funded Enterprises**	**5523**	**86389181**	**12822905**	**5887355**
国有企业	State－owned Enterprises	28	3745765	439021	942998
集体企业	Collective－owned Enterprises	3	5093	984	1031
股份合作企业	Cooperative Enterprises	－	－	－	－
联营企业	Joint Ownership Enterprises	5	5782	279	2180
国有联营企业	State Joint Ownership Enterprises	－	－	－	－
国有与集体联营企业	Joint State－collective Enterprises	3	4169	196	1402
有限责任公司	Limited Liability Corporations	869	33131746	5990213	1754966
国有独资公司	State－funded Corporations	46	2650218	810394	217682
其他有限责任公司	Other Limited Liability Corporations	823	30481528	5179818	1537285
股份有限公司	Share－holding Corporations Ltd.	76	8651840	1481894	520417
私营企业	Private Enterprises	4531	40833972	4909727	2663310
私营独资企业	Private－funded Enterprises	25	158306	23390	21925
私营合伙企业	Private Partnership Enterprises	－	－	－	－
私营有限责任公司	Private Limited Liability Corporations	4475	40137717	4788674	2564157
私营股份有限公司	Private Share－holding Corporations Ltd.	30	536560	97151	77221
其他企业	Other Enterprises	10	14102	438	2233
2. 港、澳、台商投资企业	**Enterprises With Investment from Hong Kong, Macao and Taiwan**	**84**	**4820595**	**445607**	**417868**
合资经营企业(港或澳、台资)	Joint－venture Enterprises (With Funds from Hong Kong, Macao and Taiwan)	22	703907	29598	144260
合作经营企业(港或澳、台资)	Coorperative Enterprises (With Funds from Hong Kong, Macao and Taiwan)	2	39177	－	12057
港、澳、台商独资经营企业	Enterprises With Sole Investment from Hong Kong, Macao and Taiwan	54	1910321	350905	143899
港、澳、台商投资股份有限公司	Share－holding Corporations Ltd. With Investment from Hong Kong, Macao and Taiwan	4	2033464	14058	113343
其他港澳台投资企业	Other Enterprises With Investment from Hong Kong, Macao and Taiwan	2	133726	51047	4309
3. 外商投资企业	**Enterprises With Foreign Investment**	**169**	**6828671**	**905771**	**574404**
中外合资经营企业	Joint－venture Enterprises	45	726179	121111	180133
中外合作经营企业	Cooperation Enterprises	4	390450	2901	7020
外资企业	Enterprises With Sole Foreign Investment	116	5217485	761248	341887
外商投资股份有限公司	Share－holding Corporations Ltd. With Foreign Investment	3	368182	13319	42117

批发零售贸易企业财务状况（2020 年）

Wholesale and Retail Trades by Status of Registration（2020）

（10000 yuan）

累计折旧 Accumulated Depreciation	本年折旧 Depreciation	资产总计 Total Assets	负债合计 Total Liabilities	所有者权益合计 Creditors′ Equity
2849719	**391125**	**136137170**	**96311320**	**39795118**
2402516	**319626**	**121685588**	**87079581**	**34584583**
470345	8667	5824106	3583558	2240549
621	47	5502	1615	3887
–	–	–	–	–
945	127	7290	816	6475
–	–	–	–	–
582	67	5245	480	4765
676736	107371	46877834	32624733	14226886
57394	7564	3430802	2333059	1097449
619342	99807	43447033	30291674	13129437
202241	29681	14073446	7574121	6499291
1051285	173660	54878264	43281594	11601597
3300	1201	208940	138140	70667
–	–	–	–	–
1018840	169344	53639336	42435630	11208766
29141	3112	1028549	706620	321928
296	61	18090	13093	4897
179205	**31140**	**6086543**	**3224006**	**2853229**
74357	5239	1011873	542400	471165
7649	-1493	71963	27848	44114
46430	12226	2555992	1844846	700146
50116	14525	2304615	758238	1546378
653	643	142100	50673	91427
267998	**40359**	**8365039**	**6007733**	**2357306**
90363	15155	1136333	503290	633043
3519	498	397800	373866	23934
153679	22325	6048762	4717682	1331080
18648	2203	608557	304481	304076

单位:万元

8－05 续表

项　　目	Item	营业收入 Revenue of Business	主营业务收入 Main Revenue of Business	营业成本 Cost of Business	税金及附加 Sales Tax and Extra Charges
批发零售贸易业企业合计	**Total**	**279908027**	**277020435**	**264656222**	**551071**
1. 内资企业	**Domestic－funded Enterprises**	**257146052**	**254693936**	**244712723**	**488611**
国有企业	State－owned Enterprises	13421779	13086636	12227191	262977
集体企业	Collective－owned Enterprises	19753	19736	18325	24
股份合作企业	Cooperative Enterprises	－	－	－	－
联营企业	Joint Ownership Enterprises	35307	35299	27404	124
国有联营企业	State Joint Ownership Enterprises	－	－	－	－
国有与集体联营企业	Joint State－collective Enterprises	22447	22447	17680	75
有限责任公司	Limited Liability Corporations	106752557	105752426	102835454	91968
国有独资公司	State－funded Corporations	8134671	8108639	7983974	4237
其他有限责任公司	Other Limited Liability Corporations	98617886	97643787	94851480	87731
股份有限公司	Share－holding Corporations Ltd.	22397886	22249396	21281646	18831
私营企业	Private Enterprises	114493163	113535283	108298143	114677
私营独资企业	Private－funded Enterprises	530388	528049	512584	234
私营合伙企业	Private Partnership Enterprises	－	－	－	－
私营有限责任公司	Private Limited Liability Corporations	112810432	111863459	106716754	113554
私营股份有限公司	Private Share－holding Corporations Ltd.	1148762	1140194	1067619	888
其他企业	Other Enterprises	24145	13698	23403	4
2. 港、澳、台商投资企业	**Enterprises With Investment from Hong Kong, Macao and Taiwan**	**8496175**	**8265709**	**6977224**	**29217**
合资经营企业(港或澳、台资)	Joint－venture Enterprises (With Funds from Hong Kong, Macao and Taiwan)	1100396	1043708	906907	11468
合作经营企业(港或澳、台资)	Coorperative Enterprises (With Funds from Hong Kong, Macao and Taiwan)	52786	52786	45983	202
港、澳、台商独资经营企业	Enterprises With Sole Investment from Hong Kong, Macao and Taiwan	4721415	4600352	4085195	9345
港、澳、台商投资股份有限公司	Share－holding Corporations Ltd. With Investment from Hong Kong, Macao and Taiwan	2062292	2010292	1577678	6152
其他港澳台投资企业	Other Enterprises With Investment from Hong Kong, Macao and Taiwan	559286	558571	361462	2051
3. 外商投资企业	**Enterprises With Foreign Investment**	**14265800**	**14060790**	**12966275**	**33242**
中外合资经营企业	Joint－venture Enterprises	2992930	2930525	2582282	3861
中外合作经营企业	Cooperation Enterprises	98365	65667	80836	2453
外资企业	Enterprises With Sole Foreign Investment	10566369	10457040	9833141	25216
外商投资股份有限公司	Share－holding Corporations Ltd. With Foreign Investment	290475	290450	178535	1354

continued (10000 yuan)

销售费用 Cost of Sales	管理费用 Administration Cost	财务费用 Financil Cost	营业利润 Management Profits	利润总额 Total Profits	所得税费用 Income Tax Expense	从事批发和零售业活动的从业人员平均人数(人) Average Number of Employees (person) engaged in wholesale and retail activities
8234717	**3618386**	**1017118**	**5077445**	**5265561**	**832460**	**299925**
6598079	**2964543**	**972290**	**4093045**	**4277499**	**708872**	**251590**
357183	137960	-6510	602936	621091	120588	7678
432	321	-44	694	696	120	21
–	–	–	–	–	–	–
1935	58	-72	5862	5863	1423	78
–	–	–	–	–	–	–
1413	48	-69	3301	3303	820	49
2126767	819809	320594	1537790	1644307	264837	68416
89854	54227	27478	42666	67776	14595	2725
2036913	765581	293116	1495124	1576531	250242	65691
489614	260230	73242	819290	829593	83841	15264
3622067	1745726	585032	1126008	1175345	238052	160054
2333	5830	2813	25038	25020	585	473
–	–	–	–	–	–	–
3582027	1711275	553994	1091376	1139540	235143	155360
34047	28331	28206	11168	12345	2324	4209
82	262	41	352	488	2	67
885679	**361962**	**32400**	**594096**	**596208**	**62101**	**26173**
57809	47444	3299	111419	114082	20360	2300
2479	4077	89	-4	-145	438	263
462744	207140	16303	-54523	-55023	12241	13218
228178	81537	12568	512712	512839	22900	9228
134469	21764	141	24491	24455	6162	1164
750960	**291881**	**12428**	**390305**	**391854**	**61487**	**22162**
270666	63409	6953	133082	137154	19754	8089
9608	2294	2209	937	883	250	415
367986	199492	-1821	244683	242315	39144	12532
83676	23877	1990	10447	10262	2095	1045

8－06 按国民经济行业分限额以上

Main Financial Indicators of Enterprises Above Designated

单位:万元

项目	Item	法人企业数(个) Number of Enterprises (unit)	年末资产负债 Assets and Liabilities		
			流动资产合计 Circulating Funds	存货 Inventory	固定资产原价 Orginal Value of Fixed Assets
总　计	**Total**	**5776**	**98038447**	**14174282**	**6879628**
一、批发业	**Wholesale**	**4330**	**86196319**	**11782760**	**4718509**
农、林、牧产品批发	Wholesale of Farm, Forestry and Animal Husbandry Products	51	807633	120865	46304
食品、饮料及烟草制品批发	Wholesale of Food, Beverages and Tobaccos	354	8918533	1588269	618197
纺织、服装及家庭用品批发	Wholesale of Textile Products, Garments and Household Articles	935	10296324	1358470	575263
文化、体育用品及器材批发	Wholesale of Cultural and Sports Goods	187	2013651	574093	107764
医药及医疗器材批发	Wholesale of Medicines and Medical Appliances	286	5540000	1015712	349022
矿产品、建材及化工产品批发	Wholesale of Mineral Products, Building and Chemical Materials	1669	44942366	5343254	2358376
机械设备、五金产品及电子产品批发	Wholesale of Machinery, Hardware and Electronic Products	734	11053431	1502691	583871
#汽车、摩托车及零配件批发	Wholesale of Automobiles, Motorcycle and Parts	170	3661306	307946	125838
其他批发业	Other	114	2624380	279406	79711
二、零售业	**Retail Trade**	**1446**	**11842128**	**2391522**	**2161120**
综合零售	Comprehensive Retail Trade	123	3467997	325057	965206
食品、饮料及烟草制品专门零售	Specialism Retail of Food, Beverages and Tobaccos	112	221709	30015	34774
纺织、服装及日用品专门零售	Specialism Retail of Textile Products, Garments, Shoes and Caps	84	512471	109615	86415
文化、体育用品及器材专门零售	Specialism Retail of Cultural and Sports Goods	47	315859	90585	85024
医药及医疗器材专门零售	Specialism Retail of Medicines and Medical Appliances	47	315859	90585	85024
汽车、摩托车、燃料及零配件专门零售	Specialism Retail of Automobiles, Motorcycle, Fuels and Parts	563	3076417	879946	684660
#汽车零售	Specialism Retail of Automobiles	383	2580813	831225	470720
家用电器及电子产品专门零售	Specialism Retail of Household Electric Appliances, and Electronic Products	104	628843	161657	45541
五金、家具及室内装饰材料专门零售	Specialism Retail of Hardware and Upholstery Materials	27	113880	25280	69885
货摊、无店铺及其他零售业	Stall, Non－shop and Other Retails	303	3210746	667460	164994

批发零售贸易企业财务状况(2020年)
Size in Wholesale and Retail Trades by Sector(2020)

(10000 yuan)

累计折旧 Accumulated Depreciation	本年折旧 Depreciation	资产总计 Total Assets	负债合计 Total Liabilities	所有者权益合计 Creditors´ Equity
2849719	**391125**	**136137170**	**96311320**	**39795118**
1952479	**228574**	**120047673**	**84838488**	**35195576**
17412	1609	1329573	884056	445418
266821	39963	10801181	6549863	4249604
226259	30257	12448278	9692654	2756718
52098	4360	2563434	1844323	719110
142995	26723	7727172	4838708	2884572
980826	76453	68122471	48203986	19902390
252354	44679	14192305	10352517	3847549
64439	10079	4355054	3755785	610786
13715	4529	2863259	2472380	390216
897239	**162552**	**16089497**	**11472832**	**4599541**
429606	83687	5344564	3633993	1710571
14911	4179	273596	189922	85825
41131	6427	653410	495956	146694
37907	2896	386423	279727	106897
37907	2896	386423	279727	106897
266177	45863	4511843	2965489	1544594
188570	34956	3345401	2579869	766135
28689	2869	775543	547028	228465
24968	3559	177798	117026	56138
39402	11102	3633895	2989402	642120

项　目	Item	营业收入 Revenue of Business	主营业务收入 Main Revenue of Business	营业成本 Cost of Business	税金及附加 Sales Tax and Extra Charges
总　计	**Total**	**279908027**	**277020435**	**264656222**	**551071**
一、批发业	**Wholesale**	**247786116**	**245629582**	**237479250**	**438342**
农、林、牧产品批发业	Wholesale of Farm , Forestry and Animal Husbandry Products	1464492	1441609	1425208	888
食品、饮料、烟草制品批发	Wholesale of Food, Beverages and Tobaccos	16425168	16116488	14360594	270844
纺织、服装及家庭用品批发	Wholesale of Textile Products, Garments and Household Articles	26346684	26082035	24524624	39372
文化、体育用品及器材批发	Wholesale of Cultural and Sports Goods	4495091	4478933	4212299	3931
医药及医疗器材批发	Wholesale of Medicines and Medical Appliances	10684405	10628788	9629409	17867
矿产品、建材及化工产品批发	Wholesale of Mineral Products, Building and Chemical Materials	154949302	153976084	151820647	77366
机械设备、五金产品及电子产品批发	Wholesale of Machinery, Hardware and Electronic Products	28001111	27622466	26433399	24497
#汽车、摩托车及零配件批发	Wholesale of Automobiles, Motorcycle and Parts	10887188	10699155	10412698	8686
其他批发业	Other	5419862	5283181	5073071	3578
二、零售业	**Retail Trade**	**32121911**	**31390853**	**27176972**	**112729**
综合零售	Comprehensive Retail Trade	5985360	5671876	4936538	26562
食品、饮料及烟草制品专门零售	Specialism Retail of Food, Beverages and Tobaccos	494259	487991	423069	948
纺织、服装及日用品专门零售	Specialism Retail of Textile Products, Garments, Shoes and Caps	774030	748812	481444	3781
文化、体育用品及器材专门零售	Specialism Retail of Cultural and Sports Goods	281916	277543	217573	2430
医药及医疗器材专门零售	Specialism Retail of Medicines and Medical Appliances	281916	277543	217573	2430
汽车、摩托车、燃料及零配件专门零售	Specialism Retail of Automobiles, Motorcycle, Fuels and Parts	12472500	12289450	11432182	47577
#汽车零售	Specialism Retail of Automobiles	9914538	9771446	9251110	30218
家用电器及电子产品专门零售	Specialism Retail of Household Electric Applianes, and Electronic Products	1234623	1218091	1115283	1454
五金、家具及室内装饰材料专门零售	Specialism Retail of Hardware and Upholstery Materials	210996	208368	135544	853
货摊、无店铺及其他零售业	Stall, Non - shop and Other Retails	9812377	9640720	7727890	27357

continued (10000 yuan)

销售费用 Cost of Sales	管理费用 Administration Cost	财务费用 Financil Cost	营业利润 Management Profits	利润总额 Total Profits	所得税费用 Income Tax Expense	从事批发和零售业活动的从业人员平均人数(人) Average Number of Employees (person) engaged in wholesale and retail activities
8234717	**3618386**	**1017118**	**5077445**	**5265561**	**832460**	**299925**
4906463	**2693267**	**944873**	**4322232**	**4494696**	**640091**	**178414**
14287	26534	20182	11965	15731	2848	1226
879593	346829	12292	991312	1031366	160761	36114
985750	492024	129788	279027	304974	79939	43568
108172	83238	14465	66721	69996	14624	6407
555686	288113	45552	350816	390255	54960	18134
1354914	889268	616662	2270753	2309608	243432	37170
785438	468386	101635	324029	341744	70949	30231
377997	147240	10006	-38253	-25195	11141	8730
222623	98877	4297	27609	31022	12579	5564
3328254	**925119**	**72245**	**755213**	**770865**	**192369**	**121511**
683739	214918	17487	270030	299053	54391	40096
53795	30108	771	-2955	-4493	1213	4350
196981	46947	2604	33634	35899	14820	8161
36508	18349	-1043	8099	9090	125	2985
36508	18349	-1043	8099	9090	125	2985
468760	231013	36032	305764	314494	78272	26226
285476	183926	31681	144203	152756	39835	21822
87234	38285	6000	-8536	-8015	1337	8484
44286	23902	1676	4170	4589	2710	1547
1656702	284626	7936	128066	102922	35089	20980

单位：万元

地 区	Region	企业法人数（个）Number of Enterprises (unit)	商品销售总额 Total Sales of Commodities	主营业务收入 Main Revenue of Business	营业成本 Cost of Business	税金及附加 Sales Tax and Extra Charges
全 市	**Total**	**5776**	**303955685**	**277020435**	**264656222**	**551071**
市 区	Urban District	5437	299758449	273219257	261189538	546217
#上城区	Shangcheng	490	33362987	37411374	35723759	287628
下城区	Xiacheng	519	57798749	50742631	49212777	60426
江干区	Jianggan	495	41289503	36460202	34911034	25980
拱墅区	Gongshu	424	26473449	23631702	22712418	24763
西湖区	Xihu	396	17443897	14349222	12942118	21449
高新（滨江）区	Hi－Tech(Binjiang)	454	28600133	25644928	24137607	39341
萧山区	Xiaoshan	1015	45559767	40127543	38912318	31661
萧山本级	Xiaoshan	874	41798440	36787263	35752384	28593
余杭区	Yuhang	779	27991042	25823851	24768448	30157
富阳区	Fuyang	399	10937891	9781679	9397915	9044
临安区	Lin'an	163	2401377	2130141	2054596	1756
西湖风景名胜区	The West Lake Scenic Zone	14	146170	128199	116605	171
钱塘新区	Qiantang New Area	430	11514811	10328065	9459877	16910
桐庐县	Tonglu	157	1367065	1236002	1087461	1962
淳安县	Chun'an	87	2021540	1817161	1691878	2088
建德市	Jiande	95	808631	748016	687345	803

批发零售业主要指标(2020 年)
and Retail Trades by Region(2020)

(10000 yuan)

销售费用 Cost of Sales	管理费用 Administration Cost	财务费用 Financil Cost	利润总额 Total Profits	应交增值税 Value Added Tax Payable	从事批发和零售业活动从业人员平均人数(人) Average Number of Employees (person) engaged in wholesale and retail activities
8234717	**3618386**	**1017118**	**5265561**	**1569605**	**299925**
8026989	3553489	1001626	5122593	1536823	289962
833249	442485	75423	1082326	3411721	26456
864206	461131	144353	999946	1890136	33184
935031	370532	65160	407681	1409533	34528
552168	311854	187773	399628	921778	26860
844944	348733	106950	676456	1268494	36066
1211922	351208	89227	317099	1406544	29983
860873	385738	132420	451731	150135	34146
700269	335935	122402	449038	1292029	30802
900139	484009	89952	356488	1919857	40126
263418	119015	45543	100742	434773	8808
36843	38507	12926	109741	88729	3433
6096	5235	237	2448	12191	559
878705	284847	61679	221000	1312444	19157
85390	29979	9239	43986	134321	3343
89863	22672	4263	80403	138834	4683
32476	12246	1990	18578	54661	1937

8－08 按注册类型、行业分限额以上
Main Financial Indicators of Hotels and Catering Services

单位:万元

项　　目	Item	法人企业数(个) Number of Enterprises (unit)	年末资产负债 Assets and Liabilities 流动资产合计 Circulating Funds	存　货 Inventory	固定资产原价 Orginal Value of Fixed Assets
总　计	**Total**	**1136**	**2922124**	**201898**	**3340905**
(一)按登记注册类型分组	**Grouped By Registered Type**				
1. 内资企业	**Domestic－funded Enterprises**	**1095**	**2464737**	**159715**	**2612448**
国有企业	State－owned Enterprises	31	85247	2231	303802
集体企业	Collective－owned Enterprises	7	10802	353	36321
股份合作企业	Cooperative Enterprises	－	－	－	－
联营企业	Joint Ownership Enterprises	－	－	－	－
有限责任公司	Limited Liability Corporations	161	1046662	104355	1207656
股份有限公司	Share－holding Corporations Ltd.	7	203375	1521	74101
私营企业	Private Enterprises	887	1115783	51160	983760
2. 港、澳、台商投资企业	**Enterprises With Investment from Hong Kong, Macao and Taiwan**	**17**	**295041**	**15637**	**438595**
3. 外商投资企业	**Enterprises With Foreign Investment**	**24**	**162346**	**26546**	**289862**
(二)按国民经济行业分组	**Grouped By Sector**				
1. 住宿业	**Lodging**	**510**	**2157017**	**166529**	**2779161**
旅游饭店	Restaurants for Junketing	279	1953941	163213	2618181
一般旅馆	General Hotel	226	199326	3245	159299
民宿服务	Homestay Service	5	3751	71	1681
2. 餐饮业	**Catering Services**	**626**	**765106**	**35369**	**561744**
正餐服务	Dinner Services	549	601162	23272	397811
快餐服务	Short Order Services	31	107535	8082	146750
饮料及冷饮服务	Beverages and Services	27	21090	2764	9273
餐饮配送及外卖送餐服务	Catering Distribution and Delivery Service	11	13070	907	3175
其他餐饮业	Others Catering Services	8	22250	344	4736

住宿业和餐饮业财务状况(2020 年)

Enterprises Above Designated Size by Status of Registration and Sector(2020)

(10000 yuan)

累计折旧 Accumulated Depreciation	本年折旧 Depreciation	资产总计 Total Assets	负债合计 Total Liabilities	所有者权益合计 Creditors´ Equity
1558021	**159320**	**6349746**	**4861407**	**1500152**
1244994	**124734**	**5210560**	**3857169**	**1363381**
148606	14181	258855	67415	191439
24711	615	28536	22095	6441
–	–	–	–	–
–	–	–	–	–
540678	45232	2165135	1436311	720458
48748	3817	366541	105041	261500
477824	60582	2385852	2224792	179416
170718	**20157**	**681799**	**639152**	**44773**
142309	**14428**	**457387**	**365086**	**91998**
1285413	**122583**	**4778965**	**3528456**	**1269964**
1196080	112617	4361565	3199067	1184079
89031	9857	405093	322595	80372
302	110	12307	6794	5513
272608	**36736**	**1570781**	**1332951**	**230189**
192646	29854	1136435	973814	154980
70798	4960	352424	283265	69159
3707	1199	37417	47253	–9836
2117	294	14699	10638	4061
3339	430	29807	17981	11826

单位:万元

8－08　续表

项　　目	Item	营业收入 Revenue of Business	主营业务收　入 Main Revenue of Business	税金及附加 Sales Tax and Extra Charges
总　　计	**Total**	**3158630**	**3082072**	**5416**
(一)按登记注册类型分组	**Grouped By Registered Type**			
1. 内资企业	**Domestic－funded Enterprises**	**2224953**	**2159304**	**4962**
国有企业	State－owned Enterprises	99715	96316	585
集体企业	Collective－owned Enterprises	9855	9296	21
股份合作企业	Cooperative Enterprises	－	－	－
联营企业	Joint Ownership Enterprises	－	－	－
有限责任公司	Limited Liability Corporations	558138	531497	3186
股份有限公司	Share－holding Corporations Ltd.	114231	110583	207
私营企业	Private Enterprises	1437910	1406508	928
2. 港、澳、台商投资企业	**Enterprises With Investment from Hong Kong, Macao and Taiwan**	**238899**	**236035**	**204**
3. 外商投资企业	**Enterprises With Foreign Investment**	**694778**	**686733**	**250**
(二)按国民经济行业分组	**Grouped By Sector**			
1. 住宿业	**Lodging**	**1025853**	**971307**	**4397**
旅游饭店	Restaurants for Junketing	815455	772450	3921
一般旅馆	General Hotel	207633	196092	472
民宿服务	Homestay Service	2765	2765	4
2. 餐饮	**Catering Services**	**2132777**	**2110765**	**1019**
正餐服务	Dinner Services	1156942	1140178	741
快餐服务	Short Order Services	793210	789881	217
饮料及冷饮服务	Beverages and Services	98890	96973	37
餐饮配送及外卖送餐服务	Catering Distribution and Delivery Service	33989	33989	10
其他餐饮业	Others Catering Services	49746	49744	14

continued (10000 yuan)

销售费用 Cost of Sales	管理费用 Administration Cost	财务费用 Financil Cost	营业利润 Management Profits	利润总额 Total Profits	所得税费用 Income Tax Expense	从事住宿和餐饮业活动的从业人员平均人数(人) Average Number of Employees (person) engaged in hotel and catering activities
1112214	**639522**	**81377**	**-39421**	**-18861**	**42129**	**114187**
810063	**516382**	**51274**	**-89381**	**-66026**	**16505**	**79191**
38932	43084	-558	-9034	-7650	318	3808
4375	3078	6	-913	-683	10	493
-	-	-	-	-	-	-
-	-	-	-	-	-	-
211548	135299	22831	-8997	-1928	4485	23196
69463	20750	-3201	5208	5587	1345	4489
484496	311444	32198	-74253	-59971	10345	46988
128379	**39286**	**27223**	**-33079**	**-33582**	**143**	**13683**
173773	**83855**	**2880**	**83039**	**80746**	**25481**	**21313**
422968	**407658**	**63785**	**-166690**	**-153839**	**4554**	**41544**
350910	333490	59426	-133868	-123444	3688	34020
71078	73278	4309	-32823	-30488	855	7409
980	891	49	2	94	11	115
689246	**231864**	**17592**	**127269**	**134977**	**37575**	**72643**
395369	145845	14433	28388	36679	11324	37780
240645	67188	2862	99211	97894	24598	29970
29478	11306	175	-740	-352	1401	2851
5031	4458	28	68	431	32	802
18724	3067	94	342	325	220	1240

8-09 按登记注册类型和国民经济行业分限额以上住宿业和餐饮业经营情况(2020年)

Management Conditions of Hotels and Catering Services Enterprises Above Designated Size by Status of Registration and Sector(2020)

单位:万元 (10000 yuan)

项 目	Item	法人企业(个) Number of Enterprises (unit)	营业额 Revenue of Business	客房收入 Revenue of Guest Rooms	餐费收入 Revenue of Catering Services	商品销售额 Revenue of Goods Sales
一、按登记注册类型分	**Grouped By Registered Type**					
总　计	**Total**	**1136**	**3245549**	**561021**	**2424367**	**66266**
1. 内资企业	**Domestic - funded Enterprises**	**1095**	**2267560**	**507498**	**1523554**	**64113**
国有企业	State - owned Enterprises	31	102714	43829	46012	778
集体企业	Collective - owned Enterprises	7	10342	4934	3339	37
股份合作企业	Cooperative Enterprises	-	-	-	-	-
联营企业	Joint Ownership Enterprises	-	-	-	-	-
有限责任公司	Limited Liability Corporations	161	561571	149121	298640	43047
国有独资公司	State - funded Corporations	22	115675	29130	56505	2284
其他有限责任公司	Other Limited Liability Corporations	139	445897	119991	242135	40763
股份有限公司	Share - holding Corporations Ltd.	7	119102	37458	51458	2148
私营企业	Private Enterprises	887	1468543	270372	1120861	17991
私营独资企业	Private - funded Enterprises	8	5961	-	5955	-
私营合伙企业	Private Partnership Enterprises	4	3997	-	3845	-
私营有限责任公司	Private Limited Liability Corporations	873	1440877	269644	1094093	17991
私营股份有限公司	Private Share - holding Corporations Ltd.	2	17708	728	16967	-

单位:万元　　8-09　续表　continued　　(10000 yuan)

项　目	Item	法人企业(个) Number of Enterprises (unit)	营业额 Revenue of Business	客房收入 Revenue of Guest Rooms	餐费收入 Revenue of Catering Services	商品销售额 Revenue of Goods Sales
2. 港、澳、台商投资企业	**Enterprises With Investment from Hong Kong, Macao and Taiwan**	**17**	**249269**	**23251**	**222507**	**8**
合资经营企业(港或澳、台资)	Joint - venture Enterprises (With Funds from Hong Kong, Macao and Taiwan)	9	63546	18900	42199	4
合作经营企业(港或澳、台资)	Coorperative Enterprises (With Funds from Hong Kong, Macao and Taiwan)	–	–	–	–	–
港、澳、台商独资经营企业	Enterprises With Sole Investment from Hong Kong, Macao and Taiwan	7	185074	4091	179934	4
港、澳、台商投资股份有限公司	Share - holding Corporations Ltd. With Investment from Hong Kong, Macao and Taiwan	–	–	–	–	–
3. 外商投资企业	**Enterprises With Foreign Investment**	**24**	**728721**	**30272**	**678305**	**2145**
中外合资经营企业	Joint - venture Enterprises	3	628969	7503	620673	29
中外合作经营企业	Cooperation Enterprises	–	–	–	–	–
外资企业	Enterprises With Sole Foreign Investment	20	86556	17207	57292	1487
外商投资股份有限公司	Share - holding Corporations Ltd. With Foreign Investment	–	–	–	–	–
二、按国民经济行业分	**Grouped By Sector**					
总　计	**Total**	**1136**	**3245549**	**561021**	**2424367**	**66266**
1. 住宿业	**Lodging**	**510**	**1035603**	**536120**	**354718**	**8648**
旅游饭店	Restaurants for Junketing	279	820511	379858	322811	6925
一般旅馆	General Hotel	226	212257	154363	31015	1702
民宿服务	Homestay Service	5	2836	1899	893	21
2. 餐饮业	**Catering Services**	**626**	**2209946**	**24901**	**2069649**	**57618**
正餐服务	Dinner Services	549	1183411	24901	1062599	53153
快餐服务	Short Order Services	31	837405	–	828476	1581
饮料及冷饮服务	Beverages and Services	27	102827	–	94987	2859
餐饮配送及外卖送餐服务	Catering Distribution and Delivery Service	11	34189	–	31473	25
其他餐饮业	Others Catering Services	8	52114	–	52114	–

8－10 分地区限额以上
Main Indicators of Lodging

单位:万元

地　区	Region	企业法人数（个）Number of Enterprises（unit）	营业额 Revenue of Business	客房收入 Revenue of Guest Rooms	餐费收入 Revenue of Catering Services	主营业务收入 Main Revenue of Business
全　市	**Total**	**1136**	**3245549**	**561021**	**2424367**	**3082072**
市　区	Urban District	1025	3115584	498068	2366927	2961595
#上城区	Shangcheng	179	581065	83657	453176	548416
下城区	Xiacheng	99	396066	49879	308693	374306
江干区	Jianggan	106	216249	48031	148612	205510
拱墅区	Gongshu	81	157027	27114	108304	151702
西湖区	Xihu	136	895822	50683	795736	853791
高新(滨江)区	Hi－Tech(Binjiang)	53	101103	21085	76747	96680
萧山区	Xiaoshan	97	314360	92061	177878	294627
萧山本级	Xiaoshan	89	301776	90046	168753	282950
余杭区	Yuhang	73	120684	32467	80534	120665
富阳区	Fuyang	41	42152	12652	26076	40476
临安区	Lin'an	32	29202	14020	14158	26759
西湖风景名胜区	The West Lake Scenic Zone	63	176092	55581	110856	170774
钱塘新区	Qiantang New Area	73	98345	12855	75283	89567
桐庐县	Tonglu	31	30654	9582	17560	26919
淳安县	Chun'an	57	74306	41775	27421	69688
建德市	Jiande	23	25006	11596	12458	23870

住宿餐饮业主要指标(2020 年)

and Catering by Region(2020)

(10000 yuan)

税金及附加 Sales Tax and Extra Charges	销售费用 Cost of Sales	管理费用 Administration Cost	财务费用 Financil Cost	利润总额 Total Profits	从事住宿和餐饮业活动从业人员平均人数(人) Average Number of Employees (person) engaged in hotel and catering activities
5416	**1112214**	**639522**	**81377**	**-18861**	**114187**
5287	1062403	584858	70646	2328	107816
924	241927	92267	26223	18753	17567
1134	165504	53936	12743	-21189	17006
277	69454	49716	2292	-5118	6520
432	59708	33991	1805	-10485	5000
898	214607	106435	2725	93960	30448
33	22287	27417	1846	-7293	2927
291	140695	77726	11934	-24264	12484
284	137570	74049	11912	-24209	11992
120	31143	34674	3046	-7279	4276
149	11283	12192	4920	-7606	1827
48	9471	7041	2177	-1969	1514
954	70543	75085	109	-21650	6061
35	28907	18058	850	-3588	2678
-220	7355	20134	2836	-13225	1466
322	31714	28767	6731	-5810	3624
26	10743	5763	1165	-2154	1281

8－11 分行业、类型规模以上
Main Indicators of Service Enterprises

单位:亿元

项　　目	Item	单位数(个) Number of Enterprise (Unit)	资产总计 Total Assets	固定资产原价 Orginal Value of Fixed Assets
总　计	**Total**	**4660**	**31764**	**5564**
按登记注册类型分	**Grouped By Registered Type**			
国有企业	State－owned Enterprises	67	757	156
集体企业	Collective－owned Enterprises	51	453	152
股份合作企业	Cooperative Enterprises	9	92	49
其他联营企业	Other Joint Ownership Enterprises	–	–	–
其他有限责任公司	Other Limited Liability Corporations	846	10061	2164
股份有限公司	Share－holding Corporations Ltd.	185	3208	406
私营企业	Private Enterprises	3054	4729	647
其他企业	Other Enterprises	23	22	6
港澳台商投资企业	Enterprises With Investment from Hong Kong, Macao and Taiwan	123	8195	1083
外商投资企业	Enterprises With Foreign Investment	156	1847	537
按国民经济行业分	**Grouped by Sector**			
交通运输、仓储和邮政业	Transportation,Storage and Post	728	4779	1704
信息传输、软件和信息技术服务业	Information Transmission,Softuare and Information Technology	1068	12557	1683
房地产业	Real Estate	538	3904	488
租赁和商务服务业	Leasing and Business Services	972	4936	726
科学研究和技术服务业	Scientific Research and Technical Service	633	1907	196
水利、环境和公共设施管理业	Water Conservancy,Environment and Public Utility	100	2720	611
居民服务、修理和其他服务业	Service for the Residents and Other Service Sector	152	65	14
教育	Education	74	64	18
卫生和社会工作	Health Care and Social Welfare	165	133	26
文化、体育和娱乐业	Culture,Sports and Entertainment	230	700	98

服务业企业主要经济指标(2020 年)
Above Designated Size by Sector and Type(2020)

(100 million yuan)

其中:本年折旧 Depreciation	负债合计 Total Liabilities	所有者权益合计 Total Owners´ Equities	营业收入 Revenue of Business	营业成本 Operating Costs	营业税金及附加 Sales Taxes and Extra Charges in Main Business
446	**17059**	**14704**	**15116**	**9614**	**55**
5	266	491	231	211	1
4	164	289	26	14	2
1	25	66	6	1	1
–	–	–	–	–	–
102	5902	4159	2793	2101	12
26	1441	1767	448	291	2
68	3152	1577	4500	3150	15
1	16	6	26	16	–
180	3983	4212	4194	1147	15
42	1004	843	2505	2356	5
95	2891	1888	1911	1807	5
239	6330	6227	9403	4806	27
18	2104	1800	427	291	9
48	2805	2131	1459	1207	8
15	1063	844	1343	1079	5
17	1489	1230	130	109	1
1	45	20	73	51	–
2	49	15	62	34	–
3	80	52	135	86	–
8	204	496	173	144	1

单位:亿元　　8－11　续表

项　目	Item	销售费用 Cost of Sales	管理费用 Administration Cost	财务费用 Financil Cost
总　计	**Total**	**972**	**2042**	**50**
按登记注册类型分	**Grouped By Registered Type**			
国有企业	State－owned Enterprises	6	17	－8
集体企业	Collective－owned Enterprises	1	12	－
股份合作企业	Cooperative Enterprises	－	3	－
其他联营企业	Other Joint Ownership Enterprises	－	－	－
其他有限责任公司	Other Limited Liability Corporations	94	396	55
股份有限公司	Share－holding Corporations Ltd.	41	56	2
私营企业	Private Enterprises	260	336	27
其他企业	Other Enterprises	4	4	－
港澳台商投资企业	Enterprises With Investment from Hong Kong, Macao and Taiwan	488	1102	－28
外商投资企业	Enterprises With Foreign Investment	63	80	－4
按国民经济行业分	**Grouped by Sector**			
交通运输、仓储和邮政业	Transportation,Storage and Post	31	77	51
信息传输、软件和信息技术服务业	Information Transmission,Softuare and Information Technology	776	1606	－59
房地产业	Real Estate	20	58	22
租赁和商务服务业	Leasing and Business Services	74	116	26
科学研究和技术服务业	Scientific Research and Technical Service	22	105	－
水利、环境和公共设施管理业	Water Conservancy,Environment and Public Utility	3	15	15
居民服务、修理和其他服务业	Service for the Residents and Other Service Sector	7	12	－
教育	Education	14	10	－
卫生和社会工作	Health Care and Social Welfare	15	19	1
文化、体育和娱乐业	Culture,Sports and Entertainment	11	24	－7

continued (100 million yuan)

营业利润 Management Profits	利润总额 Total Profits	所得税费用 Income Tax Expense	应付职工薪酬 Payroll Payable	应交增值税 Value Added Tax Payable	平均用工人数（万人） Average Number of Employed Persons(10000 Persons)
2371	**2451**	**274**	**1936**	**305**	**96**
7	8	1	42	4	3
-1	-	-	4	1	-
2	1	-	-	-	-
-	-	-	-	-	-
206	229	27	433	53	23
96	96	4	108	11	6
553	564	57	545	92	43
2	2	1	11	-	1
1456	1478	134	584	118	9
9	29	43	122	19	6
68	84	17	199	32	14
1961	2014	210	1081	189	27
71	75	14	111	18	14
126	128	11	178	32	17
110	112	14	212	26	11
1	3	2	38	2	3
2	2	1	25	1	4
3	4	1	26	-	2
16	16	3	33	-	2
12	14	1	34	3	2

8－12　规模以上服务业企业主要经济指标(2014－2020年)
Main Indicators of Service Enterprises Above Designated Size(2014－2020)

单位:亿元　(100 million yuan)

项　目	Item	2014	2015	2016	2017	2018	2019	2020
单位数(个)	Number of Enterprises(Unit)	4393	3238	3486	3744	4145	4303	4660
资产总计	Total Assets	14340	15412	18951	20198	27522	29337	31764
固定资产原价	Orginal Value of Fixed Assets	2716	2847	3129	3657	4319	4915	5564
本年折旧	Depreciation	156	177	207	234	303	396	446
负债合计	Total Liabilities	7181	7463	9134	10063	14317	15205	17059
所有者权益合计	Total Owners´Equities	7160	7949	9816	10135	13235	14132	14704
营业收入	Revenue of Business	4353	5236	6639	8557	11158	12866	15116
营业成本	Main Cost of Business	2650	3215	4111	5410	7280	8102	9614
营业税金及附加	Sales Taxes and Extra Charges in Main Business	58	59	47	47	54	61	55
销售费用	Cost of Sales	257	314	341	457	651	724	972
管理费用	Administration Cost	621	765	932	1223	1747	2064	2042
财务费用	Financil Cost	62	65	43	53	37	58	50
营业利润	Management Profits	858	1020	1352	1636	1812	1994	2371
利润总额	Total Profits	934	1110	1443	1689	1853	2073	2451
所得税费用	Income Tax Costs	123	110	174	196	192	240	274
应付职工薪酬	Employee benefits Payable	588	718	904	1123	1344	1599	1936
应交增值税	Value Added Tax Payable	107	106	153	194	216	253	305
平均用工人数(万人)	Average Number of Employed Persons	60.29	63.22	68.92	76.24	81.15	85.43	96.43

8 - 13　私营企业、个体工商户登记注册情况(主要年份)

Statistics on Private Enterprises and Individual Business Registration (main years)

年度　　year	在册私营企业(户) Registered Private Enterprise (unit)	注册资金(万元) Registered Capital (10,000 yuan)	在册个体工商户(户) Registered Individual Business (unit)	注册资金(万元) Registered Capital (10,000 yuan)
2013 年	225219	70699701	327961	2392950
2014 年	276005	101081913	345327	2693164
2015 年	334732	150653768	386127	3330334
2016 年	400586	266020927	426028	3743654
2017 年	480986	417947655	471374	4498107
2018 年	554683	494453994	510198	5410789
2019 年	632298	548095350	610074	7517273
2020 年	678469	561289945	659054	8502960

主要统计指标解释

社会消费品零售总额 指各种经济类型的批发零售贸易业、住宿餐饮业对城乡居民和社会集团的消费品零售额总和。这个指标反映通过各种商品流通渠道向居民和社会集团供应的生活消费品来满足他们生活需要，是研究人民生活、社会消费品购买力、货币流通等问题的重要指标。社会消费品零售额包括:(1)售给城乡居民作为生活用的商品和修建房屋用的建筑材料;(2)售给机关、团体、学校、部队、企业、事业单位的职工食堂各种食品、燃料;(3)售给部队干部、战士生活用的粮食、副食品、衣着品、日用品、燃料;(4)售给来华的外国人、华侨、港澳台同胞的消费品;(5)售给社会集团的办公用品、纸张、帐册、文印用品、计算工具、书刊和奖品;公共用品和纺织品、针织品;学校用的教学用具;文体用品;非专用的劳动保护用品，如工作服、套袖、围裙、手套、毛巾、肥皂等;日用百货和杂品，包括职工食堂用的餐具、炊具、设备和清洁卫生工具等;家具、设备、日用电器、电讯设备、电影器材和照相器材等;取暖用的设备和燃料、防暑、降温的饮料;非生产经营用的交通工具，如小轿车、面包车、工具车、卡车和油料;零星修理的各种零配件、材料、工具、建筑材料等;举办各种招待会、茶话会、宴会用的烟酒茶和各种食品及馈赠的礼品;从公费医疗经费中开支的中、西药品、中药材和医疗器材以及其他非生产性设备和用品。

限额以上批发零售业 指批发业年主营业务收入在2000万元及以上，零售业年主营业务收入在500万元及以上的各种经济类型商贸企业。

商品销售总额 指对本企业(单位)以外的单位和个人出售(包括对国(境)外直接出口)的商品金额。这个指标反映批发零售贸易业在国内市场上销售商品以及出口商品的总量。商品销售总额包括:(1)售给城乡居民和社会集团消费用的商品;(2)售给工业、农业、建筑业、运输邮电业、批发零售贸易业、餐饮业、服务业等作为生产、经营使用的商品;(3)售给批发零售贸易业作为转卖或加工后转卖的商品;(4)对国(境)外直接出口的商品，不包括:出售本企业(单位)自用的废旧包装用品，未通过买卖行为付出的商品，经本单位介绍，由买卖双方直接结算，本单位只收取手续费的业务，购货退出的商品以及商品损耗和损失等。

规模以上服务业企业 辖区内年营业收入2000万元及以上服务业法人单位。包括:交通运输、仓储和邮政业，信息传输、软件和信息技术服务业，水利、环境和公共设施管理业三个门类和卫生行业大类。辖区内年营业收入1000万元及以上服务业法人单位。包括:租赁和商务服务业，科学研究和技术服务业，教育三个门类，以及物业管理、房地产中介服务、房地产租赁经营和其他房地产业四个行业小类。辖区内年营业收入500万元及以上服务业法人单位。包括:居民服务、修理和其他服务业，文化、体育和娱乐业两个门类，以及社会工作行业大类。

Explanatory Notes on Main Statistical Indicators

Total Retail Sales of Consumer Goods refer to the sum of retail sales of consumer goods sold by wholesale and retail trade, catering and lodging industry of various economic types to urban and rural residents and social groups. This indicator is used to show the supply of consumer goods through various channels to residents and social groups to meet their needs in life, and is very important for the study on people's livelihood, on the purchasing power of consumer goods and on the circulation of money. The total retail sales of consumer goods include: (1) commodities sold to urban and rural residents for their daily use and building materials sold to them for the construction or repair of houses; (2) food and fuels sold to canteens of government organs, organizations, schools, troops, enterprises and institutions;(3) grains, non – staple food, clothing, daily articles and fuels sold to military, personnel for their daily use; (4) consumer goods sold to foreigners, overseas Chinese, and Chinese compatriots form Taiwan, Hong Kong and Macao during their stay in the mainland of China; (5) commodities sold to social groups, including office appliances, paper, account books, printing articles, calculators, newspapers, magazines and prizes; public articles, textiles and knit goods; school teaching equipment; cultural and sports articles; non special labor protection articles like working clothes, sleeves, aprons, gloves, towel sand soaps; commodities and miscellaneous goods for daily use including tableware, cooking utensils, equipment and cleaning articles for canteens; furnishings, appliances, household electrical appliances, communications facilities, film and photograph equipment; heating facilities, fuels and cooling beverages preventing heatstroke; vehicles (not for business use) such as cars, vans, tool cars, trucks and oils; parts, fittings, materials, instruments and building materials in ordinary repair, tobaccos, alcohols, teas, foods and presents for all kinds of reception meetings and banquets; Chinese and Western medicines, herbs and medical facilities and other non – production goods and equipment paid by public medical fund.

Wholesale and Retail Trade Above Designated Size refer to business enterprises of various economic types engaged in wholesale trade with year main business revenue over 20 million Yuan, and in retail sale trade with year main business revenue over 5 million Yuan.

Total Sales of Commodities refer to the amount of commodities sold by enterprises to other units and individuals (including direct export). This indictor is used to show the total value of commodities sold at domestic markets and exported. It includes: (1) commodities sold to urban and rural residents and social groups for consumption; (2) commodities sold for production and management of industry, agriculture, construction, transportation, post and telecommunications, wholesale and retail trades, catering trade and service industry; (3) commodities sold to wholesale and retail establishment for re – selling, with or without further processing; (4) commodities for direct export, excluding waste packaging materials used by the establishments(units) themselves, commodities transferred without buying or selling procedures, businesses directly settled by both parties through introduction of units who only charge commission, rejected commodities in the purchase, loss in commodities, etc.

Service industry enterprises above designated size service industry legal entities with an annual operating income of 20 million yuan and above in the jurisdiction. Including health industry category and other three categories: transportation, warehousing and postal industry; information transmission, software and information technology service industry; water conservancy, environment and public facilities management industry. Service industry legal entities with annual business income of 10 million yuan and above in the jurisdiction. Including three categories and four sub – categories: leasing and business service industry, scientific research and technical service industry, education; and property management, real estate intermediary services, real estate leasing operation and other real estate industry. Service industry legal entities with an annual business income of 5 million yuan and above in the jurisdiction. Including social work industry category and other 2 categories: Resident service, repair and other service industries; culture, sports and entertainment industries.

九、对外经济旅游

FOREIGN ECONOMIC COOPERATION AND TOURISM

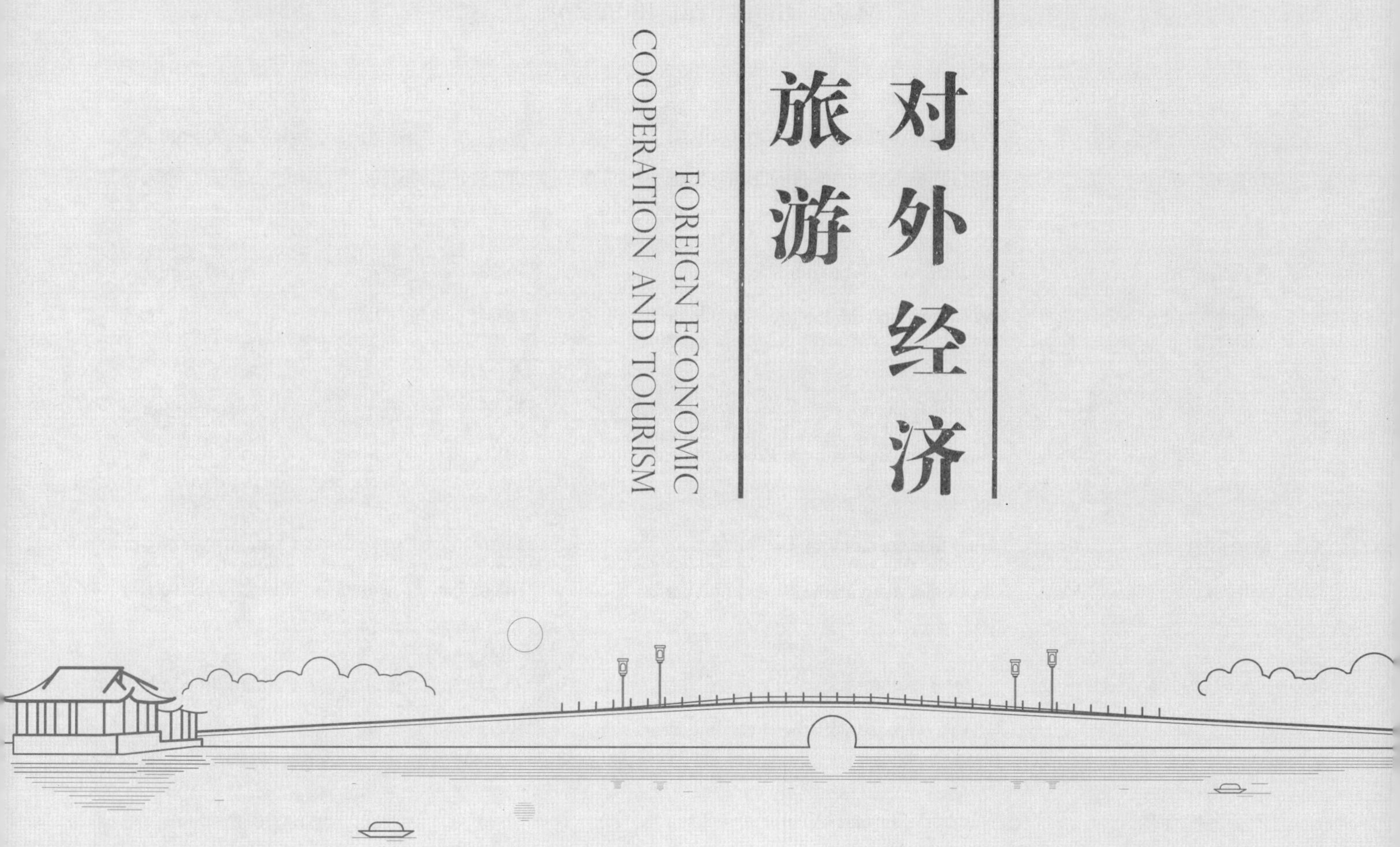

9 对外经济、旅游
Foreign Economic Cooperation and Tourism

主要统计指标
Major Statistical Indicators

实际利用外资金额	Foreign Investments Actually Utilized	72.0	亿美元	(USD 100 million)
为上年	As Compared with the Preceding Year	117.5	%	(%)
进出口总额	Total Imports and Exports	856.10	亿美元	(USD 100 million)
为上年	As Compared with the Preceding Year	105.4	%	(%)
# 出口总额	Total Exports	532.85	亿美元	(USD 100 million)
为上年	As Compared with the Preceding Year	101.6	%	(%)
进出口总额	Total Imports and Exports	5934.16	亿元	(100 million yuan)
为上年	As Compared with the Preceding Year	105.9	%	(%)
# 出口总额	Total Exports	3693.23	亿元	(100 million yuan)
为上年	As Compared with the Preceding Year	102.1	%	(%)
入境过夜游客	Number of Oversea Visitor Arrivals	14.3	万人次	(10000 person-times)
为上年	As Compared with the Preceding Year	12.6	%	(%)
旅游外汇收入	Total Foreign Exchange Earnings from International Tourism	0.59	亿美元	(USD 100 million)
为上年	As Compared with the Preceding Year	8.0	%	(%)

9-01 外商直接投资情况(1978-2020年)
Foreign Direct Investment(1978-2020)

单位:万美元 (USD 10000)

年份 Year	项目个数(个) Number of Projects (unit)	协议总投资额 Total Investments of Agreements	协议利用外资金额 Contracted Foreign Investment	实际利用外资金额 Foreign Investments Actually Utilized
1978				
1979				
1980	3	153	128	
1981				
1982				
1983	2	356	100	
1984	9	6932	2697	
1985	21	6638	1731	907
1986	9	5722	2017	683
1987	10	2685	1256	1470
1988	23	6781	2734	696
1989	34	3897	1569	1860
1990	68	7817	3951	751
1991	121	11107	5551	2129
1992	583	125224	60915	9678
1993	1078	222325	121947	35713
1994	624	174406	110541	41098
1995	427	136662	90207	42659
1996	221	108150	70982	53651
1997	174	51682	27888	41187
1998	216	98219	51400	38425
1999	212	83416	56742	42025
2000	315	89781	64548	43093
2001	483	154447	103023	50324
2002	587	247888	96720	52186
2003	869	432660	200104	100850
2004	802	629727	307746	140982
2005	756	770941	400503	171274
2006	747	1080602	537986	225536
2007	574	854907	558059	280181
2008	483	862523	622788	331154
2009	554	948323	696486	401370
2010	545	1188055	770911	435627
2011	500	1291015	817108	472230
2012	510	1342616	826516	496061
2013	415	1419926	913144	527633
2014	408	1329217	723838	633460
2015	475	1649709	1038042	711253
2016	462	1503411	847841	720915
2017	575	1877119	1069651	661001
2018	744	2545689	1565483	682658
2019	735	3066139	1321928	612818
2020	804	3622167	1059312	720184

9-02 分行业外商直接投资情况(2020年)
Foreign Direct Investment by Sector(2020)

单位:万美元 (USD 10,000)

行 业 Sector	项目数(个) Projects (unit)	占总数 % Proportion (%)	实际利用外资金额 Foreign Investments Actually Utilized	占总数(%) Proportion (%)
合 计 **Total**	**804**	**100.00**	**720184**	**100.00**
第一产业	**1**	**0.12**	**16**	**-**
农 业 Agriculture	1	0.12	16	-
第二产业	**74**	**9.20**	**232710**	**32.31**
采矿业 Mining	-	-	-	-
制造业 Manufacturing	70	8.71	221147	30.71
电力、燃气及水生产和供应业 Production & Supply of Electricity, Gas & Water	2	0.25	626	0.09
建筑业 Construction	2	0.25	10937	1.52
第三产业	**729**	**90.67**	**487458**	**67.69**
交通运输、仓储和邮政业 Transportation, Storage and Post	1	0.12	17641	2.45
信息传输、软件和信息技术服务业 Information Transmission, Softuare and Information Technology	231	28.73	156874	21.78
批发和零售贸易、餐饮业 Whole sale and Retail Tvade. Catering Services	147	18.28	19320	2.68
金融业 Banking and Insurance	6	0.75	47404	6.58
房地产业 Real Estate	12	1.49	161098	22.37
租赁和商务服务业 Leasing and Business Services	131	16.29	31847	4.42
科学研究和技术服务业 Scientific Research and Technical Service	136	16.92	47219	6.56
其他行业 Others	65	8.08	6055	0.84

9－03 分国别(地区)外商直接投资情况(2020年)
Foreign Direct Investment by Region or Territory(2020)

单位:万美元 (USD 10000)

国别(地区)	Country (territory)	历年累计 Accumulated 项目(个) Projects (unit)	历年累计 总投资额 Total Investments	历年累计 协议外资金额 Total Contracted Foreign Investments	2020年 In Year 2020 项目(个) Projects (unit)	2020年 总投资额 Total Investments	2020年 协议外资金额 Total Contracted Foreign Investments	2020年 实际利用外资 Foreign Investments Actually Utilized
合　计	**Total**	**16209**	**27965546**	**15157358**	**804**	**3622167**	**1059312**	**720184**
#中国香港	#Hong Kong China	7024	20423059	10722606	303	3169094	842102	639748
中国澳门	Macao China	84	82636	49427	2	－1345	15	－
中国台湾	Taiwan China	1774	520624	285070	94	31129	23049	492
日本	Japan	847	765555	307546	23	121438	29087	6982
泰国	Thailand	47	15419	5703	2	2003	1995	－
马来西亚	Malaysia	99	51341	34481	－		－	5
新加坡	Singapore	402	693553	398971	20	19998	5191	10980
印度	India	49	7039	6357	3	840	808	－
韩国	Republic of Korea	446	197848	103682	24	22175	16619	7145
德国	Germany	250	148500	84168	11	2428	632	12
法国	France	164	94202	49857	9	16668	2775	48
意大利	Italy	244	157937	76310	7	328	268	－
荷兰	Netherlands	104	115643	29560	5	2082	2030	4021
英国	Britain	265	275300	176166	17	5262	9945	9976
西班牙	Spain	83	71094	28012	4	763	565	16
奥地利	Austria	29	44581	34436	1	1375	1367	505
俄罗斯联邦	The Russion Federation	28	3586	1690	6	92	48	－
英属维尔京群岛	The British Virgin Islands	611	1734360	915443	8	97381	108680	13684
加拿大	Canada	311	117979	76741	30	4032	1274	96
美国	U. S. A	2010	1451112	667489	79	69889	12956	3749
澳大利亚	Australia	257	112443	87120	16	3552	2369	7
新西兰	New Zealand	51	13745	9880	4	－27	346	－

9－04　分地区外商直接投资情况(2020年)
Foreign Direct Investment by Region(2020)

单位:万美元　　(USD 10000)

区　域　　Region		批准项目个数(个) Number of Projects(unit)		实际利用外资金额 Foreign Investments Actually Utilized	
		2020年 In Year 2020	历年累计 Accumulated Until the End of 2020	2020年 In Year 2020	历年累计 Accumulated Until the End of 2020
全　市	**Total**	**804**	**16209**	**720184**	**8783983**
市　区	Urban District	782	15097	694821	8294671
#上城区	Shangcheng	30	861	59464	394823
下城区	Xiacheng	39	925	62089	290070
江干区	Jianggan	67	968	59527	450615
拱墅区	Gongshu	72	1144	52995	549284
西湖区	Xihu	90	1416	66904	735081
高新(滨江)区	Hi－Tech(Binjiang)	125	1562	69647	1024150
萧山区	Xiaoshan	137	2219	84000	1371269
余杭区	Yuhang	122	2000	107711	1029888
富阳区	Fuyang	19	806	28100	377162
临安区	Lin'an	14	486	16200	241928
钱塘新区	Qiantang New Area	65	262	88184	328449
桐庐县	Tonglu	7	585	14213	214186
淳安县	Chun'an	3	229	1013	102742
建德市	Jiande	12	298	11150	135278

9-05 特色小镇发展情况(2020年)
Statistics on Characteristic Towns(2020)

	企业数（家）Number of Enterprises (unit)	本年新入驻企业数（家）Number of new Enterprises to enter this year (unit)	"新四军"人数（个）Number of XinSiJun (unit)	固定资产投资（不包括商业住宅和商业综合体项目）（亿元）Investment in Fixed Assets (Excluding commercial housing and commercial complex projects) (100 million yuan)
合　计 Total	**46635**	**8442**	**20660**	**400**
省级特色小镇创建对象 Provincial Characteristic Towns to Create Objects	40340	7790	19911	345
省级特色小镇培育对象 Provincial Characteristic Towns to Cultivate Objects	6295	652	749	55

注:"新四军"创业人员数:包括大学生创业者、大企业高管及其他连续创业者、科技人员创业者、留学归国人员创业者等创业人员数。包括个体工商户和企业中有技术、资本入股的人员。

a)"XinSiJun" Entrepreneurs: including college student entrepreneurs, big business executives and other serial entrepreneurs, tech entrepreneurs, overseas returnees entrepreneurs and so on. Also including people with technical capital and equity of individual industrial and commercial businesses or enterprises.

9-05 续表 continued

	特色产业投资（亿元）Characteristic Industry Investment (100 million yuan)	工业企业营业收入（亿元）Industrial Enterprise Revenues in Main Business (100 million yuan)	服务业营业收入（亿元）Service Revenues (100 million yuan)	税收收入（亿元）Tax Revenues (100 million yuan)
合　计 Total	**298**	**3015**	**4404**	**557**
省级特色小镇创建对象 Provincial Characteristic Towns to Create Objects	255	2859	4277	531
省级特色小镇培育对象 Provincial Characteristic Towns to Cultivate Objects	43	156	127	26

9－06 国家级开发区

The Construction of National －

项　目	Item
规划面积　（平方公里）	Area of planning　(sq. km)
已开发面积　（平方公里）	Area of Development　(sq. km)
历年累计基础设施投资额　（亿元）	Accumulative Total Investments in Infrastructure　(100 million yuan)
历年累计批准进区企业　（个）	Accumulative Number of Enterprises Approved　(unit)
#三资企业　（个）	Foreign Investments Enter－prises　(unit)
历年累计协议利用外资　（亿美元）	Accumulative Total Foreign Investments of Agreements　(USD 100 million)
历年累计实际利用外资　（亿美元）	Accumulative Total Foreign Investments Actually Used　(USD 100 million)
年末实有投产企业个数　（个）	Number of Enterprises in Production or Operation at the Year－end　(unit)
#三资企业　（个）	Foreign Investments Enter－prises　(unit)
当年规模以上工业总产值　（亿元）	Gross Industrial Output Value of the Year　(100 million yuan)
当年规模以上企业主营业务收入　（亿元）	Fulfilled Profits and Tax of the Year　(100 million yuan)
当年规模以上企业实现利润　（亿元）	Fulfilled Profits of the Enterprises above the Designated Size of the Year　(100 million yuan)
当年出口创汇　（亿美元）	Foreign Exchange Earmings of Export of the Year　(USD 100 million)
当年财政总收入　（亿元）	Total Financial Revenue of the Year　(100 million yuan)
# 税收收入　（亿元）	Tax Revenue　(unit)

建设发展情况(2020 年)
Class Development Zones(2020)

合计 Total	杭州高新技术开发区 Hangzhou High - tech Development Zone	萧山经济技术开发区 Xiaoshan Economic and Technological Development Zone	富阳经济技术开发区 Fuyang Economic and Technological Development Zone	余杭经济技术开发区 Yuhang Economic and Technological Development Zone	临江国家高新区 Linjiang Nationd High - Tech Zone
817.53	12.12	58.41	106.04	109.26	531.70
266.49	12.12	47.20	42.17	47.00	118.00
3555.59	456.69	482.83	930.03	607.32	1078.72
-	73170	-	25702	58333	48092
4016.00	900	701	584	494	1337
-	-	126.46	39.47	45.96	261.98
385.83	102.66	67.07	31.95	34.02	150.13
160728.00	33271	13417	7615	58333	48092
-	900	453	226	494	-
8879.20	2473.20	863.62	989.66	1595.76	2956.96
22042.35	8742.50	3857.29	2650.00	3685.29	3107.27
1569.51	768.79	158.60	90.41	248.71	302.99
256.58	84.04	33.64	16.92	51.72	70.26
1081.54	358.43	243.83	116.68	172.36	190.25
1015.50	348.28	223.54	88.73	172.36	182.59

9－07 进出口情况(1990－2020 年)
Imports and Exports (1990－2020)

年 份 Year	亿美元 USD 100 million						亿元 100 million yuan					
	进出口 Exports And Imports		出口 Exports		进口 Imports		进出口 Exports And Imports		出口 Exports		进口 Imports	
	总值 Total Value	为上年% As Compared with the Preceding Year(%)	总值 Total Value	为上年% As Compared with the Preceding Year(%)	总值 Total Value	为上年% As Compared with the Preceding Year(%)	总值 Total Value	为上年% As Compared with the Preceding Year(%)	总值 Total Value	为上年% As Compared with the Preceding Year(%)	总值 Total Value	为上年% As Compared with the Preceding Year(%)
1990	1.45	172.6	0.99	198.0	0.46	135.3						
1991	2.18	150.3	1.48	149.5	0.70	152.2						
1992	3.42	156.9	2.16	146.0	1.26	180.0						
1993	8.73	255.3	4.92	227.8	3.81	302.4						
1994	34.96	400.5	26.11	530.7	8.85	232.3						
1995	45.18	129.2	33.18	127.1	12.00	135.6						
1996	43.52	96.3	31.11	93.8	12.41	103.4						
1997	48.83	112.2	37.43	120.3	11.40	91.8						
1998	59.73	122.3	44.16	118.0	15.57	136.6						
1999	73.40	122.9	50.79	115.0	22.61	145.3						
2000	104.76	142.7	69.65	137.1	35.11	155.3						
2001	112.98	107.9	72.84	104.6	40.14	114.3						
2002	131.07	116.0	84.81	116.4	46.26	115.3						
2003	182.38	139.2	109.55	129.2	72.83	157.4						
2004	244.96	134.3	151.75	138.6	93.21	128.0						
2005	298.70	121.9	198.04	130.5	100.66	108.0						
2006	389.09	130.3	262.28	132.4	126.81	126.0						
2007	434.26	111.7	299.66	114.3	134.60	106.2						
2008	480.65	110.7	336.14	112.2	144.51	107.4						
2009	404.20	84.1	271.80	80.9	132.40	91.6						
2010	523.55	129.5	353.37	130.0	170.18	128.6	3551.87		2397.67		1154.20	
2011	639.72	122.2	415.21	117.5	224.50	131.9	4152.76	116.9	2696.47	112.5	1456.28	126.2
2012	616.83	96.4	412.62	99.4	204.22	91.0	3893.23	93.8	2604.88	96.6	1288.35	88.5
2013	650.71	105.5	447.66	108.5	203.05	99.5	4037.01	103.7	2777.31	106.6	1259.70	97.8
2014	679.98	104.5	491.66	109.8	188.32	92.8	4177.24	103.5	3020.29	108.7	1156.95	91.8
2015	665.66	97.9	500.67	101.8	165.00	87.7	4132.43	99.0	3108.03	102.9	1024.40	88.7
2016	679.92	102.2	502.59	100.5	177.34	107.6	4485.97	108.7	3313.80	106.7	1172.17	114.6
2017	750.65	110.4	509.95	101.5	240.70	135.7	5085.08	113.3	3455.61	104.3	1629.46	138.8
2018	795.56	106.0	518.23	101.8	277.33	114.8	5245.28	103.1	3417.11	99.0	1828.17	111.8
2019	811.54	102.0	523.83	101.1	287.71	103.7	5596.81	106.7	3612.66	105.7	1984.14	108.5
2020	856.10	105.4	532.85	101.6	323.25	112.3	5934.16	105.9	3693.23	102.1	2240.93	112.9

9－08 分经济类型进出口情况(2020年)

Statistics on Imports and Exports by Econimic Type(2020)

单位:亿美元 (USD 100 million)

项　　目	Item	2020年 In Year 2020	为上年(%) As Compared with the Preceding Year(%)
全市进出口总值	Total Exports And Imports	856.10	105.4
一、出口总额	Exports	532.85	101.6
1. 国有企业	State－owned Enterprises	56.17	95.5
2. 三资企业	Foreign Investment Enterprises	100.51	95.3
(1)中外合作企业	Cooperation Enterprises	0.27	67.7
(2)中外合资企业	Joint－Venture Enterprises	44.39	94.6
(3)外商独资企业	Enterprises With Sole Foreign Investment	55.85	96.0
3. 集体企业	Collective－owned Enterprises	15.02	96.2
4. 私营企业	Private Enterprises	358.35	105.7
二、进口总额	Imports	323.25	112.3

9-09 分地区外贸进出口情况(2020年)
Imports and Exports by Region(2020)

单位:万美元 (USD 10000)

区域	Region	进出口总值 Total Imports and Exports	为上年(%) As Compared with the Preceding Year(%)	出口总值 Exports of This Year	为上年(%) As Compared with the Preceding Year(%)	进口总值 Imports of This Year	为上年(%) As Compared with the Preceding Year(%)
全市合计	**Total**	**8560995**	**105.4**	**5328482**	**101.6**	**3232513**	**112.3**
#不含省属	#Non-provincial	7849063	104.1	4977443	102.2	2871620	107.6
#上城区	Shangcheng	349490	117.3	156261	105.8	193229	128.7
下城区	Xiacheng	740388	121.6	296923	101.1	443465	140.7
江干区	Jianggan	447547	114.2	283368	116.5	164179	110.4
拱墅区	Gongshu	219774	110.8	150303	96.9	69471	160.3
西湖区	Xihu	421106	106.8	346219	104.2	74887	121.1
高新(滨江)区	Hi-Tech(Binjiang)	1161852	103.3	786572	110.7	375280	90.5
萧山区	Xiaoshan	1139767	93.8	879911	94.8	259856	90.4
余杭区	Yuhang	766374	110.2	712160	111.1	54213	100.3
富阳区	Fuyang	423847	103.6	193368	104.2	230478	103.0
临安区	Lin'an	259590	104.1	187842	104.0	71748	104.4
钱塘新区	Qiantang New Area	1287105	104.8	702177	103.9	584928	105.8
桐庐县	Tonglu	108617	99.8	101262	101.3	7355	83.4
淳安县	Chun'an	18525	95.0	16489	104.3	2037	55.1
建德市	Jiande	120050	122.7	110028	121.3	10021	140.3

9－10 分地区外贸进出口总值(2004－2020 年)
Total Value of Imports and Exports by Region(2004－2020)

单位:万美元 (USD 10000)

年份 Year	全市 Whole City	市区 Urban District 合计 Total	#萧山区 Xiaoshan	余杭区 Yuhang	富阳区 Fuyang	临安区 Lin'an	桐庐县 Tonglu	淳安县 Chun'an	建德市 Jiande
2004	2449671	2364434	414374	88538	52399	28918	32333	4461	19525
2005	2986993	2892191	510950	128999	72357	33262	30489	5211	25841
2006	3890853	3769910	610201	183930	81616	41492	38522	6797	34132
2007	4342666	4181699	795487	255534	105765	55542	48811	8319	48295
2008	4806503	4545719	953377	324421	126829	74862	71753	12478	101692
2009	4041991	3821965	829827	285496	116158	70454	60064	12039	77470
2010	5235549	4946409	1135326	385736	166652	101387	73919	17183	96651
2011	6397180	6044765	1432742	484903	216575	132729	93464	20459	105763
2012	6168325	5814547	1367290	512531	224446	142340	103153	21604	86681
2013	6507102	6115754	1408929	555640	265788	165094	119539	19692	87023
2014	6799775	6355378	1384823	601220	284980	193001	133392	23802	94202
2015	6656636	6178381	1189039	537405	285540	209150	147326	20814	100965
2016	6799241	6313076	1120689	520195	273306	223014	139150	18377	105623
2017	7506524	7295048	1079155	577771	372442	274535	110464	16843	84169
2018	7352678	7108994	1199436	701156	426099	238136	118296	18005	107382
2019	8115399	7889427	1214129	694110	429135	246122	108729	19382	97860
2020	8560995	8313802	1139767	766374	423847	259590	108617	18525	120050

9－11 外贸出口分国别(地区)情况(2020年)

Export by Country or Region(2020)

单位:万美元 (USD 10000)

国 别 (地区)	Country (territory)	2020年 In Year 2020	为上年(%) As Compared with the Preceding Year(%)
合 计	**Total**	**5328482**	**101.6**
#中国香港	Hong Kong China	98393	112.4
中国台湾	Taiwan China	55625	87.6
美国	U. S. A	972936	105.1
日本	Japan	323374	94.6
德国	Germany	242138	116.8
英国	Britain	187498	94.9
印度	India	199835	92.7
越南	Vietnam	180806	91.4
韩国	Republic of Korea	163000	97.8
荷兰	Netherlands	163610	113.9
意大利	Italy	104940	96.0
法国	France	148617	127.5
俄罗斯	Russia	139481	109.9
澳大利亚	Australia	122766	108.3
印度尼西亚	Indonesia	95855	83.2
西班牙	Spain	100352	112.8
加拿大	Canada	96831	102.2
巴西	Brazil	114977	101.2
墨西哥	Mexico	100790	95.8
泰国	Thailand	93770	98.3
"一带一路"国家(地区)	Countries along the Belt and Road	1688706	98.8

9-12 进出口货物分贸易方式总值表(2020年)
Total Value Table of Import and Export Goods by Trade Mode(2020)

单位:万美元 (USD 10,000)

贸易方式 Trade Mode	出口 Export		进口 Import	
	2020年 In Year 2020	为上年(%) As Compared with the Preceding Year(%)	2020年 In Year 2020	为上年(%) As Compared with the Preceding Year(%)
总值 Total Value	**5328482.13**	**101.6**	**3232512.94**	**112.3**
一般贸易 General Trade	4577165.33	102.2	2736265.35	111.9
来料加工装配贸易 Processing and Assembling Trade with Supplied Materials	30583.41	95.0	26097.29	97.6
进料加工贸易 Imported Materials Processing	596095.66	97.7	272252.32	108.5
外商投资企业作为投资进口的设备物品 Equipments and Goods Imported by Foreign-invested Enterprises as Investment	-	-	1835.66	251.0
保税监管场所进出境货物 Import and Export Cargos at Bonded Supervision Place	731.13	243.0	70283.52	136.0
海关特殊监管区域物流货物 Logistics Goods in Areas under Customs Special Supervision	20251.91	187.3	107183.87	131.4
海关特殊监管区域进口设备 Import Equipments in Areas under Customs Special Supervision	-	-	1041.96	79.0
华侨、港澳台同胞、外籍华人捐赠物资 Materials Donated by Overseas Chinese, Compatriots from Hong Kong, Macao and Taiwan, and Foreign Nationality Overseas	11921.49	-	2583.26	-
对外承包工程出口货物 Export Goods of Foreign Contracted Projects	49017.34	123.3	-	-
其他贸易 Other Trade	42715.84	56.7	14964.99	75.6

9-13 主要商品出口情况(2020年)
Major Commodity Exports(2020)

单位:万美元 (Unit: Ten Thousand U.S. Dollars)

项目名	Item	2020年 In Year 2020	为上年(%) As Compared with the Preceding Year(%)
机电产品	Mechanical and Electrical Products	2396105.38	103.7
高新技术产品	High-tech Products	938143.81	113.7
文化产品	Cultural Products	307255.19	106.1
农产品	Agricultural Products	113471.69	86.4
服装及衣着附件	Clothing and Clothing Accessories	417225.03	82.8
纺织纱线、织物及其制品	Textile Yarns, Fabrics and Their Products	691561.71	106.1
鞋靴	Footwear	40248.22	74.5
家具及其零件	Furniture and Its Parts	169983.51	99.7
塑料制品	lastic Products	155116.74	112.8
灯具、照明装置及其零件	Lamps, Lighting Devices and Their Parts	58357.64	99.3
箱包及类似容器	Bags and Similar Containers	36175.49	63.2
汽车零配件	Automobile Parts	159137.37	84.3
钢材	Steel	144813.44	107.0
船舶	Boats and Ships	2371.89	122.0
医药材及药品	Medicinal Materials and Drugs	153389.34	172.8
电线及电缆	Wire and Cable	57978.75	88.7
水海产品	Aquatic Products	3963.90	61.7

9－14 旅游发展情况(1995－2020 年)

Statistics on Tourism(1995－2020)

年 份 Year	旅游总收入 (亿元) Total Tourism Revenue (100 million yuan)	国内旅游收入 (亿元) Domestic Earnings (100 million yuan)	旅游外汇收入 (亿美元) Foreign Exchange Earnings from International Tourism (USD 100 million)	旅游总人数 (万人次) Total Tourists (10000 person－times)	国内游客人数 (万人次) Domestic Tourists (10000 person－times)
1995	106.0	94.3	1.45	2148	2104
1996	136.5	122.6	1.67	2055	2009
1997	158.8	142.1	2.01	2150	2100
1998	163.4	146.0	2.10	2172	2121
1999	186.0	166.7	2.37	2266	2207
2000	214.3	190.0	2.92	2376	2305
2001	249.7	218.9	3.37	2592	2510
2002	294.4	254.8	4.77	2758	2652
2003	325.9	290.9	4.22	2862	2776
2004	410.1	361.2	5.97	3139	3016
2005	465.1	403.6	7.58	3417	3266
2006	543.7	471.2	9.09	3864	3682
2007	630.1	548.6	11.19	4320	4112
2008	707.2	617.2	12.96	4773	4552
2009	803.1	708.9	13.80	5324	5094
2010	1025.7	910.9	16.90	6581	6305
2011	1191.0	1063.8	19.60	7487	7181
2012	1392.3	1253.2	22.02	8568	8237
2013	1603.7	1469.9	21.60	9725	9409
2014	1886.3	1743.9	23.18	10933	10606
2015	2200.7	2019.7	29.31	12382	12040
2016	2571.8	2362.6	31.49	14059	13696
2017	3041.3	2802.1	35.43	16287	15884
2018	3589.1	3335.6	38.31	18403	17983
2019	4004.5	3953.7	7.37	20814	20700
2020	3335.4	3331.3	0.59	17573	17559

注:自 2019 年开始,入境旅游口径调整为"入境过夜游客",2018 年以前为"境外旅游者人数"。

a) Since 2019, the caliber of inbound tourism has been adjusted to "inbound overnight tourists", which was "the number of overseas tourists" before 2018.

9－15 境外旅游者人数(1978－2020 年)

Number of International Tourists (1978－2020)

单位:人次 (person－times)

年份 Year	合计 Total	#外国人 Foreigners	港澳台同胞 Compatriots from Hong Kong, Macao and Taiwan	平均逗留天数 Average days of Staying
1978	53475	728	26648	
1979	84914	44714	39131	2.59
1980	124960	61710	61382	2.70
1981	154745	87727	65014	2.71
1982	152897	89100	61314	2.49
1983	160564	97803	59625	2.18
1984	179200	105771	70915	2.12
1985	238385	156311	75063	2.18
1986	266370	170960	87092	2.38
1987	300603	183477	100078	2.38
1988	349246	149512	159745	2.08
1989	248502	66094	163589	2.08
1990	388345	86621	268131	2.09
1991	390197	136809	229690	2.00
1992	489578	183781	267256	2.03
1993	459620	199796	234640	2.06
1994	337362	201692	124346	2.10
1995	441262	249418	177236	2.06
1996	462313	273477	178845	2.07
1997	504276	288949	205267	2.20
1998	507243	261353	231609	2.20
1999	591853	324625	257978	2.09
2000	707148	400906	306242	2.15
2001	819438	447689	371749	2.41
2002	1056266	631576	424690	2.50
2003	861163	482073	379090	2.72
2004	1234063	791616	442447	2.59
2005	1513585	1020840	492745	2.63
2006	1820171	1236792	583379	2.57
2007	2085997	1453650	632347	2.67
2008	2213329	1543665	669654	2.73
2009	2304045	1572838	731207	2.87
2010	2757147	1878528	878619	2.94
2011	3063140	2108263	954877	2.96
2012	3311225	2298763	1012462	2.95
2013	3160058	2198187	961871	2.93
2014	3261337	2254866	1006471	2.93
2015	3415619	2378461	1037158	2.99
2016	3632252	2556247	1076005	3.14
2017	4022309	2849993	1172316	3.25
2018	4205063	2990183	1214056	2.80
2019	1133143	839504	293639	3.20
2020	143084	113640	29444	2.35

注:从 1995 年起为全市数。自 2019 年开始,全省入境旅游统计口径调整为"入境过夜游客",根据省文旅厅数据,我市 2018 年接待入境旅游者人次为 107.23 万人次。2018 年以前为"境外旅游者人数"。

a) Data in this table has included the tourists of whole municipality since 1995. Since 2019, the statistical caliber of inbound tourism in the whole province has been adjusted to "inbound overnight tourists". According to the data from the Zhejiang Provincial Department of Culture and Tourism, Hangzhou received 1.0723 million person/times inbound tourists in 2018. which was "the number of overseas tourists" before 2018.

9-16 接待境外游客及居民出境旅游情况(2016-2020年)
Number of International Tourists and Outbound Tourists(2016-2020)

项　目	Item	2016年 In Year 2016	2017年 In Year 2017	2018年 In Year 2018	2019年 In Year 2019	2020年 In Year 2020
一、接待境外游客	**International Tourists**					
全年接待人数(人次)	**Number of Foreign Tourists(person-times)**	**3632252**	**4022309**	**4205063**	**1133143**	**143084**
#外国人	#Foreigners	2556247	2849993	2990183	839504	113640
港澳台同胞	Compatriots From Hong Kong, Macao and Taiwan	1076005	1172316	1214056	293639	29444
全年接待人天数(人天)	**Total Person-days (person-days)**	**11414114**	**13092273**	**14694611**	**2991120**	**336562**
#外国人	#Foreigners	8409339	9545816	10727681	2312566	264402
港澳台同胞	Compatriots From Hong Kong, Macao and Taiwan	3004775	3545457	3966930	678553	72159
平均逗留天数(天)	**Average Days of Staying (days)**	**3.14**	**3.25**	**2.8**	**3.2**	**2.4**
#外国人	#Foreigners	3.29	3.35	2.8	3.2	2.3
港澳台同胞	Compatriots From Hong Kong, Macao and Taiwan	2.79	3.02	2.6	2.8	2.5
旅游外汇总收入(万美元)	**Total Foreign Exchange Earnings From International Tourism (USD 10000)**	**314944**	**354286**	**383063**	**73660**	**5903**
二、居民出境旅游	**Outbound Tourism**					
居民出境旅游人数(人次)	**Outbound Tourists(Person-time)**	**1598969**	**1730474**	**2125332**	**2186500**	**87742**

注:从1995年起为全市数。自2019年开始,全省入境旅游统计口径调整为"入境过夜游客",根据省文旅厅数据,我市2018年接待入境旅游者人次为107.23万人次。2018年以前为"境外旅游者人数"。

a) Data in this table has included the tourists of whole municipality since 1995. Since 2019, the statistical caliber of inbound tourism in the whole province has been adjusted to "inbound overnight tourists". According to the data from the Zhejiang Provincial Department of Culture and Tourism, Hangzhou received 1.0723 million person/times inbound tourists in 2018. which was "the number of overseas tourists" before 2018.

9－17　接待境外游客分国别（地区）情况（2019－2020 年）
Number of International Tourists by Country or Territory（2019－2020）

单位：人次　　　　（person－times）

国　别（地区）	Country（territory）	2020 年 In Year 2020	2019 年 In Year 2019	为上年（%） As Compared with the Preceding Year（%）
合　计	**Total**	**143084**	**1133143**	**12.63%**
#中国香港	#Hong Kong China	14108	106739	13.22%
中国澳门	Macao China	1532	11269	13.59%
中国台湾	Taiwan China	13804	175631	7.86%
日本	Japan	3421	62631	5.46%
美国	U. S. A	4955	140771	3.52%
新加坡	Singapore	1195	31601	3.78%
澳大利亚	Australia	1214	29094	4.17%
泰国	Thailand	675	17756	3.80%
意大利	Italy	401	12513	3.20%
荷兰	Netherlands	378	13008	2.91%
西班牙	Spain	1685	9160	18.40%
马来西亚	Malaysia	17689	36486	48.48%
韩国	Republic of Korea	2827	111195	2.54%
法国	France	840	17003	4.94%
德国	Germany	1157	28429	4.07%
加拿大	Canada	1422	27422	5.19%
英国	Britain	979	23608	4.15%
印度尼西亚	Indonesia	14521	11185	129.83%
印度	India	440	17434	2.52%
菲律宾	Filipine	116	4821	2.41%

注：自 2019 年开始，全省入境旅游统计口径调整为“入境过夜游客”，该表 2018 年数据已调整为同口径。

a) Since 2019, the statistical caliber of inbound tourism in the whole province has been adjusted to " inbound overnight tourists" , The data of 2018 in the table has been adjusted to the same caliber.

主要统计指标解释

利用外资 指我市政府部门,企业和其他经济组织通过对外借款,吸收外商直接投资以及用其他方式筹措的境外现汇、设备、技术等。

外商直接投资 是指外国企业和经济组织或个人(包括华侨、港澳台胞以及我国在境外注册的企业)按我国有关政策、法规,用现汇、实物、技术等在我市境内开办外商独资企业、与我市境内的企业或经济组织共同举办中外合资经营企业、合作经营企业或者合作开发资源的投资(包括外商投资收益的再投资)以及经政府有关部门批准的项目投资总额内,企业从境外借入的资金。

进出口总额 海关进出口总额指实际进出我国国境的货物总金额。包括对外贸易实际进出口货物,来料加工装配进出口货物,国家间、联合国及国际组织无偿援助物资和赠送品,华侨、港澳台同胞和外籍华人捐赠品,租赁期满归承租人所有的租赁货物,进料加工进出口货物,边境地方贸易及边境地区小额贸易进出口货物(边民互市贸易除外),中外合资经营企业、中外合作经营企业、外商独资经营企业进出口货物和公用物品,到、离岸价格在规定限额以上的进出口货样和广告品(无商业价值、无使用价值和免费提供出口的除外),从保税仓库提取在中国境内销售的进口货物,以及其他进出口货物。进出口总额以观察一个国家在对外贸易方面的总规模。我国规定出口货物按离岸价格统计,进口货物按到岸价格统计。

境外旅游者人数 指来我市参观、访问、旅行、探亲、访友、休养、考察、参加会议和从事经济、科技、文化、教育、体育、宗教等活动的外国人、华侨、港澳和台湾同胞的人数。不包括外国在我市的常驻机构,如使领馆、通讯社、企业办事处的工作人员;来我市常住的外国专家、留学生以及在岸逗留不过夜人员。

境外旅游(外汇)收入 指入境旅游的外国人、华侨、港澳台同胞在杭州旅游过程中发生的一切旅游支出,对我市来说就是境外旅游(外汇)收入。

Explanatory Notes on Main Statistical Indicators

Utilization of Foreign Capital refers to foreign spot exchange, equipment and technology financed by foreign loans, foreign direct investment and other forms undertaken by Hangzhou government, enterprises and other economic units.

Foreign Direct Investment refers to the investments inside China by foreign enterprises and economic organizations or individuals (including overseas Chinese, compatriots from Hong Kong, Macao and Taiwan, and Chinese enterprises registered abroad) , following the relevant policies and laws of China, to establish wholly foreign owned enterprises, Sino foreign joint ventures and cooperative enterprises, or to explore resources jointly with enterprises or economic organizations in Hangzhou with spot exchange, material objects and technology. It also includes the re – investment of the foreign entrepreneurs with the profits gained from the investment and funds that enterprises borrow from abroad in the total investment of projects approved by the relevant department of the government.

Total Imports and Exports refer to the value of commodities imported into and exported from the boundary of China. It includes the actual imports and exports through foreign trades, imported and exported goods processed and assembled with supplied materials, supplies and gifts as aid given gratis between countries and by the United Nations and other international organizations, and contributions donated by overseas Chinese, compatriots in Hong Kong, Macao and Chinese foreign citizenship, leasing commodities belong to tenants at the end of leasing period, the imported and exported commodities processed with imported materials, commodities trading in border areas (excluding mutual exchange goods), the imported and exported commodities and articles for public use of the Sino – foreign joint ventures, cooperative enterprises and wholly foreign owned enterprises. It also includes imported or exported samples and advertising goods whose CIF or FOB value are beyond the permitted ceiling (excluding goods without trading or use value and exported free) , imported goods sold in China from bonded warehouses and other imported or exported goods. This indicator is used to observe the total size of external trade in a country. In accordance with the stipulation of Chinese government, imports are calculated at CIF, while exports are calculated at FOB.

Number of International Tourists refers to foreigners, overseas Chinese and compatriots from Hong Kong, Macao and Taiwan, who come to Hangzhou for sightseeing, visits, tours, family reunions, vacations, study tours, conferences and other activities of business, scientific and technological, cultural, educational and religious natures. It does not include employees of permanent offices of foreign countries in our city such as embassies, consulates, news agencies and offices of foreign companies, or long – term foreign experts or students residing in Hangzhou, or persons in transition without spending a night in Hangzhou.

Foreign Exchange Earnings from Overseas Tourism refer to the total expenditures of foreigners, overseas Chinese, Chinese compatriots from Hong Kong, Macao and Taiwan during their stay in Hangzhou, which are, for Hangzhou, foreign exchange earnings from overseas tourism.

十、财政、金融保险

FINANCE,BANKING AND INSURANCE

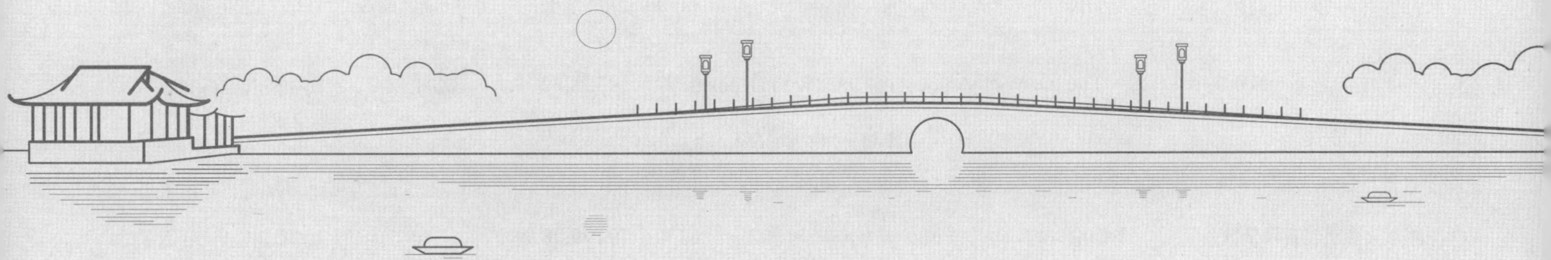

10 财政、金融、保险
Finance, Banking and Insurance

主要统计指标
Major Statistical Indicators

财政总收入	Total Financial Revenue	3854.19	亿元	(100 million yuan)
为上年	As Compared with the Preceding Year	105.6	%	(%)
一般公共预算收入	General Public Budget Revenue	2093.39	亿元	(100 million yuan)
为上年	As Compared with the Preceding Year	106.5	%	(%)
一般公共预算支出	General Public Financial Budgetary Expenditure	2069.66	亿元	(100 million yuan)
为上年	As Compared with the Preceding Year	106.0	%	(%)
年末金融机构各项存款余额	Balance of Deposits of Financial Institutions at Year-end	54246.47	亿元	(100 million yuan)
为上年	As Compared with the Preceding Year	119.8	%	(%)
# 住户存款余额	The Increased Amount of Household Deposits	14398.12	亿元	(100 million yuan)
为上年	As Compared with the Preceding Year	121.0	%	(%)
年末金融机构各项贷款余额	Balance of Loans of Financial Institutions at Year-end	49799.28	亿元	(100 million yuan)
为上年	As Compared with the Preceding Year	117.9	%	(%)

10－01 财政收入及支出(1978－2020年)

Financial Revenue and Expenditure (1978－2020)

单位:万元 (10000 yuan)

年 份 Year	财政总收入 Financial Revenue		一般公共预算收入 General Public Budget Revenue		一般公共预算支出 General Public Budget Expenditure	
	全 市 Total	市 区 Urban District	全 市 Total	市 区 Urban District	全 市 Total	市 区 Urban District
1978	94102	73396	–	–	16170	7779
1979	103259	81885	–	–	20334	11289
1980	118529	94015	–	–	21726	11867
1981	128564	100645	–	–	23964	13891
1982	140510	107298	–	–	24945	13687
1983	153941	116559	–	–	32765	17822
1984	172996	130757	–	–	46937	28710
1985	186472	131923	–	–	57710	35435
1986	205952	141943	–	–	73213	43959
1987	226262	152268	–	–	70717	41011
1988	246961	161208	–	–	95655	53031
1989	255003	156649	–	–	113571	61534
1990	252503	149904	–	–	118167	62587
1991	267597	158130	–	–	123134	62403
1992	286394	168341	–	–	132814	65984
1993	394946	233670	–	–	185168	90545
1994	484597	300014	197292	116733	215415	102430
1995	551262	339828	230431	135041	249050	120084
1996	635334	414557	268438	169987	302390	151016
1997	740725	485650	312797	196885	363834	197054
1998	869824	585615	368484	236269	424478	237221
1999	1026577	689394	449593	288002	563524	335243
2000	1428519	970937	691891	599910	734328	445698
2001	1884608	1612225	1042789	884738	1049330	849479
2002	2571408	2235021	1183153	1022964	1410199	1166298
2003	3297091	2861459	1503888	1290778	1635948	1340463
2004	3957516	3488744	1974523	1712813	1956282	1602303
2005	5207930	4584112	2504565	2172575	2383344	1957619
2006	6244906	5484645	3013888	2616084	2754809	2254347
2007	7884237	6929667	3916195	3421403	3357153	2747060
2008	9105489	7991043	4553531	3972842	4196674	3454599
2009	10194264	8965758	5207899	4535191	4903983	4000324
2010	12454323	10988265	6713413	5894414	6165836	4988197
2011	14889206	13009046	7851524	6822765	7475004	5971740
2012	16278879	14244888	8599875	7475989	7862800	6222930
2013	17349750	15157584	9452020	8207264	8557370	6662314
2014	19201076	17750305	10273169	9426504	9611771	8077961
2015	22387456	20738698	12338820	11360166	12054777	10235061
2016	25584128	23844189	14023826	12988095	14043065	12019355
2017	29212996	28010839	15674169	14979182	15409156	13968866
2018	34574596	33198717	18250616	17466268	17170834	15573258
2019	36500413	35006136	19659731	18800198	19528530	17796386
2020	38541929	37001224	20933893	20021700	20696554	18772405

单位:万元

指标	Item	全市 Total	市区 Urban District	上城区 Shangcheng
财政总收入合计	**Total**	**38541929**	**37001224**	**1605656**
一、一般公共预算收入	General Public Budget Revenue	20933893	20021700	794640
(一)税收收入	Tax Revenue	19785952	18961337	758725
1. 国内增值税	Domestic Value－added Tax	6283057	6001708	248355
其中:改征增值税	Newly Changed Value－added Tax	3815351	3692451	161199
2. 企业所得税	Corporate Income Tax	3997302	3834553	211013
3. 个人所得税	Individual Income Tax	1999483	1934690	160891
4. 资源税	Resource tax	18557	11514	－
5. 城市维护建设税	City Construction and Maintenance Tax	1138295	1103693	36085
6. 房产税	Real Estate Tax	672537	652456	45704
7. 印花税	Stamp tax	329993	318568	16636
8. 城镇土地使用税	Urban Land Use Tax	143926	130115	3663
9. 土地增值税	Land Appreciation Tax	1609298	1564057	35978
10. 车船税	Vehicle and vessel tax	127466	109100	35
11. 耕地占用税	Tax on the Use of Arable Land	417613	383633	－
12. 契税	Contract Tax	3031748	2902751	－
13. 环境保护税	Environmental protection tax	2120	1327	4
14. 其他税收	Others Tax	14557	13172	361
(二)非税收入	Non－tax Revenue	1147941	1060363	35915
1. 专项收入	Special Revenue	934996	893032	29123
#教育费附加	Revenue from Extra－Charges for Education	437692	419331	13048
地方教育附加收入	Local Education Additional Revenue	291859	279639	8699
残疾人就业保障金收入	Employment Security for The Disabled Revenue	150037	144523	7373
教育资金收入	Educational Fund Revenue	500	－	－
农田水利建设资金收入	Fund in The Farmland Irrigation Construction Revenue	35594	35274	－
2. 行政事业性收费收入	Income from Administrative Fees	167184	158222	－
3. 罚没收入	Penalty and Confiscatory Income	214645	195820	6650
4. 国有资本经营收入	Revenue of state－owned capital	－469821	－465121	－
#国有企业计划亏损补贴	Subsides to Loss－making of state－owned Enterprises	－474590	－469890	－
5. 国有资源(资产)有偿使用收入	Compensation for the Use of Seate－owned Assets Income	242891	221478	142
6. 政府住房基金收入	Government Housing Fund Income	51801	50715	－
7. 其他收入	Others Revenue	6245	6217	－
二、上划中央"四税"小计	Subtotal Revenue of Central Government	17608036	16979524	811016
1. 消费税	Consumption Tax	2329796	2323947	4804
2. 增值税	Value Added Tax	6283057	6001708	248355
3. 企业所得税	Corporate Income Tax	5995956	5751832	316520
4. 个人所得税	Individual Income Tax	2999227	2902037	241337

注:萧山区不含托管在钱塘新区的街道数据。

总收入(2020 年)

Revenue by Region(2020)

(10000 yuan)

下城区 Xiacheng	江干区 Jianggan	拱墅区 Gongshu	西湖区 Xihu	高新(滨江)区 Hi - Tech (Binjiang)	萧山区 Xiaoshan
1456845	**1966868**	**1543907**	**3177725**	**3584324**	**4610327**
812344	1076575	867308	1619799	1827504	3000273
760115	1043010	813248	1521330	1725954	2770494
279073	385493	346243	588023	647687	737268
160949	277026	189039	429446	308612	435772
153530	255388	163621	278648	421296	443631
85914	76567	51398	366280	317594	128114
–	–		–	–	2389
48654	56469	54935	81973	140568	133456
42218	73142	38659	70467	69988	64370
21575	19323	17799	30937	29606	46450
1458	3837	1926	8447	4614	25760
60146	171738	136383	94731	90806	420010
67135	17	11	326	5	19190
–	–		–	–	84799
–	–		–	–	663285
1	8	5	14	3	210
411	1028	2268	1484	3787	1562
52229	33565	54060	98469	101550	229779
40871	42039	40539	72275	95854	105288
17549	20366	20663	35200	47474	51663
11744	13542	13758	23464	31953	34292
11576	8121	6028	13351	16426	18460
–	–		–	–	–
–	–		–	–	–
4530	–	2784	7068	–	72171
6415	11094	10459	9001	5212	44501
–	-20000	–	–	–	-34001
–	-20000	–	–	–	-34001
413	403	278	10125	484	35881
–	–	–	–	–	5197
–	29	–	–	–	742
644501	890293	676599	1557926	1756820	1610054
6262	6867	7827	2511	798	15168
279073	385493	346243	588023	647687	737268
230295	383082	245432	417972	631944	665447
128871	114851	77097	549420	476391	192171

a) Figures of Xiaoshan District don't include districts which under administered by Qiantang New Area.

指 标	Item	余杭区 Yuhang	富阳区 Fuyang
财政总收入合计	**Total**	**8259080**	**1387234**
一、一般公共预算收入	General Public Budget Revenue	4410638	901379
(一)税收收入	Tax Revenue	4331263	854920
1. 国内增值税	Domestic Value－added Tax	1205175	265140
其中:改征增值税	Newly Changed Value－added Tax	853497	120777
2. 企业所得税	Corporate Income Tax	1214755	106178
3. 个人所得税	Individual Income Tax	540399	39873
4. 资源税	Resource tax	93	6719
5. 城市维护建设税	City Construction and Maintenance Tax	169719	39834
6. 房产税	Real Estate Tax	95058	33825
7. 印花税	Stamp tax	45548	14404
8. 城镇土地使用税	Urban Land Use Tax	24449	26661
9. 土地增值税	Land Appreciation Tax	288872	71353
10. 车船税	Vehicle and vessel tax	10672	5777
11. 耕地占用税	Tax on the Use of Arable Land	217286	17571
12. 契税	Contract Tax	517453	227097
13. 环境保护税	Environmental protection tax	187	396
14. 其他税收	Others Tax	1597	92
(二)非税收入	Non－tax Revenue	79375	46459
1. 专项收入	Special Revenue	123340	30517
#教育费附加	Revenue from Extra－Charges for Education	60214	14787
地方教育附加收入	Local Education Additional Revenue	40609	9878
残疾人就业保障金收入	Employment Security for The Disabled Revenue	20675	3614
教育资金收入	Educational Fund Revenue	－	－
农田水利建设资金收入	Fund in The Farmland Irrigation Construction Revenue	－	－
2. 行政事业性收费收入	Income from Administrative Fees	292	24323
3. 罚没收入	Penalty and Confiscatory Income	14828	11696
4. 国有资本经营收入	Revenue of state－owned capital	－70000	－40447
#国有企业计划亏损补贴	Subsides to Loss－making of state－owned Enterprises	－70000	－40447
5. 国有资源(资产)有偿使用收入	Compensation for the Use of Seate－owned Assets Income	10844	18557
6. 政府住房基金收入	Government Housing Fund Income	71	1813
7. 其他收入	Others Revenue	－	－
二、上划中央"四税"小计	Subtotal Revenue of Central Government	3848442	485855
1. 消费税	Consumption Tax	10535	1638
2. 增值税	Value added Tax	1205175	265140
3. 企业所得税	Corporate Income Tax	1822133	159267
4. 个人所得税	Individual Income Tax	810599	59810

continued (10000 yuan)

临安区 Lin'an	钱塘新区 Qiantang New Area	西湖风景名胜区 The West Lake Scenic Zone	桐庐县 Tonglu	淳安县 Chun'an	建德市 Jiande
1096011	**1902535**	**136632**	**583038**	**401307**	**556360**
685550	1003047	69506	342245	227682	342266
679136	926383	65310	313768	208326	302521
188479	427307	18538	117464	63662	100223
104062	92733	13688	41657	41709	39534
110513	216220	25453	48972	51907	61870
36012	53184	6930	33207	19738	11848
2313	–	–	1132	411	5500
35632	72677	3778	13788	7067	13747
20017	61789	8910	7715	4494	7872
9534	19731	1043	5513	2418	3494
12922	14507	653	4505	1928	7378
99276	59038	–	20608	12439	12194
4209	1722	1	3942	3167	11257
26405	–	–	17793	2526	13661
133217	–	–	38073	38184	52740
76	161	–	308	10	475
531	47	4	748	375	262
6414	76664	4196	28477	19356	39745
34175	55540	2982	15543	7740	18681
14174	27879	1357	7477	3911	6973
9428	18588	904	4985	2577	4658
5414	9050	721	2075	1059	2380
–	–	–	–	–	500
–	–	–	–	–	320
4264	11925	5	1301	5205	2456
9547	4425	329	8200	3834	6791
-83127	3354	–	–	–	-4700
-84542	–	–	–	–	-4700
36423	1316	880	3405	1846	16162
89	–	–	–	731	355
5043	104	–	28	–	–
410461	899488	67126	240793	173625	214094
2194	68075	13	60	2495	3294
188479	427307	18538	117464	63662	100223
165770	324330	38180	73458	77861	92805
54018	79776	10395	49811	29607	17772

10－03 分地区一般公共

General Public

单位:万元

指　　标	Item	全　市 Total	市　区 Urban District	上城区 Shangcheng
一般公共预算支出	**General Public Budget Expenditure**	**20696554**	**18772405**	**524299**
一、一般公共服务	Expenditure for General Public Services	1903776	1734087	58143
二、国防	Expenditure for National Defense	11396	9957	26
三、共安全	Expenditure for Public Security	1257777	1159227	48110
四、教育	Expenditure for Education	4042682	3691653	117471
其中:教育费附加支出	Expenditure on Extra－Charges for Educations	255443	241831	5094
五、科学技术	Expenditure for Science and Technology	1443254	1375130	20029
六、文化旅游体育与传媒	Expenditure for Culture, Sports and Media	400728	361965	6649
七、社会保障和就业	Expenditure for Social Safety Net and Employment Effort	2531543	2318836	81053
八、卫生健康	Expenditure for Medical and Health Care and Birth Control	1490008	1281861	26100
九、节能环保	Expenditure for Energy Conservation Environmental Protection	533234	453283	1045
十、城乡社区	Expenditure for Urban and Rural Community	2705431	2601925	68890
十一、农林水	Expenditure for Agriculture, Forestry and Water Conservancy	1029656	803671	2371
十二、交通运输	Expenditure for Transsportation	583462	432836	17479
十三、资源勘探工业信息等	Resources Exploration Information, etc	828444	812260	8788
十四、商业服务业等	Expenditure for Commercial Service Industry	530055	512145	13060
十五、金融	Expenditure for Financial Supervision	80600	78626	17084
十六、援助其他地区	Expenditure for Aiding Other Territories	158750	151639	15185
十七、自然资源海洋气象等	Expenditure for Land, Ocean and Meteorological Services	177203	131399	1087
十八、住房保障	Expenditure on Housing Support	401739	350724	16440
十九、粮油物资储备	Expenditure for Grain and Oil Reservation and other Materials Services	46543	40560	–
二十、灾害防治及应急管理	(缺英文)	89436	75622	1862
二十一、债务付息	Expenditure for Interest Payment	382879	327883	2990
二十二、债务发行费用	Expenditure for Interest Payment and issue costs of Government debt	3045	2925	15
二十三、其他	Other Expenditure	64913	64191	422

注:萧山区不含托管在钱塘新区的街道数据。

预算支出（2020 年）

Expenditure by Region（2020）

（10000 yuan）

下城区 Xiacheng	江干区 Jianggan	拱墅区 Gongshu	西湖区 Xihu	高新（滨江）区 Hi – Tech（Binjiang）	萧山区 Xiaoshan
542954	**823687**	**606054**	**1095492**	**1263429**	**2756453**
62607	76249	69186	84916	45771	278393
348	32	27	1520	–	2957
61784	59623	64861	83727	45720	139695
118899	207580	161017	276583	249654	568534
3492	16188	14128	19672	40000	48874
19236	68846	42098	62660	298345	145631
9841	12968	6136	14045	32713	38256
108579	104519	76495	156630	145446	172876
31670	45733	36018	88124	36037	228232
675	8623	4668	1153	6414	90285
58820	139233	100965	199229	221680	404908
1318	7748	996	19810	10800	164548
4580	135	–	–	–	76704
3118	1404	710	45530	73216	153939
22174	7733	6222	3662	14474	91396
2706	136	3250	2152	3799	2411
–	–	1670	9360	20154	23243
1579	2350	2097	6418	2673	35473
28144	41336	27631	29888	27034	67177
–	100	–	120	–	2979
1016	1111	1280	5607	2845	8738
5841	13344	710	4049	19920	57872
19	215	17	117	224	708
–	24669	–	192	6510	1498

a) Figures of Xiaoshan District don't include subdistricts which under administered by Qiantang New Area.

单位:万元 10－03 续表

指 标	Item	余杭区 Yuhang	富阳区 Fuyang
一般公共预算支出	**General Public Budget Expenditure**	**4136350**	**1025150**
一、一般公共服务	Expenditure for General Public Services	409048	106226
二、国防	Expenditure for National Defense	2310	47
三、公共安全	Expenditure for Public Security	142185	56390
四、教育	Expenditure for Education	760069	237423
其中:教育费附加支出	Expenditure on Extra－Charges for Educations	57349	25042
五、科学技术	Expenditure for Science and Technology	247255	56365
六、文化旅游体育与传媒	Expenditure for Culture, Sports and Media	72304	19352
七、社会保障和就业	Expenditure for Social Safety Net and Employment Effort	393314	78199
八、卫生健康	Expenditure for Medical and Health Care and Birth Control	245305	124567
九、节能环保	Expenditure for Energy Conservation Environmental Protection	109070	26055
十、城乡社区	Expenditure for Urban and Rural Community	757138	38208
十一、农林水	Expenditure for Agriculture, Forestry and Water Conservancy	197005	88699
十二、交通运输	Expenditure for Trarssportation	53072	78689
十三、资源勘探工业信息等	Resources Exploration Information, etc	268387	6429
十四、商业服务业等	Expenditure for Commercial Service Industry	304560	13239
十五、金融	Expenditure for Financial Supervision	8550	1448
十六、援助其他地区	Expenditure for Aiding Other Territories	24076	7597
十七、自然资源海洋气象等	Expenditure for Land, Ocean and Meteorological Services	21887	10759
十八、住房保障	Expenditure on Housing Support	22010	37209
十九、粮油物资储备	Expenditure for Grain and Oil Reservation and other Materials Services	4123	1401
二十、灾害防治及应急管理	(缺英文)	14795	4879
二十一、债务付息	Expenditure for Interest Payment	68093	31816
二十二、债务发行费用	Expenditure for Interest Payment and issue costs of Government debt	515	153
二十三、其他	Other Expenditure	11279	–

continued (10000 yuan)

临安区 Lin'an	钱塘新区 Qiantang New Area	西湖风景名胜区 The West Lake Scenic Zone	桐庐县 Tonglu	淳安县 Chun'an	建德市 Jiande
904676	**1250772**	**141381**	**564082**	**766825**	**593242**
84342	109839	8691	40346	67147	62196
405	127	10	577	276	586
46032	61468	18476	34629	30082	33839
175602	214519	4551	150977	94685	105367
1704	–	409	6903	4398	2311
36185	94362	386	30285	11163	26676
16351	4028	9669	15654	11952	11157
148130	39394	9482	58548	85229	68930
77562	29399	4589	79565	69108	59474
30514	75881	71	10231	59550	10170
53576	267287	80496	19942	42778	40786
89727	41045	1829	59815	90485	75685
40642	20494	–	16897	112465	21264
17126	188106	26	1008	11935	3241
6032	18260	531	6195	7737	3978
1065	426	11	1011	530	433
6518	3031	228	5905	–	1206
10013	5897	262	4411	15589	25804
27536	22070	2020	12409	21542	17064
1058	1101	–	2323	2328	1332
18390	8954	53	4459	6582	2773
17817	37531	–	8823	25633	20540
53	353	–	72	29	19
–	7200	–	–	–	722

10－04 分税种、支出科目财政收支情况(2014－2020 年)

Local Public Financial Budgetary Expenditure by Tax and Expenditure Account(2014－2020)

单位:万元 (10000 yuan)

指标 Item	2014	2015	2016	2017	2018	2019	2020
财政总收入合计 Total	**19201076**	**22387456**	**25584128**	**29212996**	**34574596**	**36500413**	**38541929**
一、一般公共预算收入 General Public Budget Revenue	10273169	12338820	14023826	15674169	18250616	19659731	20933893
(一)税收收入 Tax Revenue	9952111	11259532	12892210	14171594	16512101	17911758	19785952
1. 国内增值税 Domestic Value－added Tax	1224336	1301043	2097640	2969672	3222118	6464435	6283057
改征增值税 Newly Changed Value－added Tax	837724	1000427	1705813	2693559	3354083	3293607	3815351
2. 营业税 Business Tax	2650471	3094627	1988053	5288	16053		
3. 企业所得税 Corporate Income Tax	1723639	1928567	2215439	2702212	3230360	3762660	3997302
4. 个人所得税 Individual Income Tax	681449	920917	1155176	1461998	1863436	1813506	1999483
5. 城市维护建设税 City Construction and Maintenance Tax	693932	792815	890160	984315	1133495	1117782	1138295
6. 房产税 Real Estate Tax	378171	398528	443407	557952	663805	589684	672537
7. 城镇土地使用税 Urban Land Use Tax		155914	147437	205548	172024	116652	143926
8. 土地增值税 Land Appreciation Tax		551468	851760	975587	931792	1639773	1609298
9. 耕地占用税 Tax on the Use of Arable Land	72117	64426	40610	37784	31261	119847	417613
10. 契税 Contract Tax	805656	761861	1056441	1205784	1474897	1839509	3031748
11. 其他税收 Others Tax	884616	288939	300274	371895	418777	447910	492693
(二)非税收入 Non－tax Revenue	321058	1079288	1131616	1502575	1738515	1747973	1147941
1. 专项收入 Special Revenue	278423	1073893	1102959	1180199	1293351	1173121	934996
2. 行政事业性收费收入 Income from Administrative Fees	13988	12213	10968	48079	111730	101292	167184

单位:万元　　10－04　续表　continued　　(10000 yuan)

指标 Item	2014	2015	2016	2017	2018	2019	2020
3. 罚没收入 Penalty and Confiscatory Income	148190	149897	160147	218482	328202	279899	214645
4. 国有资本经营收入 Revenue of state－owned capital						－198006	－469821
#国有企业计划亏损补贴 Subsides to Loss－making of state－owned Enterprises	－147887	－197823	－250873	－174529	－230413	－198299	－474590
5. 国有资源(资产)有偿使用收入 Compensation for the Use of Seate－owned Assets Income	27927	38904	58175	101288	146357	292317	242891
6. 政府住房基金收入 Government Housing Fund Income	－	－	47.46	128247	79003	92493	51801
7. 其他收入 Others Revenue	417	2204	47146	809	10285	6857	6245
二、一般公共预算支出 General Public Budget Expenditure	9611771	12054777	14043065	15409156	17170834	19528530	20696554
1. 一般公共服务 Expenditure for General Public Services	892027	1011605	1125425	1311829	1503663	1708207	1903776
2. 教育 Expenditure for Education	1826924	2234425	2530114	2792968	3154350	3635648	4042682
3. 科学技术 Expenditure for Science and Technology	524082	701490	749190	923236	1182090	1481879	1443254
4. 文化旅游体育与传媒 Expenditure for Culture, Sports and Media	242375	449192	283936	309282	332192	389757	400728
5. 社会保障和就业 Expenditure for Social Safety Net and Employment Effort	1082564	1309862	1492895	1731704	2043585	2292860	2531543
6. 卫生健康 Expenditure for Medical and Health Care and Birth Control	716754	766328	970504	1123291	1107731	1300003	1490008
7. 节能环保 Expenditure for Energy Conservation Environmental Protection	300159	445749	408576	377904	360033	471506	533234
8. 城乡社区 Expenditure for Urban and Rural Community	1143602	1586419	2338331	2736428	2930114	3308192	2705431
9. 农林水 Expenditure for Agriculture, Forestry and Water Conservancy	562286	880440	914373	896205	942335	1053876	1029656
10. 交通运输 Expenditure for Trarssportation	306032	389625	518178	515070	754753	743181	583462
11. 住房保障 Expenditure on Housing Support	93521	122825	219590	286287	227453	229186	401739

10－05 金融机构存、贷款余额(1949－2020年)

Balance of Deposits and Loans of Financial Institutions (1949－2020)

单位:万元 (10000 yuan)

年份 Year \ 项目 Item	各项存款合计 Deposits Total	住户存款 Household Deposits	城镇住户存款 Urban Household Deposits	各项贷款合计 Loans Total
1949	241			131
1950	2044			63
1951	5475			2214
1952	7727			4533
1953	7806			7693
1954	7358			14900
1955	8996			10697
1956	8751			9674
1957	14878			11494
1958	10898			26220
1959	17912			46141
1960	17303			61064
1961	18943			45856
1962	22739			33740
1963	21725			24558
1964	23522			24721
1965	25415			29611
1966	28844			41399
1967	31748			44880
1968	36039			53683
1969	30962			56059
1970	35967			68278
1971	41903			72507
1972	44029			77571
1973	59975			106073
1974	63586			118245
1975	70118			123201
1976	74508			128047
1977	87634			128238
1978	86824	20714	17056	136759
1979	108998	28937	22640	135713
1980	180707	40447	30896	174153
1981	226949	51440	38889	236678
1982	262156	67192	50113	216040
1983	303130	86635	64736	236203
1984	388305	115766	85439	329195
1985	484999	159596	115592	580180
1986	635514	222110	153572	769841
1987	776105	302762	207505	967477
1988	839680	351943	241839	1145989
1989	1017087	501592	346318	1338984

单位:万元　　　　10－05　续表　continued　　　　(10000 Yuan)

项目 Item / 年份 Year	各项存款合计 Deposits Total	住户存款 Household Deposits	城镇住户存款 Urban Household Deposits	各项贷款合计 Loans Total
1990	1646165	697515	479031	1803266
1991	2036334	904490	616308	2136903
1992	2652966	1144737	763309	2651983
1993	3469954	1563328	1048413	3415527
1994	5061345	2394370	1642498	4450932
1995	7079650	3423379	2448787	5672105
1996	9619291	4638458	3459439	7434243
1997	12251840	5583306	4229591	9388500
1998	14948225	6701158	5155548	11620537
1999	17886717	7425967	5760527	14937506
2000	20884723	7885579	6151084	16866431
2001	26215100	9418400	7396800	20877000
2002	33731500	11834000	9492300	27523800
2003	46527300	15899600	13079600	38187000
2004	57072000	18351700	15016100	48000400
2005	67487200	21916600	17960100	55453000
2006	78555500	25552400	20789600	66038600
2007	93109600	26348300	21154300	84306800
2008	113333500	34765900	27584600	100690500
2009	142842104	42869189	34027871	131133023
2010	170843548	49909744	39352353	150787269
2011	183965719	55474824	43464332	165737441
2012	201487672	60899841	46965391	180908011
2013	221747107	64085856	47733077	193504605
2014	244505093	67672009	49107745	213168315
2015	298638294	76177515	55659016	233279520
2016	333860429	84932733	62521938	261689982
2017	364832373	86705977	63076960	292709406
2018	398104954	101985223	75755331	365982478
2019	452869942	119012969	–	422451656
2020	542464720	143981152	–	497992776

注:1. 1989 年以前数据均为银行机构存贷款,1990 年及以后年份数据为调整后金融机构存贷款。2003 年起金融机构存贷款为本外币合并数据。

2. 2015 年起,各项存款和各项贷款分类调整。

3. 2019 年起,不再区分城镇住户和农村住户。

a) Data before 1989 belonged to banking system, data after 1990 adjusted for deposits and loans of financial institutions, data of 2003 included both RMB and foreign currency.

b) Since 2015, the classification in deposits and Loans has been adjusted.

c) Since 2019, no distinction are made between urban and rural households.

10－06 市区金融机构存、贷款余额(1978－2020 年)

Balance of Deposits and Loans of Financial Institutions of Urban District(1978－2020)

单位:万元 (10000 yuan)

项目 Item / 年份 Year	各项存款 Deposits	住户存款 Household Deposits	城镇住户存款 Urban Household Deposits	各项贷款 Loans
1978	58372	13774	13246	101144
1979	73720	18055	17241	98792
1980	134275	24702	23282	121231
1981	172721	31358	29345	170539
1982	198350	39756	37047	142091
1983	226160	50439	46833	155297
1984	293145	66108	61934	194977
1985	359825	89114	82868	418214
1986	458142	115818	106703	557763
1987	565429	156704	142642	714313
1988	610601	180341	163466	846998
1989	737388	256238	229518	1000731
1990	1062574	354316	297390	1271779
1991	1309462	451756	397322	1469671
1992	1695011	572660	479248	1774158
1993	2263969	762234	662234	2298124
1994	3383877	1242379	1085363	3033010
1995	4851774	1853512	1639875	3907199
1996	6828786	2734904	2371657	5350499
1997	8831147	3287475	2873638	6772221
1998	10785066	3905602	3440607	8615412
1999	13051806	4336058	3835542	11462505
2000	15436286	4620235	4101716	13105849
2001	23765400	7976400	6460200	19237800
2002	30638400	10139800	8370100	25476700
2003	42522000	13834200	11693000	30297500
2004	52542100	16014700	13479900	44517600
2005	62249500	19231800	16208400	51455900
2006	72269600	22391800	18737800	61190700
2007	86197300	23124600	19132300	78456200
2008	104930100	30665200	24996500	93838100
2009	131800234	37837816	30801878	121473548
2010	156776515	43676938	35370599	138671334
2011	168052916	48263525	38996516	151756838
2012	183719227	52347969	41789531	156426086
2013	201596137	54488059	42142666	175670366
2014	222558892	57202595	43243610	191888081
2015	284321331	68516344	51360093	222078475
2016	317723682	76306727	57718389	249684325
2017	345461303	77416526	57941703	278049912
2018	385383821	94991531	71808820	354926592
2019	437946336	110826488	－	409258262
2020	524892599	134701696	－	481800206

注:1. 2018 年起,市区数据包含临安区。

2. 2019 年起,不再区分城镇住户和农村住户。

a) Since 2018, data of urban District Includes Lin'an district.

b) Since 2019, no distinction are made between urban and rural households.

10－07 住户(本外币)存款余额(2020 年末)

Balance of Savings Deposits(RMB and Foreign Currency) of Rural and Urban Residents(End of 2020)

单位:万元 (10000 yuan)

地区	Region	总计 Total	
		2020 年末 At the End of Year 2020	为上年(%) As Compared with the Preceding Year(%)
全　市	**Total**	**143981152**	**120.98**
市　区	Urban District	134701696	121.54
#萧山区	Xiaoshan	23161659	115.75
余杭区	Yuhang	17574772	118.97
富阳区	Fuyang	6627104	112.71
临安区	Lin'an	4699654	118.05
桐庐县	Tonglu	3681875	115.54
淳安县	Chun'an	2142054	109.50
建德市	Jiande	3455527	113.54

10－08　全市金融机构本外币

Balance of Deposits and Loans(RMB and Foreign Currency)

单位:万元

指　标	Item	全　市 Total 绝对值 Absolute Value	全　市 Total 为上年(%) As Compared with the Preceding Year(%)	市　区 Urban District 小计 Subtotal
一、各项存款	**Deposits**	**542464720**	**119.78**	**524892599**
(一)境内存款	Domestic Deposits	526845271	118.07	509303561
1.住户存款	Household Deposits	143981152	120.98	134701696
(1)活期存款	Current Deposits	60024112	118.09	56737553
(2)定期及其他存款	Term and Other Deposits	83957040	123.13	77964144
2.非金融企业存款	Non　financial Enterprise Deposits	249348339	122.95	243864752
(1)活期存款	Current Deposits	94825971	124.31	91329532
(2)定期及其他存款	Term and Other Deposits	154522368	122.13	152535221
3.广义政府存款	General Government Deposits	90250314	96.59	87510798
(1)财政性存款	Treasury Deposits	18134152	98.02	17907609
(2)机关团体存款	Organization Deposits	72116162	96.24	69603189
4.非银行业金融机构存款	Non－banking Financial Institutions Deposits	43265466	139.77	43226314
(二)境外存款	Overseas Deposits	15619450	234.38	15589038
二、各项贷款	**Loans**	**497992776**	**117.88**	**481800206**
(一)境内贷款	Domestic Loans	494666330	118.03	478473832
1.住户贷款	Household Loans	204287771	123.68	196239571
(1)短期贷款	Short－term Loans	75737279	127.79	73855789
(2)中长期贷款	Medium and Long term Loans	128550492	121.37	122383783
2.非金融企业及机关团体贷款	Non－financial Enterprise and Organization Loans	290212515	114.37	282068217
(1)短期贷款	Short－term Loans	90127405	111.08	87638224
(2)中长期贷款	Medium and Long term Loans	171945095	117.10	166407088
(3)票据融资	Note Financing	18498601	113.68	18381490
(4)融资租赁	Finance lease	9442384	101.39	9442384
(5)各项垫款	Advance Money	199030	99.93	199030
3.非银行业金融机构贷款	Non－banking Financial Institutions Loans	166044	100.61	166044
(二)境外贷款	Overseas Loans	3326446	99.25	3326374

存、贷款余额(2020 年末)
of Financial Institutions(End of 2020)

(10000 yuan)

				桐庐县 Tonglu	淳安县 Chun'an	建德市 Jiande
萧山区 Xiaoshan	余杭区 Yuhang	富阳区 Fuyang	临安区 Lin'an			
55286076	**42494701**	**15691178**	**11711751**	**7169536**	**3949212**	**6453373**
55038061	42418739	15679378	11707820	7142466	3947904	6451340
23161659	17574772	6627104	4699654	3681875	2142054	3455527
7162125	5976478	2778126	1963467	1256496	863192	1166872
15999534	11598294	3848978	2736186	2425379	1278863	2288655
21021851	15431033	6520789	5124538	2385513	949988	2148085
8348453	6590846	2806934	2438164	1498217	611278	1386943
12673398	8840187	3713855	2686374	887296	338710	761142
10615156	9140962	2023613	1883550	1070975	855819	812721
1204028	1603931	257653	201288	125398	49242	51903
9411128	7537031	1765960	1682261	945577	806577	760819
239395	271972	507872	78	4102	43	35007
248015	75962	11799	3932	27070	1308	2033
50964121	**31655512**	**18121168**	**9745427**	**6970558**	**3576551**	**5645461**
50919618	31654184	18121057	9745047	6970558	3576479	5645461
17953348	13809249	7294230	5177591	3210278	2116848	2721074
3430006	2568632	1336096	1059853	717788	441921	721782
14523342	11240617	5958134	4117738	2492491	1674927	1999291
32946270	17844935	10826827	4567456	3760280	1459631	2924387
14132478	5809645	4650804	1242328	1185495	396396	907289
18104219	11263321	5948312	3156407	2543796	1034080	1960131
694017	771969	227580	168429	30989	29155	56967
–	–	–	–	–	–	–
15556	–	130	292	–	–	–
20000	–	–	–	–	–	–
44503	1328	111	380	–	72	–

10－09 金融机构人民币

Balance of RMB Deposits and Loans

单位:万元

指 标	Item	全 市 Total 绝对值 Absolute Value	为上年(%) As Compared with the Preceding Year(%)	市 区 Urban District 小计 Subtotal
一、各项存款	**Deposits**	**518930345**	**118.12**	**501682382**
(一)境内存款	Domestic Deposits	517934308	118.10	500693126
1. 住户存款	Household Deposits	141936258	121.29	132766335
(1)活期存款	Current Deposits	58979740	118.14	55707921
(2)定期及其他存款	Term and Other Deposits	82956518	123.64	77058414
2. 非金融企业存款	Non－financial Enterprise Deposits	242538315	122.94	237241057
(1)活期存款	Current Deposits	89683049	123.66	86331492
(2)定期及其他存款	Term and Other Deposits	152855266	122.52	150909564
3. 广义政府存款	General Government Deposits	90226766	96.62	87491854
(1)财政性存款	Treasury Deposits	18134152	98.02	17907609
(2)机关团体存款	Organization Deposits	72092614	96.27	69584246
4. 非银行业金融机构存款	Non－banking Financial Institutions Deposits	43232969	140.14	43193880
(二)境外存款	Overseas Deposits	996037	127.84	989256
二、各项贷款	**Loans**	**491846035**	**118.39**	**475670403**
(一)境内贷款	Domestic Loans	491017772	118.42	474842212
1. 住户贷款	Household Loans	204281578	123.68	196233431
(1)短期贷款	Short－term Loans	75731254	127.81	73849815
(2)中长期贷款	Medium and Long term Loans	128550325	121.37	122383616
2. 非金融企业及机关团体贷款	Non－financial Enterprise and Organization Loans	286570149	114.94	278442737
(1)短期贷款	Short－term Loans	88126201	111.93	85650709
(2)中长期贷款	Medium and Long term Loans	170377988	117.65	164843179
(3)票据融资	Note Financing	18498601	113.68	18381490
(4)融资租赁	Finance lease	9442384	101.39	9442384
(5)各项垫款	Advance Money	124976	71.19	124976
3. 非银行业金融机构贷款	Non－banking Financial Institutions Loans	166044	100.61	166044
(二)境外贷款	Overseas Loans	828263	101.80	828191

存、贷款余额(2020 年末)
of Financial Institutions(End of 2020)

(10000 yuan)

萧山区 Xiaoshan	余杭区 Yuhang	富阳区 Fuyang	临安区 Lin'an	桐庐县 Tonglu	淳安县 Chun'an	建德市 Jiande
54089043	**42012206**	**15519934**	**11548648**	**6947256**	**3929937**	**6370771**
54024932	41950810	15516456	11544909	6943182	3928664	6369336
23050353	17511126	6599503	4685103	3585242	2138228	3446452
7100164	5934409	2760116	1954595	1249312	860399	1162109
15950189	11576717	3839387	2730508	2335930	1277830	2284344
20122223	15028457	6385940	4976468	2282863	938506	2075891
7815521	6228862	2692528	2301493	1422184	601801	1327572
12306702	8799595	3693412	2674975	860678	336705	748319
10613372	9139256	2023142	1883260	1070975	851888	812048
1204028	1603931	257653	201288	125398	49242	51903
9409344	7535326	1765489	1681972	945577	802646	760146
238985	271970	507872	78	4102	43	34944
64110	61395	3479	3739	4074	1272	1435
50762735	**31621475**	**18098831**	**9728498**	**6965822**	**3576397**	**5633413**
50757381	31620148	18098720	9728118	6965822	3576324	5633413
17953100	13809136	7294122	5177514	3210254	2116836	2721059
3429758	2568520	1336032	1059777	717763	441909	721767
14523342	11240616	5958090	4117737	2492491	1674927	1999291
32784281	17811011	10804598	4550604	3755569	1459489	2912355
13970489	5783766	4633147	1225476	1180784	396254	898454
18104219	11255277	5943740	3156407	2543796	1034080	1956934
694017	771969	227580	168429	30989	29155	56967
–	–	–	–	–	–	–
15556	–	130	292	–	–	–
20000	–	–	–	–	–	–
5354	1328	111	380	–	72	–

10－10　金融机构人民币信贷收支表(资金来源,2014－2020年)

Credit Funds Balance Sheet of Financial Institutions (RMB, Sources of Funds, 2014－2020)

单位:亿元　　　　(100 million yuan)

项　目	Item	2014	2015	2016	2017	2018	2019	2020
资金来源合计	**All Sources**	**25404**	**30190**	**36882**	**38680**	**42616**	**48922**	**58318**
一、各项存款	Deposits	25722	29003	32515	35322	38810	43932	51893
(一)境内存款	Domestic Deposits	25642	28946	32441	35271	38718	43854	51793
1.住户存款	Household Deposits	7224	7507	8313	8503	9981	11702	14194
2.非金融企业存款	Non－financial Enterprise Deposits	11509	12437	13854	15557	16819	19729	24254
3.广义政府存款	General Government Deposits	4219	4675	5789	7162	8442	9339	9023
4.非银行业金融机构存款	Non－banking Financial Institutions Deposits	2691	4327	4485	4049	3477	3085	4323
(二)境外存款	Overseas Deposits	80	57	74	51	92	78	100
二、金融债券	Bonds	168	240	343	439	378	542	570
三、卖出回购资产	Sell Repurchase Assets	–	–	–	5	1	–	–
四、借款及非银行业金融机构拆入	Borrowing and Non Banking Financial Institutions Borrowing	259	0	15	3	22	44	51
五、联行往来(净)	Interbank Transactions (net)	–	–	–	–	906	1383	2441
六、应付及暂收款	Accounts Payable and Temporary Collection of Money	908	935	1008	1102	1138	1282	1465
七、各项准备	All Reserves	480	600	733	850	1021	1166	1403
八、所有者权益	Creditor's Equity	930	967	1104	1491	1831	2103	2461
其中:实收资本	Paid－in Capital	201	283	315	475	525	573	714
九、其他	Others	－3063	－1555	1163	－532	－1491	－1529	－1965

10-11 金融机构人民币信贷收支表(资金运用,2014-2020年)

Credit Funds Balance Sheet of Financial Institutions (RMB,Use of Funds,2014-2020)

单位:亿元 (100 million yuan)

项 目	Item	2014	2015	2016	2017	2018	2019	2020
资金运用合计		**25404**	**30190**	**36882**	**38680**	**42616**	**48922**	**58318**
一、各项存款	**Deposits**	**20388**	**22395**	**25465**	**28574**	**35878**	**41546**	**49185**
(一)境内贷款	**Domestic Loans**	**20382**	**22373**	**25431**	**28552**	**35812**	**41464**	**49102**
1. 住户贷款	**Household Loans**	**4918**	**5858**	**7800**	**9653**	**13945**	**16516**	**20428**
(1)短期贷款	Short-term Loans	1770	1874	1998	2351	5338	5925	7573
(2)中长期贷款	Medium and Long term Loans	3148	3984	5801	7302	8607	10591	12855
2. 非金融企业及机关团体贷款	**Non-financial Enterprise and Organization Loans**	**15432**	**16502**	**17613**	**18868**	**21862**	**24931**	**28657**
(1)短期贷款	Short-term Loans	6910	6944	7083	7183	7440	7873	8813
(2)中长期贷款	Medium and Long term Loans	7145	7539	8023	9970	12388	14482	17038
(3)票据融资	Note Financing	732	1311	1679	819	1126	1627	1850
(4)融资租赁	Finance lease	589	664	783	865	875	931	944
(5)各项垫款	Advance Money	56	44	45	31	32	18	12
3. 非银行业金融机构贷款	**Non-banking Financial Institutions Deposits**	**32**	**12**	**18**	**32**	**5**	**17**	**17**
(二)境外贷款	**Overseas Loans**	**6**	**22**	**34**	**21**	**66**	**81**	**83**
二、债券投资	**Bond Investment**	**1668**	**2006**	**2033**	**2694**	**3240**	**4020**	**5619**
三、股权及其他投资	**Equity and other Investment**	**1077**	**1738**	**2642**	**2805**	**2495**	**2321**	**2402**
四、买入返售资产	**Bug Assets Repurchased**	**337**	**63**	**48**	**87**	**348**	**254**	**288**
五、存放非银行业金融机构款项	**Deposit of non Banking Financial Institutions**	**0**	**1**	**1**	**1**	**1**	**1**	**1**
六、联行往来(净)	**Interbank Transactions (net)**	**1316**	**3374**	**5961**	**3831**	-	-	-
七、金银占款	**Funds Outstanding for Gold and Silver**	-	-	-	-	-	-	-
八、外汇买卖	**Foreign Exchange Trading**	**-34**	**-7**	-	-	-	-	-
九、应收及预付款	**Collectable Account and Advance Payment**	**421**	**392**	**489**	**431**	**405**	**501**	**546**
十、投资性房地产	**Investment Property**	**3**	**3**	**6**	**6**	**8**	**7**	**7**
十一、固定资产	**Fitness Assets**	**229**	**226**	**237**	**250**	**243**	**271**	**270**

10－12 保险业务情况(2018－2020年)

Statistics on Insurance Business(2018－2020)

单位:万元 (10000 yuan)

指 标	Item	原保险保费收入 Original insurance premium income			赔付金额 Indemnity Expenditure		
		2018	2019	2020	2018	2019	2020
全市总计	**Total**	**6636184**	**8462670**	**9644446**	**2028187**	**2430755**	**2646389**
为上年%	As Compared with the Preceding Year(%)	104.7	127.5	114.0	119.6	119.9	108.9
一、财产保险	Property Insurance	2171005	2479772	2608215	1274718	1526217	1551639
企业财产险	Enterprise Property Insurance	102228	115355	124850	43599	68244	81685
家庭财产险	Family Property Insurance	16095	24345	25767	4445	6808	5786
机动车辆险	Transportation Equipment Insurance	1421091	1427142	1466591	886742	917104	877885
工程险	Project Insurance	45065	45007	51647	6234	12625	27588
责任险	Responsibilihty Insurance	134739	275356	261909	55074	136641	124049
信用险	Export Credit Insurance	147775	147038	216330	109388	98022	146377
保证险	Guarantee Insurance	121959	192314	189773	39312	73051	91995
船舶险	Shipping Insurance	5223	6814	6595	5434	3570	4042
货运险	Cargo Insurance	102036	96766	97187	76928	69951	66975
特殊风险保险	Special Pisks Insurance	10717	7718	10705	234	22085	2269
农业保险	Agriculture Insurance	25425	26714	29705	19569	25432	22823
其他险	Other	38650	115202	127156	27761	92682	100165
二、人身险	Personal Insurance	4465179	5982897	7036231	753469	904538	1094751
寿险	Life Insurance	3420019	4711382	5458429	520054	588620	581472
意外伤害险	Accidental Insurance	235145	259426	239642	56872	66799	82269
健康险	Health Insurance	810016	1012089	1338160	176543	249119	431011

主要统计指标解释

财政收入 包括:(1)各项税收。主要有增值税、营业税、土地增值税、城市维护建设税、资源税、城市土地使用税、印花税、个人所得税、企业所得税、关税和耕地占用税等。

(2)专项收入包括征收排污费、征收城市水资源费收入,教育费附加收入等。

存款 企业、机关、团体或居民根据可以收回的原则,把货币资金存入银行或其他信用机构保管并取得一定利息的一种信用活动形式。根据存款对象的不同可划分为企业存款、财政存款、机关团体存款、基本建设存款、城镇储蓄存款、农村存款等科目。它是银行信贷资金的主要来源。

贷款 银行或其他信用机构根据必须归还的原则,按一定利率,为企业、个人等提供资金的一种信用活动形式。我国银行贷款分为流动资金贷款、固定资产贷款、城乡个体工商户贷款、城乡个体工商户贷款以及农业贷款等科目。

Explanatory Notes on Main Statistical Indicators

Financial Revenue includes: (1) various tax revenues, mainly including value added tax, business tax, land value added tax, tax on city maintenance and construction, resources tax, tax on use of urban land, stamp tax, personal income tax, enterprise income tax, tariff and tax on occupancy of cultivated land, etc. (2) Special revenues, including revenue collected from imposing fee on sewage treatment and on urban water resources, and extra charges for education, etc.

Deposit is a form of credit activity that enterprises, institutions, organizations or residents deposit money into banks or other credit institutions for safekeeping and interest earning under the recoverable principle. According to different depositors, deposits are divided into enterprise deposits, treasury deposits, deposits of institutions and groups, capital construction deposits, urban savings deposits, rural deposits and other deposits. It is the major source of bank credit funds.

Loan is a form of credit activity that banks or other credit institutions provide funds at certain interest rate to enterprises and individuals in the light of the principle of unconditional repayment. Loans from Chinese banks include circulating capital loans, fixed assets loans, loans to urban and rural individuals engaged in industrial and commercial business and agricultural loans.

十一、城市建设环境保护

URBAN CONSTRUCTION AND ENVIRONMENTAL PROTECTION

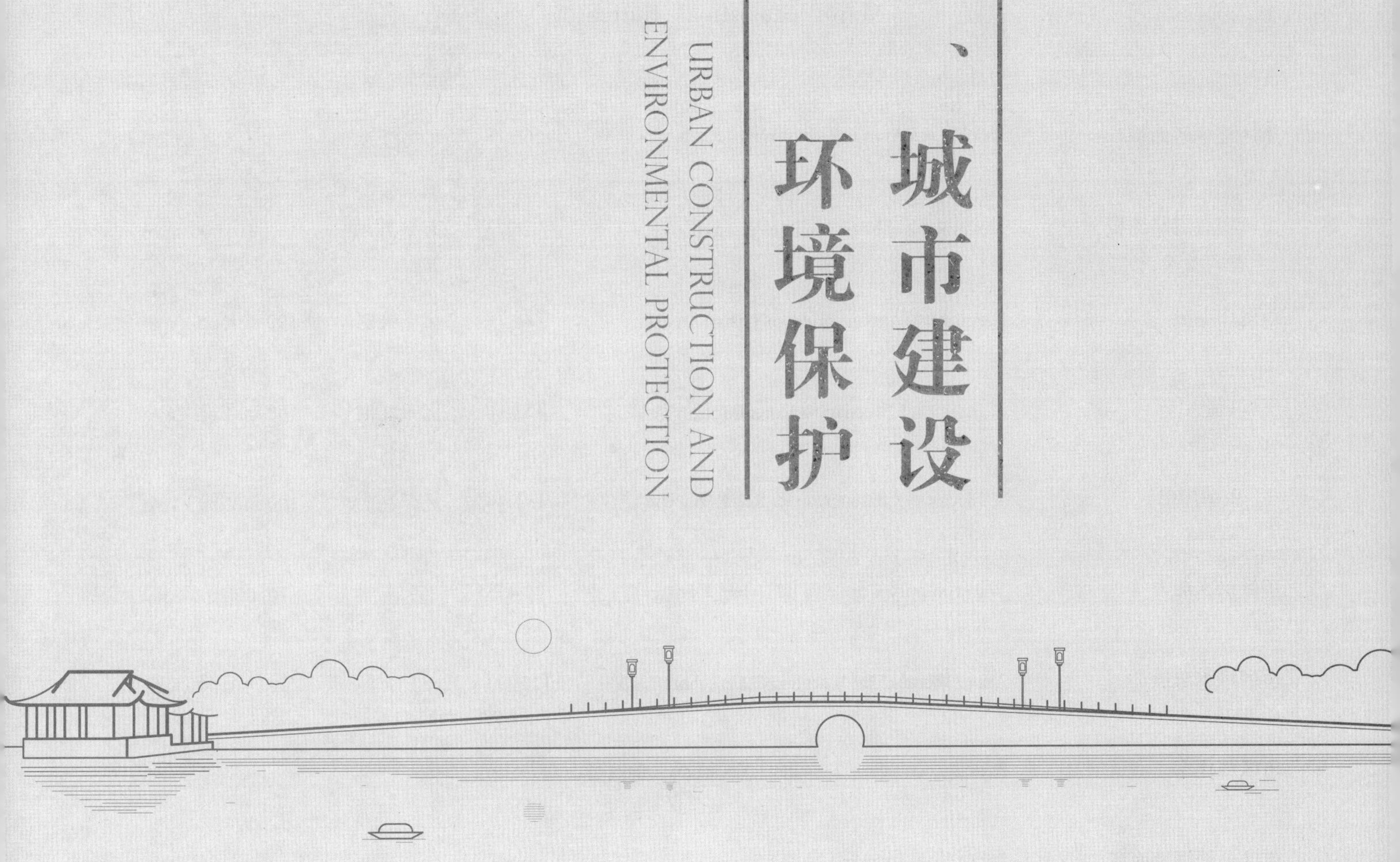

11 城市建设、环境保护
Urban Construction and Environmental Protection

主要统计指标
Major Statistical Indicators

市区建成区面积	Developed Area in Urban District	666.18	平方千米	(sq.km)
市区实有道路面积	Area of Roads in Urban District at Year-end	10073	万平方米	(10, 000 sq.m)
市区用电量	Electricity Consumption of Urban District	728.74	亿千瓦时	(100 million kW/h)
# 工业用电	Industrial Electricity Consumption	357.19	亿千瓦时	(100 million kW/h)
生活用电	Electricity Consumption for Residential Use	131.46	亿千瓦时	(100 million kW/h)
市区供水能力	Water-supply Capacity of Urban District	455	万吨/日	(10, 000 tons/day)
市区供水总量	Annual Volume of Tap Water Supplied in Urban District	120992	万吨	(10, 000 tons)
市区气化率	Percentage of Population with Access to Gas in Urban District	100	%	(%)
市区公园绿地面积	Park Green Area in Urban District	9951	公顷	(hectare)
市区空气质量达标(AQI < 100)天数	The Number of Days of Air Quality Reaching(AQI<100) the Standards	334	天	(day)

11－01　市区公共交通情况(2013－2020年)

Public Transportation in Urban Districts(2013－2020)

指　标	Item	2013	2014	2015	2016	2017	2018	2019	2020
一、轨道交通	**Rail Transit**								
年末运营线路总长度（千米）	Length of Operating Routes (year－end) (km)	47.97	66.30	81.50	81.50	117.60	117.60	135.40	306.30
客运总量（万人次）	Passenger Traffic (10,000 person－times)	9237	14521	22348	26877	33986	52985	63202	58241
二、公共汽车	**Bus**								
年末运营线路条数（条）	Number of Operating Routes (year－end) (unit)	645	703	756	758	937	1152	1140	1307
年末运营线路总长度（千米）	Length of Operating Routes (year－end) (km)	11445	12032	12791	13866	16819	21460	18547	25947
#BRT线路长度（千米）	BRT line length (km)	122	113	128	151	151	132	289	132
年末运营公共汽车（辆）	Number of Public Transportation Vehicles(year－end) (unit)	8249	8656	8555	8770	9672	11272	10708	10866
#无轨电车（辆）	Number of Operating Trolleys (unit)	101	115	150	150	150	150	85	85
客运总量（万人次）	Passenger Traffic (10,000 person－times)	132221	140928	142312	141441	151263	158753	155496	70392
三、出租汽车	**Tax**								
年末实有出租汽车数（辆）	Number of Taxis(year－end) (unit)	10904	11913	11963	12209	13233	14125	14133	14093

11－02 市区城市供电、供水情况(1949－2020 年)
Electricity and Water Supply in Urban Districts(1949－2020)

年 份 Year	供电总量 Power Supply			供水总量 Water Supply		
	合计(亿千瓦时) Total (100 million kWh)	#工业用电 Industrial	#生活用电 Residents´living	合计(万吨) Total (10000 tons)	#生产用水 Production	#生活用水 Residents´living
1949	0.24	0.15	0.08	191	25	166
1950	–	–	–	–	–	–
1951	–	–	–	–	–	–
1952	0.43	0.35	0.06	229	65	164
1953	0.53	0.43	0.07	353	109	244
1954	0.67	0.57	0.08	452	148	304
1955	0.66	0.55	0.08	540	162	378
1956	0.82	0.68	0.10	714	249	464
1957	0.90	0.72	0.12	845	310	535
1958	1.47	1.27	0.13	1264	622	642
1959	2.18	1.91	0.16	2097	1259	838
1960	2.94	2.61	0.17	2909	1834	1075
1961	2.73	2.37	0.18	2647	1600	1047
1962	2.50	2.06	0.21	2556	1465	1091
1963	2.56	2.09	0.23	2561	1440	1121
1964	3.00	2.50	0.25	2924	1679	1244
1965	3.49	2.97	0.26	3164	1937	1227
1966	4.02	3.46	0.27	3669	2392	1277
1967	3.74	3.11	0.51	3892	2388	1504
1968	–	–	–	3891	2369	1522
1969	4.15	3.48	0.58	4766	3100	1666
1970	4.68	4.00	0.59	4972	3360	1578
1971	5.34	4.49	0.70	5978	4072	1868
1972	5.80	4.95	0.72	6548	4440	2018
1973	5.94	5.05	0.77	6755	4562	2193
1974	5.15	4.20	0.81	6725	4482	2243
1975	4.93	3.94	0.85	7007	4707	2300
1976	5.40	4.33	0.92	7379	4992	2387
1977	7.57	5.72	1.02	8140	5498	2642
1978	8.01	6.52	1.26	9072	6116	2956
1979	9.04	7.23	1.54	10548	6813	3388
1980	10.25	8.73	1.17	11199	7359	3840
1981	10.87	8.98	1.45	12662	7943	4718
1982	11.62	9.41	1.70	13761	8272	5380
1983	12.60	10.13	1.88	14226	8211	6015
1984	13.70	10.72	2.24	15586	8713	6800
1985	14.94	11.18	2.34	17484	8599	8144
1986	15.85	12.96	0.78	17894	8527	9367
1987	16.97	13.56	1.04	18911	9424	9487
1988	17.95	13.96	1.30	19806	10028	9764
1989	18.51	14.20	1.51	20733	8780	11941

11－02　续表　continued

年　份 Year	供电总量 Power Supply			供水总量 Water Supply		
	合计(亿千瓦时) Total (100 million kWh)	#工业用电 Industrial	#生活用电 Residents´living	合计(万吨) Total (10000 tons)	#生产用水 Production	#生活用水 Residents´living
1990	19.95	14.89	1.86	22290	8945	13301
1991	21.16	15.69	1.99	22772	9223	13522
1992	23.34	17.04	2.31	24412	10052	14338
1993	25.70	18.21	2.69	25333	10022	15289
1994	29.49	19.68	3.57	25902	9707	16195
1995	31.41	20.89	4.07	27740	9380	18336
1996	35.41	21.67	5.26	27216	8845	18125
1997	42.39	25.82	6.32	26513	7593	18920
1998	48.46	28.58	7.67	26593	8075	17838
1999	51.19	29.55	7.90	25504	7395	18109
2000	60.19	33.52	9.86	33725	8100	19410
2001	133.12	92.99	16.79	52000	18324	25710
2002	156.61	110.31	18.76	53372	18180	31408
2003	190.12	131.87	23.67	59180	21796	30743
2004	207.75	146.56	23.89	62265	23544	29187
2005	244.78	172.56	27.98	73331	27327	35220
2006	279.94	197.61	32.53	64764	20258	33979
2007	313.47	219.92	36.86	66753	19519	33682
2008	325.75	221.28	41.15	68178	19354	35902
2009	346.93	230.20	45.31	69499	16671	37274
2010	392.64	258.35	50.74	53565	11479	30978
2011	432.57	282.95	55.49	52660	11884	22384
2012	444.95	278.93	63.62	58183	12478	22861
2013	484.05	296.08	71.52	60747	13005	23733
2014	552.71	355.06	72.56	66172	14792	26894
2015	559.54	345.23	78.27	66760	14902	26162
2016	583.96	337.04	93.03	65087	14161	25078
2017	673.73	389.00	105.29	83192	16157	33960
2018	724.31	397.72	117.67	88568	15866	35778
2019	738.88	381.96	125.83	99156	21534	40117
2020	728.74	357.19	131.46	120992	29601	49606

11－03 市区市政建设情况(2013－2020年)
Public Utilities in Urban Districts(2013－2020)

指 标	Item	2013	2014	2015	2016	2017	2018	2019	2020
一、市政建设	**Urban Infrastructure**								
建成区面积(平方公里)	Constructed Area (sq. m)	462.48	495.22	506.09	541.38	591.08	615.22	648.46	666.18
年末实有道路面积(万平方米)	Area of Roads (year－end) (10,000 sq. m)	5426	6145	6540	6932	8291	8840	9341	10073
年末实有道路长度(公里)	Length of Roads(year end) (km)	2479	2748	2991	3075	3550	3783	3990	4323
年末实有桥梁数(座)	Number of Bridges(year－end) (unit)	1165	1235	1337	1353	1443	1473	1545	1705
排水管道长度(公里)	Length of Drainage Pipelines (km)	4455	5012	5370	5944	8614	8924	9125	9434
城市污水排放量(万立方米)	Volume of Sewage Drained (10,000 cu. m)	48432	53111	56974	57916	69834	74438	80447	82795
城市污水处理总量(万立方米)	the Total Volume of Urban Sewage Treatment (10,000 cu. m)	46251	50318	54137	55061	66516	71364	77245	80406
二、城市液化气	**Urban Liquefied Petroleum Gas**								
供气总量 (万吨)	Total Volume of Liquefied Petroleum Gas Supply (10,000 tons)	11.92	9.87	12.38	13.14	12.86	13.28	12.24	11.17
#家庭用气(万吨)	Supply for Residential Use (10,000 tons)	4.70	5.08	6.08	5.90	6.48	5.81	5.15	6.98
三、人工煤气及天然气	**Coal Gas and Natural Gas**								
家庭用气总量(万立方米)	Total Volume of Coal Gas Consumed (10,000 cu. m)	13869	18019	20659	21878	23614	26506	32907	50843
家庭用气户数(万户)	Residential Households with Access to Gas (10,000 households)	91.08	111.30	130.69	139.03	153.17	172.81	187.85	200.30
四、全社会气化率 %	**Percentage of Population with Access to Gas** (%)	**100**	**100**	**100**	**100**	**100**	**100**	**100**	**100**

11－04 市区园林绿化情况(2013－2020年)
Urban Forestation(2013－2020)

指 标	Item	2013	2014	2015	2016	2017	2018	2019	2020
建城区绿化覆盖面积(公顷)	The Green Areas Coveraged in Constructed Areas (hectare)	18606	20031	20464	22035	23620	24999	26312	28885
建城区园林绿地面积(公顷)	Total Area of Parks, Gardens and Green Areas in Constructed Areas (hectare)	17071	18386	18949	20118	21726	22886	23986	26249
#公园绿地(公顷)	Public Green Area (hectare)	5820	6304	7640	8118	8770	8976	9246	9951
建城区绿化覆盖率(%)	Rate of the Green Areas Coveraged in Constructed Areas (%)	40.23	40.57	40.43	40.70	39.96	40.63	40.58	43.36
公园景点个数(个)	Number of Parks and Scenic Resorts (unit)	190	207	217	222	245	251	260	305
公园景点面积(公顷)	Area of Parks and Scenic Resorts (hectare)	2094	2298	2488	2754	3074	3150	3208	3539

11-05 环境保护情况(2020年)

Statistics on Environmental Protection(2020)

指标名称		Item		全市 Whole City	市区 Urban District
工业废水排放量	(万吨)	Industrial Wastewater Emissions	(10,000 tons)	14221.55	13145.42
工业废水中COD排放量	(吨)	COD Emissions in Industrial Wastewater	(tons)	6049.79	3958.62
工业废水中氨氮排放量	(吨)	Ammonia emissions in Industrial wastewater	(tons)	131.28	99.23
工业二氧化硫产生量	(吨)	Industrial Sulfur Dioxide Produced	(tons)	59091.77	52122.77
工业二氧化硫排放量	(吨)	Industrial Emissions of Sulfur Dioxide	(tons)	3973.00	2588.10
工业氮氧化物排放量	(吨)	Industrial Nitrogen Oxide Emissions	(tons)	16055.79	9705.24
工业烟(粉)产生量	(吨)	Industrial Smoke (Powder) Production	(tons)	3507799.56	1786745.01
工业烟(粉)尘排放量	(吨)	Industrial Smoke, Powder and Dust Emissions	(tons)	10411.02	5359.68
一般工业固体废物综合利用率	(%)	Comprehensive Utilization Rate of General Industrial Solid Waste	(%)	99.03	98.99
城市污水集中处理率	(%)	Centralized Treatment Rate of Urban Sewage	(%)	97.06	97.11
城市生活垃圾无害化处理率	(%)	Harmless Treatment Rate of City's Living Garbage	(%)	100	100
空气质量优良天数	(天)	Air Quality Days	(days)	-	334
集中式饮用水源地水质达标率	(%)	Compliance Rate of Centralized Sources of Drinking Water	(%)	100	100

主要统计指标解释

自来水生产能力　指年底城建部门管理的自来水厂实际生产能力。

生活用水量　指居民日常生活与公共福利设施的用水量。包括居民、饮食店、旅馆、医院、理发店、浴池、洗衣店、游泳池、商店、学校、机关、部队等单位的用水量。

供气总量　指全年售给各类用户的全部煤气量。包括工业用量、家庭用量和其他用量。

年末实有道路长度　指除土路外，路面经过铺装宽度在3.5米以上的道路，包括高级、次高级道路和普通道路。

城市桥梁　指城市范围内，修建在河道上的桥梁和道路与道路立交、道路跨越铁路的立交桥，以及人行天桥。包括永久性桥和半永久性桥，不包括临时性桥、铁路桥、涵洞。

营运线路长度　指设置的固定营运线路的长度，包括郊区营运线路长度。不包括临时行驶的线路长度。

用水普及率　指城市用水的非农业人口数（不包括临时人口和流动人口）与城市非农业人口总数之比。计算公式为：

$$用水普及率=\frac{城市用水非农业人口数}{城市非农业人口数}\times 100\%$$

城市园林绿地面积　指城市公共绿地、专用绿地、生产绿地、防护绿地、郊区风景名胜区的全部面积。

公园绿地面积　指供游览休息的各种公园、动物园、植物园、陵园以及花园、游园和供游览休息用的林荫道绿地、广场绿地。不包括一般栽植的行道树及林荫道的面积。

Explanatory Notes on Main Statistical Indicators

Production Capacity of Tap Water refers to the actual production capacity of the waterworks administered by the urban construction department at the year end.

Domestic water consumption refers to the water consumption of residents daily life and public welfare facilities, including the consumption of residents, restaurants, hotels, hospitals, barber shops, public bathhouses, laundries, swimming pools, shops, schools, institutions, army and other units.

Total Gas Supply refers to the total volume of gas sold to users in a year, including the gas for industrial use, family use and others.

Length of Roads at the Year End refers to the length of roads with pavement width more than 3.5 meters except unsurfaced roads, including high quality, medium quality and ordinary roads.

Urban Bridges refer to bridges over river courses, overpasses crossing roads or railways and passenger footbridge sin urban areas. Permanent and semi – permanent bridges are included. Temporary bridges, railway bridges and culverts are excluded.

Length of Operation Line refers to the length of the roads in fixed operation, including the suburb one, but excluding the temporary one.

Urban Water Popularity rate refers to the ratio of the urban non – agricultural population (excluding temporary and floating population) using tap water to the total urban non – agricultural population. The formula is as follows:

$$\text{Urban Water Popularity rate} = \frac{\text{Urban Non – agricultural Population Using Tap Water}}{\text{Urban Non – agricultural Population}} \times 100\%$$

Area of Urban Gardens and Green Lands refers to the total area of urban public green land, special green land, production green land, protection green land and suburban scenic spots.

Park Green Area refers to the area of various parks, zoos, botanical gardens, cemeteries, gardens, and boulevard and square green land for sightseeing and rest. Areas of street trees and boulevards are excluded.

十二、科技、教育 文化、卫生、体育

SCIENCE AND TECHNOLOGY,EDUCATION, CULTURE,PUBLIC HEALTHAND SPORTS

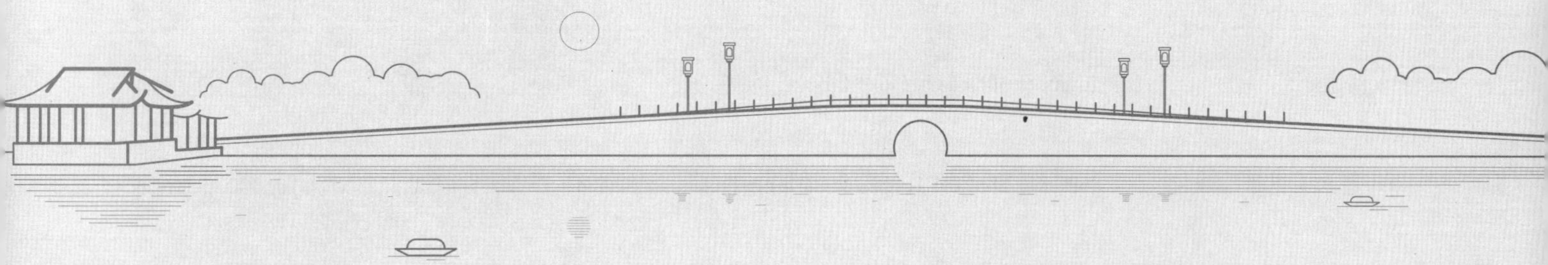

12

科技、教育、文化、卫生、体育
Science and Technology, Education, Culture, Public Health and Sports

主要统计指标
Major Statistical Indicators

高等学校数	Number of Regular Institution of Higher Education	40	个	(unit)
高等学校在校学生数	Number of Students in Regular Institution of Higher Education	55.06	万人	(10, 000 person)
高中在校学生数	Number of Students in Senior High Schools	12.46	万人	(10, 000 person)
初中在校学生数	Number of Students in Junior High Schools	24.94	万人	(10, 000 person)
小学在校学生数	Number of Students in Primary Schools	64.53	万人	(10, 000 person)
医疗病床数	Number of Beds in Health Institutions	9.01	万张	(10, 000 bed)
# 医院	Number of Beds in Hospitals	8.43	万张	(10, 000 bed)
卫生技术人员数	Number of Medical Technical Personnel	13.43	万人	(10, 000 person)
# 执业(助理)医师	Number of Licensed (Assistant) Doctors	5.11	万人	(10, 000 person)
公共图书馆	Public Library	15	个	(unit)

12－01 科技活动情况（2014－2020 年）
Statistics on Scientific and Technological Activities（2014－2020）

指 标 Item	2014	2015	2016	2017	2018	2019	2020
一、全社会科技活动 The Scientific and Technological Activities in Whole Society							
研究与试验发展活动折合全时人员（人年）Full－time Equivalent of R&D Personnel	90193	94323	94696	103245	109507	126275	149424
研究与试验发展经费支出（亿元）R&D Expenditure（0.1 billion Yuan）	274.00	302.19	346.36	396.82	464.25	530.42	578.79
研究与试验发展经费支出与 GDP 之比（%）The Proportion of R&D Expenditure in GDP（%）	2.98	3.01	3.06	3.15	3.25	3.44	3.59
二、规模以上工业科技活动 The Scientific and Technological Activities of Industrial Enterprises Above Designated Size							
有研究与试验发展活动企业数（个）The Number of Enterprises with R&D Activities（Unit）	1518	1671	1753	1819	1784	2075	2553
研究与试验发展项目数（个）The Number of R&D Projects（Unit）	7383	8265	8943	10000	10102	12430	15507
企业有科技机构（个）Scientific and Technological Institutions of Enterprises（Unit）	1346	1354	1410	1611	1567	1904	2242
科技机构仪器和设备原价（亿元）Original Value of Equipment in Scientific and Technological Institutions（0.1 billion Yuan）	99.61	100.73	126.23	142.78	156	172.41	201.9
研究与试验发展人员（万人）R&D Personnel（10,000）	7.41	8.01	7.92	8.39	9.29	9.68	10.78
每万名从业人员中研究与试验发展活动人员数（人）The Number of R&D Personnel per 10,000 Employees（Person）	644	724	743	794	906	961	1061
研究与试验发展经费支出（亿元）R&D Expenditure（0.1 billion Yuan）	177.39	198.06	215.03	241.93	268.28	296.90	307.23
研究与试验发展经费支出占营业收入的比例（%）The Proportion of R&D Expenditure in Business Income（%）	1.33	1.55	1.70	1.78	1.77	1.86	1.96

12－02　全社会 R&D 经费投入情况(2012－2020 年)
R&D Investment of the Whole Society(2012－2020)

单位:亿元　(100 million yuan)

年　份 Year	总计 Total	按执行部门分　By Sector			
		研究机构 Research and Development Institutions	高等院校 Colleges and Universties	规模以上工业企业 Industrial Enterprises above Designated Size	其他 Others
2012	228.00	14.96	38.12	143.47	31.44
2013	248.73	15.91	39.78	160.21	32.83
2014	274.00	17.34	42.06	177.39	37.21
2015	302.19	20.88	46.04	198.06	37.21
2016	346.36	16.55	40.79	215.03	73.99
2017	396.82	18.04	44.56	241.93	92.29
2018	464.25	26.35	49.93	268.28	119.69
2019	530.42	29.17	62.60	296.90	141.75
2020	578.79	32.80	71.00	307.23	167.76

12-03 规模以上工业企业 R&D 经费投入情况(2012-2020 年)

Basic Statistics on R&D Investment of Industrial Enterprises above Designated Size(2012-2020)

单位:亿元 (100 million yuan)

年份 Year	总计 Total	按经费来源分 By Source			
		政府资金 Government Funds	企业资金 Self-raised Funds by Enterprise	境外资金 Overseas Funds	其他资金 Other
2012	143.47	4.63	137.73	0.41	0.70
2013	160.21	4.35	154.42	0.26	1.19
2014	177.39	5.24	171.18	0.10	0.89
2015	198.06	5.35	191.03	0.24	1.43
2016	215.03	3.88	209.98	0.08	1.09
2017	241.93	7.73	233.04	0.22	0.94
2018	268.28	6.31	261.25	0.41	0.21
2019	296.90	5.65	291.25	-	-
2020	307.23	3.70	303.01	0.41	0.11

12－04 规模以上工业企业 R&D 经费投入情况（2020 年）

Basic Statistics on R&D Investment of Industrial Enterprises above Designated Size(2020)

项目	Item	有 R&D 活动的企业数（个）	企业办研发机构（个）	企业办机构仪器和设备原价（亿元）	R&D 人员（万人）	R&D 经费支出（亿元）
总　计	**Total**	**2553**	**2242**	**201.90**	**10.78**	**307.23**
按企业规模分	**Grouped by Size of Enterprises**					
大型企业	Large	94	119	62.74	3.88	152.47
中型企业	Medium－sized	386	404	65.66	2.77	74.16
小微企业	Small	2073	1719	73.50	4.13	80.60
按登记注册类型分	**Grouped by Status of Registration**					
国有企业	State－owned Enterprises	2	1	0.06	…	0.03
集体企业	Collective－owned Enterprises	2	5	0.67	0.01	0.09
股份合作企业	Cooperative Enterprises		3	0.04		
联营企业	Joint Ownership Enterprises					
有限责任公司	Limited Liability Corporations	253	237	27.45	1.54	49.23
股份有限公司	Share－holding Corporations Ltd.	198	255	46.50	2.83	93.95
私营企业	Private Enterprises	1802	1474	75.93	4.48	94.14
外商及港澳台投资企业	Enterprises with Investment from Foreign、Hong Kong、Macao and Taiwan	296	267	51.25	1.92	69.79
其他企业	Other Enterprises					

12－05 分地区、行业规模以上单位年末人才资源(2020年)
Trained Personnel Resource of Units above Designated Size by Region(2020)

单位:人 (person)

项 目	Item	合计 Total	非私营单位 Non－Private	#专业技术人员 Technical Personnel	非私营单位 Non－Private	#技术工人 Technical Workers	非私营单位 Non－Private
全市	**Whole City**	**2258214**	**1050185**	**673870**	**355745**	**1158960**	**509831**
市区	Urban District	2098557	1008359	649321	349891	1047795	481961
#上城区	Shangcheng	80406	46950	31663	18550	27844	17198
下城区	Xiacheng	128389	91204	38673	25389	62531	50122
江干区	Jianggan	126445	62652	41308	21016	52766	27932
拱墅区	Gongshu	116263	49457	35462	12686	56197	27048
西湖区	Xihu	249879	145637	95248	56234	109118	64100
高新(滨江)区	Hi－Tech(Binjiang)	268680	167539	163346	119481	51599	21326
萧山区	Xiaoshan	377000	122402	80634	28742	237695	73509
余杭区	Yuhang	346819	115035	82311	29663	199978	65491
富阳区	Fuyang	100736	41594	20518	6979	60077	27574
临安区	Lin'an	90017	27521	19249	5695	52657	16222
钱塘新区	Qiantang New Area	208344	134229	40262	25122	133685	88517
西湖风景名胜区	The West Lake Scenic Zone	5579	4139	647	334	3648	2922
桐庐县	Tonglu	86910	20635	11104	2395	64364	14595
淳安县	Chun'an	21748	7024	4223	1125	13389	4000
建德市	Jiande	50999	14167	9222	2334	33412	9275

注:2020年数据口径范围调整为规模以上单位年末人才资源。
a) Numbers in 2020 are human resources of units above designated size in the year－end.

项　目	Item	合计 Total	非私营单位 Non－Private	#专业技术人员 Technical Personnel	非私营单位 Non－Private	#技术工人 Technical Workers	非私营单位 Non－Private
按国民经济行业分组	**Total**	**2258214**	**1050185**	**673870**	**355745**	**1158960**	**509831**
农、林、牧、渔业	Farming, Forestry, Animal Husbandry and Fishery	－	－	－	－	－	－
采矿业	Mining	857	175	103	31	476	57
制造业	Manufacturing	842519	423059	174065	111948	544140	251687
电力、热力、燃气及水生产和供应业	Production & Supply of Electricity, Heat, Gas & Water	14132	12780	3344	3117	7919	7094
建筑业	Construction	525156	118051	147299	42739	315114	64091
批发和零售业	Wholesale & Retail Trades	158243	75551	38871	22085	43190	23978
交通运输、仓储和邮政业	Transportation, Storage and Posts	78531	56430	14646	9966	44958	36157
住宿和餐饮业	Hotels and Catering Services	45123	28017	4716	1964	24138	17499
信息传输、软件和信息技术服务业	Information Transmission, Software and Information Technology	207279	126539	132909	83989	39374	24466
金融业	Financial Intermediation	－	－	－	－	－	－
房地产业	Real Estate	98789	70229	21180	14646	44628	37198
租赁和商务服务业	Leasing and Business Services	100172	43793	26036	7254	52419	26245
科学研究、技术服务业	Scientific Research, Technical Services	101658	55288	77509	42860	6869	3621
水利、环境和公共设施管理业	Management of Water Conservancy, Environment and Public Facilities	24372	18134	3040	1880	18330	14567
居民服务、修理和其他服务业	Service to Households, Repair and Other Services	17683	2169	1930	309	12582	731
教育	Education	12102	6134	8454	4383	1013	371
卫生和社会工作	Health Care and Social Work	21270	5635	13733	3226	2670	1262
文化、体育和娱乐业	Culture, Sports and Entertainment	10328	8201	6035	5348	1140	807
公共管理、社会保障和社会组织	Public Management, Social Security and Social Organizations	－	－	－	－	－	－

12－06 专利申请与授权情况(2007－2020 年)
Patent Application and Authorization(2007－2020)

单位:件 (item)

年份 Year	专利申请合计 Patent Applications	发明 Inventions	实用新型 Utility Models	外观设计 Designs	专利授权合计 Patent Applications Granted	发明 Inventions	实用新型 Utility Models	外观设计 Designs
2007	13295	4592	4332	4371	7563	1320	3638	2605
2008	18549	5130	5796	7623	9831	1923	4637	3271
2009	26077	6703	9806	9568	15507	2535	5806	7166
2010	29732	7766	13108	8858	26483	3238	11888	11357
2011	40890	9717	18783	12390	29249	4511	14556	10182
2012	53785	11960	25313	16512	40651	5526	20400	14725
2013	58280	14031	25523	18726	41518	4903	23159	13456
2014	48569	14779	21711	12079	33548	5552	18147	9849
2015	60839	17777	29048	14014	46245	8296	24764	13185
2016	73546	24951	32187	16408	41052	8647	21763	10642
2017	75709	25578	35096	15035	42227	9872	21282	11073
2018	98396	36539	44963	16894	55379	10267	30891	14221
2019	113562	43357	53957	16248	61568	11748	36326	13494
2020	143912	55297	70983	17632	92399	17327	58540	16532

12－07　分地区专利申请与授权情况(2020 年)
Patent Application and Authorization by Region(2020)

单位:件　　(item)

地　区	Region	专利申请合计 Patent Applications	发明 Inventions	实用新型 Utility Models	外观设计 Designs	专利授权合计 Patent Applications Granted	发明 Inventions	实用新型 Utility Models	外观设计 Designs
全市	**Whole City**	**143912**	**55297**	**70983**	**17632**	**92399**	**17327**	**58540**	**16532**
市区	Urban District	137462	53399	67525	16538	88524	17132	55875	15517
#上城区	Shangcheng	3771	1283	1975	513	2291	312	1449	530
下城区	Xiacheng	7428	3832	3167	429	4447	1342	2666	439
江干区	Jianggan	5368	1660	2591	1117	3978	384	2282	1312
拱墅区	Gongshu	4899	1623	2529	747	3214	299	2206	709
西湖区	Xihu	18516	10939	5858	1719	12708	5223	5685	1800
高新(滨江)区	Hi－Tech(Binjiang)	24333	12883	7890	3560	13322	4034	6282	3006
萧山区	Xiaoshan	14820	3711	9562	1547	11012	621	8917	1474
余杭区	Yuhang	27643	6796	16925	3922	19127	1434	14016	3677
富阳区	Fuyang	7207	2331	4426	450	4705	824	3439	442
临安区	Lin'an	7164	1174	5250	740	4753	309	3800	644
钱塘新区	Qiantang New Area	16313	7167	7352	1794	8967	2350	5133	1484
西湖风景名胜区	The West Lake Scenic Zone								
桐庐县	Tonglu	2976	542	1820	614	2220	97	1519	604
淳安县	Chun'an	889	316	465	108	542	26	405	111
建德市	Jiande	2585	1040	1173	372	1113	72	741	300

注:西湖区含风景名胜区;萧山区不含托管在钱塘新区的街道数据。

a) Figures of Xihu include the West Lake Scenic Zone; Figures of Xiaoshan District don't include subdistricts which under administered by Qiantang New Area.

12－08　文化事业单位数(2000－2020年)
Number of Culture Institutions(2000－2020)

单位:个　　(unit)

年　份 Year	电影院 Cinemas	剧场 Theaters	剧团 Opera Troupes	文化馆 Cultural Centers	文化站 Cultural Stations	图书馆 Libraries	博物馆 Museums	展览馆 Exhibition Buildings
2000	16	9	18	13	268	10	9	1
2001	16	15	18	13	226	10	11	1
2002	18	13	18	13	221	10	11	1
2003	20	11	18	13	220	10	11	1
2004	18	16	18	13	165	10	12	1
2005	22	12	19	13	204	12	12	1
2006	22	12	19	13	197	13	12	1
2007	22	12	19	13	195	14	12	1
2008	23	12	19	13	195	14	13	1
2009	22	12	20	13	198	16	35	1
2010	31	12	21	13	199	16	65	1
2011	30	11	21	15	190	15	65	1
2012	40	11	21	15	192	15	65	1
2013	48	11	21	15	189	15	65	1
2014	66	12	21	15	189	15	65	1
2015	90	11	20	15	189	15	67	1
2016	90	11	20	15	189	15	68	1
2017	158	11	20	15	189	15	68	1
2018	158	11	20	15	189	16	76	1
2019	193	9	20	15	189	16	79	1
2020	195	6	20	15	175	15	80	1

12－09　分地区文化部门机构数(2020 年末)

Number of Culture Institutions by Region(End of 2020)

单位:个　　(unit)

指　标	Item	剧场 Theaters	剧团 Opera Troupes	文化馆 Cultural Centers	文化站 Cultural Stations	图书馆 Libraries	博物馆 Museums	展览馆 Exhibition Buildings
全市	**Total**	**6**	**20**	**15**	**175**	**15**	**80**	**1**
市区	Urban District	6	18	12	122	12	74	1
#萧山区	Xiaoshan	–	1	1	22	1	9	–
余杭区	Yuhang	1	1	1	19	1	5	–
富阳区	Fuyang	–	1	1	24	1	2	–
临安区	Lin'an	–	–	1	18	1	2	–
桐庐县	Tonglu	–	1	1	14	1	2	–
淳安县	Chun'an	–	–	1	23	1	2	–
建德市	Jiande	–	1	1	16	1	1	–

12－10 市区文化事业单位数(1978－2020年)
Culture Institutions of Urban District (1978－2020)

单位:个 (unit)

年份 Year	电影院 Cinemas	剧团 Opera Troupes	剧场 Theaters	文化馆 Cultural Centers	文化站 Cultural Stations	图书馆 Libraries	博物馆 Museums
1978	7	13	6	5	–	2	1
1979	8	14	7	5	27	2	1
1980	8	15	7	5	37	2	1
1981	8	17	7	6	40	2	1
1982	9	17	7	6	45	3	1
1983	9	15	3	6	46	3	1
1984	9	15	4	6	49	3	1
1985	8	16	9	6	47	3	2
1986	8	15	8	6	48	3	2
1987	8	15	9	6	38	3	2
1988	7	14	9	6	50	3	2
1989	7	14	9	6	48	2	2
1990	9	14	9	5	48	3	2
1991	10	14	8	5	48	3	2
1992	11	14	8	5	48	3	6
1993	10	14	9	5	42	3	6
1994	11	13	9	5	48	3	6
1995	11	13	9	5	67	3	6
1996	10	13	8	5	55	3	6
1997	10	13	8	5	52	3	6
1998	9	13	8	6	55	3	7
1999	9	13	6	6	52	3	8
2000	8	12	6	6	52	3	9
2001	49	14	11	8	89	5	11
2002	–	14	10	8	90	4	11
2003	19	14	11	13	92	4	11
2004	18	14	14	8	93	5	12
2005	16	15	10	8	94	7	12
2006	16	15	10	8	94	8	12
2007	16	15	10	8	92	9	12
2008	18	15	11	8	92	9	13
2009	15	16	11	8	95	11	34
2010	25	17	11	8	96	11	54
2011	23	17	10	10	94	10	54
2012	31	17	10	10	96	10	54
2013	31	17	11	10	94	10	54
2014	55	18	11	11	118	11	57
2015	78	18	11	11	118	11	59
2016	78	18	11	11	118	11	60
2017	146	18	11	12	136	12	61
2018	146	18	11	12	136	13	72
2019	178	18	9	12	136	13	74
2020	179	18	6	12	122	12	74

12－11 分地区艺术表演团体演出情况（2020 年）

Basic Statistics on Performance of Art Troupes by Region（2020）

指　　　标	Item	艺术表演场所演出场次（场）Number of Performances in Artistic Performance Place (scene)	艺术表演场所演出收入（万元）Income of Performances in Artistic Performance Place (10000 yuan)	剧团演出场次（场）Number of Performances of Opera Troupes (scene)	农　村（场）Rural Areas (scene)	剧团演出观众人数（万人次）Number of Spectators of Opera Troupes (10000 person－times)	剧团演出收入（万元）Income of Performances of Opera Troupes (10000 yuan)
全市	**Total**	**2035**	**2008.8**	**4229**	**1189**	**256.2**	**8114.8**
为上年(%)	As Compared with the Preceding Year (%)	122.1	113.6	98.0	100.8	86.5	99.7
市区	Urban District	2035	2008.8	3883	903	228.29	7875.2
#萧山区	Xiaoshan	-	-	50	24	4.5	-
余杭区	Yuhang	42	-	169	149	1.1	122.2
富阳区	Fuyang	-	-	101	90	8.1	132.8
临安区	Lin'an	-	-	-	-	-	-
桐庐县	Tonglu	-	-	180	120	8	119.6
淳安县	Chun'an	-	-	-	-	-	-
建德市	Jiande	-	-	166	166	19.9	120

12－12　图书出版数量(2019－2020年)

Number of Books Published(2019－2020)

项　目　Item	本版图书种数(种) Number of Publications (kind)		租型图书种数(种) Number of Publications for Lease (kind)		总印数(万册、万份) Total Printed Copies (10000 copies)		总印张(千印张) Total Printed Sheets (1000 sheets)	
	2019	2020	2019	2020	2019	2020	2019	2020
图书总计 Total	**15352**	**13623**	**386**	**387**	**44287.50**	**40857.37**	**3317561.33**	**3108869.42**
使用《中国标准书号》部分合计 Publication with "China Standard Book Number"	15237	13565	386	387	44235.00	40799.85	3312682.45	3104869.97
#哲学 Philosophy	198	144	–	–	197.38	165.74	25673.33	22417.66
社会科学总论 General Social Science	212	230	–	–	155.73	106.57	21313.83	14452.12
文化、科学、教育、体育 Culture, Science, Education and Sports	7909	7017	–	377	35506.53	33891.14	2472666.18	2423460.95
文学 Literature	2067	1939	–	–	4208.31	2978.18	384326.52	286306.25
艺术 Arts	2054	1656	–	–	885.88	768.75	104747.78	83784.20
自然科学总论 General Natural Science	21	28	–	–	18.29	18.31	3395.10	3208.41
不使用《中国标准书号》部分合计 Publications without "China Standard Book Number"	115	58	–	–	52.50	57.52	4878.88	3999.45

12－13　幼儿园基本情况(1978－2020年)

Basic Statistics on Kindergartens(1978－2020)

单位:人　　　　(person)

年　份 Year	园　数(个) Kindergartens(unit)	在园幼儿数 Number of Children	教职员工数 Teachers and Staff	教　师 Number of Full－time Teachers
1978	266	37597	2570	1439
1979	216	59245	3731	2201
1980	518	82182	4763	3398
1981	676	82808	5275	3691
1982	853	95733	6357	4269
1983	1034	95676	6271	4135
1984	1749	112095	7238	4900
1985	1743	115766	7360	5278
1986	1607	118792	7898	5659
1987	1678	133773	8622	6335
1988	1541	139883	9221	6608
1989	1397	132947	9595	6849
1990	1526	136277	9808	7167
1991	1422	150982	10472	7388
1992	1431	133773	9240	6487
1993	1328	171005	10779	7886
1994	1470	165860	10718	7891
1995	1493	149497	10102	7943
1996	1437	150587	10203	7625
1997	1504	146530	10480	7743
1998	1695	153035	10691	7956
1999	1787	156372	10719	8107
2000	2037	168414	11740	8770
2001	1249	174204	11447	7880
2002	1268	175891	11988	8086
2003	1285	176862	13702	9076
2004	1098	186472	14991	9544
2005	1188	188991	16161	10288
2006	1188	195552	17550	11053
2007	1071	212754	19330	12168
2008	1037	235867	21193	12917
2009	972	246336	22970	14211
2010	969	267352	25525	15203
2011	970	271128	27458	16023
2012	914	283421	29843	17811
2013	860	285406	32037	18945
2014	881	295036	35212	20088
2015	910	313385	38238	21404
2016	930	325495	40833	22955
2017	960	336343	43692	24628
2018	991	343646	47635	26326
2019	1020	350261	50352	27685
2020	1049	374861	54246	29646

12－14　小学基本情况（1978－2020 年）
Basic Statistics on Primary Schools（1978－2020）

单位：人　　　　　　　　　　　　　　　　　　　　　　　　　　　　　（person）

年　份 Year	学校数（个） Number of Schools （unit）	在校学生数 Enrollment	毕业生数 Graduates	教职员工数 Number of Teachers and Staff	专职教师数 Number of Full－time Teachers
1978	4959	605137	－	24103	22291
1979	4850	577811	－	25089	23220
1980	4781	560244	－	25388	22902
1981	4668	525503	－	22468	20832
1982	4528	479264	－	22213	20289
1983	4417	444301	－	20842	18945
1984	4345	427763	－	20496	18500
1985	4286	414839	－	20945	18415
1986	4250	413507	－	20796	18464
1987	4205	405856	－	21067	18751
1988	4137	426842	－	21658	19236
1989	4106	459162	－	22660	20177
1990	4077	460514	－	20542	18099
1991	3972	453055	－	20781	18369
1992	3654	450496	－	21452	19067
1993	3473	477026	－	22141	19775
1994	3352	504867	－	22751	20462
1995	3172	513988	－	23743	21380
1996	3006	525674	－	24553	22197
1997	2762	538390	－	25269	23022
1998	2395	532845	－	25718	23499
1999	1996	512874	－	26350	24120
2000	1659	485679	100405	25938	23876
2001	1354	467982	93365	25535	23179
2002	1197	456535	89752	25425	23138
2003	1044	448969	84051	25304	22955
2004	897	447971	74872	25396	23066
2005	791	458942	75337	25793	23541
2006	605	459529	79070	26040	23848
2007	437	456152	81767	26455	24251
2008	418	452143	82620	26894	24743
2009	417	445132	80441	27445	25424
2010	408	453897	76126	27881	25709
2011	409	465289	73465	27862	26395
2012	415	472613	74547	25620	27777
2013	419	483489	73682	30373	28949
2014	421	502688	73244	31490	30139
2015	443	524513	71398	32815	31280
2016	447	543038	77726	33873	32549
2017	458	560411	84615	35510	34150
2018	478	590491	78951	37316	35793
2019	489	616929	85564	39297	37708
2020	496	645302	89093	40756	39330

12－15 初中基本情况(1978－2020年)

Basic Statistics on Junior Middle Schools(1978－2020)

单位:人 (person)

年 份 Year	学校数(个) Number of Schools (unit)	在校学生数 Enrollment	毕业生数 Graduates	专职教师数 Number of Full－time Teachers
1978	254	247209	–	11978
1979	363	208484	–	11020
1980	369	204073	–	10695
1981	359	194024	–	10015
1982	367	193135	–	10107
1983	370	190221	–	9948
1984	368	192971	–	9679
1985	361	196889	–	9799
1986	376	199638	–	9821
1987	385	195426	–	10264
1988	380	170079	–	10055
1989	376	151223	–	9825
1990	382	160111	–	9564
1991	387	185590	–	10020
1992	367	212022	–	10603
1993	365	203896	–	10876
1994	371	205388	–	11495
1995	373	216300	–	12058
1996	374	229466	–	12810
1997	368	227809	–	13370
1998	359	222191	–	13493
1999	339	239174	–	13723
2000	330	269484	68347	14529
2001	314	285203	75722	15685
2002	315	282951	91056	15758
2003	316	268824	98412	15836
2004	303	252291	93042	16042
2005	289	241374	90094	16205
2006	263	235527	85436	16374
2007	262	238252	76194	16591
2008	260	244464	74827	16965
2009	252	241899	77268	17317
2010	245	236014	78379	17795
2011	246	223545	78431	17652
2012	244	215701	75489	17992
2013	241	213452	71006	18260
2014	241	213936	67988	18671
2015	243	211323	69200	18909
2016	249	215756	69674	19469
2017	251	224797	69084	20144
2018	264	235003	66949	20800
2019	269	244070	73657	21691
2020	280	249434	80451	22525

12－16　高中基本情况(1978－2020年)
Basic Statistics on Senior High Schools(1978－2020)

单位:人　　　　(person)

年　份 Year	学校数(个) Number of Schools (unit)	在校学生数 Enrollment	毕业生数 Graduates	专职教师数 Number of Full－time Teachers
1978	352	102815	–	5235
1979	182	58866	–	3471
1980	151	43661	–	3173
1981	118	34606	–	2825
1982	113	35136	–	2740
1983	111	38580	–	2740
1984	105	43167	–	2781
1985	104	47510	–	3016
1986	95	46379	–	2972
1987	92	44697	–	3006
1988	89	42196	–	2947
1989	88	39994	–	2898
1990	86	39829	–	2922
1991	82	37809	–	2896
1992	74	34620	–	2791
1993	72	32483	–	2641
1994	75	35720	–	2673
1995	72	40771	–	2880
1996	70	43692	–	3135
1997	69	47975	–	3388
1998	75	55688	–	3693
1999	82	64459	–	4172
2000	85	73049	17484	4745
2001	88	79632	22012	5262
2002	81	91635	22630	6126
2003	77	108116	25429	6879
2004	81	115303	30630	7510
2005	80	120883	34486	8041
2006	82	124177	39484	8421
2007	80	122939	39805	8542
2008	76	120294	40551	8646
2009	75	118057	41408	8751
2010	72	116983	39319	8871
2011	71	117089	38579	9061
2012	70	115652	38623	9069
2013	70	113894	37810	9125
2014	72	110478	38489	9378
2015	75	109983	37303	9630
2016	77	110431	36022	10016
2017	80	113054	34860	10430
2018	87	114324	36460	10825
2019	87	118039	36865	11161
2020	91	124563	37697	11684

12－17　中等专业学校基本情况(1978－2020 年)
Basic Statistics on Specialized Secondary Schools(1978－2020)

单位:人　　　　(person)

年　份 Year	学校数(个) Number of Schools (unit)	在校学生数 Enrollment	毕业生数 Graduates	教职员工数 Teachers and Staff	专职教师数 Number of Full－time Teachers
1978	26	8711	－	3044	1080
1979	27	11093	－	2601	1124
1980	26	9453	－	2450	1101
1981	35	7309	－	3122	1276
1982	37	8284	－	3694	1529
1983	37	10516	－	3716	1604
1984	42	13419	－	4194	1758
1985	46	16527	－	5095	1959
1986	50	19114	－	5641	2336
1987	52	20929	－	6081	2623
1988	51	22117	－	6144	2741
1989	54	23302	－	6602	2888
1990	55	23564	－	6679	2948
1991	55	23331	－	6584	2770
1992	55	26373	－	6786	2825
1993	56	30336	－	6732	2780
1994	57	36079	－	6881	2840
1995	57	42784	－	6851	2888
1996	58	49593	－	6789	2904
1997	57	51752	－	6731	2896
1998	56	55796	－	6554	2746
1999	50	52272	－	5023	2272
2000	28	45238	15674	2950	1421
2001	26	32763	15202	2053	1051
2002	14	26255	13355	1251	566
2003	13	21735	11866	1058	457
2004	11	21262	6399	869	416
2005	10	20344	6661	893	443
2006	8	12540	5830	410	184
2007	8	8927	4849	414	194
2008	8	5514	4130	345	152
2009	8	4016	2025	233	65
2010	6	3999	1092	348	151
2011	5	4071	934	369	154
2012	5	3909	1252	376	150
2013	5	3656	1215	390	158
2014	7	3974	1077	469	226
2015	7	3968	1134	494	244
2016	7	4402	982	504	262
2017	7	4566	1348	386	177
2018	6	4448	1457	381	172
2019	7	4535	1385	372	173
2020	7	4540	1470	375	181

12－18　高等学校基本情况(1978－2020年)

Basic Statistics on Regular Institutions of Higher Education(1978－2020)

单位:人　　　　(person)

年　份 Year	学校数(个) Number of Schools (unit)	招生数 Entrants	在校学生数 Enrollment	毕业生数 Graduates	教职员工数 Teachers and Staff	专职教师数 Number of Full－time Teachers
1978	9	－	13319	－	8966	3946
1979	12	－	17518	－	10182	4458
1980	13	－	23545	－	12400	5278
1981	13	－	28936	－	13090	5359
1982	13	－	25821	－	14363	6067
1983	14	－	27443	－	15267	6172
1984	16	－	31384	－	15889	6387
1985	20	－	36996	－	17507	7247
1986	22	－	40051	－	18968	7845
1987	21	－	39922	－	18965	7876
1988	21	－	40787	－	19582	8133
1989	21	－	40330	－	19680	8107
1990	21	－	39866	－	19495	8075
1991	21	－	42192	－	19489	7737
1992	19	－	43787	－	19841	7561
1993	19	－	51063	－	19787	7561
1994	19	－	59109	－	19903	7703
1995	20	－	63124	－	19883	7799
1996	20	－	66023	－	19693	7824
1997	20	－	69391	－	19540	7793
1998	17	－	76546	－	19320	7723
1999	18	－	89109	－	20136	8135
2000	32	46070	122386	17004	23791	10477
2001	33	63001	174894	22756	25805	11866
2002	34	74656	224048	27213	27307	13605
2003	35	85865	269798	41192	34508	18141
2004	36	96810	313599	53288	33325	18445
2005	36	101374	351918	63989	34816	19583
2006	36	103885	373563	80069	36929	21375
2007	36	110371	392770	90944	38843	23197
2008	36	114714	409559	97778	39762	24017
2009	36	114568	429774	96101	40420	24765
2010	37	113529	434811	101681	41582	25003
2011	38	117892	446721	104486	42222	25735
2012	38	121331	459181	107484	43216	26689
2013	38	123046	471820	108688	43992	27544
2014	38	122099	474652	110512	44710	28265
2015	39	139002	475558	125013	44825	28868
2016	39	138819	480953	128434	45512	29222
2017	39	143784	484070	128880	46337	29843
2018	40	149848	496383	131823	47124	30247
2019	40	160426	518325	132048	49020	31448
2020	40	173873	550608	134221	50983	32801

12－19 小学、幼儿园及特殊

Basic Statistics on Primary Schools,

单位:人

指　标	Item	全　市 Total	市　区 Urban District	萧山区 Xiaoshan
小　　学	**Primary Schools**			
学校数(所)	Number of Schools(unit)	496	400	82
班数(班)	Number of Classes(unit)	16795	14949	2630
在校学生数	Number of Students	645302	581430	103878
本年招生数	Number of New Students Enrollment	119957	108643	19352
本年毕业生数	Number of Graduates	89093	79177	14083
专职教师数	Full－time Teachers	39330	34901	5723
2021 年预计毕业生数	Number of Students Will Graduate in 2021	92788	82881	14873
幼儿园	**Kindergartens**			
园数(个)	Number of Kindergartens(unit)	1049	923	189
班数(班)	Number of Classes(unit)	13288	11955	2089
在园幼儿数	Number of Children	374861	337618	61432
教师数	Full－time Teachers	29646	26959	4626
盲聋哑学校	**Schools for the Blind,Deaf and Deaf－mute**			
学校数(个)	Number of Schools(unit)	2	2	－
在校学生数	Number of Students	323	323	－
本年招生数	Number of New Students Enrollment	52	52	－
本年毕业生数	Number of Graduates	68	68	－
专职教师数	Number of Full－time Teachers	162	162	－
智障者学校	**Schools for Weaken in Intelligence**			
学校数(个)	Number of Schools(unit)	12	9	1
在校学生数	Number of Students	1294	1155	264
本年招生数	Number of New Students Enrollment	151	138	23
本年毕业生数	Number of Graduates	173	160	26
专职教师数	Number of Full－time Teachers	417	384	73
工读学校	**Reformatory Schools**			
学校数(个)	Number of Schools(unit)	1	1	－
在校学生数	Number of Students	443	443	－
本年招生数	Number of New Students Enrollment	296	296	－
本年毕业生数	Number of Graduates	254	254	－
专任教师数	Number of Full－time Teachers	65	65	－

教育基本情况(2020年)
Kindergartens and Special Education(2020)

(person)

余杭区 Yuhang	富阳区 Fuyang	临安区 Lin'an	桐庐县 Tonglu	淳安县 Chun'an	建德市 Jiande
59	44	41	27	39	30
3088	1245	884	658	589	599
123676	45310	33074	25603	15648	22621
24288	7700	5744	4549	2627	4138
15150	7223	4983	3920	2490	3506
6753	2808	2001	1528	1542	1359
16155	7418	5176	3830	2596	3481
158	73	81	45	41	40
2618	873	646	482	353	498
72841	26057	17820	14673	9262	13308
5899	1915	1440	969	675	1043
–	–	–	–	–	–
–	–	–	–	–	–
–	–	–	–	–	–
–	–	–	–	–	–
–	–	–	–	–	–
1	1	1	1	1	1
143	64	84	38	70	31
18	11	5	5	3	5
21	17	14	6	7	–
40	28	33	12	8	13
–	–	–	–	–	–
–	–	–	–	–	–
–	–	–	–	–	–
–	–	–	–	–	–
–	–	–	–	–	–

12－20 普通中学、职业中学

Basic Statistics on Senior, Junior High

单位:人

指 标	Item	全 市 Total	市 区 Urban District	萧山区 Xiaoshan
高 中	**Senior High Schools**			
学校数(所)	Number of Schools(unit)	91	75	12
在校学生数	Number of Students	124563	106259	20346
本年招生数	Number of New Students Enrollment	44658	38275	6869
本年毕业生数	Number of Graduates	37697	31666	6461
专职教师数	Full－time Teachers	11684	9794	1858
2021年预计毕业生数	Number of Students Will Graduate in 2021	38654	32853	6551
初 中	**Junior High Schools**			
学校数(所)	Number of Schools(unit)	280	235	46
在校学生数	Number of Students	249434	219414	38533
本年招生数	Number of New Students Enrollment	87278	77333	13106
本年毕业生数	Number of Graduates	80451	70278	13723
专职教师数	Full－time Teachers	22525	19568	3424
2021年预计毕业生数	Number of Students Will Graduate in 2021	77832	67851	12309
职业中学	**Vocational Schools**			
学校数(所)	Number of Schools(unit)	30	25	4
在校学生数	Number of Students	59030	52507	10558
本年招生数	Number of New Students Enrollment	21597	19229	3958
本年毕业生数	Number of Graduates	18506	16380	3321
专职教师数	Full－time Teachers	4702	4178	900
2021年预计毕业生数	Number of Students Will Graduate in 2021	17424	15476	3048
技工学校	**Technical Schools**			
学校数(所)	Number of schools(unit)	20	19	1
在校学生数	Number of Students	29735	28032	2621
专职教师数	Full－time Teachers	1597	1502	212

和技工学校基本情况(2020 年)

Schools and Vacational, Technical Schools(2020)

(person)

余杭区 Yuhang	富阳区 Fuyang	临安区 Lin'an	桐庐县 Tonglu	淳安县 Chun'an	建德市 Jiande
17	7	5	5	5	6
15803	12773	7261	5692	5530	7082
5732	4551	2486	2051	1844	2488
4726	4005	2287	1699	1796	2536
1554	1134	654	587	562	741
4825	4013	2295	1753	1770	2278
40	17	17	12	15	18
42254	21886	14137	11385	8386	10249
14921	7450	4931	3751	2693	3501
13297	7490	4584	3694	3057	3422
3507	1770	1070	961	944	1052
13190	7059	4369	3870	2795	3316
5	2	2	2	2	1
10805	7261	3667	2034	3016	1473
3842	2728	1346	812	1097	459
3488	2110	1104	774	955	397
766	626	329	159	253	112
3234	1996	1130	537	881	530
–	1	1	–	–	1
–	471	693	–	–	1703
–	28	50	–	–	95

12－21 各高等学校

Basic Statistics on Regular

单位:人

单位名称	Item	在校学生数 Number of students 2020	为上年(%) As Compared with the Preceding Year(%)	其中研究生 Graduate Student
全　市	**Total**	**550608**	**106.22**	**84645**
#市　区	**Urban District**	**541386**	**106.19**	**84645**
浙江大学	Zhejiang University	63404	107.35	37026
杭州电子科技大学	Hangzhou Dianzi University	22405	109.28	5441
浙江工业大学	Zhejiang Univesity of Technology	30320	105.94	10974
浙江理工大学	Zhejiang Sci－Tech University	23640	106.99	5433
浙江农林大学	Zhejiang Forestry University	18463	106.70	3233
浙江中医药大学	Zhejiang University of Traditional Chinese Medicine	13144	110.95	3043
杭州师范大学	Hangzhou Normal University	21127	105.19	3781
浙江工商大学	Zhejiang Gongshang University	21762	107.47	5416
中国美术学院	China Academy of Art	9459	103.16	2349
中国计量大学	China JiLiang University	18537	106.02	2762
浙江科技学院	Hangzhou Application Engineering and TechnologyCollege	18196	103.06	1275
浙江广播电视大学	Zhejiang Radio & TV University	9700	108.00	
浙江水利水电专科学校	Zhejiang Water Conservancy and Hydroelectricity College	10382	109.94	－
浙江财经大学	Zhejiang University of Finance and Economics	17361	106.55	2671
浙江警察学院	Zhejiang Police College	3522	97.75	－
浙江传媒学院	Zhejiang Institute of Media and Communications	14305	101.95	323
浙江树人大学	Zhejiang Shuren University	17991	106.54	－
浙江大学城市学院	Zhejiang University City College	11301	97.21	－

基本情况（2020 年）
Institutions of Higher Education(2020)

(person)

本年招生数 Entrants	其中研究生 Graduate Student	本年毕业生数 Graduates	其中研究生 Graduate Student	教职员工数 Number of Teachers and Staff 合计 Total	专职教师 Full - time Teachers
173873	**31865**	**134221**	**17690**	**50983**	**32801**
170832	**31865**	**132000**	**17690**	**50446**	**32331**
18331	12031	12338	6757	9463	4063
7001	2250	4878	1288	2584	1632
9071	4307	7042	2748	3236	2300
6852	2339	5291	1124	2239	1651
5343	1391	4068	676	1700	1214
3955	1314	2604	703	1426	935
6077	1662	4980	1037	2503	1653
6622	2177	4975	1352	2020	1600
2575	788	2194	461	1094	647
5455	1310	4291	616	1793	1262
4718	609	3824	138	1463	1168
4237				274	77
3882	–	2855	–	746	502
4925	1046	3870	514	1656	1156
945	–	1018	–	473	249
3841	201	3182	98	1438	964
5420	–	4307	–	1007	825
2776	–	3057	–	1060	715

12-22 各级成人教育

Basic Statistics on

单位：人

指　标	Item	成人高等学历教育 Higher Education for Adults	成人高校 Adult Institutions of Higher Education	普通高校成人高等学历教育 Adult Higher Education in Ordinary Universities
全　市	**Total**			
学校数(所)	Number of Schools(unit)	3	3	-
在校学生数	Number of Students	145785	9700	136085
本年招生数	Number of New Students Enrollment	76925	4237	72688
本年毕业生数	Number of Graduates	48883	2992	45891
教职员工数	Number of Teachers and Staff	425	425	-
#专职教师	#Full-time Teachers	166	166	-
市　区	**Urban District**			
学校数(所)	Number of Schools(unit)	3	3	-
在校学生数	Number of Students	145785	9700	136085
本年招生数	Number of New Students Enrollment	76925	4237	72688
本年毕业生数	Number of Graduates	48883	2992	45891
教职员工数	Number of Teachers and Staff	425	425	-
#专职教师	#Full-time Teachers	166	166	-

基本情况(2020 年)
Various Adult Education(2020)

(person)

成人中等学历教育 Adult Secondary Education	成人中等专业 Adult Secondary Specialized	成人中学 Secondary Schools for Adults
5	5	
18022	18022	
8516	8516	
5700	5700	
657	657	
314	314	
5	5	
18022	18022	
8516	8516	
5700	5700	
657	657	
314	314	

12－23 医疗卫生机构数(1978－2020年)

Number of Health Institutions(1978－2020)

单位:个　　　　(unit)

年 份 Year	全市合计 Total	医 院 Hospitals	市区合计 Urban District	医 院 Hospitals
1978	1361	421	689	45
1979	1390	426	696	50
1980	1381	425	675	51
1981	1476	424	749	51
1982	1540	432	798	56
1983	1540	435	800	58
1984	1574	437	807	54
1985	1582	404	787	47
1986	1636	407	826	53
1987	1693	420	865	55
1988	1710	438	878	55
1989	1721	443	882	57
1990	1738	440	890	58
1991	1789	441	889	58
1992	1767	436	885	58
1993	1730	403	882	68
1994	1717	416	882	72
1995	1712	414	883	72
1996	1712	416	893	83
1997	1711	411	891	81
1998	1491	419	757	89
1999	1530	400	789	85
2000	1599	396	853	85
2001	1496	391	1072	191
2002	1817	116	1277	88
2003	1901	99	1323	73
2004	1985	114	1396	87
2005	2196	127	1604	97
2006	2570	134	1886	107
2007	2607	138	1872	104
2008	2544	141	1813	108
2009	2687	144	1887	111
2010	2819	151	1906	113
2011	2958	167	1992	122
2012	3017	198	2004	146
2013	4139	208	2233	156
2014	4198	218	2763	173
2015	4428	244	2982	198
2016	4691	277	3214	226
2017	4933	302	3906	273
2018	5377	316	4338	282
2019	5925	343	4857	304
2020	5675	353	4609	312

12－24 医疗病床数(1978－2020年)

Number of Beds in Health Institutions(1978－2020)

单位:张 (bed)

年 份 Year	全 市 Total	医 院 Hospitals	市 区 Urban District	医 院 Hospitals
1978	14042	11704	6588	5789
1979	15124	12682	7335	6282
1980	16317	13478	8244	6940
1981	17408	13576	9646	7185
1982	17179	14350	9194	7580
1983	17338	14584	9411	7833
1984	17694	14691	9536	7867
1985	19637	15010	11095	7933
1986	20555	16035	11657	8448
1987	21465	16770	12203	8863
1988	23394	17954	13204	9651
1989	24111	18363	13581	9773
1990	24121	18879	13219	10041
1991	24966	19444	13968	10437
1992	25606	20243	14206	10821
1993	25653	20884	14058	10982
1994	25984	20870	14231	11045
1995	26684	21360	14731	11336
1996	28141	22217	15427	12132
1997	26616	22341	15076	12190
1998	27327	23110	15530	12766
1999	26713	22952	14988	12691
2000	27166	23303	15496	13068
2001	27063	23520	20523	17770
2002	27609	22797	21200	18667
2003	29144	22036	22641	18205
2004	31738	24444	25008	20338
2005	33251	25907	26732	21931
2006	33972	27186	27172	23184
2007	36928	29987	29884	25664
2008	38114	31416	30663	26882
2009	40226	33094	32412	28031
2010	42828	36148	34693	30639
2011	45291	39363	36633	33291
2012	49471	44019	40534	37383
2013	52056	46636	42506	39489
2014	55779	50805	48406	44639
2015	63632	58400	55540	51672
2016	69452	63994	60666	56522
2017	75948	70187	69057	64524
2018	81215	75186	73481	68765
2019	85708	79957	77680	73202
2020	90057	84251	81927	77353

12－25　分种类分地区

Number of

单位:个

指　　标	Item	全　　市 Total	市　　区 Urban District
总　　计	**Total**	**5675**	**4609**
一、医院	**Number of Hospitals**	**353**	**312**
1. 综合医院	General Hospitals	166	147
2. 中医医院	Hospitals of Chinese Medicine	42	35
3. 中西医结合医院	Chinese Therapeutics with Western	8	7
4. 专科医院	Specialized Hospitals	114	101
#口腔医院	Hospitals for Mouth	24	23
眼科医院	Hospitals for Eye	10	7
耳鼻喉科医院	ENT Hospitals	–	–
肿瘤医院	Tumor Hospitals	2	2
心血管病医院	Cardiovascular Hospitals	2	2
胸科医院	Chest Hospitals	–	–
血液病医院	Blood Diseases Hospitals	–	–
妇产(科)医院	Hospitals for Pregnant Woman	12	12
儿童医院	Children Hospitals	5	5
精神病医院	Mental Hospitals	9	6
传染病医院	Hospitals for Infectious Diseases	1	1
皮肤病医院	Dermatology Hospital	5	5
结核病医院	Tuberculosis Hospitals	–	–
麻风病医院	Leprosy Hospitals	–	–
职业病医院	Occupational Disease Hospitals	–	–
骨科医院	Orthopaedics Hospitals	4	3
康复医院	Healing Hospitals	16	13
整形外科医院	Plastic Hospitals	2	2
美容医院	Beauty Hospitals	13	13
其他专科医院	Other Special Hospitals	9	7
5. 护理院	Nursing Centers	23	22
二、基层医疗卫生机构	**Community Medical Institutions**	**5215**	**4209**
1. 社区卫生服务中心(站)	Health Service Centers for Community	1306	1133
#社区卫生服务中心	Health Service Centers	135	127
社区卫生服务站	Health Service Stations	1171	1006
2. 卫生院	Health Service Centers	81	30
#街道卫生院	Rural Township Hospitals in Subdistrict	–	–
乡镇卫生院	Rural Township Hospitals in Country	81	30
3. 村卫生室	Health Offices in Village	759	243
4. 门诊部	Clinics	799	748
5. 诊所、卫生所、医务室、护理站	Other Health Care Institutions	2270	2055
三、专业公共卫生机构	**Professional Public Health Institutions**	**56**	**40**
疾病预防控制中心	Centers for Disease Prevention and Control	16	13
专科疾病防治所(所、站)	Specialized Centers for Disease Prevention and Control(stations)	2	–
健康教育所(站、中心)	Education Center for Health(stations)	–	–
妇幼保健院(所、站)	Maternity and Child Care Centers(stations)	10	7
急救中心(站)	First－aid Centers(stations)	10	6
采供血机构	Blood Supplying Agencies	3	2
卫生监督所	Institutions of Public Health Inspection	13	10
计划生育服务机构	Family Planning Service Institutions	2	2
四、其他卫生机构	**Other Health Care Institutions**	**51**	**48**
疗养院	Sanatoriums	8	8
医学科学研究机构	Research Institutions of Medical Science	–	–
医学在职培训机构	Medical Training Organization for Incumbent	3	2
临床检验中心(所、站)	Clinical Laboratory Center	–	–
统计信息中心	Statistical Information Centers	–	–
其他	Other	40	38

医疗卫生机构数(2020 年末)
Health Institutions(End of 2020)

(unit)

萧山区 Xiaoshan	余杭区 Yuhang	富阳区 Fuyang	临安区 Lin'an	桐庐县 Tonglu	淳安县 Chun'an	建德市 Jiande
892	**832**	**215**	**502**	**350**	**323**	**393**
59	**33**	**15**	**29**	**19**	**12**	**10**
46	16	6	14	11	5	3
5	2	4	10	3	2	2
–	1	1	–	–	–	1
7	10	4	4	5	5	3
2	3	1	1	–	1	–
–	–	1	–	1	1	1
–	–	–	–	–	–	–
–	–	–	–	–	–	–
–	–	–	–	–	–	–
–	–	–	–	–	–	–
–	–	–	–	–	–	–
–	1	–	–	–	–	–
–	1	–	–	–	–	–
–	3	1	1	1	1	1
–	–	–	–	–	–	–
1	–	–	–	–	–	–
–	–	–	–	–	–	–
–	–	–	–	–	–	–
–	–	–	–	–	–	–
–	2	–	–	1	–	–
1	–	1	–	1	1	1
–	–	–	–	–	–	–
–	–	–	1	–	–	–
3	–	–	1	1	1	–
1	4	–	1	–	–	1
820	**780**	**192**	**469**	**326**	**304**	**376**
327	194	157	83	107	48	18
29	20	25	5	4	2	2
298	174	132	78	103	46	16
–	–	10	20	10	21	20
–	–	–	–	–	–	–
–	–	10	20	10	21	20
96	–	–	147	118	170	228
92	111	24	21	29	7	15
305	475	1	198	62	58	95
7	**4**	**4**	**4**	**3**	**7**	**6**
2	1	1	1	1	1	1
–	–	–	–	–	1	1
–	–	–	–	–	–	–
–	1	1	1	1	1	1
2	1	1	1	–	3	1
1	–	–	–	–	–	1
1	1	1	1	1	1	1
1	–	–	–	–	–	–
6	**15**	**4**	**–**	**2**	**–**	**1**
1	1	4	–	–	–	–
–	–	–	–	–	–	1
–	1	–	–	–	–	1
–	–	–	–	–	–	–
–	–	–	–	–	–	–
5	13	–	–	2	–	–

12－26 分种类分地区

Total Number of

单位：张

指　　标	Item	全　　市 Total	市区 Urban District
总　　计	**Total**	**90057**	**81927**
一、医院	**Number of Hospitals**	**84251**	**77353**
1. 综合医院	General Hospitals	45249	41540
2. 中医医院	Hospitals of Chinese Medicine	12384	10637
3. 中西医结合医院	Chinese Therapeutics with Western	5588	5327
4. 专科医院	Specialized Hospitals	17394	16233
#口腔医院	Stomatology Hospitals	369	354
眼科医院	Ophthalmology Hospitals	324	234
耳鼻喉科医院	ENT Hospitals	–	–
肿瘤医院	Tumor Hospitals	2558	2558
心血管病医院	Cardiovascular Hospitals	502	502
胸科医院	Chest Hospitals	–	–
血液病医院	Blood Diseases Hospitals	–	–
妇产(科)医院	Hospitals for Pregnant Woman	2040	2040
儿童医院	Children Hospitals	1922	1922
精神病医院	Mental Hospitals	2820	2248
传染病医院	Hospitals for Infectious Diseases	700	700
皮肤病医院	Dermatology Hospital	197	197
结核病医院	Tuberculosis Hospitals	–	–
麻风病医院	Leprosy Hospitals	–	–
职业病医院	Occupational Disease Hospitals	–	–
骨科医院	Orthopaedics Hospitals	619	573
康复医院	Healing Hospitals	3806	3439
整形外科医院	Plastic Hospitals	136	136
美容医院	Beauty Hospitals	255	255
其他专科医院	Other Special Hospitals	1146	1075
5. 护理院	Nursing Centers	3636	3616
二、基层医疗卫生机构	**Community Medical Institutions**	**3676**	**2992**
1. 社区卫生服务中心(站)	Health Service Centers for Community	2822	2772
#社区卫生服务中心	Health Service Centers	2822	2772
社区卫生服务站	Health Service Stations	–	–
2. 卫生院	Health Service Centers	777	143
#街道卫生院	Rural Township Hospitals in Subdistrict	–	–
乡镇卫生院	Rural Township Hospitals in Country	777	143
3. 村卫生室	Health Offices in Village	–	–
4. 门诊部	Clinics	77	77
5. 诊所、卫生所、医务室、护理站	Other Health Care Institutions	–	–
三、专业公共卫生机构	**Professional Public Health Institutions**	**1217**	**669**
疾病预防控制中心	Centers for Disease Prevention and Control	–	–
专科疾病防治所(所、站)	Specialized Centers for Disease Prevention and Control(stations)	200	0
健康教育所(站、中心)	Education Center for Health(stations)	–	–
妇幼保健院(所、站)	Maternity and Child Care Centers(stations)	993	655
急救中心(站)	First – aid Centers(stations)	24	14
采供血机构	Blood Supplying Agencies	–	–
卫生监督所(中心)	Institutions of Public Health Inspection	–	–
计划生育服务机构	Family Planning Service Institutions	–	–
四、其他卫生机构	**Other Health Care Institutions**	**913**	**913**
#疗养院	Sanatoriums	–	–
医学科学研究机构	Research Institutions of Medical Science	–	–
医学在职培训机构	Medical Training Organization for Incumbent	–	–
临床检验中心(所、站)	Clinical Laboratory Center	–	–
统计信息中心	Statistical Information Centers	–	–
其他	Other	–	–

医疗病床数(2020 年末)

Beds in Health Institutions(End of 2020)

(bed)

萧山区 Xiaoshan	余杭区 Yuhang	富阳区 Fuyang	临安区 Lin'an	桐庐县 Tonglu	淳安县 Chun'an	建德市 Jiande
11141	**7135**	**4230**	**3229**	**2551**	**2670**	**2909**
10731	**5826**	**3213**	**3092**	**2263**	**2401**	**2234**
8014	3121	1517	1881	1540	1180	989
1882	617	1158	912	506	801	440
–	330	76	–	–	–	261
785	1203	462	249	217	420	524
30	30	15	25	–	15	–
–	–	20	–	20	25	45
–	–	–	–	–	–	–
–	–	–	–	–	–	–
–	–	–	–	–	–	–
–	–	–	–	–	–	–
–	–	–	–	–	–	–
–	45	–	–	–	–	–
–	50	–	–	–	–	–
–	685	327	182	–	180	392
–	–	–	–	–	–	–
40	–	–	–	–	–	–
–	–	–	–	–	–	–
–	–	–	–	–	–	–
–	–	–	–	–	–	–
–	393	–	–	46	–	–
20	–	100	–	100	180	87
–	–	–	–	–	–	–
–	–	–	22	–	–	–
695	–	–	20	51	20	–
50	555	–	50	–	–	20
350	**779**	**371**	**93**	**190**	**119**	**375**
321	779	265	56	22	–	28
321	779	265	56	22	–	28
–	–	–	–	–	–	–
–	–	106	37	168	119	347
–	–	–	–	–	–	–
–	–	106	37	168	119	347
–	–	–	–	–	–	–
29	–	–	–	–	–	–
–	–	–	–	–	–	–
0	**310**	**312**	**44**	**98**	**150**	**300**
–	–	–	–	–	–	–
–	–	–	–	–	–	200
–	–	–	–	–	–	–
–	310	312	30	98	150	90
–	–	–	14	–	–	10
–	–	–	–	–	–	–
–	–	–	–	–	–	–
–	–	–	–	–	–	–
60	**220**	**334**	**–**	**–**	**–**	**–**
–	–	–	–	–	–	–
–	–	–	–	–	–	–
–	–	–	–	–	–	–
–	–	–	–	–	–	–
–	–	–	–	–	–	–
–	–	–	–	–	–	–

12－27 医院诊疗

Number of

指　　标	Item	机构数(个) Number of Institutions (unit)	诊疗人次数(万人次) Total Number of Patients Treate (10000 person－times)
总　　计	**Total**	**5675**	**12698.73**
一、医院	**Number of Hospitals**	**353**	**6695.88**
1. 综合医院	General Hospitals	166	4026.60
2. 中医医院	Hospitals of Chinese Medicine	42	1067.53
3. 中西医结合医院	Chinese Therapeutics with Western	8	489.35
4. 专科医院	Specialized Hospitals	114	1106.15
#口腔医院	Stomatology Hospitals	24	196.45
眼科医院	Ophthalmology Hospitals	10	35.99
耳鼻喉科医院	ENT Hospitals	–	–
肿瘤医院	Tumor Hospitals	2	69.69
心血管病医院	Cardiovascular Hospitals	2	38.57
胸科医院	Chest Hospitals	–	–
血液病医院	Blood Diseases Hospitals	–	–
妇产(科)医院	Hospitals for Pregnant Woman	12	224.53
儿童医院	Children Hospitals	5	286.60
精神病医院	Mental Hospitals	9	55.09
传染病医院	Hospitals for Infectious Diseases	1	54.44
皮肤病医院	Dermatology Hospital	5	22.92
结核病医院	Tuberculosis Hospitals	–	–
麻风病医院	Leprosy Hospitals	–	–
职业病医院	Occupational Disease Hospitals	–	–
骨科医院	Orthopaedics Hospitals	4	18.19
康复医院	Healing Hospitals	16	13.03
整形外科医院	Plastic Hospitals	2	4.69
美容医院	Beauty Hospitals	13	75.07
其他专科医院	Other Special Hospitals	9	10.91
5. 护理院	Nursing Centers	23	6.24
二、基层医疗卫生机构	**Community Medical Institutions**	**5215**	**5765.15**
1. 社区卫生服务中心(站)	Health Service Centers for Community	1306	3511.63
#社区卫生服务中心	Health Service Centers	135	3444.91
社区卫生服务站	Health Service Stations	1171	66.71
2. 卫生院	Health Service Centers	81	566.45
#乡镇卫生院	Rural Township Hospitals in Country	81	566.45
3. 村卫生室	Health Offices in Village	759	99.87
4. 门诊部	Clinics	799	935.58
5. 诊所、卫生所、医务室	Other Health Care Institutions	2270	651.61
三、专业公共卫生机构	**Professional Public Health Institutions**	**56**	**221.95**
专科疾病防治院(所、站)	Specialized Centers for Disease Prevention and Control(stations)	2	8.06
妇幼保健院(所、站)	Maternity and Child Care Centers(stations)	10	198.42
四、其他机构	**Other Institutions**	**51**	**15.76**
疗养院	Sanatoriums	8	15.76

次数和入院人数（2020 年）
Hospital Patients(2020)

门、急诊人次数(万人次) Out - Patients and Emergency Patients (10000 person - times)	入院人数 (人) Hospital Admissions(person)	每百门急诊次入院人数(人) Hospital Admissions Per 100 Patient - time (person)
12268.34	**2504913**	**2.31**
6635.25	**2408643**	**3.63**
4016.81	1479819	3.68
1062.28	302621	2.85
484.86	137064	2.83
1065.76	469696	4.41
167.23	1354	0.08
34.45	11756	3.41
-	-	-
69.69	156104	22.40
34.06	8102	2.38
-	-	-
-	-	-
221.20	107890	4.88
286.14	78339	2.74
55.05	28827	5.24
54.08	15490	2.86
22.92	894	0.39
-	-	-
-	-	-
-	-	-
18.19	11296	6.21
12.73	20380	16.01
4.69	2883	6.15
75.07	14029	1.87
10.27	12352	12.03
5.55	19443	35.05
5403.05	**20690**	**0.05**
3403.83	10041	0.03
3337.11	10041	0.03
66.71	-	-
547.23	10120	0.18
547.23	10120	0.18
97.90	-	-
720.13	529	-
633.95	-	-
217.34	**58229**	**2.88**
8.06	917	1.14
193.82	57312	2.96
12.70	**17351**	**13.67**
12.70	17351	13.67

12－28 卫生事业

Total Number of

单位:人

指　　标	Item	全　　市 Total	市　　区 Urban District
总　　计	**Total**	**164991**	**151446**
一、卫生技术人员	Number of Medical Technical Personnel	134258	122937
1. 执业(助理)医师	Licensed (Assistant) Doctor	51135	46884
#执业医师	Licensed Doctor	47520	43906
2. 注册护士	Registered Nurse	58542	54024
3. 药剂师	Druggist	7885	6994
4. 技师人员	Checking Member	7257	6640
#检验师	Docimaster	5056	4607
5. 其他	Others	9439	8395
二、其他技术人员	Other Medical Technical Personnel	8825	8419
三、管理人员	Managerial Personnel	7275	6779
四、工勤人员	Logistics Worker	14156	13119

人员数(2020 年末)

Medical Technical Personnel(End of 2020)

(person)

萧山区 Xiaoshan	余杭区 Yuhang	富阳区 Fuyang	临安区 Lin'an	桐庐县 Tonglu	淳安县 Chun'an	建德市 Jiande
20055	**14596**	**7024**	**6024**	**5302**	**3697**	**4546**
16243	11806	5879	4952	4443	3041	3837
6118	4662	2326	2070	1717	1184	1350
5475	4212	2020	1795	1462	1020	1132
6846	4664	2301	1837	1662	1236	1620
1121	685	307	342	354	243	294
710	775	291	268	232	170	215
500	576	183	183	172	121	156
1448	1020	654	435	478	208	358
810	544	477	419	160	116	130
1069	734	263	185	259	86	151
1831	1512	405	379	429	302	306

12－29 卫生技术人员(1978－2020年)

Number of Medical Technical Personnel(1978－2020)

单位:人 (person)

年 份 Year	全 市 Total	执业(助理)医师 Number of Licensed (Assistant) Doctors	注册护士 Registered Nurses	市 区 Urban District	执业(助理)医师 Number of Licensed (Assistant) Doctors	注册护士 Registered Nurses
1978	19059	7375	3483	10867	4346	2510
1979	20060	7539	3536	11779	4733	2632
1980	21110	8311	3885	12376	5179	2804
1981	22737	9284	4139	13697	5946	3032
1982	23558	9883	4369	14221	6204	3193
1983	24914	10833	4562	15213	6990	3352
1984	25648	11291	4817	15807	7393	3487
1985	25593	11503	5071	15840	7644	3705
1986	26489	12623	5391	16543	8239	3940
1987	27663	12369	5805	17361	8329	4156
1988	28676	13674	6938	18022	8710	4801
1989	29791	14177	7348	18619	9146	5085
1990	30990	14483	7822	19231	9374	5397
1991	32169	14858	8153	19630	9494	5610
1992	32628	14842	8417	19690	9373	5736
1993	33172	15181	8643	19708	9499	5797
1994	33964	15465	8979	19907	9472	5940
1995	34245	16465	9531	19943	9607	6249
1996	34946	16789	9794	20695	9889	6508
1997	35423	17112	10019	20728	9902	6571
1998	35857	16022	10577	21035	9452	6788
1999	35256	16668	10587	20519	9610	6856
2000	35487	16317	11186	20344	9050	7300
2001	36643	16994	11576	28293	12968	9343
2002	37193	16092	11922	28818	12332	9653
2003	39019	16614	12460	30299	12731	10161
2004	39816	16770	13248	30886	12894	10840
2005	42353	17833	14514	33206	13802	12034
2006	45375	18831	15557	35904	14689	12986
2007	49780	20701	17455	39860	16290	14601
2008	52379	21223	18702	42015	16747	15556
2009	56270	22753	20997	45219	17996	17530
2010	61117	24345	23418	49232	19414	19481
2011	65869	25773	25231	53008	20566	20949
2012	71618	27369	28382	57971	22004	23760
2013	78340	29686	30996	63359	23886	25808
2014	85614	31977	34724	74064	27675	30528
2015	93036	34832	38182	80799	30316	33672
2016	101194	38172	42011	88076	33344	37154
2017	110395	41833	46343	100478	38333	42580
2018	117425	44896	49911	106923	41105	45838
2019	126995	48962	55004	115959	44842	50639
2020	134258	51135	58542	122937	46884	54024

12－30 体育运动情况(2016－2020 年)
Basic Statistics on Sports Activities(2016－2020)

单位:人 (person)

指　　标	Item	2016 年	2017 年	2018 年	2019 年	2020 年
一、年末体委工作人员数	**Workers in Sports Commissions at Year－end**	**705**	**696**	**687**	**615**	**599**
#教练员	#Full－time Coaches	152	157	163	153	159
二、等级裁判员发展人数	**Number of Referees in Grades**	**78**	**110**	**－**	**－**	**298**
#女	#Female	44	60	－	－	106
一级裁判员	First Grade Referees	28	－	－	－	－
二级裁判员	Second Grade Referees	50	110	－	－	298
三级裁判员	Third Grade Referees	－	－	－	－	－
三、等级运动员发展人数	**Number of Athletes in Grades**	**469**	**509**	**364**	**478**	**329**
#女	#Female	182	223	139	179	127
一级运动员	First Grade Athlete	78	113	－	－	－
二级运动员	Second Grade Athlete	391	396	364	478	328
三级运动员	Third Grade Athlete	－	－	－	－	－

主要统计指标解释

文化事业机构　指从事专业文化工作和为专业文化工作服务的独立建制的单独核算的单位。不包括这些单位另外举办独立核算的其他机构和各部门的业余文化组织。

艺术表演团体　指从事戏曲、音乐、舞蹈、杂技等专业艺术表演，有独立帐户，实行单独核算的团体。不包括半工半艺、半农半艺和民间职业剧团。

普通高等学校　指按照国家规定的设置标准和审批程序批准举办，通过国家统一招生考试，招收高中毕业生为主要培养对象，实施高等教育的全日制大学、独立设置的学院和高等专科学校、短期职业大学。

成人高等学校　指按照国家有关规定审批，招收通过全国成人高教统一招生考试的具有高中毕业或同等学历的在职从业人员利用脱产、半脱产、业余或函授等多种形式对其实施高等学历教育，培养高等教育专科或本科毕业水平的专门人才，修业年限、课程设置和总学时数均按高等学历教育要求付诸实施的学校。包括广播电视大学、职工高等学校、农民高等学校、管理干部学院、教育学院、独立设置的函授学院等。

小学学龄儿童入学率　指调查范围内已入小学学习的学龄儿童占校内外学龄儿童总数(包括弱智儿童在内，但不包括盲聋哑儿童)的比重。计算公式：

$$\text{小学学龄儿童入学率}=\frac{\text{已入学的小学学龄儿童数}}{\text{校内外小学学龄儿童总数}}*100\%$$

等级运动员人数　指经考核正式批准授予等级运动员称号的人数。运动员等级分为国际级运动健将、运动健将、一级运动员、二级运动员、三级运动员、少年级运动员。

等级裁判员人数　指经考核正式批准授予等级裁判员称号的人数。裁判员等级分为国际裁判、国家级裁判、一级裁判、二级裁判、三级裁判。

卫生机构　卫生机构是指从卫生行政部门取得《医疗机构执业许可证》，或从民政、工商行政、机构编制管理部门取得法人单位登记证书，为社会提供医疗保健、疾病控制、卫生监督等服务或从事医学科研、医学教育等卫生单位和卫生社会团体。不包括卫生行政机构、香港和澳门特别行政区以及台湾所属卫生机构。

卫生技术人员　卫生技术人员包括执业(助理)医师、注册护士、药剂人员、检验和影像技师(士、员)等卫生专业人员。

执业(助理)医师、执业(中)药师和注册护士　执业(助理)医师、执业(中)药师和注册护士是指领取医师、药师执业证书和注册护士证书的人员。不包括从事管理工作的医师、药师和护士。

Explanatory Notes on Main Statistical Indicators

Culture Institutions refer to units specialized in cultural development or service, which have independent organizational system and accounting system, excluding other self – accounting establishments run by these units and amateur cultural groups established by various departments.

Art Troupe refers to the troupe engaged in drama, music, dance, acrobatics or other art performance with independent accounts in banks and self accounting system, excluding the troupes which are engaged partly in industrial or agricultural activities and partly in art performance, and folk professional troupes.

Regular Institutions of Higher Education refer to full – time universities, independent colleges, high professional schools and short – term professional universities which are set up according to the government evaluation and approval procedures, recruit high school graduates as main training objects through the national unified entrance examination and, provide higher education courses.

Adult Higher Education Institutions refer to educational establishments, which are set up in line with government relevant rules and approval, enroll staff and workers with senior secondary school or equivalent education through the national unified entrance examination of adult higher education, provide higher education courses in many forms, such as full – time, part – time, spare – time, or correspondence to cultivate specialized talents with the graduation level of junior college or undergraduate, and implement the length of schooling, curriculum and total class hours according to the requirements of higher education. It includes Radio and TV universities, high education schools for staff and workers and for peasants, colleges for management cadres, pedagogical colleges, and independent correspondence colleges.

Enrollment Rate of Primary School – age Children refer to the proportion of primary school – age children enrolled at primary schools to primary school – age children both in and outside schools within the scope of investigation (including retarded children, but excluding blind, deaf and mute children). The formula is:

$$\text{Enrollment Rate of Primary School – age Children} = \frac{\text{Number of primary School – age Children at Primary Schools}}{\text{Total Number of Primary School – age Children Both in and Outside schools}} \times 100\%$$

Number of Grade Athletes refers to the number of athletes who have been given titles through examination. They are classified as international masters of sports, masters of sports, first – grade, second – grade and third – grade sportsmen and young athletes.

Number of Grade Referees refers to the number of referees who have been given titles after examination. They are classified as international referees, national referees and referees of the first, second and third grades.

Health Institutions refer to health institutions and society organization that get the practice license of medical institution from the health administration department, or get registration certificate of legal entity from civil administration, industry and business administration or organization management department, and offer medical treatment, disease control, supervision of sanitation for society or are engaged in medical research and medical education. It excludes health administration department and Institutions of Hong Kong, Macao, and Taiwan.

Medical Technical Personnel include licensed (assistant) doctor, registered nurse, druggist, checking members and photo artificer.

Licensed (Assistant) Doctor, Licensed Druggist and Registered Nurse refers to the doctor, druggist and nurse who get the practice certificate. Those engaged in management are excluded.

十三、人民生活 物价、民政

PEOPLE' S LIVELIHOOD, PRICE INDICES AND CIVIL ADMINISTRATION

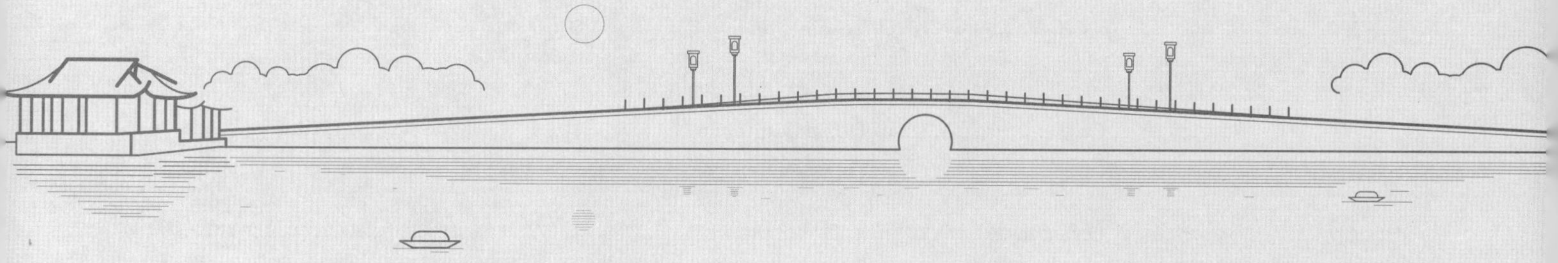

13 人民生活、物价、民政
People's Livelihood, Price Indices and Civil Administration

主要统计指标
Major Statistical Indicators

非私营单位就业人员工资总额	Total Wages of Employed Persons of Non-private Units	3676.74	亿元	(100 million yuan)
非私营单位就业人员平均工资	Annual Average Wages of Employed Persons of Non-private Units	128308	元	(yuan)
全体居民人均可支配收入	Per Capita Disposable Income of Urban and Rural Residents	61879	元	(yuan)
为上年	As Compared with the Preceding Year	104.4	%	(%)
城镇常住居民人均可支配收入	Per Capita Disposable Income of Permanent Urban Residents	68666	元	(yuan)
为上年	As Compared with the Preceding Year	103.9	%	(%)
农村常住居民人均可支配收入	Per Capita Disposable Income of Permanent Rural Residents	38700	元	(yuan)
为上年	As Compared with the Preceding Year	106.7	%	(%)
市区居民消费价格指数	Consume Price Index of Urban District	102.1	上年=100	(Preceding Year=100)
市区商品零售价格指数	Commodity Retail Price Index of Urban District	100.9	上年=100	(Preceding Year=100)
工业生产者出厂价格指数	Producer Price Indices for Industrial Products	97.5	上年=100	(Preceding Year=100)

13－01　居民家庭人均收入支出（2018－2020年）
Per Capita Income and Expenditure of Households（2018－2020）

单位：元　　　　　　　　　　　　　　　　　　　　　　　　　　　　　　　　（yuan）

项　目 Item	全体居民 Urban and Rural Residents			城镇常住居民 Permanent Urban Residents			农村常住居民 Permanent Rural Residents		
	2018	2019	2020	2018	2019	2020	2018	2019	2020
一、可支配收入 Disposable Income	54348	59261	61879	61172	66068	68666	33193	36255	38700
工资性收入 Icome from Wages and salaries	31355	34136	36014	35084	37845	39720	19796	21601	23359
经营净收入 Net Buisness Income	6084	6584	6446	5298	5849	5640	8521	9067	9196
财产净收入 Net Income from Property	7202	8111	8235	9080	10045	10182	1380	1574	1586
转移净收入 Net Income from Transfer	9707	10430	11184	11710	12329	13124	3496	4013	4559
二、消费支出 Expenditure	37369	40016	38235	41615	44076	41916	24203	26296	25664
食品烟酒 Food,Tobacco and Liquor	9278	9833	9901	10160	10651	10717	6542	7067	7114
衣着 Clothing	2185	2182	1972	2470	2432	2177	1301	1339	1272
居住 Residence	9939	10204	10658	10971	11081	11434	6739	7242	8006
生活用品及服务 Daily Necessities and Services	2195	2089	2092	2468	2300	2288	1351	1375	1423
交通通信 Transportation and Communication	6140	6761	6253	6743	7446	6883	4269	4444	4101
教育文化娱乐 Education, Cultural and Recreation Service	3625	4149	3242	4196	4765	3704	1856	2070	1664
医疗保健 Medicine and Medical Service	2929	3636	3215	3335	4057	3651	1670	2210	1729
其他用品及服务 Other Supplies and Services	1078	1162	902	1272	1344	1062	475	549	355

13－02 城镇住户调查情况(1978－2020 年)
Basic Conditions of Urban Households (1978－2020)

年份 Year	调查户数(户) Number of Households Surveyed (household)	平均每户人口(人) Average Household Size (person)	平均每户就业人数(人) Average Number of Employed Persons Per Household(person)	年人均可支配收入(元) Per Capita Annual Disposable Income (yuan)	年人均消费支出(元) Per Capita Annual Consumption Expenditure(yuan)	人均住房建筑面积(平方米) Per Capita Living Space in City Areas (sq. m)
1978	28	4.20	2.89	338	301	
1979	28	4.19	2.77	396	365	
1980	28	4.18	2.79	521	491	
1981	100	3.97	2.37	540	513	
1982	100	3.90	2.35	532	532	
1983	100	3.90	2.42	578	535	11.7
1984	100	3.90	2.36	729	679	12.4
1985	150	3.53	2.26	1026	908	12.9
1986	150	3.49	2.27	1169	1072	13.2
1987	150	3.42	2.25	1260	1118	14.1
1988	200	3.41	2.16	1565	1515	14.1
1989	200	3.40	2.15	1764	1615	14.1
1990	200	3.37	2.15	1985	1685	14.5
1991	200	3.40	2.20	2128	1894	14.4
1992	200	3.28	2.14	2580	2296	14.8
1993	200	3.21	2.10	3525	3183	14.9
1994	200	3.31	2.10	5249	4559	15.9
1995	200	3.20	2.05	6301	5559	15.6
1996	200	3.20	2.00	7206	6095	15.9
1997	200	3.14	1.99	7896	6766	16.5
1998	300	3.12	1.93	8465	7235	18.8
1999	300	3.11	1.92	9085	7424	19.5
2000	300	3.10	1.83	9668	7790	19.9
2001	440	2.98	1.72	10896	8968	20.7
2002	500	2.93	1.53	11778	9215	21.7
2003	500	2.92	1.51	12898	9950	22.9
2004	500	2.92	1.48	14565	11213	23.7
2005	600	2.84	1.42	16601	13438	27.6
2006	600	2.81	1.44	19027	14472	28.0
2007	600	2.72	1.45	21689	14896	28.8
2008	600	2.75	1.29	24104	16719	29.9
2009	600	2.68	1.25	26864	18595	30.8
2010	600	2.70	1.25	30035	20219	30.9
2011	600	2.71	1.32	34065	22642	33.7
2012	600	2.69	1.31	37511	22800	34.4
2013	1920	2.79	1.51	40925	30659	34.9
2014	1920	2.79	1.53	44632	32165	35.1
2015	1920	2.79	1.48	48316	33818	35.5
2016	1920	2.80	1.49	52185	35686	35.8
2017	1920	2.91	1.48	56276	38179	36.4
2018	2250	2.93	1.50	61172	41615	37.3
2019	2250	2.96	1.53	66068	44076	38.2
2020	2250	2.94	1.47	68666	41916	39.3

注:2000 年及以前为主城区数据;2001－2012 年为包括萧山区和余杭区在内的市区数据;2013－2020 年为包括所有区、县(市)城乡住户一体化改革后新口径数据。

a) The data on the table include the main urban districts before 2000; The data include Xiaoshan district and Yuhang district in 2001－2012; The date include all districts and counties since 2013; The data in this table are calculated at new rage by the results of integrated survey of urban households and rural households sine 2013.

13－03　城镇居民家庭平均每百户耐用消费品拥有量(2012－2020 年)

Number of Major Durable Consumer Goods Owned Per 100 Urban Households(2012－2020)

项　目 Item		2012	2013	2014	2015	2016	2017	2018	2019	2020
家用汽车 Family Car	(辆) (unit)	34.3	40.2	45.4	48.7	52.3	55.8	59.7	62.6	65.3
摩托车 Motorcycle	(辆) (unit)	4.0	6.6	6.8	5.4	5.0	4.8	7.0	6.2	5.4
电冰箱 Refrigerator	(台) (unit)	102.5	88.0	92.3	92.2	97.6	99.9	107.0	110.0	110.1
洗衣机 Washing Machine	(台) (unit)	96.6	82.6	86.8	86.9	92.6	94.6	98.5	102.3	102.4
热水器 Water Heater	(台) (unit)	105.4	89.4	93.7	95.5	101.4	105.2	109.2	114.0	115.2
空调器 Air Conditioner	(台) (unit)	214.7	189.6	201.5	207.3	226.6	235.3	243.2	250.2	252.2
彩色电视机 Color TV Set	(台) (unit)	178.4	166.4	174.0	174.1	183.1	187.3	187.9	193.8	191.9
摄像机	(架) (unit)	12.4	10.0	10.5	10.5	10.3	–	–	–	–
照相机 Camera	(架) (unit)	63.5	50.6	54.4	51.5	48.4	49.9	34.9	28.9	27.6
计算机 Computer	(台) (unit)	112.2	103.7	110.6	110.1	112.0	115.1	100.5	89.8	90.6
#接入互联网的计算机 of which:Internet－connected computer	(台) (unit)	98.6	92.5	100.2	99.8	100.8	104.9	92.9	86.0	87.3
固定电话 Telephone	(部) (set)	83.6	51.6	54.2	50.7	47.3	45.9	28.9	19.8	17.6
移动电话 Mobile Phone	(部) (set)	213.1	217.4	227.9	229.9	242.1	245.4	258.3	259.0	260.3
#接入互联网的移动电话 of which:Internet－connected Mobile Phone	(部) (set)	–	125.1	140.8	155.8	175.3	191.4	212.9	223.6	233.2

注:2012 年为包括萧山区和余杭区在内的市区数据;2013－2020 年为包括所有区、县(市)城乡住户一体化改革后新口径数据。
a)The data include Xiaoshan district and Yuhang district in 2012;The date include all districts and counties since 2013;The data in this table are calculated at new rage by the results of integrated survey of urban households and rural households sine 2013.

13－04 农村住户调查情况(1978－2020年)

Basic Conditions of Rural Households(1978－2020)

年 份 Year	调查户数(户) Number of Households Surveyed (household)	平均每户人口(人) Average Number of Residents per Household (person)	平均每户就业人数(人) Average Number of Employed Persons Per Household (person)	人均可支配收入(元) Per Capita Annual Disposable Income of Rural Households (yuan)	人均消费支出(元) Per Capita Annual Consumption Expenditure (yuan)	人均住房建筑面积(平方米) Per Capita Floor Space (sq. m)
1978				162		
1979				204		
1980	60	4.72	2.93	250	287	23.3
1981	60	4.60	2.70	333	294	25.2
1982	60	4.43	2.73	405	328	26.3
1983	170	4.55	2.85	395	355	29.9
1984	170	4.44	2.81	510	416	31.7
1985	420	4.40	2.88	624	542	29.9
1986	620	4.39	2.88	675	601	31.3
1987	620	4.34	2.86	820	714	33.1
1988	620	4.26	2.87	996	925	35.5
1989	620	4.17	2.85	1117	1011	36.8
1990	620	4.16	2.89	1171	923	39.6
1991	620	4.03	2.81	1308	1018	38.0
1992	620	4.01	2.81	1493	1129	37.5
1993	540	3.91	2.76	1748	1276	37.1
1994	630	3.85	2.35	2267	1884	37.8
1995	630	3.87	2.30	3012	2373	40.5
1996	630	3.81	2.77	3482	2772	42.2
1997	630	3.87	2.86	3785	2762	42.0
1998	630	3.87	2.88	4006	2858	46.2
1999	630	3.80	2.80	4209	2851	48.0
2000	630	3.61	2.59	4894	3393	49.0
2001	630	3.57	2.53	5330	3909	52.0
2002	630	3.53	2.53	5708	4444	52.7
2003	670	3.48	2.53	6250	5142	54.7
2004	670	3.48	2.54	6950	5608	58.9
2005	1100	3.34	2.34	7655	6004	66.0
2006	1100	3.63	2.52	8515	6901	66.5
2007	1100	3.60	2.61	9549	7568	68.0
2008	1100	3.56	2.58	10692	8446	69.7
2009	1100	3.57	2.59	11822	9065	70.7
2010	1100	3.58	2.59	13186	10267	71.2
2011	1100	3.46	2.49	15245	12125	72.5
2012	1100	3.45	2.50	17017	13612	71.0
2013	1280	3.38	2.03	21208	16021	66.9
2014	1280	3.35	2.05	23555	17816	67.9
2015	1280	3.36	2.02	25719	19334	68.8
2016	1280	3.38	2.04	27908	20563	69.9
2017	1280	3.38	2.03	30397	21983	70.9
2018	950	3.40	2.05	33193	24203	72.5
2019	950	3.42	2.01	36255	26296	74.1
2020	950	3.44	2.03	38700	25664	75.5

注:2013－2020年为城乡住户一体化改革后新口径数据。

a) The data in this table are calculated at new rage by the results of integrated survey of urban households and rural households sine 2013.

13－05　农村居民家庭平均每百户耐用消费品拥有量(2012－2020年)
Number of Major Durable Consumer Goods Owned Per 100 Rural Households(2012－2020)

项　　目	Item	2012	2013	2014	2015	2016	2017	2018	2019	2020
家用汽车　（辆）	Family Car　(Unit)	27.5	28.8	34.3	38.2	42.4	46.5	50.9	52.7	54.9
摩托车　（辆）	Motorcycle　(Unit)	42.6	33.5	32.7	30.7	26.0	24.5	20.4	18.8	17.7
电冰箱　（台）	Refrigerator　(Unit)	101.8	93.8	99.5	103.9	109.0	112.0	121.8	124.4	125.6
洗衣机　（台）	Washing Machine　(Unit)	87.8	78.3	82.7	86.4	92.5	96.0	100.6	103.4	104.1
热水器　（台）	Water Heater　(Unit)	90.9	79.3	85.9	93.2	103.2	109.9	121.1	124.0	127.6
空调机　（台）	Air Conditioner　(Unit)	143.3	122.9	135.9	147.6	168.2	186.7	206.4	211.4	211.6
彩色电视机　（台）	Color TV Set　(Unit)	210.6	186.0	196.1	202.0	213.5	220.3	223.5	217.0	220.0
摄像机　（架）	(unit)	1.3	1.8	2.3	2.5	2.9	2.4	－	－	－
照相机　（架）	Camera　(Unit)	26.5	21.1	21.1	19.6	19.8	17.4	10.5	9.7	10.3
计算机　（台）	Personal Computer　(Unit)	60.4	59.3	67.3	69.6	75.0	76.4	70.4	60.2	61.3
#接入互联网的计算机　（台）	of which: Internet－connected computer　(Unit)	51.8	51.5	59.8	64.2	68.5	70.2	65.0	57.4	59.4
固定电话　（部）	Telephone　(Set)	－	49.6	52.7	46.4	35.0	31.8	23.0	16.1	14.2
移动电话　（部）	Mobile Phone　(Set)	253.1	235.5	244.6	253.8	265.2	274.5	286.4	267.9	270.9
#接入互联网的移动电话　（部）	of which: Internet－connected Mobile Phone　(Set)	－	106.0	121.2	141.7	172.2	200.8	214.7	209.6	231.8

注:2013－2020年为城乡住户一体化改革后新口径数据。

a) The data in this table are calculated at new rage by the results of integrated survey of urban households and rural households since 2013.

13－06 就业人员工资总额(1978－2020年)

Total Wages of Employed Persons(1978－2020)

单位:万元 (10000 yuan)

年份 Year	全市(非私营及规上私营) Total (includes Non－private Units and private units above designated size)	非私营单位 Non－private	市区(非私营及规上私营) Urban District(includes Non－private Units and private units above designated size)	非私营单位 Non－private
1978		43775		28256
1979		52127		34318
1980		67918		45574
1981		72896		48809
1982		75584		50959
1983		78336		52909
1984		102223		69135
1985		130114		87774
1986		157471		105995
1987		180077		121003
1988		230868		152859
1989		253956		167055
1990		277910		182985
1991		313906		209052
1992		377614		253653
1993		534537		359041
1994		772236		521669
1995		890488		615450
1996		973592		683244
1997		1073862		762957
1998		1112718		803264
1999		1180947		864418
2000		1267524		949872
2001		1481659		1279749
2002		1614676		1398222
2003		1867776		1617504
2004	2844691	2188159	2313930	1859164
2005	3711915	2970200	3112937	2584779
2006	4526841	3811735	3830043	3338568
2007	6233799	4954813	5256791	4317965
2008	8592198	6416424	7338932	5679543
2009	9909330	7549145	8475547	6665279
2010	12305726	9330552	10531483	8238017
2011	15012179	11222834	12934215	9954506
2012	19540005	14839012	17115217	13217453
2013	23604682	17582336	20762852	15820468
2014	26630950	19822713	24629017	18551986
2015	28884146	21523984	26718242	20179320
2016	32370091	24176045	29918514	22617274
2017	35985206	26467155	34266225	25422943
2018	39952564	28646933	38177817	27526523
2019	45772971	32985194	43842112	31754987
2020	–	36767377	–	–

注:口径范围,1997年及以前为全市全部职工,1998－2012为在岗职工,2013年起为就业人员。2004年起包含规模以上私营单位。

a) Data on this table refer to wages of all employees before 1997, that refer to all staff and workers in 1998－2012, and refer to employed persons since 2013. Data on this bill includes Private units above designated size since 2004.

13－07 就业人员年平均工资(1978－2020 年)
Average Annual Wages of Employed Persons(1978－2020)

单位:元 (yuan)

年 份 Year	全市(非私营及规上私营) Total (includes Non－private Units and private units above designated size)	非私营单位 Non－private	市区(非私营及规上私营) Urban District(includes Non－private Units and private units above designated size)	非私营单位 Non－private	市区全社会在岗职工 The Fully Employed Persons in Urban Districts	全社会就业人员
1978		597		642		
1979		643		692		
1980		777		814		
1981		783		810		
1982		791		809		
1983		813		835		
1984		1036		1071		
1985		1266		1316		
1986		1469		1536		
1987		1616		1690		
1988		1986		2073		
1989		2173		2261		
1990		2382		2486		
1991		2586		2706		
1992		3071		3233		
1993		4220		4561		
1994		6118		6597		
1995		7156		7786		
1996		7966		7851		
1997		9108		10048		
1998		10555		11512		
1999		12187		13225		
2000		14257		15454		
2001		18319		18962	18205	
2002		21418		22091	19749	
2003		24668		25535	20113	
2004	21879	28891	24204	30719	22235	
2005	24685	31069	26366	32166	22645	
2006	27620	32791	29397	33967	23581	
2007	29864	36496	31625	37991	25489	
2008	32513	40193	34107	41501	27863	
2009	35638	43947	37270	45149	30480	
2010	39772	48772	41303	49938	34330	
2011	45775	54408	47695	55958	38837	
2012	51077	56417	52610	57548	42493	
2013	55124	63664	56857	64941	46831	
2014	60904	69209	61924	70034	51449	
2015	66322	76073	67569	77061	55908	
2016	73390	85022	74589	85767	61174	
2017	80482	93891	81440	94430	67047	
2018	88752	103798	89762	104479	–	72951
2019	101069	117339	102289	118337	–	80817
2020	–	128308	–	–	–	–

注:口径范围,1997 年及以前为全市全部职工,1998－2012 为在岗职工,2013 年起为就业人员。2004 年起包含规模以上私营单位。2015 年富阳纳入市区统计范围;2017 年临安纳入市区统计范围。

a) Data on this table refer to wages of all employees before 1997, that refer to all staff and workers in 1998－2012, and refer to employed persons since 2013. Data on this bill includes Private units above designated size since 2004. Fuyang was included in urban statistics since 2015, Lin'an was included in ruban statistics since2017.

13－08　规模以上单位就业人员工资总额(2020年)

Total Wages of Employed Persons of Units Above Designated Size(2020)

单位：万元　　　　(10000 yuan)

项　目 Item		就业人员工资总额 Total Wages of Employed Persons	非私营 Non－private	在岗职工工资总额 Total Wages of Fully Employed Staff and Workers	非私营 Non－private	其他就业人员工资总额 Total Wages of Other Employed Persons	非私营 Non－private
全市总计	**Whole city Total**	**32303795**	**18697802**	**31569951**	**18384117**	**733843**	**313686**
市区总计	Urban District	30965116	18225616	30262117	17916089	702999	309527
#上城区	Shangcheng	1411403	950958	1374845	930625	36558	20334
下城区	Xiacheng	1868261	1354764	1804314	1304479	63947	50285
江干区	Jianggan	1930797	1039934	1895807	1022143	34990	17792
拱墅区	Gongshu	1617297	741914	1584010	724201	33287	17712
西湖区	Xihu	4186114	2615453	4090321	2563495	95793	51958
高新(滨江)区	Hi－Tech(Binjiang)	6109529	4299396	6021743	4273294	87786	26102
萧山区	Xiaoshan	4135135	1849968	4011850	1799987	123285	49981
余杭区	Yuhang	5241610	2828968	5108239	2815616	133371	13352
富阳区	Fuyang	934404	426801	924816	424113	9588	2688
临安区	Lin'an	861585	330813	850175	325299	11410	5514
钱塘新区	Qiantang New Area	2571232	1711840	2501669	1660622	69563	51218
西湖风景名胜区	The West Lake Scenic Zone	97749	74807	94330	72215	3419	2593
桐庐县	Tonglu	656251	198841	647437	196458	8813	2383
淳安县	Chun'an	240350	94427	229265	93440	11085	987
建德市	Jiande	442078	178919	431132	178130	10946	789

注:2020年数据口径范围调整为规模以上单位就业人员工资总额。
a) Numbers in 2020 are the total wages of employees in units above designated size.

项 目 Item	就业人员工资总额 Total Wages of Employed Persons	非私营 Non－private	在岗职工工资总额 Total Wages of Fully Employed Staff and Workers	非私营 Non－private	其他就业人员工资总额 Total Wages of Other Employed Persons	非私营 Non－private
按国民经济行业分组 Grouped by Sector	**32303795**	**18697802**	**31569951**	**18384117**	**733843**	**313686**
农、林、牧、渔业 Farming, Forestry, Animal Husbandry & Fishery	–	–	–	–	–	–
采矿业 Mining	11089	3266	10971	3266	118	
制造业 Manufacturing	9204626	5495587	9079537	5413865	125090	81722
电力、热力、燃气及水生产和供应业 Production & Supply of Electricity, Heat, Gas & Water	250830	236065	248918	234220	1912	1845
建筑业 Construction	4940210	1394098	4672315	1342447	267895	51651
批发和零售业 Wholesale & Retail Trades	3068317	1773597	3002311	1725930	66006	47667
交通运输、仓储和邮政业 Transportation, Storage and Post	1479372	1026214	1463459	1016693	15913	9521
住宿和餐饮业 Hotels and Catering Services	622149	362451	589650	341142	32499	21310
信息传输、软件和信息技术服务业 Information Transmission, Software and Information Technology	6768866	4951182	6742069	4933295	26796	17888
金融业 Financial Intermediation	–	–	–	–	–	–
房地产业 Real Estate	1636351	976592	1591109	945923	45242	30669
租赁和商务服务业 Leasing and Business Services	1435815	667528	1357002	653407	78814	14122
科学研究、技术服务业 Scientific Research, Technical Services	1668790	1129727	1635381	1105196	33409	24532
水利、环境和公共设施管理业 Management of Water Conservancy, Environment and Public Facilities	291936	222958	289606	221681	2330	1277
居民服务、修理和其他服务业 Service to Honseholds, Repair and Other Services	202187	83227	189887	83047	12300	180
教育 Education	204816	117270	199684	114243	5132	3027
卫生和社会工作 Health Care and Social Work	282321	68990	269042	64662	13279	4328
文化、体育和娱乐业 Culture, Sports and Entertainment	236120	189050	229012	185102	7108	3948
公共管理、社会保障和社会组织 Public Management, Social Security and Social Organizations	–	–	–	–	–	–

13－09　规模以上单位就业人员平均工资(2020年)

Average Annual Wages of Employed Persons of Units Above Designated Size(2020)

单位:元　　　　(yuan)

项目	Item	就业人员 Total employment	非私营单位 Non－private	在岗职工 Staff and Workers	非私营单位 Non－private
全市	**Total**	**103596**	**128707**	**105632**	**131940**
市区	Urban District	105834	145946	107994	148689
#上城区	Shangcheng	108027	129742	109984	132341
下城区	Xiacheng	98868	107293	103467	114615
江干区	Jianggan	105301	122970	107163	125737
拱墅区	Gongshu	93476	101819	94990	104643
西湖区	Xihu	109730	114324	112651	117070
高新(滨江)区	Hi－Tech(Binjiang)	169169	209351	170322	210470
萧山区	Xiaoshan	81683	99190	82211	99833
余杭区	Yuhang	112533	183082	115795	184179
富阳区	Fuyang	77062	88739	77378	89045
临安区	Lin'an	77773	101723	77920	101834
钱塘新区	Qiantang New Area	88170	97084	91416	102989
西湖风景名胜区	The West Lake Scenic Zone	85059	94287	85189	94140
桐庐县	Tonglu	70261	83726	70516	83652
淳安县	Chun'an	66913	77020	67850	77447
建德市	Jiande	70031	90868	70845	91237

注:2020年数据口径范围调整为规模以上单位就业人员平均工资。

a) Numbers in 2020 are the average wages of employees in units above designated size.

项目 Item	就业人员 Total employment	非私营单位 Non-private	在岗职工 Staff and Workers	非私营单位 Non-private
按国民经济行业分组 Grouped by Sector	**103596**	**128707**	**105632**	**131940**
农、林、牧、渔业 Farming, Forestry, Animal Husbandry & Fishery	-	-	-	-
采矿业 Mining	73245	93320	73584	93320
制造业 Manufacturing	92101	108547	93175	110980
电力、热力、燃气及水生产和供应业 Production & Supply of Electricity, Heat, Gas & Water	147686	154584	148963	156043
建筑业 Construction	69170	82453	70198	82834
批发和零售业 Wholesale & Retail Trades	102262	125800	104333	130877
交通运输、仓储和邮政业 Transportation, Storage and Post	108304	120359	109699	122240
住宿和餐饮业 Hotels and Catering Services	56212	56554	60192	63583
信息传输、软件和信息技术服务业 Information Transmission, Software and Information Technology	250915	291831	252298	293715
金融业 Financial Intermediation	-	-	-	-
房地产业 Real Estate	96332	89670	98377	91245
租赁和商务服务业 Leasing and Business Services	87058	86859	86864	86999
科学研究、技术服务业 Scientific Research, Technical Services	154330	195868	155437	197385
水利、环境和公共设施管理业 Management of Water Conservancy, Environment and Public Facilities	88422	110195	89299	110647
居民服务、修理和其他服务业 Service to Households, Repair and Other Services	57158	62727	56470	62828
教育 Education	119280	149236	122958	156177
卫生和社会工业 Health Care and Social Work	112974	106928	113808	108003
文化、体育和娱乐业 Culture, Sports and Entertainment	151505	179842	153206	182510
公共管理、社会保障和社会组织 Public Management, Social Security and Social Organizations	-	-	-	-

13-10 市区消费价格指数(1978-2020年)
Consumer Price Indices in Urban District(1978-2020)

(上年=100) (Preceding Year=100)

年份 Year	居民消费价格指数 Consumer Price Index	商品零售价格指数 Retail Price Index
1978	100.1	100.1
1979	100.4	100.9
1980	100.8	109.3
1981	102.0	102.0
1982	102.0	102.3
1983	102.1	102.3
1984	103.1	103.1
1985	117.2	117.5
1986	106.0	106.1
1987	110.5	111.3
1988	121.9	123.4
1989	117.8	118.2
1990	104.6	104.4
1991	107.5	106.9
1992	110.4	110.2
1993	121.4	117.3
1994	121.5	118.8
1995	116.5	113.3
1996	110.5	107.2
1997	106.7	102.4
1998	101.8	99.8
1999	100.4	98.2
2000	100.8	98.3
2001	99.5	95.3
2002	98.8	97.9
2003	99.5	98.1
2004	102.5	101.6
2005	101.7	100.3
2006	101.2	100.2
2007	103.5	103.1
2008	104.9	106.0
2009	98.6	98.6
2010	103.9	103.7
2011	104.8	104.4
2012	102.5	101.9
2013	102.5	101.5
2014	102.0	100.8
2015	101.8	100.2
2016	102.6	101.5
2017	102.5	101.0
2018	102.3	102.0
2019	103.1	103.1
2020	102.1	100.9

13-11 市区居民消费价格分类指数(2019-2020年)

Consumer Price Indices by Category in Urban District(2019-2020)

(上年=100) (Preceding Year=100)

项目	Item	2019	2020
居民消费价格总指数	**Consumer Price Index**	**103.1**	**102.1**
一、食品烟酒	**Food, Tobacco and Liquor**	**106.3**	**106.9**
1. 食品	Food	107.9	108.9
(1)粮食	Grain	101.1	101.7
(2)薯类	Tubers	106.1	98.0
(3)豆类	Beans	109.9	102.7
(4)食用油	Edible Oil and Fats	102.6	99.4
(5)菜	Vegetables	103.1	101.5
(6)畜肉类	Meat of Livestock	123.1	136.7
(7)禽肉类	Meat of Poultry	108.2	108.8
(8)水产品	Aquatic Products	99.1	102.6
(9)蛋类	Eggs	105.6	97.4
(10)奶类	Milk	104.1	99.9
(11)干鲜瓜果类	Dried and Fresh Melons and Fruits	112.8	94.0
(12)糖果糕点类	Candy and Cake	101.2	104.0
(13)调味品	Flavoring	105.7	102.5
(14)其他食品类	Other Foods	101.9	105.8
2. 茶及饮料	Tea and Beverages	104.6	101.8
3. 烟酒	Tobacco and Liquor	100.8	99.6
4. 在外餐饮	Dining Out	104.8	104.9
二、衣着	**Clothing**	**101.3**	**100.1**
1. 服装	Garments	101.8	100.0
2. 服装材料	Garments Material	100.0	100.2
3. 其他衣着及配件	Other Clothing and Parts	99.4	103.2
4. 衣着加工服务费	Clothing Manufacturing Services	103.7	109.4

项　　目	Item	2019	2020
5. 鞋类	Footwear	99.0	98.9
三、居住	**Residence**	**100.9**	**99.7**
1. 租赁房房租	Rent of Rental Housing	101.9	99.8
2. 住房保养维修及管理	Housing Maintenance and Management	100.3	101.7
3. 水电燃料	Water, Electricity and Fuels	100.7	98.9
4. 自有住房	Private Housing	101.0	99.5
四、生活用品及服务	**Articles for Daily Use and Services**	**103.0**	**103.1**
1. 家具及室内装饰品	Furniture and Interior Decorations	102.3	102.9
2. 家用器具	Home Appliances	99.4	97.8
3. 家用纺织品	Home Textiles	102.2	105.2
4. 家庭日用杂品	Daily Use Household Articles	105.4	105.5
5. 个人护理用品	Personal - care Supplies	106.0	104.7
6. 家庭服务	Household Services	103.7	106.2
五、交通和通信	**Transport and Communications**	**99.0**	**96.6**
1. 交通	Transport	98.6	95.3
2. 通信	Communications	100.0	99.7
六、教育文化和娱乐	**Education, Culture and Recreation**	**104.3**	**101.7**
1. 教育	Education	103.5	105.0
2. 文化娱乐	Cultural and Recreation	105.4	97.7
七、医疗保健	**Health Care**	**107.0**	**103.1**
1. 药品及医疗器具	Medicine and Medical Instrument	111.3	99.4
2. 医疗服务	Medical Services	104.1	105.6
八、其他用品和服务	**Other Articles and Services**	**102.8**	**103.8**
1. 其他用品类	Other Articles	104.7	107.1
2. 其他服务类	Other Services	101.6	101.7

13-12 市区零售价格分类指数(2019-2020年)
Retail Price Indices by Category in Urban District(2019-2020)

(上年=100) (Preceding Year=100)

项目	Item	2019	2020
商品零售价格指数	**Retail Price Index**	**103.1**	**100.9**
一、食品	**Food**	**106.8**	**107.5**
1. 粮食	Grain	101.1	101.7
2. 薯类	Tubers	106.1	98.0
3. 豆类	Beans	109.9	102.7
4. 食用油	Edible Oil and Fats	102.6	99.4
5. 菜	Vegetables	103.1	101.5
6. 畜肉类	Meat of Livestock	123.1	136.7
7. 禽肉类	Meat of Poultry	108.2	108.8
8. 水产品	Aquatic Products	99.1	102.5
9. 蛋类	Eggs	105.6	97.4
10. 奶类	Milk	104.1	99.9
11. 干鲜瓜果类	Dried and Fresh Melons and Fruits	112.8	94.0
12. 糖果糕点类	Candy and Cake	101.2	104.0
13. 调味品	Flavoring	105.4	102.4
14. 其他食品类	Other Foods	101.9	105.8
15. 在外餐饮	Dining out	104.8	104.9
二、饮料、烟酒	**Beverages, Tobacco and Liquor**	**101.8**	**100.0**
1. 茶及饮料	Tea and Beverages	104.6	101.8
2. 烟草	Tobacco	100.0	100.2
3. 酒类	Liquor	102.6	98.3
三、服装、鞋帽	**Garments, Shoes and Hats**	**101.2**	**99.9**
1. 服装	Garments	101.8	100.0
2. 鞋帽袜	Footgear and Hat	99.4	99.2
3. 其他衣着配件	Other Clothing and Parts	95.2	104.2
四、纺织品	**Textiles**	**101.6**	**103.4**
1. 服装材料	Garments Material	100.0	100.2
2. 床上用品	Bedding	102.5	105.0
五、家用电器及音像器材	**Household Appliances, Music and Video Equipment**	**98.6**	**97.5**
1. 家庭设备	Household Equipment	99.8	97.2
2. 文娱用耐用消费品	Durable Consumer Goods for Entertainment	97.2	97.5

项　目	Item	2019	2020
3. 专业音像器材	Audio and Video Equipment	93.9	99.1
六、文化办公用品	**Cultural and office Appliances**	**100.9**	**97.9**
七、日用品	**Articles for Daily Use**	**104.6**	**102.4**
1. 日用百货	General Merchandise for Daily Use	107.0	102.4
2. 厨具餐具茶具	Kitchen Ware, Table Ware, Tea Set	107.1	105.8
3. 清洗用品	Cleaning Supplies	103.0	102.0
4. 其他日用品	Other Articles for Daily Use	100.0	99.8
八、体育娱乐用品	**Sports and Recreation Articles**	**102.7**	**102.2**
1. 体育户外用品	Sports Outdoor Products	97.7	105.8
2. 娱乐用品	Recreation Articles	104.7	100.9
九、交通、通信用品	**Transportation and Communication Appliances**	**100.1**	**98.1**
1. 交通运输机械	Transportation Vehicles	100.0	97.3
2. 通信器材	Equipment of Communication	101.0	102.4
十、家具	**Furniture**	**103.2**	**102.7**
十一、化妆品	**Cosmetics**	**106.7**	**106.3**
十二、金银饰品	**Gold and Silver Ornaments**	**107.3**	**111.3**
十三、中西药品及医疗保健用品	**Traditional Chinese and Western Medicine and Health Care Articles**	**111.2**	**99.2**
1. 医疗卫生器具	Medical Instruments and Articles	103.2	103.3
2. 中药	Traditional Chinese Medicines	103.4	101.3
3. 西药	Western Medicines	109.2	96.9
4. 保健器具及用品	Articles for Health Care	122.0	101.1
十四、书报杂志及电子出版物	**Books, Newspapers, Magazines and Electronic Publications**	**104.7**	**102.2**
1. 教材及参考书	Teaching Materials and Reference Books	103.5	106.2
2. 书报杂志	Books, Newspapers and Magazines	110.1	101.0
3. 计算机办公软件	Computer Office Software	96.2	98.9
十五、燃料	**Fuels**	**97.0**	**90.8**
1. 煤炭及制品	Coal and Coal Products	99.0	100.9
2. 石油及制品	Oil and Oil Products	96.8	89.6
十六、建筑材料及五金电料	**Building Materials and Hardware**	**100.7**	**100.1**
1. 建筑装潢材料	Building Decoration Materials	100.3	99.5
2. 五金水暖	Hardware	102.0	101.8

13－13　工业生产者出厂价格指数(2013－2020年)

Producer Price Indices for Industrial Products(2013－2020)

(上年＝100)　　(Preceding Year＝100)

项　目 Item	2013	2014	2015	2016	2017	2018	2019	2020
工业生产者出厂价格总指数 Total Producer Price Indices for Industrial Products	**98.5**	**98.6**	**96.5**	**99.2**	**104.4**	**102.4**	**99.0**	**97.5**
一、按轻重工业分 Grouped by Industries								
轻工业 Light Industry	**99.9**	**99.2**	**97.4**	**99.8**	**104.0**	**102.0**	**98.1**	**96.3**
以农产品为原料 Made from Agricultural Products	100.8	99.9	98.5	99.8	102.6	101.6	98.6	97.8
以非农产品为原料 Made from Non－agricultural Products	98.4	98.2	95.8	99.8	106.1	102.5	97.2	94.1
重工业 Heavy Industry	**97.5**	**98.2**	**95.8**	**98.7**	**104.6**	**102.6**	**99.6**	**98.3**
采掘 Mining & Quarrying Industry	101.0	104.2	94.9	97.3	100.6	101.7	96.9	96.0
原料 Raw Materials Industry	97.5	96.7	92.5	96.4	106.7	102.3	100.0	95.4
加工 Manufacturing Industry	97.5	98.5	96.7	99.4	104.1	102.7	99.5	99.0
二、按二大部类分 Grouped by Means of Producting and Consumer Goods								
生产资料 Means of Production	**97.8**	**98.0**	**95.3**	**98.8**	**105.8**	**103.0**	**98.4**	**96.7**
采掘 Mining	101.0	104.2	94.9	97.3	100.6	101.7	96.9	96.0
原料 Raw Materials	96.5	95.7	91.0	96.1	109.9	103.2	95.8	90.9
加工 Manufacture	98.2	98.7	96.6	99.6	104.7	103.0	99.2	98.3
生活资料 Consumer Goods	**100.6**	**100.6**	**100.1**	**100.1**	**99.9**	**100.3**	**100.8**	**100.0**
食品 Foods	101.0	101.1	100.9	100.0	99.4	100.2	101.1	99.1
衣着 Clothing	102.0	100.1	100.1	101.1	99.9	101.3	99.6	100.2
一般日用品 Articles for Daily Use	99.8	100.7	99.9	100.5	100.4	99.7	101.1	100.5
耐用消费品 Durable Consumer Goods	99.6	100.0	99.2	99.1	99.7	100.7	100.6	100.3

项　　目 Item	2013	2014	2015	2016	2017	2018	2019	2020
三、按工业部门分 Grouped by Industrial Sector								
冶金工业 Metallurgical Industry	95.4	96.2	93.2	101.7	115.0	103.9	97.7	101.6
电力工业 Power Industry	99.1	99.6	98.2	97.8	100.2	100.9	100.9	97.7
煤炭及炼焦工业 Coal and Coking Industry								
石油工业 Petroleum Industry	100.5	100.5	92.4	87.7	97.9	101.6	111.1	90.5
化学工业 Chemical Industry	97.3	95.8	92.7	97.3	107.8	103.4	96.2	91.1
机械工业 Machine Building Industry	98.1	98.9	97.6	99.4	101.4	100.2	99.3	98.8
建材材料工业 Building Materials Industry	97.3	103.0	94.0	96.3	111.5	123.1	105.4	102.5
森林工业 Timber Industry	101.0	101.3	99.9	98.9	100.9	100.5	100.0	99.2
食品工业 Food Industry	101.2	100.5	100.2	100.2	99.6	100.4	101.2	99.4
纺织工业 Textile Industry	101.1	98.9	96.3	100.1	103.5	101.7	97.8	96.0
缝纫工业 Tailoring Industry	102.6	100.5	99.8	99.6	99.6	101.2	99.6	100.1
皮革工业 Leather Industry	101.1	101.0	100.4	100.5	101.3	101.4	100.2	101.1
造纸工业 Paper Industry	96.3	99.7	98.5	98.9	109.8	103.0	93.2	97.0
文教艺术用品工业 Cultural, Educational & Handicrafts Articles	100.0	98.8	98.9	99.5	99.7	97.9	98.0	99.4
其它工业 Others	101.3	104.6	102.9	105.5	102.5	103.0	105.4	105.4

13－14　工业生产者购进价格指数(2013－2020年)

Purchasing Price Indices for Industrial Producers(2013－2020)

(上年＝100)　　(Preceding Year＝100)

项　目 Item	2013	2014	2015	2016	2017	2018	2019	2020
工业生产者购进价格指数 Purchasing Price Index for Industrial Producers	**97.3**	**97.3**	**92.9**	**98.9**	**108.4**	**103.7**	**96.8**	**96.1**
燃料动力类 Fuel and Power	96.9	99.0	95.1	93.6	105.7	103.1	99.3	93.7
黑色金属材料类 Ferrous and Metals	95.0	92.4	85.9	100.9	115.5	106.8	97.6	99.1
1. 钢材 Rolled－steel	95.4	92.5	86.3	101.0	115.9	106.8	97.4	99.0
2. 其他 Other	90.1	90.3	80.5	98.2	106.8	105.1	100.7	100.7
有色金属材料及电线类 Non－ferrous Metals and Electric Wire	93.7	94.5	92.2	101.3	114.7	101.3	99.8	106.9
化工原料类 Chemical Raw Materials	97.0	97.7	91.7	100.8	110.9	105.4	91.9	89.8
木材及纸浆类 Wood and Paper Pulps	98.8	98.5	98.5	99.8	111.6	104.4	92.9	97.3
建筑材料及非金属类 Building Materials	99.4	105.7	96.9	99.0	117.1	120.9	102.7	100.3
农副产品类 Farm and Sideline Products	98.4	100.4	99.3	99.3	106.9	96.5	97.4	98.0
其他工业原材料及半成品类 Other Industrial Raw Materials and Semi－products	97.8	98.9	96.7	98.8	102.7	101.1	98.0	98.4
纺织原料类 Textile Raw Materials	101.9	99.9	97.1	98.8	104.8	101.9	98.6	96.2

13-15 住宅销售价格指数(2020年)
Residential Sales Price Indices(2020)

月份	Month	新建商品住宅 New Residential Commodities Building		二手住宅 The Second-hand Residence	
		上月=100 Last month=100	上年同期=100 Preceding Year=100	上月=100 Last month=100	上年同期=100 Preceding Year=100
一月	January	100.3	105.0	100.1	103.0
二月	February	99.9	104.4	100.0	103.1
二月	March	101.3	105.4	100.7	103.1
四月	April	100.9	105.2	101.0	103.2
五月	May	100.7	105.1	100.8	102.7
六月	June	101.2	105.2	101.0	103.3
七月	July	100.2	104.9	101.3	104.6
八月	August	100.4	105.3	100.7	105.4
九月	September	100.0	105.1	100.3	105.9
十月	October	100.0	105.2	100.3	106.4
十一月	November	99.8	105.1	100.1	106.5
十二月	December	99.7	104.5	100.5	106.9

13－16　分地区社会办福利院情况（2020年末）
Basic Statistics on Welfare Homes by Region（End of 2020）

地区 Region	单位（个）Homes（unit）	职工（人）Staff and Workers（person）	床位数（张）Beds（bed）	在院人数（人）Persons Housed（person）	老人（人）Seniors（person）
全市 Total	**330**	**6610**	**75848**	**35516**	**35100**
市区 Urban District	235	5882	65366	31386	30970
#萧山区 Xiaoshan	43	1476	8947	4251	4211
余杭区 Yuhang	22	197	9921	5857	5811
富阳区 Fuyang	34	546	5943	2121	2107
临安区 Lin'an	37	240	5600	1378	1355
桐庐县 Tonglu	37	256	3582	955	955
淳安县 Chun'an	34	280	3099	1333	1333
建德市 Jiande	24	192	3801	1842	1842

注：萧山区不含托管在钱塘新区的街道数据。

a）Figures of Xiaoshan District don't include districts which under administered by Qiantang New Area.

13－17 分地区优抚对象

Number of Persons Receiving

单位:人

指　　标 Item	全　市 Total	市　区 Urban District	上城区 Shangcheng	下城区 Xiacheng	江干区 Jianggan
享受定期抚恤金人数 Number of Persons Receiving Periodical Commiseration	5048	3746	249	238	228
烈属遗属 Number of Martyr Kinsfolk	181	90	3	1	2
牺牲军人遗属 Number of the Sacrifice Soldiers	89	61	1	-	-
病故军人遗属 Number of Kinsfolks of the Illness－died Soldiers	166	115	4	-	6
残疾军人	4612	3480	241	237	220
享受定期补助人数 Number of Persons Enjoying Regular Subsidies	43634	30397	61	63	745
在乡复员军人 Rural Demobilized Soldier	981	622	4	6	5
优待优抚对象带病回乡退伍军人 Number of Rural Veterans with Illness Receiving Subsiders	2702	1525	2	3	15
优待优抚对象人数	48682	34143	310	301	973

人员情况(2020 年)
Public Subsidies by Region(2020)

(person)

拱墅区 Gongshu	西湖区 Xihu	高新(滨江)区 Hi-Tech (Binjiang)	钱塘新区 Qiantang	萧山区 Xiaoshan	余杭区 Yuhang	富阳区 Fuyang	临安区 Lin'an	桐庐县 Tonglu	淳安县 Chun'an	建德市 Jiande
223	563	93	87	622	490	589	364	392	380	530
1	8	3	4	10	9	26	23	25	33	33
–	5	–	1	7	8	35	4	15	5	8
3	8	1	3	23	19	36	12	18	19	14
219	542	89	79	582	454	492	325	334	323	475
281	1665	662	1621	8719	5271	5958	5351	4798	3749	4690
9	19	12	26	101	141	152	147	115	108	136
2	17	12	61	305	186	761	161	637	174	366
504	2228	755	1708	9341	5761	6547	5715	5190	4129	5220

13-18 市、县级社会

Basic Statistics on Institutions and

单位:个

指标 Item		全市 Total	市区 Urban District	萧山区 Xiaoshan
合计	**Total**	**3435**	**2572**	**313**
按活动区域分	**Grouped by Region**			
地级社团	Municipal - level Societies	786	786	
县级社团	County - level Societies	2649	1786	313
按性质分	**Grouped by Category**			
科技与研究	Technology and Research	148	107	19
生态环境	Ecological Envirenment	25	23	4
教育	Education	39	33	2
卫生	Health	99	93	9
社会服务	Social Services	574	295	93
文化	Culture	343	271	49
体育	Sport	356	310	36
法律	Law	14	11	1
工商业服务	Industry and Business Services	944	841	24
宗教	Religion	46	34	7
农业及农村发展	Agricure and Rural Development	180	114	13
职业及从业组织	Vocational and Business Organizations	148	148	18
国际及涉外组织	International and Foreign Organizations	4	4	-
其他	Other	515	288	38

团体机构情况（2020 年）

Organizations at County Level（2020）

（unit）

余杭区 Yuhang	富阳区 Fuyang	临安区 Lin'an	桐庐县 Tonglu	淳安县 Chun'an	建德市 Jiande
242	**241**	**252**	**248**	**377**	**238**
242	241	252	248	377	238
20	17	12	15	22	4
1	–	4	1	1	–
1	2	3	2	–	4
11	3	29	–	1	5
11	15	13	4	274	1
25	25	27	10	26	36
25	25	27	5	12	29
–	1	1	–	1	2
80	58	31	59	22	22
4	4	3	5	3	4
19	29	44	15	15	36
6	28	41	–	–	–
–	–	2	–	–	–
39	34	15	132	–	95

13－19　社会保障情况(2013－2020年)
Social Security(2013－2020)

单位:万人　　(10000 persons)

项　目 Item	2013	2014	2015	2016	2017	2018	2019	2020
城镇登记失业人员 Number of the Registered Unemployed Persons in Urban	4.60	4.03	3.67	3.72	3.76	4.27	5.32	9.41
城镇登记失业率(%) The Registered Rate of Unemployment in Urban (%)	1.85	1.84	1.74	1.72	1.70	1.60	1.80	2.42
失业人员再就业 The Re－employed Persons of Unemployment	13.13	13.50	14.22	11.48	11.04	11.31	6.37	3.44
职工基本养老保险参保人数 Number of Persons in the Basic Pension Program in Urban	530.70	559.48	569.09	575.98	628.32	671.07	704.69	751.54
失业保险参保人数 Number of Persons in the Unemployment Insurance Program	316.36	331.83	349.42	374.16	413.20	459.37	486.65	523.46
职工基本医疗保险参保人数 Number of Persons in the Basic Medical Insurance Program	448.35	469.40	500.21	529.32	580.50	632.66	671.12	713.49
工伤保险参保人数 Number of Persons in the Work－injure Insurance Program	394.82	406.65	418.17	428.41	462.44	520.12	556.67	633.36
生育保险参保人数 Number of Persons in the Bear Insurance Program	292.01	309.23	324.59	349.33	390.73	430.43	457.01	514.88
城乡居民养老保险(障)人数 Number of Persons in the Urban and Rural old－age Security	106.40	103.97	99.45	95.51	88.68	85.09	83.61	81.01
城乡居民参加医疗保险人数 Number of urban and rural residents participated in medical insurance	373.93	370.81	370.50	368.21	373.93	359.74	364.75	364.60

13－20 分地区社会保障情况(2020年末)

Social Security by Region(End of 2020)

单位:人　　(persons)

指标 Item	职工基本养老保险参保人数 Number of Employed Persons in the Basic Pension Program	职工基本医疗保险参保人数 Number of Persons in the Basic Medical Insurance Program	工伤保险参保人数 Number of Persons in the Work－injure Insurance Program	生育保险参保人数 Number of Persons in the Bear Insurance Program	失业保险参保人数 Number of Persons in the Unemployment Insurance Program
全　市 Total	**7515404**	**7134934**	**6333582**	**5148839**	**5234553**
市　区 Urban District	6947275	6659365	5945213	4883005	4976693
桐庐县 Tonglu	231772	194176	150195	117867	115410
淳安县 Chun′an	110737	110602	93578	54609	51469
建德市 Jiande	225620	170791	144596	93358	90981

主要统计指标解释

就业人员劳动报酬 指各单位在一定时期内直接支付给本单位全部就业人员的劳动报酬总额。

在岗职工工资总额 指各单位在一定时期内直接支付给本单位全部在岗职工的劳动报酬总额。

工资总额的计算原则应以直接支付给职工的全部劳动报酬为根据。各单位支付给本单位全部职工的劳动报酬,不论是计入成本的还是不计入成本的,不论是以货币形式支付还是以实物形式支付的,不论是单位自筹的资金还是上级(或政府财政部门)下拨的资金,不论是厂级单位筹集的资金还是下属车间(科室)及附属经营单位筹集的资金,均应列入工资总额计算的范围。

在岗职工平均工资 指各单位的在岗职工在一定时期内平均每人所得的工资额。它表明一定时期内在岗职工工资收入的高低程度,是反映在岗职工工资水平的主要指标。计算公式为:

$$\text{在岗职工平均工资}=\frac{\text{报告期实际支付的全部在岗职工工资总额}}{\text{报告期全部在岗职工平均人数}}$$

全社会单位 包括独立核算的机关、事业单位,非私营企业和私营企业,但不含个体工商户。

离休、退休、退职人员 指正式办理了离休、退休、退职手续,并享受相应的离休、退休、退职待遇的人员。

保险福利费用 指企业、事业、机关单位在工资以外实际支付给职工和离休、退休、退职人员个人以及用于集体的劳动保险和福利费用。

社会福利事业单位 指集中收养社会孤、老、残、幼的机构。包括由民政部门管理的社会福利院、儿童福利院、精神病人福利院和城镇集体办的福利院,以及农村集体举办的敬老院。

社会福利事业单位收养人数 包括民政部门管理和城镇及农村集体举办的社会福利事业单位中收养的老人,少年儿童,缺乏生活自理能力的残疾人员和精神病人。

商品零售价格指数 是反映城乡商品零售价格变动趋势的一种经济指数。零售物价的调整变动直接影响到城乡居民的生活支出和国家的财政收入,影响居民购买力和市场供需平衡,影响消费与积累的比例。因此,计算零售价格指数,可以从一个侧面对上述经济活动进行观察和分析。

居民消费价格指数 是反映一定时期内城乡居民所购买的生活消费品价格和服务项目价格变动趋势和程度的相对数。是综合了城市居民消费价格指数和农民消费价格指数计算取得。利用居民消费价格指数,可以观察和分析消费品的零售价格和服务价格变动对城乡居民实际生活支出的影响程度。

工业生产者出厂价格指数 是反映全部工业产品出厂价格总水平的变动趋势和程度的相对数。其中除包括工业企业售给商业、外贸、物资部门的产品外,还包括售给工业和其他部门的生产资料以及直接售给居民的生活消费品。通过工业生产价格指数能观察出厂价格变动对工业总产值的影响。

Explanatory Notes on Main Statistical Indicators

Labour Remuneration of Employees refers to total remuneration payment by various units to all their employees during a certain period of time.

Total Wages of On – the – job Staff and Workers refer to the total remuneration payment by various units to all their on – the – job staff and workers during a certain period of time.

The calculation of total wages should be based on the total remuneration payment directly paid to staff and workers. All wages and salaries and other payments to staff and workers should be calculated in, whether they are include in cost or not, paid in money or in kind, raised by the unit itself or allocated by the superior (or the financial department of the government), raised by the factory level units or by subordinate workshops (departments) and affiliated business units.

Average Wage of On – the – job Staff and Workers refers to the average wage per person during a certain period of time for on – the – job staff and workers in all units, which is a main indicator to reflect the general level of wage income of on – the – job staff and workers during a certain period of time. It is calculated as follows:

$$\text{Average Wage of On – the – job Staff and Workers} = \frac{\text{Total wages of on – the – job staff and workers actually paid in Reference Period}}{\text{Number of on – the – job Staff and workers in Reference period}}$$

Units of Whole Society includes independent accounting units of government organizations and institutions, non – private and private enterprises, but excludes individual business.

Retired and Resigned Person refers to persons who have formally gone through the formalities for their retirement or quitting from work and enjoy the corresponding treatments.

Insurance and Welfare Funds refers to labour insurance and welfare funds paid by enterprises, organizations and institutions to their staff and workers as well as retired and resigned persons individually in addition to their wages and salaries, and for collective use.

Social Welfare Institutions refer to institutions for centralized adoption of orphans, the elderly, the disabled and the young. It includes social welfare institutions run by civil affairs department, children welfare institutions, welfare institutions for mental patients, collective – owned welfare institutions and old people´s home in rural areas.

Number of People Taken in by Social Welfare Institutions refers to the number of old people, children, disabled persons and mental patients who lack self – care ability taken in by social welfare institutions run by civil affairs departments and collective units in urban and rural areas.

Retail Price Index reflects the general change in retail prices of commodities. The change and adjustment in retail prices directly affect the living expenditure of urban and rural residents, government revenue, purchasing power of residents and the equilibrium of market supply and demand, and the ratio of consumption to accumulation. Therefore, the calculation of retail price index is useful in observing and analyzing the above economic activities from one aspect.

Consumer Price Index reflects the trend and degree of changes in prices of consumer goods and services purchased by urban and rural residents in a certain period, and is a composite index derived from the urban consumer price index and the rural consumer price index. Consumer price index can be used to observe and analyze the impact of the change of consumer price and service price on actual expenditure for living cost of urban and rural residents.

Ex – factory Price Index of Industrial Products reflects the trend and degree of changes in general ex – factory prices of all industrial products, including products sold by industrial enterprise to commerce, foreign trade and materials departments, means of production sold to industry and other sectors, as well as consumer goods sold to residents. It can be used to analyze the impact of ex – factory prices on gross industrial output value.

中国统计出版社有限公司最新图书简目

（仅供参考，以实际出版为准）

统计资料

中国统计年鉴　中国统计摘要　中国第三产业统计年鉴
中国第三次全国农业普查综合资料　国际统计年鉴　金砖国家联合统计手册
中国－东盟国家统计手册　中国农村统计年鉴　中国县域统计年鉴
中国农产品价格调查年鉴　中国城市统计年鉴　中国价格统计年鉴
中国贸易外经统计年鉴　中国零售和餐饮连锁企业统计年鉴　中国商品交易市场统计年鉴
大中型批发零售和住宿餐饮企业统计年鉴　中国住户调查年鉴　中国工业统计年鉴
中国环境统计年鉴　中国能源统计年鉴　中国建筑业统计年鉴
中国房地产统计年鉴　中国投资领域统计年鉴　长江经济带发展统计年鉴
中国人口和就业统计年鉴　中国劳动统计年鉴　中国社会统计年鉴
中国科技统计年鉴　中国高技术产业统计年鉴　全国企业创新调查年鉴
中国文化及相关产业统计年鉴　中国妇女儿童状况统计资料　中国青年发展状况统计年鉴
中国基本单位统计年鉴　中国教育统计年鉴　中国教育经费统计年鉴
中国民族统计年鉴　中国残疾人事业统计年鉴　中国电力统计年鉴

省级综合统计年鉴系列

北京　天津　河北　山西　内蒙古　辽宁　吉林　黑龙江　上海　江苏　浙江　安徽　福建　江西　山东　河南　湖北　湖南
广东　广西　海南　重庆　四川　贵州　云南　西藏　陕西　甘肃　青海　宁夏　新疆　新疆生产建设兵团

市（县）级综合统计年鉴系列

滨海新区　石家庄　唐山　邯郸　邢台　保定　承德　沧州　衡水　太原　大同　晋城　晋中　长治　忻州　朔州　临汾　运城
阳泉　吕梁　呼和浩特　包头　鄂尔多斯　赤峰　大连　长春　四平　延吉　延边　哈尔滨　齐齐哈尔　黑龙江垦区　浦东新区
南京　无锡　徐州　常州　苏州　南通　淮安　盐城　扬州　镇江　宿迁　江阴　丹阳　海门　张家港　通州　如东　杭州　宁波
绍兴　台州　温州　金华　嘉兴　湖州　丽水　舟山　合肥　安庆　福州　厦门　漳州　宁德　龙岩　莆田　泉州　三明　南平
思明　南昌　上饶　抚州　赣州　九江　景德镇　宁都　济南　青岛　枣庄　潍坊　聊城　郑州　洛阳　三门峡　南阳　商丘
平顶山　信阳　济源　武汉　宜昌　十堰　荆州　荆门　咸宁　黄冈　长沙　广州　东莞　惠州　深圳　汕尾　珠海　南宁　桂林
柳州　防城港　贵港　梧州　玉林　钦州　海口　三亚　儋州　成都　贵阳　毕节　黔南　昆明　文山　德宏　西安　安康　延安
汉中　渭南　商洛　榆林　银川　兰州　庆阳　乌鲁木齐

调查年鉴系列

天津　内蒙古　上海　河南　湖北　湖南　广西　重庆　四川　云南　甘肃　宁夏　南宁　桂林　贵港　昆明

统计方法应用/实用手册

Python 数据分析基础（第二版）　非参数统计（第五版）　现代金融投资统计分析（第四版）
国民经济核算初级教程（第二版）　国民经济核算教程（第五版）　概率统计基础
全国统计专业技术资格考试系列考试用书：统计业务知识（第四版修订版）　统计业务知识学习指导与习题
全国统计专业技术资格考试系列考试用书：统计相关知识（第四版）　统计相关知识学习指导与习题

统计通俗读物/统计科普图书

领导干部统计知识问答（第二版）　统计公文写作及会议办理实用手册　大数据在统计工作中的应用案例汇编
中国国民经济核算知识问答（修订版）　地区生产总值核算国际比较研究　新中国统计制度方法的发展与改革

重点图书

第七次全国人口普查年鉴　第四次全国经济普查地图集　中国经济普查年鉴 2018
新编英汉汉英统计大词典　中国国民经济核算体系 2016　国民经济行业分类注释
挑大学选专业 2020—考研择校指南　挑大学选专业 2020—高考志愿填报指南　中华医学统计百科全书

HANGZHOU

STATISTICAL YEARBOOK

杭州统计年鉴